Children's Reading Comprehension and Assessment

Center for Improvement of Early Reading Achievement
CIERA
Steven A. Stahl, University of Illinois
Susan B. Neuman, Temple University
P. David Pearson, University of California, Berkeley
Series Editors

Barbara M. Taylor and P. David Pearson
Teaching Reading: Effective Schools, Accomplished Teachers

Anne van Kleeck, Steven A. Stahl, and Eurydice B. Bauer
On Reading Books to Children: Parents and Teachers

Scott G. Paris and Steven A. Stahl
Children's Reading Comprehension and Assessment

Children's Reading Comprehension and Assessment

Edited by

Scott G. Paris
University of Michigan

Steven A. Stahl
University of Illinois

Routledge
Taylor & Francis Group
New York   London

First published by
Lawrence Erlbaum Associates,
10 Industrial Avenue
Mahwah, NJ 07430
Reprinted 2010 by Routledge

Routledge
Taylor & Francis Group
270 Madison Avenue
New York, NY 10016

Routledge
Taylor & Francis Group
2 Park Square
Milton Park.Abingdon
Oxon OX14 4RN

Cover design by Sean Sciarrone

Library of Congress Cataloging-in-Publication Data

Children's reading comprehension and assessment / edited by Scott G. Paris,
   Steven A. Stahl.
           p.   cm.
   Includes bibliographical references and index.
ISBN 0-8058-4655-7 (cloth : alk. paper)
ISBN 0-8058-4656-5 (pbk. : alk. paper)
1. Reading comprehension. 2. Reading—Ability testing.   I. Paris, Scott G.,
   1946– .   II. Stahl, Steven A.
LB1050.45.C87   2004
372.47—dc22

                                        2004052067
                                        CIP

Dedication

This book is dedicated to the memory of Steve Stahl, our colleague and friend, who passed away in May 2004. Steve was an important part of CIERA for many years. In some ways, he was the keel of our ship, providing our crew direction and steady balance during turbulent times in the field of reading research. He was instrumental in organizing and editing this volume, and he worked with all the authors to make this volume successful. Steve's intellectual contributions to CIERA, education, and teachers were enormous; they provide an enduring legacy to his commitment to improve literacy for everyone.

Steve Stahl was a word master. He saw incongruities and ironies with ease, and he delighted in exposing and sharing the humor in language, politics, and people. He was witty without trying, charming without pretending, and courageous without flinching. His family and friends knew these traits for years, but students, teachers, and colleagues who did not know him were often surprised and perplexed by the Harvard-educated scholar with the down-home, unassuming approach to language and life. He was the academic version of Will Rogers. Maybe that is why audiences leaned forward in their chairs when he spoke and students listened attentively in class. The intellectual insights were woven together with examples, stories, and humor.

Steve was constantly inquisitive. In his research, writing, and teaching, he was rarely satisfied that he or anyone else had solved a problem or laid an issue to rest. His review articles were rich syntheses of ideas; his research explored difficult issues; his scholarship and eloquence were abundant. Steve's legacy cannot be measured in words, even by his own prolific wit and publications. Steve lived a life dedicated to education, a passionate belief that we all could help children and society by promoting literacy in every person. His commitment to teachers and students was part of his character, just as much as his mastery of language. That he discovered a way to combine his passions in a career was a benefit to untold thousands of teachers and students who never met him.

This volume is just one of many of Steve's intellectual contributions to the field of literacy, but sadly it is one of his last. He worked tirelessly for CIERA and brought energy, vision, and integrity to every task. On behalf of all the contributors to this volume and his colleagues at CIERA, we dedicate this work to Steve Stahl and we honor his devotion to literacy and education.

Contents

       of Multiple Item Formats to Assess Reading Comprehension
       Jay R. Campbell

16 Dimensions Affecting the Assessment of Reading   369
       Comprehension
       *David J. Francis, Jack M. Fletcher, Hugh W. Catts,
       and J. Bruce Tomblin*

17 The Influence of Large-Scale Assessment of Reading   395
       Comprehension on Classroom Practice: A Commentary
       Karen K. Wixson and Joanne F. Carlisle

       Author Index   407

       Subject Index   417

Foreword

P. David Pearson
University of California, Berkeley

Just the right book at just the right time—that is how I regard this latest and last volume in the CIERA portfolio of contributions to the field of reading research. In placing reading comprehension at the top of the scholarly agenda for reading research, this volume continues a recent tradition of contributions reminding us of what reading is all about—making meaning in response to a written text. It can rightfully take its place alongside other recent "classics" that have championed the cause of reading comprehension including Walter Kintsch's 1998 landmark update on our theoretical and empirical knowledge of the essential cognitive processes involved in comprehension, the policy-oriented initiative of the Rand Reading Study Group (Snow, 2002), and a handful of important books about comprehension instruction led by the Block and Pressley (2001) volume documenting our knowledge base about solid instructional activities.

If this book had been published in 1989, I would have said that it provided a wonderful continuation of the exquisite work on comprehension (e.g., basic processes, instructional practices, and assessment) spearheaded by the folks at the Center for the Study of Reading during the 1970s and 1980s. Because the volume appeared in 2005, I am forced to contextualize it differently. Now, after an ebb of nearly two decades in which other research and policy agendas—first the radical constructivism of whole language and its siblings and then the re-emergence of basic skills of decoding and fluency—dominated our academic discourse in the field of reading, reading comprehension is re-emerging as a significant player in scholarship, practice, and policy. I say welcome back to center stage! The book is balanced on many dimensions. It is a balance of past, present, and future—with a nostalgic reverie of past efforts to understand comprehension and operationalize it through assessment in chapter 2, clear expositions of current trends in theory and assessment in chapter 3 (Kintsch & Kintsch) and chapter 1 (Anne Sweet), and projections about future trends and needs by nearly every author of every chapter. It is a balance of emphases on theory, practice, and policy. In fact, as one moves through the chapters, there is a definite movement from theory (Part 1 and chapters in Part 2) to practice (in Parts 2 and 3) to policy (the issues of wide-scale assessment in Part 4). Although the intent of the book was to focus most prominently on comprehension assessment, it turned out that instruction (especially in Part 3) and contextual factors (Parts 2 and 3) worked their way into the deliberations. Given the important link between instruction and assessment and the ever-present influence of context, this linkage, whether intentional or unintentional, is a welcome addition to the volume. Finally, it is a good balance of reports of different traditions of scholarship—ranging from hard core psychometric analyses, especially in chapter 6 (Paris and colleagues) and chapter 15 (Francis and colleagues), to policy analyses of the consequences of assessment (chapter 13 by Salinger and chapter 15 by Wixson and Carlisle), to mixed methodological analyses in the remainder of the chapters.

The book will prove extremely useful to other scholars of reading comprehension, especially those who would like to join the movement to conduct empirical research to better understand current comprehension assessments, both their strengths and weaknesses or causes and consequences, and to improve assessments by making them both more theory-friendly and user-friendly. It may seem contradictory to apply both of these standards, strong connections to theory *and* everyday classroom practice, but I would argue that we cannot have one without the other. An assessment that is too grounded in current classroom practices runs the risk of reifying a set of curricular and instructional practices that are woefully undertheorized and pedagogically misguided. Why? Because a lot of mainstream practice in teaching/facilitating comprehension is conceptually misguided; namely, a long tradition of aligning our standards and goals to a scope and sequence of comprehension skills that bears little resemblance to the cognitive reality of comprehension processes. Just as surely, assessments that err on the side of theory may result in theoretically impeccable tools that no one can or will use.

Three themes dominate this book, and I wish I could claim credit for discerning them, but I cannot for they have been unearthed by virtually all of the commentaries that close each of the four parts of the book. Duke (Part 1), Calfee and Miller (Part 2), Pressley and Hilden (Part 3), and Wixson and Carlisle (Part 4) have summarized and situated the more empirically grounded pieces in each of the four sections in exemplary fashion. They have provided contextual fabric for understanding each chapter as well as the net contributions of their respective sections. In fact, I recommend that they be read *before* reading the chapters they synthesize. A quick perusal of these syntheses will convince you that the themes are consistent within and across parts—the crying need for theory, the nonunitary nature of comprehension processes and/or assessment, and the need for a system of comprehension assessments.

I have already made my pitch for theory; clearly, I believe that without it, the field will continue to commit the sins of the past. As far as the nonunitary nature of comprehension as a fundamental cognitive process or as an assessment phenomenon, I both agree and disagree. I agree with all of the commentators that comprehension varies according to topical domain, contextual factors, and task demands, rendering it idiosyncratic, interpretive, and situational—but I think that the variation we witness is highly predictable and governed by higher order principles of cognitive organization and processes as well as motivational factors. Comprehension, I believe, is like most things in human experience—what appears similar at one level of analysis will appear different at another; conversely, what seems different at one level will appear similar at another. As for the need for systems of assessment, I could not agree more. When we place too much burden on a single tool, format, approach, or task, we run the risk of invalidating it—because an assessment valid for one purpose may not be valid for another. The search for an assessment that will be all things to all people is, always has been, and will continue to be fruitless and misguided. We are better advised to seek assessments that are optimally matched to particular situations and purposes. It will not be simple to meet that challenge, but the seductive simplicity of a silver bullet, a single solution, should be avoided at all costs.

I cannot close this foreword without commenting on the two professional losses marked by the publication of this volume. Institutionally, this volume, along with a recent issue of *Elementary School Journal* (2005), are the last published vestiges of CIERA, the Center for the Improvement of Early Reading Achievement, which was devoted to understanding the contexts that shape our capacity to support young children's reading development. Roughly half of the contributors to this volume were involved in CIERA's research portfolio, several in enacting CIERA's research agenda on assessment, and others in promoting instruction that impacts comprehension. I am pleased that such a prestigious and important volume would serve to close this important chapter on reading research. This volume will serve as one of CIERA's most lasting legacies.

More importantly, it marks the tragic loss of our dear friend and colleague, Steve Stahl, who, along with Scott Paris, undertook the daunting task of editing this volume. I echo the tribute paid posthumously to Steve by Scott. I cannot think of a more fitting tribute to our colleague than to be a part of a book that honors what is most central to the mysteries he spent most of his professional life unraveling—the secrets of reading.

REFERENCES

Block, C., & Pressley, M. (Eds.). (2001). *Comprehension instruction: Research-based best practices*. New York: Guilford Press.

Editors. (2005). *Elementary School Journal, 105*(2), 129–243.

Kintsch, W. (1998). *Comprehension: A paradigm for cognition*. Cambridge, UK: Cambridge University Press.

Snow, C. (2002). *Reading for understanding: Toward an R&D program in reading comprehension*. Washington DC: Rand Corporation.

Preface

Reading is remarkable. For some children, learning to read seems effortless and rapid, whereas for others, it can be an arduous and frustrating chore. Reading may not be rocket science, as some pundits note, but understanding how children learn to read, how to teach reading, and how to help struggling readers have been remarkably stubborn puzzles. Researchers, educators, and policy makers have devoted an enormous amount of energy and resources at the turn of this millennium to provide proven practices and evidence-based policies that will promote literacy for all children. It is a remarkable challenge considering that many children in America go to school without speaking English fluently, without adequate nutrition and safety, without adult tuition at home, and without preschool literacy experiences that prepare them to read. The cognitive mysteries surrounding teaching and learning to read may be solved long before the social and economic obstacles that thwart literacy are removed, but it will require concerted effort and scientific innovation from professionals in many disciplines. Indeed, the children who are most at risk for low literacy will need remarkable resources: personal tutoring, motivating materials, daily instruction, and genuine opportunities to learn.

There has been a renewed dedication to improve children's reading, in the United States and throughout the world. Literacy is an essential skill in an interconnected world of advanced technology. Social progress and economic growth depend on an educated population. Research on reading must be viewed within these historical and global contexts to appreciate the importance of literacy for individuals, communities, and nations. Likewise, this volume must be considered in context. The Center for the Improvement of Early Reading Achievement (CIERA) was begun in 1996 when Elfrieda Hiebert at the

University of Michigan and David Pearson at Michigan State University organized a coalition of researchers around the country to propose a national reading research center to the Office of Educational Research and Improvement (OERI). Many of the contributors to this volume wrote the grant proposal, conducted the original studies, and witnessed rapid changes in the field of reading. About that time, Snow, Burns, and Griffin (1998) published an influential book, *Preventing Reading Difficulties*, that described the developmental course of early reading. The Report of the National Reading Panel (2000) identified the alphabetic principle, phonemic awareness, fluency, vocabulary, and comprehension as five essential reading components. These components were the foundation of reading instruction and assessment practices in the No Child Left Behind (NCLB) Act in 2001 that had a profound impact on reading assessment and instruction in schools across the USA. By the time CIERA closed its doors in 2003, even OERI had been transformed into the Institute of Education Sciences (IES). It was an era of remarkable changes.

CIERA researchers disseminated research results and practical advice in numerous ways. We created materials such as *Every Child A Reader* (Hiebert, Pearson, Taylor, Richardson, & Paris, 1998), provided web-based resources and bibliographies, conducted annual Summer Institutes for educators, and produced several edited volumes including; Van Kleeck, Stahl, and Bauer, *On Reading Books to Children* (2003), Taylor and Pearson, *Teaching Reading: Effective Schools, Accomplished Teachers* (2002), and Hoffman and Schallert, *The Texts in Elementary Classrooms* (2004). This volume on reading comprehension is part of the CIERA series and is designed to summarize current knowledge about instruction and assessment of reading comprehension in young children. The volume emerged from a conference held in October 2002 in Michigan that provided a lively and intense exchange of ideas. Joanne Carlisle and Steve Stahl, as CIERA codirectors, organized and led the conference. The focus on comprehension is a natural complement to the emphasis in the 1990s on basic decoding skills, and many chapters reconsider and extend the research on reading comprehension conducted in the 1980s. Comprehension is a timely focus, partly because it was neglected during an era focused on enabling skills of beginning readers and partly because it is crucial for reasoning about text. It was the cutting-edge topic of 2002 and will remain important in the future.

The authors in this volume examine what it means to understand text and how comprehension can be assessed. The first section provides a national and historical context to the study of reading comprehension. The second section examines how vocabulary, motivation, and expertise influence comprehension and considers the developmental course and correlates of comprehension. Chapters in the third section consider how schools focus on comprehension for instruction and assessment. The fourth section includes chapters on large-scale assessment that analyze how test formats and psychometric characteristics influence measures of reading comprehension. At the end of each section is a commentary that reviews chapters in that section, critiques the main points, and synthesizes critical issues.

The fundamental issues about reading comprehension and how to assess it will not be solved quickly. Like many issues in the development and pedagogy of reading, they are complex and resistant to simple solutions. The diversity of reading skills and backgrounds among children is matched by the enormous range of expertise among teachers and resources among schools. Variable conditions for reading may require variable solutions for instruction and assessment. Researchers must devise methods to study and understand these interactions. Teachers must design differentiated plans for instruction and assessment. Parents and policymakers need to understand that not all practical decisions can be based on scientific evidence and that not all evidence is unequivocal. These are remarkable challenges motivated by a desire to see the joy and pride in a young child who asks, "Do you want to listen to me read this book?" We hope this volume stretches current thinking and establishes new boundaries so that innovative approaches to instructing and assessing children's reading comprehension flourish in the future.

REFERENCES

Hiebert, E. H., Pearson, P. D., Taylor, B. M., Richardson, V., & Paris, S. G. (1998). *Every child a reader.* Ann Arbor, MI: The Center for the Improvement of Early Reading Achievement.

Hoffman, J., & Schallert, D. (Eds.). (2004). *The texts in elementary classrooms.* Mahwah, NJ: Lawrence Erlbaum Associates.

No Child Left Behind Act of 2001. (2002). Pub. L. No. 107–110, paragraph 115 Stat, 1425.

Report of the National Reading Panel. (2000). *Teaching children to read: An evidence-based assessment of the scientific research literature on reading and its implications for reading instruction.* Washington, DC: National Institute of Child Health and Human Development and U.S. Department of Education.

Snow, C. E., Burns, M. S., & Griffin, P. (1998). *Preventing reading difficulties in young children.* Washington, DC: National Academy Press.

Taylor, B. M., & Pearson, P. D. (Eds.). (2002). *Teaching reading: Effective schools, accomplished teachers.* Mahwah, NJ: Lawrence Erlbaum Associates.

Van Kleeck, A. V., Stahl, S., & Bauer, E. B. (Eds.). (2003). *On reading books to children.* Mahwah, NJ: Lawrence Erlbaum Associates.

Part I

Historical and Theoretical Foundations

1

Assessment of Reading Comprehension: The RAND Reading Study Group Vision

Anne P. Sweet
U.S. Department of Education

The assessment of reading comprehension is a critical component of any national research effort aimed at improving our understandings about what is reading comprehension and how it can best be taught. The core of this chapter, excerpted from *Reading for Understanding: Toward an R&D Program in Reading Comprehension* (2002), was written by the RAND Reading Study Groups for the Department of Education's Office of Educational Research and Improvement (OERI) and designed to inform the development of a research agenda for reading. In 1999, Kent McGuire, then assistant secretary for OERI, launched an agenda-setting effort for federal education research, focused on mathematics and reading education and managed by the RAND Corporation. Two study groups were formed, each charged with identifying the most pressing needs in its particular area.

The RAND Reading Study Group (RRSG) was composed of 14 experts,[1] representing a range of disciplinary and methodological perspectives on the field of reading. This group functioned as an expert panel for little more than 2 years (2000–2002) to establish a convergent perspective on what is known about reading, what are the most urgent tasks in developing an integrated research base, and

---

[1] Members of the Rand Reading Study Group (RRSG) were Donna Alvermann, Janice Dole, Jack Fletcher, Georgia Earnest Garcia, Irene Gaskins, Art Graesser, John Guthrie, Michael Kamil, William Nagy, Annemarie Sullivan Palincsar, Catherine Snow (RRSG Chair), Dorothy Strickland, Frank Vellutino and Joanna Williams. Anne P. Sweet was the RAND reading study director.

what needs to be done to improve reading outcomes. The study group formulated an initial draft of a report in the summer of 2000 which was used to solicit commentary and guidance to the committee in devising its final report. That report was published early in 2002 as a book entitled *Reading for Understanding: Toward an R&D Program in Reading Comprehension* (RAND Reading Study Group, 2002). The RRSG report served its primary purpose by providing the impetus for OERI to create a whole new Program of Research on Reading Comprehension (PRRC), under the leadership of successor OERI assistant secretary, Grover J. Whitehurst.

We have made enormous progress over the last 25 years in understanding how to teach aspects of reading. We know about the role of phonological awareness in cracking the alphabetic code, the value of explicit instruction in teaching sound-letter relations, and the importance of reading practice in creating fluency. Measures of these constructs (phonological awareness, letter-sound relations, and fluency), on average, render good approximations of these skills. The same cannot be said for measures of reading comprehension.

THE STUDY GROUP'S ANALYSIS

Understanding the nature of the problem of reading comprehension requires having available good data identifying which readers can successfully undertake which activities with which texts. Such data are not available, in part because the widely used comprehension assessments are inadequate. Further, the improvement of instruction relies crucially on the availability of information about the effectiveness of instruction. Teachers need reliable and valid assessments tied closely to their curricula so that they can see which students are learning as expected and which need extra help. In addition, schools, districts, and states are increasingly calling for reliable and valid assessments that reflect progress toward general benchmarks of reading, writing, and mathematics ability. For the area of reading comprehension, good assessments that are tied to curriculum as well as good assessments of general comprehension capacity are sorely needed. These assessments need to be constructed in accordance with the many advances in psychometric theory.

WHAT WE ALREADY KNOW
ABOUT COMPREHENSION ASSESSMENTS

Currently available assessments in the field of reading comprehension generate persistent complaints that these instruments

- inadequately represent the complexity of the target domain.
- conflate comprehension with vocabulary, domain-specific knowledge, word reading ability, and other reader capacities involved in comprehension.
- do not rest on an understanding of reading comprehension as a developmental process or as a product of instruction.
- do not examine the assumptions underlying the relation of successful performance to the dominant group's interests and values.
- are not useful for teachers.
- tend to narrow the curriculum.
- are unidimensional and method-dependent, often failing to address even minimal criteria for reliability and validity.

Indeed, most currently used comprehension assessments reflect the purpose for which they were originally developed—to sort children on a single dimension by using a single method. Even more important, however, is that none of the currently available comprehension assessments is based in a viable or articulated theory of comprehension. In addition, none can give us a detailed or convincing picture of how serious is the problem of comprehension achievement in the United States. These considerations, as well as the thinking about the nature of reading comprehension represented in this document, create a demand for new kinds of assessment strategies and instruments that (a) more robustly reflect the dynamic, developmental nature of comprehension; (b) represent adequately the interactions among the dimensions of reader, activity, text, and context; and (c) satisfy criteria set forth in psychometric theory.

Currently, widely used comprehension assessments are heavily focused on only a few tasks: reading for immediate recall, reading for the gist of the meaning, and reading to infer or disambiguate word meaning. Assessment procedures to evaluate learners' capacities to modify old or build new knowledge structures, to use information acquired while reading to solve a problem, to evaluate texts on particular criteria, or to become absorbed in reading and develop affective or aesthetic responses to text, have occasionally been developed for particular research programs but have not influenced standard assessment practices. Because knowledge, application, and engagement are the crucial consequences of reading with comprehension, assessments that reflect all three are needed. Further, the absence of attention to these consequences in widely used reading assessments diminishes the emphasis on them in instructional practices as well.

WHAT WE NEED IN THE AREA
OF COMPREHENSION ASSESSMENTS

The entire research enterprise sketched out in this report depends on having a more adequate system of instrumentation for assessing reading comprehension. A satisfactory assessment system is a prerequisite to making progress with all aspects of the research agenda we propose. Thus we argue that investing in improved assessments has very high priority. It is clear that we cannot even sketch the seriousness of the problem of reading comprehension in the United States or the nature of the decline in comprehension outcomes that is the source of much worry until we have an assessment system that can be used across the developmental range of interest and that assesses the same construct across that range.

Assessing the effect of changes in instruction depends on having valid, reliable, and sensitive assessments. The effect of assessment on instruction is a question that constitutes a research agenda of its own, particularly in this highly accountability-oriented era of education reform. However, the power of high-stakes assessments over instruction and curriculum can be somewhat mitigated if teachers have available alternative assessment options that give them more useful information.

Any system of reading assessments should reflect the full array of important reading comprehension consequences. We argue that a research program to establish expectable levels of performance for children of different ages and grades on this full array of consequences is necessary. Such a program is a prerequisite to developing performance criteria at different age and grade levels and to pursuing questions about reader differences associated with instructional histories, social class, language, and culture in reading comprehension outcomes.

Although the reading comprehension consequences defined earlier constitute the basis for designing a comprehension assessment that would reflect success, our view suggests that assessments designed to reflect readers' cognitive, motivational, and linguistic resources as they approach a reading activity are also necessary. For instance, when the outcomes assessment identifies children who are performing below par, process assessments could help indicate why their reading comprehension is poor. Further, diagnostic assessments are crucial in dissecting the effect of particular instructional or intervention practices. Ideally, we would move ultimately toward assessment systems that can also reflect the dynamic nature of comprehension, for example, by assessing increments of knowledge about vocabulary and particular target domains that result from interaction with particular texts.

We see the development of an assessment system for reading comprehension as having a very high priority. Such a system should be based in contemporary approaches to test development and evaluation. We recognize that developing a comprehensive, reliable, and valid assessment system is a long-term project. Crucial for such a system are the criteria for judging performance across the developmental span. Nonetheless, a substantial start could be made in the short run, either by targeting the assessment of outcomes and reader resources as a major task of the research agenda or by encouraging the development of prototype assessments for outcomes and reader resources within other research efforts (such as research focused on instructional efficacy). Such an effort is central to pursuing larger research agendas, such as longitudinal work to create a picture of the development of reading comprehension, a large-scale effort to determine how U.S. children are functioning as readers, or a systematic pursuit of differences in reading comprehension performance related to cultural background, social class, and language status.

The approach to assessment proposed here differs from current approaches to reading assessment in that it would both grow out of and contribute to the development of an appropriately rich and elaborated theory of reading comprehension. Assessment procedures generated by this approach are thus more likely to be influenced and changed by theoretically grounded reading research. Our approach also highly values the utility of assessment for instruction. Of course, comprehensive assessment systems can place high demands of time on students and teachers; thus, we have an obligation to develop assessments that are embedded in and supportive of instruction, rather than limited to serving the needs of researchers.

A comprehensive assessment program reflecting the thinking about reading comprehension presented here would have to satisfy many requirements that have not been addressed by any assessment instruments, while also satisfying the standard psychometric criteria. The minimum requirements for such a system follow:

- Capacity to reflect authentic outcomes—Although any particular assessment may not reflect the full array of consequences, the inclusion of a wider array than that currently being tested is crucial. For example, students' beliefs about reading and about themselves as readers may support or obstruct their optimal development as comprehenders; teachers may benefit enormously from having ways to elicit and assess such beliefs.
- Congruence between assessments and the processes involved in comprehension—Assessments that target particular operations involved in comprehension must be available, in the interest of revealing interindividual

and intraindividual differences that might inform our understanding of the comprehension process and of outcome differences. The dimensionality of the instruments in relation to theory should be clearly apparent.

• Developmental sensitivity—Any assessment system needs to be sensitive across the full developmental range of interest and to reflect developmentally central phenomena related to comprehension. Assessments of young children's reading tend to focus on word reading rather than on comprehension. Assessments of listening comprehension and of oral language production, both of which are highly related to reading comprehension, are rare and tend not to be included in reading assessment systems despite their clear relevance. The available listening comprehension assessments for young children do not reflect children's rich oral language-processing capacities because they reflect neither the full complexity of their sentence processing nor the domain of discourse skills.

• Capacity to identify individual children as poor comprehenders—An effective assessment system should be able to identify individual children as poor comprehenders, not only in terms of prerequisite skills such as fluency in word identification and decoding, but also in terms of cognitive deficits and gaps in relevant knowledge (background, domain specific, etc.) that might adversely affect reading and comprehension, even in children who have adequate word-level skills. It is also critically important that such a system be able to identify early any child who is apt to encounter difficulties in reading comprehension because of limited resources to carry out one or another operation involved in comprehension.

• Capacity to identify subtypes of poor comprehenders—Reading comprehension is complexly determined. It therefore follows that comprehension difficulties could come about because of deficiencies in one or another of the components of comprehension specified in the model. Thus, an effective assessment system should be able to identify subtypes of poor comprehenders in terms of the components and desired outcomes of comprehension. It should also be capable of identifying both intraindividual and interindividual differences in acquiring the knowledge and skills necessary for becoming a good comprehender.

• Instructional sensitivity—Two major purposes for assessments are to inform instruction and to reflect the effect of instruction or intervention. Thus, an effective assessment system should provide not only important information about a child's relative standing in appropriate normative populations (school, state, and national norms groups), but also important information about the child's relative strengths and weaknesses for purposes of educational planning.

- Openness to intraindividual differences—Understanding the performance of an individual often requires attending to differences in performance across activities with varying purposes and with a variety of texts and text types.
- Usefulness for instructional decision making—Assessments can inform instructional practice if they are designed to identify domains that instruction might target, rather than to provide summary scores useful only for comparison with other learners' scores. Another aspect of utility for instructional decision making is the transparency of the information provided by the test given to teachers without technical training.
- Adaptability with respect to individual, social, linguistic, and cultural variation—Good tests of reading comprehension, of listening comprehension, and of oral language production target authentic outcomes and reflect key component processes. If performance on a task reflects differences owing to individual, social, linguistic, or cultural variations that are not directly related to reading comprehension performance, the tests are inadequate for the purposes of the research agenda we propose here.
- A basis in measurement theory and psychometrics—This basis should address reliability within scales and over time, as well as multiple components of validity at the item level, concurrently with other measures and predictively relative to the longer-term development of reading proficiency. Studies of the dimensionality of the instruments in relation to the theory underpinning their construction are particularly important. Test construction and evaluation of instruments are important areas of investigation and are highly relevant to our proposed research agenda.

Clearly, no single assessment would meet all these criteria. Instead, we propose an integrated system of assessments, some of which may be particularly appropriate for particular groups (e.g., emergent or beginning readers, older struggling readers, second-language readers, or readers with a particular interest in dinosaurs). Furthermore, the various assessments included in the system would address different purposes, such as a portmanteau assessment for accountability or screening purposes, diagnostic assessments for guiding intervention, curriculum-linked assessments for guiding instruction, and so on. Given that we are proposing multiple assessments, we believe that studies of their dimensionality and of the interrelations of these dimensions across measures are especially critical.

A sample of issues that would certainly arise in the process of developing a comprehensive assessment system for reading comprehension follows:

- The effect of various response formats on performance.

- Variation in performance across types of text.
- The effect of nonprint information.
- The effect of various formats and accommodations on the test performance of learners of English as a second language.
- Variation in performance across a variety of types of discourse and genres, including hypertext.
- The effect on performance of specifying different purposes for reading.
- The capacity to differentiate domain-specific and reading-general operations.
- The need to reflect performance on literacy tasks typical of electronic reading, such as retrieval.
- The capacity to explore issues that go outside the traditional rubric of comprehension, such as scanning, intertextuality, domain-specific strategies, and consulting illustrations.
- The reliability, validity, and dimensionality of different assessment instruments and approaches.

KEY ISSUES THE RESEARCH AGENDA SHOULD ADDRESS

The key questions and issues that a research agenda on reading assessment needs to address and that are closely connected to the RRSG's proposed areas for future instruction research, include the following:

- How can the education community measure strategic, self-regulated reading, including a student's use of such strategies as questioning, comprehension monitoring, and organizing the knowledge gained from text?
- To what extent are performance-based assessments of reading sensitive to a student's competencies in such processes as vocabulary, cognitive strategies, writing ability, oral language (syntax), reading fluency, domain-content knowledge of the texts, and such dispositions as motivation and self-efficacy for reading?
- How do we design valid and reliable measures of self-regulated, strategic reading that teachers can administer in the classroom to inform their instructional decisions?
- What informal assessments should teachers use to identify children who may need additional or modified instruction within the classroom to prevent a referral to special education services?
- How do we construct informal assessments to assist teachers in identifying how to help students who have low reading comprehension? For exam-

ple, how could teachers identify which children need to be taught specific reading strategies or supported in domain knowledge acquisition or motivational development?

• What reading comprehension assessment could be both administered efficiently by all teachers in a school and used across grades to document student growth and guide teacher decisions about the appropriate texts, tasks, contexts, and learning activities for students?

• What available measures of motivation and engagement in reading can be linked to reading competencies, related to growth over time, and used to guide classroom learning activities?

• What measures of reading fluency can be used at the levels of the individual student, the classroom, and the school and can be related to reading comprehension and reading motivation?

• Which measures of reading comprehension are sensitive to specific forms of reading instruction and intervention for all readers?

• What are the dimensions evaluated by different assessments in relation to more traditional assessments and the proposed new approaches to assessment? How well does the dimensionality map onto the theories behind the development of the assessments?

ADVANCING READING COMPREHENSION

The PRRC is the U.S. Department of Education's (OERI's) new research initiative that is designed to advance the science of reading comprehension. This program is a direct outgrow of the RRSG's report. The major objective of the PRRC is to expand scientific knowledge of how students develop proficient levels of reading comprehension, how it can be taught most optimally, and how it can be assessed in ways that reflect as well as advance our current understanding of reading comprehension and its development. In so doing, the program is designed to obtain converging empirical evidence on the development and assessment of comprehension that coheres with scientifically supported theories of the processes involved in reading comprehension. It is also designed to provide a scientific foundation for approaches to comprehension instruction that allow students to achieve proficient levels of comprehension across a range of texts and subjects.

Under the PRRC of 2002, a call for proposals was put forth that solicited research that focused on one or more of three areas of inquiry:

1. Developmental patterns of students' reading comprehension.
2. Instructional interventions for reading comprehension.

3. Measures of reading comprehension that reflect empirically justified dimensions, distinguish reader differences, and are sensitive to instructional goals.

OERI's call for research on reading comprehension under the PRRC program in 2002 is quite explicit: proposed studies are to be described by a specific conceptual framework and relevant prior empirical evidence, both of which must be clearly articulated. The research must have the potential to advance fundamental scientific knowledge that bears on the solution of important educational problems. Any research approach must incorporate a valid inference process that allows generalization beyond the study participants. The outcome is that six grants were awarded under the PRRC of 2002, totaling 6 million dollars. The funds available for the PRRC grant competition are expected to rise substantially in upcoming years. One of the biggest challenges that OERI* faces is garnering a goodly number of applicants (researchers and research collaborators) who propose to conduct the kind of comprehension research that will advance the field in significant ways. We are hopeful that you are poised to help us meet this challenge.

REFERENCE

RAND Reading Study Group. (2002). *Reading for understanding: Toward an R&D program in reading comprehension.* Washington, DC: RAND Education.

No official support or endorsement by the U.S. Department of Education is intended or should be inferred.

---

*The Institute of Education Sciences (IES) is the successor agency to OERI. Grover J. Whitehurst, who became the first IES Director, provided the leadership in OERI's new Program of Research on Reading Comprehension.

2

The Assessment of Reading Comprehension: A Review of Practices— Past, Present, and Future[1]

P. David Pearson
University of California, Berkeley

Diane N. Hamm
Michigan State University

The purpose of this chapter is to build an argument for a fresh line of inquiry into the assessment of reading comprehension. We intend to accomplish that goal by providing a rich and detailed historical account of reading comprehension, both as a theoretical phenomenon and an operational construct that lives and breathes in classrooms throughout America. We review both basic research, which deals with reading comprehension largely in its theoretical aspect, and applied research, which is much more concerned about how comprehension gets operationalized in classrooms, reading materials, and tests.

With a renewed professional interest in reading comprehension (e.g., Rand Study Group, 2001), it is an optimal time to undertake a new initiative in the area of reading comprehension assessment. For a host of reasons, many having to do with curricular politics, reading comprehension has been placed on a back burner for well over 15 years. It is time it returned to a central role in discussions of reading. To do so, it needs our rapt and collective attention at this particular

---

[1]The original version of this chapter was prepared for the RAND Corporation as a background paper for their report to the Office of Educational Research and Improvement on Reading Comprehension.

point in history. First, reading comprehension, both its instruction and its assessment, is arguably the most important outcome of reform movements designed to improve reading curriculum and instruction. Second, given the national thirst for accountability, we must have better (i.e., conceptually and psychometrically more trustworthy) tools to drive the engines of accountability at the national, state, and local level. Third, and even more important, we need better assessments so that we can respond to the pleas of teachers desperate for useful tools to assist them in meeting individual needs. It is doubly appropriate that the assessment of reading comprehension receive as much attention as the construct itself. In the final analysis, a construct is judged as much by how it is operationalized as by how it is conceptualized.

The process of text comprehension has always provoked exasperated but nonetheless enthusiastic inquiry within the research community. Comprehension, or "understanding," by its very nature, is a phenomenon that can only be assessed, examined, or observed indirectly (Johnston, 1984a; Pearson & Johnson, 1978). We talk about the "click" of comprehension that propels a reader through a text, yet we never see it directly. We can only rely on indirect symptoms and artifacts of its occurrence. People tell us that they understood, or were puzzled by, or enjoyed, or were upset by, a text. Or, more commonly, we quiz them on "the text" in some way—requiring them to recall its gist or its major details, asking specific questions about its content and purpose, or insisting on an interpretation and critique of its message. All of these tasks, however challenging or engaging they might be, are little more than the residue of the comprehension process itself. Like it or not, it is precisely this residue that scholars of comprehension and comprehension assessment must work with to improve our understanding of the construct. We see little more of comprehension than Plato saw of the shadows in the cave of reality.

Models of reading comprehension and how to assess it have evolved throughout the 20th century (see Johnston, 1984b). Many techniques of assessment have risen to prominence and then fallen out of use, some to be reincarnated decades later, usually with new twists. Our aim is to provide a thorough account of what we know about assessing reading comprehension. Where possible and appropriate, we take detours into research and theory about the comprehension process, on the grounds that conceptions of the process, because they have influenced how it is assessed, will inform our understanding. We hope to illuminate the patterns, cycles, and trends in comprehension assessment. Through these efforts, we hope to provide our readers with a means to evaluate the current state of reading assessment, which we believe has reached a critical juncture, one that can be crossed only by shaping a research agenda that will improve our capacity to create valid, fair, and informative assessments of this important phenomenon.

HISTORICAL FOUNDATIONS OF READING
COMPREHENSION ASSESSMENT

Before the Beginning

Although reading comprehension assessment as a formal, identifiable activity is a 20th century phenomenon, it has been a part of classrooms as long as there have been schools, required texts, students who are required to read them, and teachers wanting or needing to know whether students understood them. In every century and every decade, every assignment given by a teacher, every book report or chapter summary, and every conversation about a book, story, article, or chapter, has provided an opportunity for assessment. It was not until well into the 20th century that we began to seize those opportunities. There are two plausible explanations for the relatively late arrival of comprehension as an indicator of reading achievement. First, the default indicator of reading prowess in the 17th to 19th centuries was definitely oral capacity, indexed either by accuracy or by expressive fluency, in the tradition of declamation and oratory (see Mathews, 1996, or Smith, 1986, for accounts of this emphasis). Second, within ecclesiastical circles, comprehension, at least in the sense of personal understanding, was not truly valued; if it mattered, it mattered largely as a stepping stone to the more valued commodity of text memorization (see Olson, 1994, for an account of the various religious traditions in text interpretation).

The Beginning

It is well worth our effort to examine early trends in reading assessment, for they suggest that nearly all of the tools we use to measure reading comprehension today made an appearance in some way shape or form before World War II. Granted, today's formats and approaches may look more sophisticated and complex, but, as our review demonstrates, those formats were there, at least in prototypic form, long ago.

The first systematic attempts to index reading ability by measuring comprehension date back to the period just prior to World War I. Binet, as early as 1895 (cited in Johnston, 1984a), used comprehension test items, ironically, to measure intelligence rather than reading achievement. In 1916, Kelly brought us the first published comprehension assessment, the *Kansas Silent Reading Tests*. Thorndike, in his classic 1917 piece, *Reading as Reasoning: A Study of Mistakes in Paragraph Reading*, offered us our first professional glimpse "inside the head" as he tried to characterize what must have been going on in the minds of students to produce the sorts of answers they come up with when answering questions about text. As we indicated earlier, the quest to get as close as possible to the "phenomenological act of comprehension" as it occurs has always driven re-searchers to discover new and more direct indexes of reading comprehension.

The scientific movement and the changing demographic patterns of school-ing in America were both forces that shaped the way reading was conceptual-ized and assessed in the first third of the century. Schools had to accommodate rapid increases in enrollment due to waves of immigration, a rapidly industrial-izing society, the prohibition of child labor, and mandatory school attendance laws. The spike in school enrollment, coupled with a population of students with dubious literacy skills, dramatically increased the need for a cheap, effi-cient screening device to determine students' levels of literacy. During this same period, psychology struggled to gain the status of a "science" by employing the methods that governed physical sciences and research. In America, the be-haviorist schools of thought, with their focus on measurable outcomes, strongly influenced the field of psychology (Johnston, 1984a; Pearson, 2000; Resnick, 1982); quantification and objectivity were the two hallmarks to which educa-tional "science" aspired. Thus, when psychologists with their newfound scien-tific lenses were put to work creating cheap and efficient tests for beleaguered schools, the course of reading assessment was set. Group administered, multi-ple-choice, standardized tests would be the inevitable result.

The other strong influence in moving toward comprehension as a measure of reading accomplishment was the curricular shift from oral to silent reading as the dominant mode of reading activity in our classrooms. Although the first published reading assessment, circa 1914 (Gray, 1916, 1917), was an oral read-ing assessment created by William S. Gray (who eventually became a preemi-nent scholar in the reading field and the senior author of the country's most widely used reading series), most reading assessments developed in the first third of this century focused on the relatively new construct of silent reading (see Pearson, 2000; Johnston, 1984a). Unlike oral reading, which had to be tested individually and required that teachers judge the quality of responses, si-lent reading comprehension (and rate) could be tested in group settings and scored without recourse to professional judgment; only stop watches and multi-ple-choice questions were needed. In modern parlance, we would say that they moved from a "high inference" assessment tool (oral reading and retelling) to a "low inference" tool (multiple-choice tests or timed readings). Thus, it fit the demands for efficiency and scientific objectivity, themes that were part of the emerging scientism of the period. The practice proved remarkably persistent for at least another 40 or 50 years. Significant developments in reading compre-hension would occur in the second third of the century, but assessment would remain a psychometric rather than a cognitive activity until the cognitive revo-lution of the early 1970s.

It is important to note that comprehension instruction and the curricular materials teachers employed were driven by the same infrastructure of tasks used to create test items—finding main ideas, noting important details, determining sequence of events, cause–effect relations, comparing and contrasting, and drawing conclusions.[2] If these new assessments had not found a comfortable match in school curricular schemes, one wonders whether they would have survived and prospered to the degree that they did.

Intelligence and Comprehension.   Interestingly, it was difficult to tell the difference, in these early years, between reading comprehension assessments and intelligence tests. Freeman (1926) noted that Binet (1895, as cited in Johnston, 1984a) had used reading comprehension items as a part of his IQ battery. Consider, also, this item from an early (but undated) edition of a Thurstone (n.d.) intelligence test[3] (cited in Johnson, 1984a):

> Every one of us, whatever our speculative opinion, knows better than he practices, and recognizes a better law than he obeys. (Froude)

Check two of the following statements with the same meaning as the quotation above.

_____   To know right is to do the right.
_____   Our speculative opinions determine our actions.
_____   Our deeds often fall short of the actions we approve.
_____   Our ideas are in advance of our every day behavior.

Minor Anomalies and Omens of the Future.   Although behaviorism was the dominant paradigm underlying curricular and assessment work during this period, remnants of a cognitively more complex approach of the sort that Huey described near the turn of the century (Huey, 1908) made minor appearances on the assessment scene. Free recall was used by a few researchers as an index of comprehension. Starch (1915), for example, created a ratio (the number of relevant words a student remembered in a passage in comparison to the proportion of total words remembered) as an index of comprehension. Courtis (1914) developed a similar but simpler index (ratio of idea units reproduced or interpreted to the number possible). These indexes, especially the relevance index,

---

[2]This tradition of isomorphism between the infrastructure of tests and curriculum has been a persistent issue throughout the century. See, for example, Johnson & Pearson (1975), and Resnick (1982). See also Smith (1966) for an account of the expansion of reading comprehension as a curricular phenomenon.

[3]The use of more than one right answer predates the infamous a, b, c (a and b) multiple-choice format as well as the systematic use of the "more than one right answer" approach used in some state assessments in the 1980s and 1990s (Pearson et al., 1990).

foreshadow work in the 1970s and 1980s on "importance" (as indexed by the relevance of propositions to a text's ideational structure (e.g., Rumelhart, 1977). Even at this early stage, scholars recognized that recall is not the same process as making or uncovering meaning (Kelly, 1916), but recall continued to be used in research, and later in practice, as a direct index of comprehension. This use of recall would be revived in the 1970s as a retelling procedure, which would give us a window on whether students were remembering important ideas in stories (Stein & Glenn, 1977) or in the propositional data base of expository texts (Kintsch & van Dijk, 1978; Turner & Greene, 1977).

Consistent with the efficiency criterion in the new scientific education, speed was often used as an important factor in assessing comprehension. Kelly, the author of the *Kansas Silent Reading Tests* (1916), required students to complete as many of a set of 16 diverse tasks as they could in the 5 min allotted. The tasks included some "fill in the blanks," some verbal logic problems, and some procedural tasks (following directions). Monroe also used a speeded task—asking students to underline the words that answered specific questions.

We can even find foreshadowing of the error detection paradigms that were to be so widely used by psychologists investigating metacognitive processes in the 1970s through the 1990s (Markman, 1977; Winograd & Johnston, 1980). For example, Chapman (1924) asked students to detect words that were erroneous or out of place in the second half of each paragraph (presumably they did so by using, as the criterion for rejection, the set or schema for paragraph meaning that became established as they read the first half). In 1936, Eurich required students to detect "irrelevant clauses" rather than words.

Thorndike (1917) was probably the first educational psychologist to try to launch inquiry into both the complex thought processes associated with comprehension and assessment methods. He referred to reading "as reasoning," suggesting that there are many factors that comprise it: "elements in a sentence, their organization ... proper relations, selection of certain connotations and the rejection of others, and the cooperation of many forces" (Thorndike, 1917, p. 323). He proposed ideas about what should occur during "correct reading," claiming that a great many misreadings of questions and passages are produced because of underpotency or overpotency of individual words, thus violating his "correct weighting" principle: "Understanding a paragraph is like solving a problem in mathematics. It consists in selecting the right elements in the situation and putting them together in the right relations, and also with the right amount of weight or influence or force of each" (Thorndike, 1917, p. 329). Of course, he assumed that there are such things as "correct" readings. He argued further that in the act of reading, the mind must organize and analyze ideas from the text. "The vice of the poor reader is to say the words to himself without actively making judgments concerning what they reveal" (Thorndike, 1917, p. 332). Clearly for Thorndike, reading was an active and complex cognitive process. Although this perspective did not become dominant in this early period, it certainly anticipated the highly active view of the reader that would become prominent during the cognitive revolution of the 1970s.[4]

Paralleling an active line of inquiry in oral reading error analysis (see Allington, 1984) during this period, some researchers followed Thorndike's lead and tried to develop taxonomies of the kinds of errors readers make either during decoding or understanding. Touton and Berry (1931, cited in Davis, 1968) classified errors into six categories based on research on college students' (a) failure to understand the question, (b) failure to isolate elements of "an involved statement" read in context, (c) failure to associate related elements in a context, (d) failure to grasp and retain ideas essential to understanding concepts, (e) failure to see setting of the context as a whole, and (f) other irrelevant answers.

Although Goodman (1968, 1969) is rightfully credited with helping us understand that oral reading errors, or *miscues*, to use his term, can reveal much about the comprehension processes in which a student engages; there were inklings of this perspective emerging in the 1920s. Gates (1937), for example, was interested in how readers' fluency may be an indicator of one's ability and understanding. He looked at readers' "error of hesitation," that is, whether a reader stumbled over a word or phrase. Durrell (1955) and later Betts (1946) sought to use these error patterns as indicators of the level of reading material students could handle, both from a word recognition and comprehension perspective. These early scholars determined that students who misread many words (they found that 2% seems to be our outside limit—although modern scholars often go up to 5%) will have difficulty comprehending a passage. These harbingers notwithstanding, it would be another 30 years before Goodmans' (Goodman, 1968; Goodman, 1969; Goodman & Burke, 1970) miscue analysis work prompted us to take oral reading miscues seriously as a lens that would allow us to look into the windows of the mind at the comprehension process.

PSYCHOMETRICS GATHERS MOMENTUM

Two significant events in the history of assessment occurred during the 1930s and 1940s; both would have dramatic effects on reading comprehension assess-

---

[4]It is somewhat ironic that the sort of thinking exhibited in this piece did not become a dominant view in the early 1900s. Unquestionably, Thorndike (1917) was the preeminent educational psychologist of his time. Further, his work in the psychology of learning (the law of effect and the law of contiguity) became the basis of the behaviorism that dominated educational psychology and pedagogy during this period, and his work in assessment was highly influential in developing the components of classical measurement theory (reliability and validity). Somehow this more cognitively-oriented side of his work was less influential, at least in the period in which it was written.

ment. First, in 1935, IBM introduced the IBM 805 scanner, which had the potential to reduce the cost of scoring dramatically (compared to hand-scoring of multiple-choice, or "even worse," short answer and essay tests) by a factor of 10 (Johnston, 1984a). It is not insignificant that the Scholastic Aptitude Test, which, in the 1920s and early 1930s, had been mostly an essay test, was transformed into a machine-scorable multiple-choice test shortly thereafter (Resnick, 1982). This development paved the way for a new generation of multiple-choice assessments for all fields in which testing is used; reading comprehension assessment proved no exception.

Determining the Infrastructure of Reading Comprehension

The second important event was the publication, in 1944, of Frederick Davis's landmark doctoral dissertation in which he used a brand new statistical tool, factor analysis, to determine whether a set of conceptually distinct subtests of reading comprehension (entities like finding main ideas, selecting details, determining word meanings, drawing conclusions, determining cause–effect relations, distinguishing fact from opinion, and the like) were also psychometrically distinct. Factor analysis is a technique, still highly popular among traditional psychometricians, in which the covariation among "units" (usually items or subtests) is examined to discover which units tend to cluster with (i.e., covary with) which other units. Armed with this new tool, researchers were (at least theoretically) ready to answer a question that had vexed both test makers and curriculum designers for the two or three decades in which reading tests and reading curriculum had become part of the American educational landscape: Is comprehension a unitary or a multivariate construct? That is, are there distinct subcomponents, subprocesses, or "skills" that ought to be measured and perhaps taught separately? Or, alternatively, is reading better construed as a unitary process that ought to be considered holistically?

In his groundbreaking 1944 study, Davis reviewed the literature describing reading comprehension as a construct and found several hundred skills mentioned. He sorted them into nine categories (see Table 2.1) that he felt constituted conceptually distinct groups; from these he devised nine testable skills (based also in part on correlation data). Davis employed the most sophisticated factor analytic tools available (Kelley, 1935) in his search for psychometric uniqueness to match the conceptual uniqueness of his categories. Acknowledging the unreliability of some of the subtests (due among other factors to the small standard deviations and the fact that each passage had items from several cognitive categories attached to it), he was able to conclude that reading comprehension consisted of two major factors, word knowledge and "reasoning

TABLE 2.1
Davis's Nine Potential Factors

1. Word meanings	6. Text-based questions with paraphrase
2. Word meanings in context	7. Draw inferences about content
3. Follow passage organization	8. Literary devices
4. Main thought	9. Author's purpose
5. Answer specific text-based questions	

about reading," that were sufficiently powerful and reliable to guide us in the construction of tests and reading curriculum. He speculated that another three factors (comprehension of explicitly stated ideas, understanding passage organization, and detecting literary devices) had the potential, with better item development, to reveal themselves as independent factors.

Between 1944 and the early 1970s, several scholars attempted to either replicate or refute Davis's findings. Harris (1948) found only one factor among the seven he tested. Derrik (1953) found three, and they were consistent across different levels of passage length. Hunt (1957) used differential item analysis and correction formulae to adjust his correlations, finding vocabulary (i.e., word knowledge) as the single most important factor.

Partially in response to the conflicting evidence in the field, Davis (1968, 1972) replicated his earlier work but with a more sophisticated design and set of analysis tools, not to mention the newly available capacity of mainframe computers. Using a very large set of items from various publishers and his own bank of items, he constructed 40 multiple-choice questions per hypothesized skill, each derived from a separate passage.[5] From this set, he created a more psychometrically sound subset of 24 items for each skill; that is, he selected items that exhibited high correlations with the total subtest and the total test but low correlations with other subtests. Armed with this virtually optimal set of items, he tested the independence of eight distinguishable subskills remarkably similar to the set used in his 1944 study (see Table 2.2).

Davis (1968) used cross validation (the use of multiple regression weights computed in one matrix to obtain multiple correlation coefficients in a different but analogous matrix) and multiple regression analyses to determine the pro-

---

[5]The availability of items, each derived from a separate passage, represents a great psychometric advantage because the conceptual case for item independence can be made. However, as a practical matter, it is dubious that we would, could, or will ever use comprehension assessments with only one item per passage.

TABLE 2.2
Davis's Eight Potential Factors (1968)

1. Remembering word meaning	5. Drawing inferences from the content
2. Word meanings in context	6. Recognizing the author's tone, mood, and purpose
3. Understanding content stated explicitly	7. Recognizing literary techniques
4. Weaving together ideas in the content	8. Following the structure of the content

portion of common and unique variance among the subtests. Remembering word meanings explained the most (32%) unique variance. This was followed by "drawing inferences from content," with 20% unique variance. This was followed, in order of magnitude of unique variance, by "structure of the passage," "writerly techniques" and "explicit comprehension." Again, he concluded that comprehension was not a unitary factor.

During the late 1960s and early 1970s, there was a flurry of activity in this tradition. Spearitt (1972) reviewed and re-analyzed what seemed to be Davis's 1968 work, finding at least four statistically differentiable skills, only one of which appeared to be clearly unique, whereas the other three could be measuring the same general ability. Schreiner, Hieronymus, and Forsyth (1971), analyzing data from the popular Iowa Test of Basic Skills, supplemented by additional subtests measuring general cognitive and verbal skills (e.g., listening comprehension, verbal reasoning, and reading and skimming speed), found that all of the supplementary tests were statistically independent but that the various reading comprehension subtests (paragraph meaning, cause and effect, reading for inferences, and selecting main ideas) could not be statistically differentiated from one another. By the mid-1970s, we witnessed a sharp decline of this rich area of scholarship, with the general view among reading educators being that there were not nearly as many distinct subskills as the available tests and instructional programs of the era would lead one to believe. That would not, however, stop the proliferation of single skill tests, which became even more popular in the 1970s and 1980s.

Although it is difficult to trace precise causal links between this extensive work on factor analysis and the prevailing practices in reading assessment, it is worth noting that virtually all of the commercially popular reading assessments of this era (for that matter, in both preceding and following eras)[6] followed the

---

[6]The persistence and resilience of standardized reading tests is quite remarkable. As a part of our work, we traced the evolution, across several editions, of several of the most popular standardized tests. Stability clearly outshines change in the examination of the history of these tests.

practice of embedding comprehension skills that varied on some dimension of perceived cognitive complexity (finding details, inferring details, selecting or inferring main ideas, drawing inferences about characters and ideas, detecting author's craft, etc.) within a set of short passages on different topics.[7] To achieve a balanced test, developers would build a matrix in which content (in the case of reading comprehension, content is construed as the topics of the passages) was crossed with the processes (the various cognitive skills in the underlying model of reading); they would then use the matrix to monitor the "balance" of item types appearing in the final version of a commercial test.

The Cloze Procedure

In the 1950s, Wilson Taylor (1953) developed the cloze procedure as an alternative to the conventional standardized test. Taylor began with the assumption that even the process of writing multiple-choice items was subjective. Instead of introducing subjectivity by requiring test developers to determine what content and features of a passage should be assessed, Taylor developed the cloze technique, which replaces human judgment with a mechanical approach to item development. A test designer simply deletes every nth word (usually every fifth word) in a passage; the task of the examinee is to fill in each cloze blank. The more blanks filled in, the higher the comprehension score. There was a buzz of excitement about the cloze procedure during the 1960s and 1970s (see Rankin, 1965; see also Bormuth, 1966, for the most elaborate application of cloze). Cloze was touted as the scientific alternative to multiple-choice tests of reading comprehension. It was widely used as the comprehension criterion in studies of readability in the 1960s (see Bormuth, 1966). It became the cornerstone of reading assessment for ESL (English as a second language) speakers (see Bachman, 1982), where it is still widely used (Bachman, 2000).

Cloze has experienced a great deal of adaptation over the years. For example, in the classic cloze procedure, students are asked to write in their responses when every fifth word is deleted. Only exact replacement is scored as correct; synonyms will not do. However, researchers and test developers have created a modified cloze procedure using a whole host of variations:

- Allow synonyms to serve as correct answers.
- Delete only every fifth content word (leaving function words intact).
- Use an alternative to every fifth word deletion.

---

[7]Highly influential in this period was Bloom's (1956) taxonomy of the cognitive domain, in which he laid out a hierarchy of processes that presumably varied on a dimension of cognitive complexity.

- Delete words at the end of sentences and provide a set of choices from which examinees are to pick the best answer (this tack is employed in several standardized tests, including the Stanford Diagnostic Reading Test and the Degrees of Reading Power).

The unsettled question about cloze tests is whether they are measures of individual differences in comprehension or measures of the linguistic predictability of the passages to which they are applied. They have been widely criticized for this ambiguity. But perhaps the most damaging evidence in their role as indexes of reading comprehension is that they are not sensitive to "intersentential" comprehension, that is, understanding that reaches across sentences in a passage. In a classic study, Shanahan, Kamil, and Tobin (1983) created several passage variations and assessed cloze fill-in rates. In one condition, sentence order was scrambled by randomly ordering the sentences. In another condition, sentences from different passages were intermingled, and in a third condition, isolated sentences from different passages were used. There were no differences in cloze fill-in rate across any of these conditions, indicating that an individual's ability to fill in cloze blanks does not depend on passage context; in short, when people fill in cloze blanks, they do not think across sentence boundaries. In the period of the cognitive revolution of the 1980s, in which comprehension was viewed as an integrative process, a measure that did not require text integration did not fare well.

These findings notwithstanding, modified, multiple-choice versions of cloze are still alive and well in standardized tests (i.e., the Degrees of Reading Power and the Stanford Diagnostic Reading Test referred to earlier) and in ESL assessment for adults and college students (Bachman, 2000).

Passage Dependency

Beginning in the late 1960s, a new construct arose in reading assessment, one that, at the time, had the impact of a "the emperor has no clothes" epiphany. Several scholars became concerned about the fact that many of the questions of reading comprehension on standardized tests could be answered correctly without reading the passage (mainly because the information assessed was likely to exist in examinees' prior knowledge as well as in the text). This problem is particularly exacerbated in passages about everyday or common academic topics (in comparison, for example, to fictional narratives). A number of researchers (e.g., Tuinman, 1974, 1978) conducted passage dependency studies in which some participants took the test without the passage being present. The difference between the p value of an item in the two conditions (with and without text) is an index of an item's passage dependency. The logic of this construct is simple and compelling: a reader should have to read a passage to answer questions about it. Interestingly, the interest in passage dependency, like the interest in cloze, waned considerably during the cognitive revolution. In the new paradigm, prior knowledge would be embraced as one of the cornerstones of comprehension, and scholars would attempt to take prior knowledge into account rather than try to eliminate or encapsulate its impact on comprehension (see Johnston, 1984b, for an account of these attempts during the early 1980s).

THE IMPACT OF CRITERION-REFERENCED ASSESSMENT[8]

Beginning in the 1960s and lasting until the late 1980s, criterion-referenced tests (CRT) became a major force in classroom reading assessment and basal reading programs. The theoretical rationale for CRTs comes from the mastery learning work of eminent scholars such as Benjamin Bloom (1968), John Carroll (1963), and Robert Gagné. The idea behind mastery learning was that if we could just be more precise about the essential elements involved in learning any particular domain or process, we could bring most, if not all, students to higher levels of achievement, perhaps even levels where we could state with confidence that they had mastered the skill. The precision could be achieved, according to the champions of mastery learning (see Otto, 1977; Otto & Chester, 1976), by decomposing the domain or process into essential elements. Then one could teach (and test) each of the elements to mastery. To determine whether an element had been mastered, a transparent test was needed, one in which a clear criterion had been met. In CRTs, an absolute standard, such as 80% correct on a test of the particular element, not a relative standard, such as the average score of students in a given classroom, grand, school, or state, would serve as the criterion.[9]

Criterion-referenced assessments were popular throughout our schools and curricula in the 1970s and 1980s, but nowhere was their influence more dramatically felt than in basal reading materials. Starting in the early 1970s, basal programs developed criterion-referenced tests for every unit (a grouping of 6 to 8 stories plus associated activities) and every book in the series. Each successive edition of basal programs brought an increase in the number of these single component tests—tests for each phonics skill (all the beginning, middle and fi-

---

[8]For this section, we relied heavily on the treatment of these issues in Sarroub and Pearson (1998).

[9]The most compelling version of criterion-referenced assessment is domain-referenced assessment, a practice in which the items in a test are viewed as a sample from the population of items representing performance in that domain of knowledge or inquiry. Early proponents of domain referenced assessment (see Bormuth, 1970; Hively, 1974) saw great hope for this approach as a way of estimating student mastery over knowledge domains. Modern proponents (e.g., Bock, 1997) are no less enthusiastic.

nal consonant sounds, vowel patterns, and syllabication), tests for each comprehension skill (main idea, finding details, drawing conclusions, and determining cause–effect relations) at every grade level, tests for alphabetical order and using the encyclopedia, and just about any other skill one might imagine. With powerful evidence from mastery learning's application to college students (Bloom, 1968), publishers of basal programs and some niche publishers began to create and implement what came to be called skills management systems.[10] In their most meticulous application, these systems became the reading program. Students took a battery of mastery tests, practiced those skills they had not mastered (usually by completing worksheets that looked remarkably like the tests), took tests again, and continued through this cycle until they had mastered all the skills assigned to the grade level (or until the year ended). Unsurprisingly, the inclusion of these highly specific skill tests had the effect of increasing the salience of workbooks, worksheets, and other "skill materials" that students could practice in anticipation of (and as a consequence of) mastery tests. Thus, the basals of this period included two parallel systems: (a) a graded series of anthologies filled with stories and short nonfiction pieces for oral and silent reading and discussion, and (b) an embedded skills management system to guide the development of phonics, comprehension, vocabulary, and study skills. In the true mastery programs (e.g., Board of Education, City of Chicago, 1984; Otto, 1977) and in some basal programs, students who failed a particular subtest were required to practice skill sheets that looked remarkably like the mastery tests until they could achieve mastery (which was usually and arbitrarily defined as 80% correct).

For comprehension assessment, the consequences were dramatic. Even with standardized, multiple-choice assessments of the ilk studied by Davis (1968), there had been some sense that important aspects of a passage ought to be queried. But with the new criterion-referenced assessments of reading comprehension, the number of comprehension subskills increased dramatically, as did the number of specific skill tests for each of these. Clearly, in these assessments, as illustrated in Fig. 2.1, the emphasis is on the skill rather than the passage. The passage is nothing more than a vehicle that allows for an assessment of the skill. For example, Figure 1 tests a child's ability to recognize sequential order.

---

[10]The most popular of these systems was the Wisconsin Design for Reading Skill Development, followed closely by Fountain Valley. Their heyday was the decade of the 1970s, although they remained a staple, as an option, through the 1980s and 1990s and are still available as options in today's basals. For an account of the rationale behind these systems, see Otto (1977). For a critique of these programs during their ascendency, see Johnson and Pearson (1975).

The children wanted to make a book for their teacher. One girl brought a camera to school. She took a picture of each person in the class. Then they wrote their names under the pictures. One boy tied all the pages together. Then the children gave the book to their teacher.

1. What happened first?
   a. The children wrote their names
   b. Someone brought a camera to school
   c. The children gave a book to their teacher
2. What happened after the children wrote their names?
   a. A boy put the pages together
   b. The children taped their pictures
   c. A girl took pictures of each person
3. What happened last?
   a. The children wrote their names under the pictures
   b. A girl took pictures of everyone
   c. The children gave a book to their teacher

FIG. 2.1. An example of a basal reader's criterion-referenced test (adapted from the Ginn Reading Program, 1982).

The basals of the 1970s and 1980s were filled with tests like these for up to 30 different comprehension skills (Johnson & Pearson, 1975).[11] More importantly, they persisted and flourished in the face of many professional critiques of their theoretical and practical efficacy, validity, and utility (Johnson & Pearson, 1975; Valencia & Pearson, 1987b).

Standardized reading assessments also felt the impact of criterion-referenced assessment. First, several testing companies brought out their own versions of criterion-referenced assessments that could compete with those offered by start-up companies (e.g., Fountain Valley and National Computer Systems —the marketer of Wisconsin Design). Second, and perhaps more influential, most testing companies created the capacity to report scores on their standardized assessment by specific comprehension subskills (e.g., main idea, details, inferences, author's craft, etc.). In so doing, they were, in somewhat ironic a fashion, completing the goal laid out by Davis (1944) when he began his quest

[11]A related movement, domain-referenced assessment, also became popular during this period, but it did not establish a strong foothold within reading assessment. In a field like mathematics, it made sense to talk about the domain or population of all two-digit multiplication facts or the like. However, a concept such as all of the possible literal comprehension probes for stories appropriate for Grade 2 readers seems to make little sense. Only Bormuth (1970) developed anything approaching a domain-referenced approach for assessing reading comprehension in his nearly forgotten classic, *On the Theory of Achievement Test Items*.

to identify independent subprocesses of comprehension in the early 1940s. Thus, by 1985, it was possible for a school to receive not only conventional reports of the average, by grade or class, of grade norm, percentile, NCE (normal curve equivalent), or stanine scores, but also reports of the percentage of students, by grade or class, who demonstrated mastery (i.e., exceeded the cut score) on each of the component skills included in the test.

THE REVOLUTIONS BEGIN

Somewhere during this period of active psychometric work on reading assessment (between 1955 and 1975—the exact point of departure is hard to fix), the field of reading experienced a paradigm shift. The underlying theoretical perspectives of behaviorism on which reading pedagogy and reading assessment had been built throughout the century were challenged, overturned, and replaced by a succession of pretenders to the theoretical throne. Along the way, reading scholars were forced to confront fundamental shifts in the prevailing views of reading and writing that led to the creation of a variety of serious curricular alternatives to the conventional wisdom of the 1970s. Reading became an ecumenical scholarly commodity; it was embraced by scholars from many different fields of inquiry (see Pearson & Stephens, 1993, for a complete account of this phenomenon). The first to take reading under their wing were the linguists, who wanted to convince us that reading was a language process closely allied to its sibling language processes of writing, speaking, and listening. Then came the psycholinguists and the cognitive psychologists, who convinced us to seek out the underlying language and cognitive processes that enabled reading. They were soon followed soon by the sociolinguists, the philosophers, the literary critics, and the critical theorists, each bringing a critique of its immediate predecessor, each offering a new perspective to guide instructional practice, including assessment.

It is not altogether clear why reading has attracted such interest from scholars in so many other fields. One explanation is that reading is considered by so many to be a key to success in other endeavors in and out of school; this is often revealed in comments like, "Well if you don't learn to read, you can't learn other things for yourself." Another reason is that scholars in these other disciplines thought that the educationists had got it all wrong: it was time for another field to have its perspective heard. Whatever the reasons, the influence of these other scholarly traditions on reading pedagogy is significant; in fact, neither the pedagogy nor the assessment of the 1980s and 1990s can be understood without a firm grounding in the changes in worldview that these perspectives spawned.

In terms of reading comprehension assessment, three of these movements are particularly important: cognitive psychology, sociolinguistics (and more general sociocultural perspectives), and literary theory (in the form of reader response theory). Cognitive psychology spawned the first of two major shifts in comprehension assessment; the second was prompted by the joint influence sociolinguistics and literary theory.

COGNITIVE PSYCHOLOGY

In rejecting behaviorism, cognitive psychology allowed psychologists to extend constructs such as human purpose, intention, and motivation to a greater range of psychological phenomena, including perception, attention, comprehension, learning, memory, and executive control or "metacognition" of all cognitive process. All of these would have important consequences in reading pedagogy and, to a lesser extent, reading assessment.

The most notable change within psychology was that it became fashionable for psychologists, for the first time since the early part of the century, to study complex phenomena such as language and reading.[12] And in the decade of the 1970s, works by psychologists flooded the literature on basic processes in reading. One group focused on text comprehension, trying to explain how readers come to understand the underlying structure of texts. We were offered story grammars—structural accounts of the nature of narratives, complete with predictions about how those structures impede and enhance story understanding and memory (Mandler & Johnson, 1977; Rumelhart, 1977; Stein & Glenn, 1977). Others chose to focus on the expository tradition in text (e.g., Kintsch, 1974; Meyer, 1975). Like their colleagues interested in story comprehension, they believed that structural accounts of the nature of expository (informational) texts would provide valid and useful models for human text comprehension. And in a sense, both of these efforts worked. Story grammars did provide explanations for story comprehension. Analyses of the structural relations among ideas in an informational piece also provided explanations for expository text comprehension. However, neither text-analysis tradition really tackled the relation between the knowledge of the world that readers bring to text and comprehension of those texts. In other words, by focusing on structural rather than the ideational, or content, characteristics of texts, they failed to get to the heart of comprehension. That task, as it turned out, fell to one of the most popular and influential movements of the 1970s: schema theory.

Schema theory (see Anderson & Pearson, 1984; Rumelhart, 1981) is a theory about the structure of human knowledge as it is represented in memory. In our memory, schemata are like little containers into which we deposit the par-

---

[12]During this period, great homage was paid to intellectual ancestors such as Edmund Burke Huey, who, as early as 1908, recognized the cognitive complexity of reading. Voices such as Huey's, unfortunately, were not heard during the period from 1915 to 1965 when behaviorism dominated psychology and education.

ticular traces of particular experiences as well as the "ideas" that derive from those experiences. So, if we see a chair, we store that visual experience in our "chair schema." If we go to a restaurant, we store that experience in our "restaurant schema." If we attend a party, we store that experience in our "party schema," and so on.

Schema theory also provided a credible account of reading comprehension, which probably, more than any of its other features, accounted for its popularity within the reading field in the 1970s and 80s.[13] Schema theory struck a sympathetic note with researchers as well as practitioners. It provided a rich and detailed theoretical account of the everyday intuition that we understand and learn what is new in terms of what we already know. It also accounted for the everyday phenomenon of disagreements in interpreting stories, movies, and news events—we disagree with one another because we approach the phenomenon with very different background experiences and knowledge.

With respect to reading comprehension, schema theory encouraged educators to examine texts from the perspective of the knowledge and cultural backgrounds of students to evaluate the likely connections that they would be able to make between ideas inscribed[14] in the text and the schema that they would bring to the reading task. Schema theory also promoted a constructivist view of comprehension; all readers, at every moment in the reading process, construct the most coherent model of meaning for the texts they read.[15] Perhaps the most important legacy of this constructivist perspective was that it introduced ambiguity about the question of where meaning resides. Does it reside in the text? In the author's mind as she sets pen to paper? In the mind of each reader as she builds a model of meaning unique to her experience and reading? In the interaction between reader and text? Schema theory raised, but did not settle these questions.

The Impact of Cognitive Science on Assessment

The impact of this new work in comprehension on curriculum and classroom teaching was immediate. We saw huge changes in basal readers, which, even

---

[13]It is not altogether clear that schema theory is dead, especially in contexts of practice. Its role in psychological theory is undoubtedly diminished due to attacks on its efficacy as a model of memory and cognition. See McNamara, Miller, and Bransford (1991) or Spiro and Jehng (1990).

[14]Smagorinsky (2001) used the phrase *inscribed* in the text as a way of indicating that the author of the text had some specific intentions when he or she set pen to paper, thereby avoiding the thorny question of whether meaning exists "out there" outside of the minds of readers. We use the term here to avoid the very same question.

[15]Most coherent model is defined as that model which provides the best account of the "facts" of the text uncovered at a given point in time by the reader in relation to the schemata instantiated at that same point in time.

until the late 1980s, remained the core tool of classroom practice. These included the following: (a) more attention to the role of prior knowledge introducing new texts, explicit teaching of comprehension strategies; (b) attention to text structure (in the form of story maps and visual displays to capture the organizational structure of text); and (c) the introduction of metacognitive monitoring (reflecting on what one has read, said, or written to see if it makes sense; see Pearson, 2000).

The impact on assessment, in particular, the unsettled question of where meaning resides, was fairly transparent: How, with even a modicum of respect for fairness, can we use tests with single correct answers if we know that answers are influenced by experience and background knowledge? It was not long before educators began to ask questions about whether the long tradition of standardized, multiple-choice assessments could or should continue to be used as measures of program quality or teacher effectiveness.

Table 2.3 (from Valencia & Pearson, 1987b) illustrates clearly the tensions that existed between the new cognitively oriented views of the reading process and prevailing assessment praxis in the mid 1980s.

By the late 1980s, constructivist approaches to reading assessment began to emerge. These were new efforts and new perspectives, and they sought new formats and new approaches to question generation for assessments. They privileged conceptual over psychometric criteria in building new reading assessments. They emphasized the need for assessments to reflect resources such as prior knowledge, environmental clues, the text itself, and the key players involved in the reading process. They emphasized metacogntion as a reflective face of comprehension. And they championed the position that only a fresh start in assessments would give us tests to match our models of instruction.

Major Changes. Changes included longer text passages, more challenging questions, and different question formats (such as the "more than one right answer" format and open-ended questions). Reading scholars acknowledged that although all multiple-choice items include answers that are plausible under certain conditions, they do not necessarily invite reflection or interactive learning. Assessment efforts in Illinois and Michigan (see Valencia, Pearson, Peters, & Wixson, 1989) led the charge in trying to incorporate these new elements. First, in the spirit of authenticity, they included longer, and more naturally occurring or "authentic" text selections in tests. Also, both included test items that measured prior knowledge rather than trying to neutralize its effects (i.e., the passage dependency phenomenon). They also included items that were designed to measure students' use of reading strategies and their dispositions toward reading. For example, the Illinois Goal Assessment Program (1991) promoted

TABLE 2.3

A Set of Contrasts Between Cognitively-Oriented Views of Reading and Prevailing Practices in Assessing Reading Circa 1986

New Views of the Reading Process Tell Us That ...	*Yet When We Assess Reading Comprehension, We ...*
Prior knowledge is an important determinant of reading comprehension.	Mask any relation between prior knowledge and reading comprehension by using lots of short passages on lots of topics.
A complete story or text has structural and topical integrity.	Use short texts that seldom approximate the structural and topical integrity of an authentic text.
Inference is an essential part of the process of comprehending units as small as sentences.	Rely on literal comprehension text items.
The diversity in prior knowledge across individuals as well as the varied causal relations in human experiences invite many possible inferences to fit a text or question.	Use multiple-choice items with only one correct answer, even when many of the responses might, under certain conditions, be plausible.
The ability to vary reading strategies to fit the text and the situation is one hallmark of an expert reader.	Seldom assess how and when students vary the strategies they use during normal reading, studying, or when the going gets tough.
The ability to synthesize information from various parts of the text and different texts is the hallmark of an expert reader.	Rarely go beyond finding the main idea of a paragraph or passage.
The ability to ask good questions of text, as well as to answer them, is the hallmark of an expert reader.	Seldom ask students to create or select questions about a selection they may have just read.
All aspects of a reader's experience, including habits that arise from school and home, influence reading comprehension.	Rarely view information on reading habits and attitudes as important information about performance.
Reading involves the orchestration of many skills that complement one another in a variety of ways.	Use tests that fragment reading into isolated skills and report performance on each.
Skilled readers are fluent; their word identification is sufficiently automatic to allow most cognitive resources to be used for comprehension.	Rarely consider fluency as an index of skilled reading.
Learning from text involves the restructuring, application, and flexible use of knowledge in new situations.	Often ask readers to respond to the text's declarative knowledge rather than to apply it to near and far transfer tasks.

Note. This was adapted from Valencia and Pearson, 1987b, p. 731.

an interactive model of reading in which the construction of meaning became the locus around which reading strategies, dispositions toward literacy, text characteristics, and prior knowledge, revolved. The question in Fig. 2.2 illustrates the possibility of having more than one right answer (coded with a *) to the question.

Another powerful influence focused on the test development process rather than items per se. Consistent with the work on text structure from the early part of the cognitive revolution, many of the new assessments used elaborate text analyses procedures to generate structural representations of the texts (story maps for narratives and text maps for informational texts) to be used in developing comprehension assessments. Equipped with these structural representations, which were also hierarchical, test developers used criteria of structural importance to decide which subset, among the myriad of conceptual relations within a text, ought to be included in a comprehension assessment. Test writers employed this technique as a part of the test specification procedures in several state assessment efforts (Valencia et al., 1989) and in the National Assessment of Educational Progress from 1988 onward (NAEP Reading Consensus Project, 1992).

A Systematic Research Program. A fair amount of research on these new assessment practices was carried out in the 1980s, much of it conducted at the Center for the Study of Reading under the leadership of Valencia and Pearson (Pearson et al., 1990; Valencia & Pearson, 1987a; Valencia et al., 1986). For example, several candidate measures of prior knowledge were compared to a common criterion, an individual interview, to determine which exhibited the greatest concurrent validity (Pearson et al., 1990). This work was a part of a new way of dealing with the prior knowledge problem in reading comprehension assessment. As we mentioned earlier, the traditional approach to dealing with prior knowledge in standardized tests was to neutralize it. Test writers would

---

What do you think that the author Patricia Edwards Clyne wanted you to learn from reading "The Army of Two"?

A. There is safety in large numbers.
B. Keep things that you may need in the future in a safe place.
C. Lighthouses and sand dunes are dangerous places to live.
*D. It takes more than strength to win a battle.
*E. Careful thinking can sometimes make things possible that seem impossible.

FIG. 2.2. An item that has more than one right answer.

provide lots of short passages covering a wide variety of topics, the hope being that the variety would prevent any given type of individual from being consistently advantaged because of prior experiences.[16] The solution advocated in the 1960s was to use passage dependency analyses as a means of culling out items that could be answered without reading the text. The solution in these new assessments was to embrace prior knowledge as a part of the process of making meaning and then to assess it independently of comprehension so that its impact could be separately indexed.

Similar criterion validity studies were carried out for measures of comprehension monitoring, dispositions for reading, and comprehension. Although this work addressed a broad range of psychometric and conceptual issues, item format and test infrastructure is of greatest interest to the problems still lingering in the field. Central questions still plaguing us are which formats have the greatest validity as indexes of comprehension and how do the various items in a comprehension assessment cluster form independent factors.

The first analysis of interest in the Illinois work is a criterion validity study carried out in the 1986 pilot (Pearson et al., 1990). They investigated the relation between a common interview technique for assessing passage comprehension and four competing multiple-choice assessment formats. The four formats were conventional multiple choice: select as many answers as are plausible, rate each answer on a scale of plausibility, and select that subset of questions that would tap important information in the passage. These formats are described in Table 2.4.

Working with 200 eighth-graders who had taken the test in one of the four formats (50 per format) and operating under the assumption that in a perfect world, a one-on-one interview format would give us the best possible index of any students' comprehension, they conducted a Piagetian-like clinical interview (see Ginsburg, 1997) to interrogate their understanding of the same passage. Using retelling and follow-up question probes, each student received an interview score characterizing the breadth and depth of his or her comprehension. This score was used as the criterion variable to compare the common variance that each format shared with the interview. The researchers hypothesized that if comprehension consists of deep reasoning about passage content, then formats which emphasize deeper processing of content ought to be more closely related to (and hence serve as better predictors of) the ultimate interview criterion than those formats requiring lower levels of processing. The results supported the following hypothesis: the "rate each of the choices" format shared

---

[16]Note that this approach tends, on average, to favor those students who have high general verbal skills as might be indexed by an intelligence test, for example. These will be the students who will possess at least some knowledge on a wide array of topics (Johnston, 1984a, 1984b).

TABLE 2.4
Description and Examples of Response Formats
in the Illinois Pilot of 1986

"Single Correct Answers"
The standard comprehension format was a multiple-choice item where students select the one best answer to a question.

How does Ronnie reveal his interest in Anne?
Ronnie cannot decide whether to join in the conversation.
Ronnie gives Anne his treasure, the green ribbon.
Ronnie invites Anne to play baseball.
Ronnie gives Anne his soda.

"More Than One Right Answer"
The second item format was constructed to look very much like a traditional multiple-choice item but with one important difference: Students are told that there could be one, two, or even as many as three plausible responses to each question. The rationale behind such a format is that most questions do have more than one right answer. The ideas presented in stories and in nonfiction selections often have multiple causes and multiple relations with other ideas in the text or related to the text; hence, it is very constraining, if not misleading, to have to write items that allow only a single explanation for a complex relation.

How does Ronnie reveal his interest in Anne?
Ronnie cannot decide whether to join in the conversation.
Ronnie gives Anne his treasure, the green ribbon.
Ronnie gives Anne his soda.
Ronnie invites Anne to play baseball.
During the game, he catches a glimpse of the green ribbon in her hand.

"Score-Every-Response" Format
A slight variation of this "select-as-many-as-are-appropriate" format was developed for use at Grade 8 and Grade 10. Given items that have one, two, or as many as three plausible answers (as in the previous format), students must score each response option with a 2, 1, or 0 rating, where 2 indicates a *very good answer,* 1 indicates that the response is *on the right track,* and 0 represents a response that is *totally off the track.* In this format, students must deal with every response option, and they must use the defined criteria to help them distinguish levels of appropriateness:

How does Ronnie reveal his interest in Anne?
(2)(1)(0)   Ronnie cannot decide whether to join in the conversation.
(2)(1)(0)   Ronnie gives Anne his treasure, the green ribbon.
(2)(1)(0)   Ronnie gives Anne his soda.
(2)(1)(0)   Ronnie invites Anne to play baseball.
(2)(1)(0)   During the game, he catches a glimpse of the green ribbon in her hand.

"Question-Selection" Format
In the fourth format, students were presented with a list of 20 questions that might be asked about the passage they read. The task was to select approximately 10 questions that would be good to ask classmates to be sure they understood the reading selection. Students were not to answer these questions, but simply to identify good questions by marking each with a "Yes" or a "No." This item format is based on the research finding that skilled readers are better than poor readers at asking questions, both to clarify confusing points and to focus on important aspects of text.

the most variance in common with the interview score, followed, in order, by the "select-all-the-plausible-answers" format, the "conventional format," and the "select questions" format. Interestingly, the "rate-each-distracter" format also achieved the highest reliability ($\alpha = .93$).

The Illinois group also carried out two important factor analytic studies during the 1987 pilot. 2,700-plus students at each of four grade levels—3, 6, 8, and 10, with each student responding to comprehension, prior knowledge, metacognitive, and habits and attitudes items from two out of six passages, with each pair of passages occurring equally often in a matrix sampling plan. Using exploratory factor analysis, a three-factor solution emerged consistently across all passage pairs. Essentially the metacognitive and the habits and attitudes items each defined an independent factor with the third factor being a combination of the comprehension and prior knowledge items. Given the centrality of prior knowledge in the underlying schema-theoretic models on which the assessment was built, the clustering of knowledge and comprehension items was not a surprise. However, it must be acknowledged that the reliability of the prior knowledge scale, when calibrated at the individual level, was much lower than the reliability of the other tests.

In a second factor analysis, the group investigated whether responses to individual comprehension items across the 16 pairs of passages tended to cluster more by cognitive category or passage. Using a combination of exploratory and confirmatory factor analyses, they were unable to achieve any clustering by cognitive category. For all 16 passage pairs, passage, not cognitive process, emerged as the single explanatory factor. This led them to conclude that topical knowledge, not cognitive process, was a more salient factor in explaining variance in reading comprehension.

Sentence Verification Task. Another novel assessment approach emerging from the cognitive science work of the 1970s was the sentence verification task (SVT). It was developed by Royer and his colleagues (Royer, 1987; Royer, & Cunningham, 1981; Royer, Hastings, & Hook, 1979; Royer, Kulhavy, Lee, & Peterson, 1986; Royer, Lynch, Hambleton, & Bulgarelli,1984) to provide a measure of reading comprehension that was not, like so many multiple-choice standardized tests, dependent on external factors such as intelligence or prior knowledge. They have also championed it as a task that teachers can adapt to assess comprehension of specific texts used in their classrooms. One of its other attributes is that, like the cloze task, SVTs can be created using a procedure that involves relatively few inferences and judgments on the part of the test developer. Once a passage has been selected, item development is quite algorithmic. The test developer selects a passage, such as the one about down pillows.

One wonderful thing about grandparents, Tim decided, was the stories they could tell about his parents when they had been young. His favorite story about his mother was the famous pillow caper.

"Nowadays," Grandma said, "a feather pillow is something of a rarity or a luxury. Most people seem content with polyester fillings and such. When your mother was small, we had nothing but feather stuffed in our house. You don't know what comfort is until you've sunk your head into 3,000 bits of goose down.

"Once when your mother had nothing to do, she saw the point of one little feather sticking out of a tiny hole in the corner of her pillow. She pulled it out and another came right along to take its place. You can image the rest of this story!"

"Yes," laughed Tim, "she pulled out all the feathers."

"I went to her room," said Grandma, "and there I found 3,000 feathers flying around. All your mother could say was: 'I didn't know there would be so many of them!'"

Then one proceeds to develop an approximately equal number of four different item types (Table 2.5).

Examples for all four item types appear in Table 2.6. All, incidentally, are derived from the previous passage. When it is administered, an examinee reads the passage and then responds to the items (selecting old or new for each) without being able to look back at the text. Thus, at least short-term memory is required to complete the task.

Royer and his colleagues have applied the SVT to texts in a number of subject matters and to a diverse array of student populations, including ESL populations. The procedure produces results that meet high psychometric standards of reliability and validity (Royer, 1987). In addition, scores on the SVT are sen-

TABLE 2.5

Item Types and Definitions for New Sentence Verification Task

Item Type	Definition
• Original:	Verbatim repetition of a sentence in the passage.
• Paraphrase:	The same meaning as an original but with lots of semantic substitutes for words in the original sentence.
• Meaning change:	Uses some of the words in the passage but in a way that changes the meaning of the original sentence.
• Distracter:	A sentence that differs in both meaning and wording from the original.

TABLE 2.6
A Sample Sentence Verification Task Comprehension Test

Choices	Items
Old New	1. Most people seem content with polyester fillings and such. (Original)
Old New	2. You don't know what comfort is until you've sunk your head into 3,000 bits of polyester. (Meaning change)
Old New	3. It is always fun visiting grandparents because they take you someplace exciting, like the zoo or the circus. (Destructer)
Old New	4. Being able to hear stories of when his mom and dad were kids was one of the great things about having grandparents around, Tim concluded. (Paraphrase)
Old New	5. His favorite grandparent was his mother's mother. (Destructer)
Old New	6. In our home, we only had pillows filled with feathers when your mom was a child. (Paraphrase)
Old New	7. "Nowadays," Grandma said, "feather pillows are very common and not considered a luxury." (Meaning change)
Old New	8. His favorite story about his father was the famous pillow caper. (Meaning change)
Old New	9. Once when your mother had nothing to do, she saw the point of one little feather sticking out of a tiny hole in the corner of her pillow. (Original)
Old New	10. "I never guessed there would be this many feathers," was the only thing she could say. (Paraphrase)
Old New	11. You can guess what happened next! (Paraphrase)
Old New	12. "I went out to the yard," said Grandma, "and there I found 3,000 feathers flying around." (Meaning change)
Old New	13. She poked it back in, but another came right along to take its place. (Meaning change)
Old New	14. "Yes," laughed Tim, "she pulled out all the feathers." (Original)
Old New	15. "I wish," said Tim, "that I could get a goose down pillow." (Distracter)

sitive to other factors that are known to affect comprehension, such as prior knowledge (Royer, Lynch, Hambleton, & Bulgarelli, 1984), overall reading skill (Royer & Hambleton, 1983), intersentential comprehension (Royer, Kulhavy, Lee, & Peterson, 1984), and text readability (Royer et al., 1979). Despite a good track record and strong grounding in both the psychometric and conceptual poles, SVT never gathered much momentum in the field. We suspect that for many educators, it flunks the prima facie test: It just does not have the look and

feel of what we mean by "comprehension assessment." After all, there is no retelling and no question answering. This lack of interest is unfortunate because
the technique, or at least some of its features, could be useful in building new,
conceptually sound, efficient, and replicable assessment procedures.

Classroom Assessment. The most significant advances in classroom comprehension assessment tools during this period also came from cognitive science. First was the spread of retellings as a tool for assessing comprehension.
Driven by the 1970s advances in our knowledge about the structure of narrative
and expository text (see Meyer & Rice, 1984), many scholars (see Irwin &
Mitchell, 1983; Morrow, 1988) developed systems for evaluating the depth and
breadth of students' text understandings based on their attempts to retell or recall what they had read. Like the formal efforts of this era, there was a conscious
attempt to take into account reader, text, and context factors in characterizing
students' retellings.

Second was the "use the think-aloud" protocol as a measure of comprehension. Think-alouds had become respectable research tools by virtue of the important work on self-reports of cognitive processes popularized by Ericsson and
Simon (1984). In attempting to characterize the nature of expertise in complex
activities, such as chess, Ericsson and Simon learned that the most effective way
inside the heads of expertise was to engage the players in thinking aloud about
the what, why, and how of their thing and actions during the activity.

This led to the wider use of think-alouds. First, they became a research tool to
get at the process, not just the product of student thinking (e.g., Hartman,
1995; Olshavsky, 1976–1977). Then, they became an instructional practice
(Baumann, Jones, & Seifert-Kessell, 1993), and finally, it was used as an assessment practice (California Learning Assessment System, 1994; Farr & Greene,
1992). With the ostensible purpose of assessing metacognitive processes during
reading, Farr and Greene (1992) engaged students in write-along tasks (a kind
of mandatory set of marginal notes prompted by a red dot at key points in the
text). Students were encouraged, as they are in think-alouds, to say (in this case,
make a few notes about) what they thought at a given point. A similar practice
was a standard part of the now defunct California Learning Assessment System
(1994): marginal notes were allowed, even encouraged, in the initial reading of
the texts, and those notes were fair game for review when the tasks were scored.
Unfortunately, with the exception of a very thorough account of the research
and theoretical background on verbal protocols by Pressley and Afflerbach
(1995), very little careful work of either a conceptual or psychometric nature on
the use of think-alouds as a viable assessment tool has emerged, although there
was one effort to evaluate different approaches to metacognitive assessment in

the special studies of the National Assessment of Educational Progress (NAEP) in 1994; in fact, this effort spawned the Farr and Greene effort.

SOCIOCULTURAL AND LITERARY PERSPECTIVES

We are not sure whether what happened next constitutes a second major shift or is better thought of as an extension of the first shift. It came so fast on the heels of the cognitive revolution that it is hard to pinpoint its precise beginning point.

Sociolinguistics

In fact, harbingers of this sociocultural revolution, emanating from sociolinguistic perspectives (see Bloome & Greene, 1984) and the rediscovery of Vygotsky (see Vygotsky, 1978; Wertsch, 1985), were around in the early to mid-1980s, even as the cognitive revolution was exercising its muscle on assessment practices. For example, in cognitively motivated teaching approaches such as reciprocal teaching, students took on more responsibility for their own learning by teaching each other. In process writing, revision, and conversation around revision, delved more deeply into the social nature of reading, writing, and understanding. Teachers used such practices to engage students to reflect on their work as well as interact with others around it. The concept of "dynamic assessment" also emerged in this period. Dynamic assessment (Feuerstein et al., 1979) allows the teacher to use student responses to a given task as a basis for determining what sort of task, accompanied by what level of support and scaffolding from the teacher, should come next. Here we see both cognitive and sociocultural influences in assessment.

These early developments notwithstanding, the next round of assessment reforms carried more direct signs of the influence of these new social perspectives of learning, including group activities for the construction of meaning and peer response for activities requiring writing in response to reading.

Literary Theory

The other influential trend was a renaissance in literary theory in the elementary classroom. One cannot understand the changes in pedagogy and assessment that occurred in the late 1980s and early 1990s without understanding the impact of literary theory, particularly reader response theory. In our secondary schools, the various traditions of literary criticism have always had a voice in the curriculum, especially in guiding discussions of classic literary works. Until the middle 1980s, the "New Criticism" (Richards, 1929) that began its ascendancy in the depression era dominated the interpretation of text for several decades. It had sent teachers and students on a search for the one "true" meaning in each text they encountered.[17] With the emergence (some would argue the re-emergence) of reader response theories, all of which gave as much authority to the reader as to either the text or the author, theoretical perspectives, along with classroom practices, changed dramatically. The basals that had been so skill-oriented in the 1970s and so comprehension-oriented in the 1980s became decidedly literature-based in the late 1980s and early 1990s. Comprehension gave way to readers' response to literature. Reader response emphasizes affect and feeling that can either augment or replace cognitive responses to the content. To use the terminology of the most influential figure in the period, Louise Rosenblatt (1978), the field moved from efferent to aesthetic response to literature. And a "transactive model" replaced the "interactive model" of reading championed by the cognitive views of the 1980s. According to Rosenblatt, meaning is created in the transaction between reader and text. This meaning, which she referred to as the "poem," is a new entity that resides above the reader-text interaction. Meaning is therefore neither subject nor object nor the interaction of the two. Instead, it is transaction, something new and different from any of its inputs and influences.[18]

Illustrating the Impact of Reading Assessment

Nowhere was the influence of these two new perspectives more prominent than in the development of the California Language Arts Framework (California Department of Education, 1987) and in the assessment systems that grew out of the framework. There was a direct attempt to infuse social, cultural, and literary perspectives into comprehension assessment processes more transparent than in the work of the California Learning Assessment System (CLAS; 1994). CLAS, which died an unhappy death via legislative mandate in the mid-1990s, nonetheless paved the way for more open assessments by emphasizing response to literature formats and the social aspects of learning. Response to literature questions articulated a more open and reflective stance toward reading rather than a skills-based approach:

- If you were explaining what this essay is about to a person who had not read it, what would you say?

---

[17]We find it most interesting that the ultimate psychometrician, Frederick Davis (e.g., 1968), was fond of referencing the New Criticism of I. A. Richards (1929) in his essays and investigations about comprehension.

[18]Rosenblatt (1978) credited the idea of transaction to John Dewey, who discussed it in many texts, including *Experience and Education* (1938).

- What do you think is important or significant about it?
- What questions do you have about it?
- This is your chance to write any other observations, questions, apprecia-
tions, and criticisms of the story" (pp. 6–9).

Response to literature formats demanded students to be able to summarize,
explain, justify, interpret, and provide evidence in their answers. In other words,
assessment of reading comprehension reached a new stage, one much more compatible with what society might expect of students in the real world. The early
work of the New Standards (see Pearson, Spalding, & Myers, 1998) had the same
goals, theoretical grounding, and format characteristics as CLAS (1994):

- Give students a chance to show their expertise in artifacts that have the benefit of the same social and cultural supports that support effective instruction.
- Let the work be interesting and relevant to students? backgrounds and
cultural heritage.
- Let the work be guided by the support of colleagues who have the students' best interests at heart.
- Let the work be borne of the same motives and conditions that prevail in
the worlds of work and social action.

If the idea that students live in multiple worlds such as home, school, and
community and are expected to relate to others across contexts grew out of the
sociocultural revolution in the late 1980s, it must be acknowledged that this
revolution had well-grounded historical precedents (see Dewey, 1938). In line
with the idea of the social nature of learning, comprehension assessment systems such as CLAS and New Standards also devised reading comprehension
tests which focused on the interconnectedness of individual learning within the
contexts of group work. Figure 2.3 is such an example.

These changes in reading assessment practices did not go unnoticed by basal
reader publishers. Beginning in the late 1980s and early 1990s, they began to incorporate these practices into their internal assessment systems, using handles
such as process tests and performance assessments (see, for example, Silver
Burdett & Ginn, 1989). Basals maintained their specific skill tests, but even
with these carryovers from the 1970s, important changes occurred—longer
passages, assessment of multiple skills per passage, and a reduction in the number of skills assessed. By the mid-1990s, basal assessments had moved even further down the performance assessment road. Even so, they never completely
eliminated the specific skill tests; instead, these new assessments were added as
optional alternatives to the more traditional tools.

Now you will be working in a group. You will be preparing yourself to do some writing later. Your group will be talking about the story you read earlier. A copy of the story is provided before the group questions if you need to refer to it. Some of the activities in this section may direct you to work alone and then share with your group, the other activities may have all of you working together. It is important to take notes of your discussion because you will be able to use these notes when you do your writing.

Read the directions and do the activities described .members of the group should take turns reading the directions. The group leader should keep the activities moving along so that you finish all the activities.

You'll have 15 minutes for these prewriting activities.

FIG. 2.3.   An activity from the California Learning Assessment System (1984).

Critiques of the New Assessments

As with other novel approaches in comprehension assessment, performance assessments came under fire as teachers and test developers struggled with issues of validity (particularly for individual scores), external accountability, reliability, and generalizability (Linn, 1999; Pearson, DeStefano, & García, 1998). Given what we know about the high stakes functions for which assessments are used to make decisions about individuals (e.g., decisions about entry into or exit from special programs or "certifying" or licensure decisions), these criticisms should not be surprising.

The Social Nature of the Assessments.   Performance assessments, probably because of their strong connection to everyday classroom activity and real-world workplace contexts, tended to encourage teachers to have students work in groups. This led to an essential dilemma: What are we to do when we know that the performance of an individual student is influenced by the work, comments, and assistance of peers or teachers? The essence of this dilemma was captured well in an essay by Gearhart et al. (1993) entitled, "Whose work is it anyway?" This "contamination" of individual student scores has prompted great concern on the part of professionals who need to make decisions about individuals. The social components of the reading process can be grounded in theories that may even deny the existence, or at least the significance, of the "individual." This makes assessment doubly difficult.

Task Generalizability.   Task generalizability, the degree to which performance on one task predicts performance on a second, is a major concern with these performance tasks. The data gathered from the first scoring of New Standards tasks (Linn, DeStefano, Burton, & Hanson, 1995) indicate that indexes of generalizability for both math and reading tasks were quite low. That essentially means that performance on any one task is not a good predictor of scores on other tasks. Shavelson and his colleagues encountered the same lack of generalizability with science tasks (Shavelson, Baxter, & Pine, 1992), as have other scholars (e.g., Linn, 1993), even on highly respected enterprises such as the advanced placement tests sponsored by the College Board. The findings in the College Board analysis are noteworthy for the incredible variability in generalizability found as a function of subject matter. For example, to achieve a generalizability coefficient of .90, estimates of testing time range from a low of 1.25 hr for Physics to over 13 hr for European History. These findings suggest that we need to measure students' performance on a large number of tasks before we can feel confident in having a stable estimate of their accomplishment in a complex area such as reading, writing, or subject matter knowledge. Findings such as these probably explain why standardized test developers have included many short passages on a wide array of topics in their comprehension assessments. They also point to a bleak future for performance assessment in reading; one wonders whether we can afford the time to administer and score the number of tasks required to achieve a stable estimate of individuals' achievement.

The Legacy.   If one examines trends in the assessment marketplace and in state initiatives, one can make predictions based on a usually reliable indicator of the latest trends in assessment. Now, in the year 2004, the revolution begun in the 1980s is over, or at least inching along in a very quiet cycle. Granted, successful implementations of authentic wide-scale assessment have been maintained in states like Maryland (Kapinus, Collier, & Kruglanski, 1994), Kentucky, and Oregon (see Pearson, Calfee, Walker-Webb, & Fleisher, 2002). However, other states (e.g., California, Wisconsin, Arizona, and Indiana) have rejected performance assessment and returned to off-the-shelf, multiple-choice, standardized reading assessments. Pearson et al. (2002) found a definite trend among states in which performance assessment is still alive to include it in a mixed model, not unlike NAEP, in which substantive, extended response items sit alongside more conventional multiple-choice items. Both these item formats accompany relatively lengthy passages. Even the more modest reforms in Illinois (the multiple-correct answer approach) were dropped in 1998 (interestingly, in favor of a NAEP-like mixed model approach). And it is the NAEP model that, in our view, is most likely to prevail. It is within the NAEP mixed model that the legacy of the reforms of the early 1990s are likely to survive, albeit in a highly protracted form. It is to the NAEP experience that we now turn our attention.

THE NATIONAL ASSESSMENT
OF EDUCATIONAL PROGRESS

It is important to give a prominent role to the reading assessments of NAEP in examining the history of reading comprehension assessment in the last quarter of the 20th century. NAEP is often regarded by people in the field as a sort of gold standard for the most forward thinking assessment practices (see Campell, Voelkl, & Donahue, 1998). NAEP has, especially in the last decade, developed a reputation for embodying our best thinking about both the conceptual and psychometric bases of assessment, especially in the area of reading.

The History of NAEP Reading Assessment

NAEP was authorized by Congress in 1963 as an effort to assess the "condition and progress of American education." The first NAEP assessment was administered in 1969, and it has grown in stature and importance from one decade to the next. Overseen by the National Assessment Governing Board and the National Center for Educational Statistics (Jones, 1996), the NAEP tests are the grades on the infamous "Nation's Report Card," which serves as an index of how states compare. It is also an index of trends in achievement.

The original plan for developing the NAEP tests was to center on open-ended constructed response items, which were to be interpreted within a "goal-free" perspective; that is, there would be little attempt to aggregate or interpret scores across items to build profiles of subdomains within a subject matter. Instead, performance data would be tied to individual items, which would be made public; the hope was that the significance of various performance data would emerge from these public forums. Two things changed quickly, however. First, for whatever reasons (economy being the most plausible), multiple-choice, not constructed response, dominated even the early years of NAEP, and they still constitute the lion's share of items (with allotted time balanced fairly equally between multiple-choice and constructed response). Second, in the early 1970s, NAEP moved quickly from its goal-free position to adopt subject matter frameworks, with the clear expectation that items would be developed to provide an overall account of performance in subject matter domains and to measure specific objectives within the framework.

In reading, revisions of frameworks have prompted changes in the reading test instrument over time, at least since the early 1970s (Salinger & Campbell, 1998). In the framework operative in the 1970s, student performance was measured against a set of objectives that looked remarkably consistent with then popular Bloom's taxonomy (1956). Students should

- Demonstrate the ability to show comprehension of what was read
- Analyze what is read, use what is read.
- Reason logically.
- Make judgments.
- Have an attitude and interest in reading.

The 1980s framework reveals several changes, some of which indicate that literature was beginning to make its mark on the objectives. Students would, according to the framework

- Value reading and literature.
- Comprehend written works.
- Respond to written works in interpretive and evaluative ways.
- Apply study skills.

In 1992, amidst the renaissance in literature as a part of the elementary and secondary curriculum, the impact of reader response theory on the NAEP framework is transparent. In fact, the "stances" readers are supposed to take are directly traceable to Langer's approach to helping teachers implement a response-based curriculum (see Langer, 1995). Langer's approach to response includes activities that get students into, through, and beyond the texts they read. In the 1992 NAEP framework, students were to be exposed to texts and items that encourage them to read to

- Form an initial understanding.
- Develop an interpretation.
- Personally reflect and respond to the reading.
- Demonstrate a critical stance.

Forming an initial understanding is remarkably like Langer's (1995) "into" stage. Developing an understanding is what Langer had in mind in her "through" stage, and personal response and critical reflection map directly onto Langer's "beyond" stage.

The Current NAEP Framework

The stances are the driving force behind the latest framework. It is worth dissecting these categories to examine what can be thought of as a theoretically well-grounded approach to item development. "Forming initial understanding" focuses on readers' initial impressions or "global understanding" (p. 11) of the text, with a broad perspective. NAEP often puts this as one of the first questions on a test. "Developing interpretation" occurs when readers are required to "extend their initial impressions to develop a more complete understanding of what they read" (p. 11) by taking information across parts of a text and focusing on specific information. In "personal response," readers are required to "connect knowledge from the text with their own personal background knowledge." In other words, how does the text relate to personal knowledge? In the last stance, "demonstrating critical stance," readers are required "to stand apart from the text and consider it objectively" (p. 12). This involves "critical evaluation, comparing and contrasting, and understanding the impact of such features as irony, humor, and organization" (p. 12). These stances are illustrated by several sample questions taken directly from the 1992 Framework booklet (see Table 2.7; NAEP Reading Consensus Project, 1992).

Neither the NAEP Reading Framework nor the NAEP item structure has changed since 1992.[19] The framework and the items are designed to allow us to understand how well American students negotiate complex interactions with text. This goal is to be achieved by the inclusion of a wide variety of text types and purposes (reading for literary experience, reading for information, and reading to perform a task), strict attention to the "four stances" described earlier, and systematic inclusion of three item types: multiple choice, short constructed response, and extended constructed response.

Issues and Problems in NAEP Reading Assessment

The Framework.   Despite the efforts of those responsible for NAEP to ensure that the reading framework reflects the latest knowledge gleaned from recent research, many criticisms abound. For example, the four stances can overlap, both conceptually and psychometrically. A simple examination of the questions suggests that often personal response and developing interpretation are a part of critical reflection; in getting to a critical position, a reader often ex-

---

[19]As this manuscript was completed, no change in the National Assessment of Educational Progress (NAEP) Reading Framework (NAEP Reading Consensus Project, 1992) had surfaced, although a task force had been assembled to consider changes.

TABLE 2.7
National Assessment of Educational Progress (NAEP) Stances

Forming Initial Understanding
- Which of the following is the best statement of the theme of the story?
- Write a paragraph telling what this article generally tells you.
- What would you tell someone about the main character?

Developing Interpretations
- How did the plot begin to develop?
- What caused the character to do this (use examples from the story to support your answer)?
- What caused this event?
- What type of person is the character (use information from the text to support your answer)?
- In what ways are these ideas important to the topic or theme?
- What will be the result of this step in the directions?
- What does the character think about ____?

Personal Reaction and Response
- How did this character change your ideas of _____?
- Do you think that ___ (say a grandmother or a child) would interpret this passage in the same way?
- How is the story like or different from your own personal experience? Explain?
- Does this description fit what you know about ___ and why?
- What does this passage/story say to you?
- Why do you think ___ (bullfrogs eat dragonflies? Is there anything else you think they might eat? What information from your own knowledge helps you answer this)?

Demonstrate Critical Stance
- Compare this article/story to that one.
- How useful would this be to ____?
- Do you agree with the author's opinion of this event?
- Does the author use (irony, personification, humor) effectively? Explain.
- What could be added to improve the author?s argument?
- Is this information needed?
- What other information would you need to find out what you don't know now?

---

amines both his or her knowledge repertoire and reads across text segments. It is interesting to note that NAEP has never reported scores by these stances, although the sample of items per category in their matrix-sampling scheme is large enough to obtain reliable estimates for each of the categories. The most plausible conclusion is that the cognitive categories do not hold up when scrutinized by factor analysis and other techniques designed to empirically determine the patterns of internal clustering. Furthermore, even expert literacy researchers cannot reliably classify items into the categories assigned by NAEP test developers (DeStefano, Pearson, & Afflerbach, 1997). Essentially, researchers judged the four types not to be discrete from one another. This failure of the cognitive stances to hold up psychometrically is reminiscent of the findings from the analyses of the Illinois assessment a decade earlier.

Item Format. Perhaps the most serious validity issue regarding test items within NAEP centers on item format. In particular, the push for achieving greater economy of testing time and scoring costs have prompted NAEP officials to fund research on the "value added question" of constructed response items; the question of interest is whether the extra expense of constructed response items is justified. That expense would be justified if and only if it could be demonstrated that constructed response items increase our capacity to assess comprehension accurately and validly—above and beyond what could be achieved only with multiple-choice items. Evidence of increased capacity could take many forms: (a) the discovery of independent factors for different formats, (b) different item information functions (a la item response theory), and (c) finding that different items elicit different levels of cognitive engagement.

Focusing on the third of these potential sources of evidence, Pearson et al. (in press) conducted several studies to determine if there are any substantive differences in cognitive processes evoked from multiple-choice and constructed-response items with the 1996 NAEP reading data. The basic methodology involves asking students to think aloud as they answer questions. Using both the item responses and the think-aloud data, researchers classify the type of thinking students were engaging in as they worked through each answer. The think-aloud produces cognitive categories, which are then scaled on a "cognitive depth" continuum. These depth indexes are used to compare depth across different item formats.

In the initial study, which was limited to existing NAEP passages and items, the research team members found few cognitive differences across the multiple-choice and constructed-response divide. Concerned that they might not have captured depth of processing adequately, they went outside the NAEP framework and item sets. First, they reframed the concept of deeper engagement using a more theoretically driven lens. Then they created the best possible test for "open-ended" constructed response items in reading by including a text type not previously studied, poetry, and tasks that were very much in the reader response tradition, discussed earlier. In addition, they wanted to see if the presence of multiple texts could also influence engagement, so they chose three thematically related poems and adapted some very open-ended constructed-response items that were much more in the spirit of the CLAS assessments discussed earlier. In scoring the new think-alouds, they discovered two new indexes of deep engagement that had not emerged in the earlier analysis (which was limited to NAEP tasks)—"multiplicity" and "intertextuality." Multiplicity occurs when an examinee assumes more than one possible stance toward an item; for example, taking the perspective of the author, then the main character, then perhaps himself or herself as a reader. Intertextuality involves linking ideas across texts (or distinctly separate segments of a single text). With these new tools for examining deeper cognitive engagement, they re-analyzed the earlier NAEP think-alouds only to discover that the data from those tasks also exhibited these two new indexes of depth, prompting them to re-analyze the earlier data set. The re-analysis indicated that the multiple-choice items elicited a significantly lower proportion of multiple and intertextual strategies than did either the short or extended constructed-response items. These data suggest that when the standard of deep engagement is relatively low, as it was in the first study, few item format differences emerge, but that when the bar for deep cognitive engagement is set higher (number of think-aloud statements exhibiting either multiplicity of stances or textual linking), item format differences emerge. Moreover, the data from the poetry task suggest that if we really want to assess deeper comprehension processes, we are better advised to develop genuine performance tasks than we are to simply transform multiple-choice items into short answer questions.

OTHER IMPORTANT DEVELOPMENTS IN THE LAST DECADE

Linking Comprehension Assessment to Book Reading Levels

Within the last decade, two separate initiatives have been tried to link performance on tests of reading comprehension to books that students ought to be able to read. Both the Degrees of Reading Power (Touchstone Applied Science Associates, 1995) and the Lexile scales (Stenner & Burdick, 1997; Stenner et al., 1987) provide this sort of service. They are able to achieve this link by placing students' scores on comprehension measures on the same scale as the readability of books and other reading materials. Scores on a particular test, then, indicate more than how an examinee's performance compares to other examinees (norm-referenced) or to some preset cutoff score (criterion-referenced). Additionally, they point to the sort of books that a student achieving a particular score ought to be able to read. Specifically, they indicate the level of difficulty (what some might call challenge) of books that students achieving a given score ought to be able to read and understand (i.e., answer 75% of a hypothetical set of comprehension questions that might be asked about the book). One might think of Lexile scores as "text referenced" measures of comprehension, although Stenner and Burdick (1997) refer to this feature as criterion-referenced.

To validate the Lexile framework, Stenner and his colleagues (Stenner & Burdick, 1997; Stenner et al., 1987) have engaged in an elaborate sequence of studies. Using the mainstays of readability formulas (word frequency and sentence length) as a way of predicting the difficulty of text, they scaled the difficulty of a wide range of cloze-like comprehension test passages and items, as illustrated in Fig. 2.4.

After administering the test items to a large set of examinees and validating the predictive power of their indexes of passage difficulty, Stenner and his colleagues created a set of formulas that allowed them to place examinee performance and text difficulty on a common scale: "An important feature of the Lexile Framework is that it provides criterion-referenced interpretations of every measure. When a person's measure is equal to the task's calibration, then the Lexile scale forecasts that the individual has a 75 percent comprehension rate on that task. When 20 such tasks are given to this person, one expects three-fourths of the responses to be correct" (Stenner & Burdick, 1997, p. 16).

Stenner and his colleagues then applied the Lexile scaling techniques to 1,780 comprehension items from nine popular standardized tests, obtaining average correlations between Lexile predictions and observed item difficulties in the mid-.90 range. The next major initiative was to validate the Lexile as a measure of text difficulty, which they accomplished by using the scale to predict the rank ordering of basal reading levels (preprimer through Grade 8 reader); the average correlation, across 11 basal series, turned out to be .97.

The final step is to apply the lexile scale to a wide range of trade books, which the Stenner group has done. Now it is possible for a teacher to receive scores from a standardized test in Lexiles as well as National Curve Equivalents (NCEs), or

---

An Example Lextile Test Item

Wilbur likes Charlotte better and better each day. Her campaign against insects seemed sensible and useful. Hardly anybody around the farm had a good word to say for a fly. Flies spent their time pestering others. The cows hated them. The horses hated them. The sheep loathed them. Mr. and Mrs. Zuckerman were always complaining about them, and putting up screens. **Everyone** _____ **about them.**

A. agreed   B. gathered   C. laughed   D. learned

FIG. 2.4.   Segment from *Charlotte's Web* by E. B. White, 1952, New York: Harper & Row.

percentiles, or grade-norms (for example, both the Stanford Achievement Test–9 and the Stanford Diagnostic Reading Test from HBJ provide Lexile score reporting options). The idea is that teachers can then use the scores to guide them in helping students select appropriate books (at least for the subset of books that have been "Lexilized").

The Degrees of Reading Power (DRP), a modified cloze test originally developed by the state of New York for state assessment purposes, has developed a similar approach to scaling books and students on a common scale, allowing teachers to use DRP scores to place students in level appropriate books. A major difference between the DRP approach and the Lexile approach is that although the DRP scale requires the use of its test, the Lexile scale can be (and has been) applied to any of several currently available standardized tests. What we have been unable to locate is any research indicating the accuracy and validity of the book matching process (e.g., some independent measure of whether the books predicted as within a child's range really were), save a few Web site testimonials from customers.

Reemergence of Skills Orientation

After a decade in which reading skill instruction was backgrounded in deference to literature-based activities that took center stage in reading instructional practices, skills have made a remarkable recovery in the past 3 years. All of the state frameworks emerging in the last few years give skills, particularly phonemic awareness and phonics skills, a prominent role, especially in the primary grades. Also, basal programs that only 7 years ago tried to hide their skills now place them prominently in student texts, workbooks, and teacher manuals. What remains to be seen is how this shift toward greater and more prominent skill inclusion will impact comprehension assessment. Will it usher in a renaissance in skills management systems and lots of specific component skill tests, such as those that characterized the criterion-referenced assessments of the 1970s? Or will the assessments in the next decade continue to carry traces of the performance assessment movement of the 1990s?

NEW INITIATIVES

Having traversed this complex and multifaceted landscape of reading comprehension assessment, we conclude this essay by offering a set of recommendations for future initiatives in this important curricular topic. These recommendations are based on our reading of the full history of reading comprehension assessment in the 20th century. Sometimes the recommendations are derived from a perceived deficit in the research (we just have not examined the question with sufficient care). Some recommendations are based on our professional judgment that it is time to revisit a question or an issue that, although carefully investigated in earlier periods, deserves a fresh look.

Interactions of Ability and Other Factors

No question is more important to address than the question of whether assessments are equally sensitive to student performance at all levels of the achievement continuum. It is possible, for example, that one approach to comprehension assessment provides a better index of comprehension for students who are still struggling with decoding and word recognition whereas another is more appropriate for students who have word level skills under automatic processing control. To take a simple example, we know that for many younger readers, as well as struggling writers and spellers at any age, the requirement to compose written responses will interfere with our capacity to obtain valid estimates of their comprehension. A number of initiatives seem appropriate at this point in time.

Ability and Response Medium. For years, we have asked students to write in response to reading, generally regarding it as a useful approach to comprehension assessment for more complex reading tasks, such as critical response to literature and critical evaluation of ideas and arguments. Yet we also know that the writing requirement can obscure some children's ability to understand and interpret text because of their poor motor skill development, inadequate spelling, and underdeveloped writing dispositions. Also, it is not unreasonable to hypothesize that certain response media differentially affect students of different abilities or proclivities. Some students, especially those who achieve well, might better show critical dispositions on paper; others, for whom writing is a chore, might shine in an oral response mode. We need studies to evaluate this potential interaction between ability and the medium of response. We could build test forms in which response mode and task complexity are systematically crossed, and then administer the different forms to populations with known reading and writing capacities.

Ensuring That Tests Measure the Entire Range of Performance. In 1992, when NAEP began to use achievement levels (Below Basic, Basic, Proficient, and Advanced) to report student achievement, a problematic feature of the NAEP assessment was unearthed. NAEP, like most state assessments, is given only at a few grades (4, 8, and 12), and when passages are selected for inclusion at a given grade level, test developers try to select passages that are "appropriate" for the grade level. Granted, test developers seek some variability in passage difficulty; however, the range of difficulty on passages remains fairly narrow. When it was announced that 40% of fourth graders in the United States scored "below basic," there were two possible explanations. Either our fourth graders truly perform that poorly, or the test is insensitive to performance differences at the low end of the achievement scale (in other words, the test has no "floor"). The issue of passage difficulty in reading, particularly its potentially depressing effect on performance of students at the lower end of the performance continuum, has been emphasized in a number of recent reports (e.g., Glaser et al., 1997). It has prompted scholars and policymakers to call for the production of easier blocks of NAEP reading items so that low-performing students can at least "make it onto the scale," or in the language of information value, so that we possess more information about the performance of low-performing students.

NAEP (as well as state assessment efforts relying on grade level passages) should be encouraged to include several blocks containing some very easy (perhaps appropriate for one or two grades below the target grade) passages to see if the distribution in the lower end of the scale can be spread out and measured more reliably and sensitively. In that way, greater meaning could be attached to terms like *below basic* (on NAEP). Interestingly, standardized testing companies have long recognized this problem and accommodated it by providing a range of passage difficulty for each form and level of the test. We suspect, however, that many state tests, because of the emphasis on grade appropriate passages, suffer the same problem encountered in NAEP. Ironically, with the Item Response Theory (IRT) models used in today's wide-scale assessment, giving lower ability students easier passages does not provide them with an unfair advantage. It just gives them a greater opportunity to land somewhere on the underlying performance scale of the test. These issues are especially relevant in dealing with aggregated scores; the reporting of individual scores is another matter.

Achievement and Skill Profiles. Just after midcentury, a few studies were conducted addressing the question of what it means to achieve at a particular level on a standardized test, say a particular grade norm score, percentile rank, or stanine. The methodology was remarkably simple but ingenious. Students took one or another standardized tests; at the same time they took a battery of specific skill tests (phonics, vocabulary, and comprehension subskills). Performances on the various skill tests were examined to build different skill profiles. The question of interest was whether those students who score within a given band of performance on a standardized reading comprehension test would exhibit similar skill profiles. In the few studies we were able to find (e.g., Naylor,

1972), the statistical tendency has shown great profile variability within a given band of performance on a comprehension test. What this suggests is that readers are using some sort of compensatory mechanisms. In other words, some readers may achieve a given level of comprehension performance by relying primarily on a rich reservoir of vocabulary knowledge to compensate for underdeveloped decoding and word recognition skills or comprehension strategies. Others may rely primarily on excellent decoding skills, test-wiseness, or comprehension strategies to compensate for weaknesses elsewhere. The compensatory hypothesis contrasts with a common alternative—the notion that some minimal threshold must be achieved on each and every prerequisite skill for comprehension to take place. Given the recent revival in skills-oriented reading instruction, studies of this ilk would be most timely. We would also be able to better address the question of the multifaceted nature of comprehension and, equally important, the relation among decoding, vocabulary, and comprehension skills. Recently, Riddle-Buly and Valencia (2002) conducted a study along these lines. First, they identified a population of "low achievers" from the Washington statewide assessment (i.e., those who scored "below the bar"—levels 1 and 2 out of 4—on-grade level reading performance). Then they administered a battery of language, vocabulary, and reading subskill assessments (e.g., phonics, word identification, and the like) to these students. What they discovered is that there are indeed many, many ways to fall below the bar. In fact, they identified several "profiles" or clusters of readers who differed dramatically in their skill infrastructures—word callers (students who decode words accurately, even automatically, but don't comprehend well), slow word callers (like their word caller counterparts but are not automatic in recognizing words), word stumblers (accurate but slow and dysfluent readers), and slow and steady comprehenders (students who eventually get the meaning but read slowly and deliberately).

Accommodations for Special Populations.   Here is an essential question: How much of an accommodation for special populations can be made before crossing the validity line and invalidating the construct the test is designed to measure? The most radical accommodation on a reading test is, of course, reading the passage and the items to the student. On the face of it, this accommodation changes a reading comprehension test into a listening comprehension assessment. The least radical accommodation, more time, probably does little to invalidate the test or the construct because most comprehension tests are designed to be untimed. Between these two extremes lies a range of popular accommodations that may, to one degree or another, erode or compromise the validity of a test. For example, what is the impact of providing a glossary or dictionary? What about reading the test items but requiring students to read the text on their own? Given the increased emphasis on full participation of all students in group assessments, it seems important to address a full range of possible accommodations, making sure to weigh increased participation against potential sources of invalidity.

Item Format

Although there exists a small corpus of careful studies that allow us to examine the relation between multiple-choice and constructed-response items, we still have a great deal to learn. Much of the problem in interpreting the current set of studies is that the research has been more opportunistic than intentional. In the prototypic study, researchers take advantage of an existing test or battery that happens to include both constructed-response and multiple-choice formats. Much rarer are studies in which the researchers have set out to evaluate both the underlying constructs and the validity of the test(s) designed to measure those constructs.

What is needed is a newer examination of the relations between multiple-choice and constructed-response items. Short of a complete evaluation of the item format construct, there are a number of useful initiatives that would allow us to answer the question of value added for performance items with greater assurance than is currently possible.

The Cognitive Demands of Multiple-Choice and Constructed-Response Items. The work of Pearson et al. (in press) and Campell (1999) has provided us with some estimate of the differential cognitive processes that examinees employ in response to different item formats, and we support more work using the basic methodology of the think-aloud verbal protocols. Although think-aloud methodology appears promising for this sort of initiative (Campbell, 1999; Pearson et al., in press; Yepes-Bayara, 1996), it is by no means the only index of cognitive functioning that we should consider. When tasks involve text reading and response, both eye-movement methodology and computer controlled text search (look-back) methodology could provide rich information about the influence of item format on the role of text in selecting and constructing responses as a part of comprehension assessment.

Rubric Research. We have placed rubric research in the format category because rubrics are unique to a particular item format—constructed-response items. Rubrics such as those used in NAEP for scoring constructed-response items in reading have been roundly criticized. It would be useful to work with NAEP or NAEP-like reading passages to evaluate different approaches to rubric development. The current NAEP rubrics are viewed by critics as too quantitative and only marginally related to the NAEP framework for reading (DeStefano et al., 1997). High dividends might result from a modest investment in creating new rubrics that are driven by the framework and then comparing the quality of information, both psychometrically and pragmatically, received when items are scored by these rubrics versus conventional rubrics. In another vein, we might examine the conceptual genesis of rubrics, paralleling Fredericksen's (1984) questions about whether transforming multiple-choice items into performance items is the same as transforming performance into multiple-choice items. Suppose the rubric for a set of constructed-response items is based on the same conception of underlying dimensions (the psychological construct) as were used to guide the development of a comparable set of multiple-choice items. Such a practice might, in fact, be a reasonable control if our goal is to examine trait equivalence across item formats; however, this practice can also constrain our thinking about the range of possible traits that might be assessed with the constructed-response format and teased out by an appropriate rubric. In other words, in achieving control for conceptual equivalence, we might be losing our capacity to uncover a large set of possible dimensions of the construct that can only be tapped by the constructed-response format. This issue could be addressed in a study in which competing rubrics were developed and used to score a common set of constructed-response items. The first rubric would be developed using a framework initially used to generate multiple-choice items and then extended to constructed-response items. The second rubric would result from a fresh perspective: subject matter experts would be asked to generate a framework and related rubrics for an assessment system consisting only of constructed-response items. The question of interest is whether the two rubrics would yield equivalent scores and or trait information.

Prior Experience and Test Format. The reader's prior experience has two possible realizations, one at the classroom-school level and one at the individual level. At the classroom-school level, it is instantiated as instructional experience (opportunity to learn). If we can be sure of the type of curricular experiences different students have experienced (e.g., emphasis on critical stance or response to literature in reading or basic decoding skills), and if we can locate populations with different curricular histories, we can test constructed-response items under optimal conditions. We can ask the following: Do students who have learned what the items are designed to measure perform at higher levels than students who have received other curricular emphases? It would be interesting, for example, to conduct a think-aloud study (along the lines of the work by Pearson et al., in press) in sites that exhibit just such a curricular contrast. At the individual level, of course, prior experience is instantiated as prior knowledge, and its impact is well documented in reading and writing assessment. It would be useful to know whether students provide more elaborate and more sophisticated responses to constructed-response prompts when they are quite knowledgeable about the topic at hand.

Transforming Items Across Formats.   When evaluating the equivalence of constructed-response and multiple-choice items, researchers sometimes begin with one set of items, say multiple-choice, and rewrite them as constructed-response, or vice-versa. In this way, they attempt to control the content and focus of the items across formats. In other studies, there is no attempt to control for content and focus; instead, researchers take advantage of an existing test that happens to contain some multiple-choice and some constructed-response items. What we need are studies in which both multiple-choice and constructed-response items are developed in ways that allow each to "put their best foot forward," so to speak. To our knowledge, Fredericksen (1984) is one of the few researchers to consider the possibility that we may be introducing a source of bias when, for example, constructed-response items are generated by transformations from an existing set of multiple-choice items. He also is one of the few researchers to develop multiple-choice items from an existing set of constructed-response items. This study would extend the logic of his dual source approach to item generation. One could accomplish such goals with a procedure along the following lines:

- Identify a domain of interest, such as reading comprehension, response to literature, mathematical power, and so forth.
- Identify one group of item writers with reputations for developing first-rate multiple-choice items; identify a second group with equally strong reputations for constructed-response items.
- Set each group to work on developing a set of items for the domain of interest.
- When each group is finished, ask them to exchange item groups and, as best they can, transform each multiple-choice item into a constructed-response item and vice-versa.
- Create matched item sets, balanced for content and format.
- Administer to students, and evaluate relations between constructed-response and multiple-choice item subsets.

Garavaglia (2000) has completed just such a study in on NAEP mathematics items in the domain of algebraic representations of everyday experience. Garavaglia found that for the run-of-the-mill constructed response items that appear in NAEP, which tend to be little more than multiple-choice items in disguise, little advantage is gained by including the constructed response format. It was only when genuine performance tasks (e.g., multiple-step, problem-solving tasks with opportunities to write about one's work) were included in the mix that one can show the value added of constructed response items. It would be interesting to transfer this methodology to reading comprehension assessment.

The Role of Passage Difficulty in Reading Assessment. In the previous section, we outlined the dimensions of this issue, but here we deal with the interaction of passage difficulty and item format. If more "accessible" blocks, comprised of easier passages, are created and if we are thoughtful about how we design and generate items across blocks, we can determine whether response format (multiple-choice versus constructed-response) or passage difficulty (or some unique combination) is responsible for the current low information yields of constructed-response items in tests like NAEP and many state tests. It might be, for example, that students have a lot more to say when it is relatively easy for them to read, digest, think about, and even critique the texts they encounter. It might also turn out that difficulty interacts with student achievement level in such a way that easy passages provide opportunities for low-achieving students to shine whereas hard passages provide just the challenge that high-achieving students need to get involved in the assessment.

Revisiting the Sentence Verification Task. The SVT has never been able to build much of a constituency, and we are not sure why. Perhaps it is because it is viewed as too cumbersome a process to use on a regular basis. Perhaps it is because it seems limited to application with shorter texts. Perhaps it is because it confounds memory with comprehension and because it puts readers in the odd circumstance of having to decide between veridical restatement (is this exactly what the text said?) and semantic equivalence (does this mean the same thing as the text said?) when deciding what to do with a paraphrase item. If these concerns can be overcome, perhaps SVT deserves another round of experimental trials to determine if it can provide teachers and schools with useful information about comprehension. Perhaps the most significant challenge to SVT is whether test developers can apply it to longer passages of the type currently used in NAEP and an increasing number of state assessments. A demonstration of its usefulness with longer passages would go a long way toward increasing its perceived utility for standardized assessments.

Mixed Model Assessments

Earlier we suggested that the current trend is toward mixed models of assessment, along the lines of NAEP and several state assessment initiatives, not to mention a few standardized tests (e.g., the SAT–9 has the capacity to mix in some constructed response items). Given the increasing popularity of this model, we need to study its conceptual, psychometric, and pragmatic characteristics very carefully. Among other things, we need to know the relative contributions of various components, using research tools along the lines of those outlined in the previous section on item format studies. However, other initiatives are also called for within this domain of inquiry.

Compensatory Approaches to Achieve Particular Cut Scores.   The New Standards Reference Exam (1998), currently marketed by HBJ, uses an interesting strategy to determine whether students meet a standard. The test is built on a mixed model, a combination of constructed responses to challenging passages and some very traditional multiple-choice responses to short passages, the stuff of which typical standardized tests are made. Test developers ask experts to determine the various combinations of scores on the multiple-choice and constructed-response portions of the test that would represent mastery of the construct. This is reminiscent of the admissions indexes used by universities to admit freshmen: different combinations of high school grade point average and SAT scores will get a student over the "admit" line—a high score on one component can compensate for a low score on the other. This raises an interesting possibility for creating comprehension scores to determine whether a particular standard (usually a cut score) has been met. Essentially this procedure caters to individual differences in item format preferences. The research question of interest is whether different combinations of scores on the two exams really can and do provide equal estimates of comprehension ability or achievement. For example, if we compared students who had achieved a common cut score with widely different patterns of reliance on constructed-response versus multiple-choice items, would we find that they both could meet a common external criterion, such as successful participation in a particular curriculum or activity (e.g., classroom discussion) or a score on a completely independent measure of comprehension.

Other (Not Readily Classifiable) Initiatives

Genre and Comprehension.   One of the great mysteries of reading assessment is the persistent gap between performance on narrative texts and informational texts. In study after study, state assessment after state assessment, students consistently achieve higher raw scores on narrative texts. The question is why? Is the difference a function of opportunity to learn (we know that elementary students are exposed to at least 10 times more narrative than expository text)? Is it due to prior knowledge (other things being equal, do students know more about the everyday experiences depicted in stories than they do the propositional knowledge in expositions)? Or is there something about the way that we assess understanding of the two genres that creates an artifactual difference (maybe we test more central ideas in stories than in nonfiction)? A close content examination of item types, focus, and relation to the texts from which they are derived, followed by some small-scale experiments, seems appropriate to determine the source of this persistent finding.

Interest, Knowledge, Comprehension and the Idea of a Level Playing Field. We know that both interest and prior knowledge (which are themselves conflated) influence comprehension, but we have not really considered the consequences of these relations for assessment, at least not in recent years. Given what we know about the lack of generalizability of performance tasks and the capacity of passage effects to overwhelm cognitive process effects, we have an ethical obligation to get inside the quagmire that resides at the intersection of interest, knowledge, and comprehension. We know that our estimate of a given student's comprehension is dependent on the passages read. Our traditional solution to the influence of topical knowledge has been to make sure that we provide students with a wide range of short passages on widely variant topics. This practice more or less guarantees that students who have high general verbal ability will do best on standardized tests (see Johnston, 1984a, 1984b). And because all students have read the same passages, we seduce ourselves into believing that we have satisfied the fairness (level playing field) criterion. Perhaps we need to consider other metaphors for fairness. What if every student reading passages for which he or she possessed the maximum level of interest and knowledge, rather than every student reading the same passages, were considered to be the default fairness criterion? In other words, what might happen if we replaced the "level playing field" with "playing to readers' strengths" as a criterion of fairness? Yet, how would we know if we are indeed capitalizing on readers' strengths? It would be useful to examine performance (perhaps something like reaching a particular performance standard) as a function of variations in student interest and knowledge, where some sort of common task could be applied to a wide range of passages. Retelling could be applied across a wide array of passages. Another possibility is a core set of common, generic, constructed-response questions; just such a set was used in 1994 NAEP special studies (as cited in Salinger & Campbell, 1998).

Examining the Consequential Validity of the Lexile Scale Framework. The Lexile scale (and the parallel DRP) holds great promise in helping teachers make difficult book placement decisions without the arduous effort of administering cumbersome benchmark book assessments or informal reading inventories. However, to our knowledge, the most important validity studies, especially for a measure that purports to impact practice, have not been conducted—examining the consequential validity of the book placements suggested by the analysis. Several studies are possible here. First, it would be interesting to compare the placement recommendations of teachers who possess different levels of experience and knowledge of children's literature with those provided by the Lexile process. Does the Lexile scale conform to the recommendations of more experienced and more knowledgeable teachers? Second, it would be useful to compare the experiences and understanding of students who read Lexile recommended books. It is one thing to make the connections to books through a common scaling procedure; it is quite another to validate the match in terms of all the cognitive, affective, and aesthetic features of a quality reading experience. In other words, can kids really read, appreciate, and benefit from books recommended by the Lexile process? And are they, in reality, more capable of reading those books than books with higher Lexile ratings?

CONCLUSION

Reading comprehension assessment has been a significant landmark in the educational landscape for just over 80 years. Its history is a remarkable story, one characterized by cycles of great hope and expectation alternating with periods of disappointment and frustration. A disappointment general to scholars throughout its history has been our persistent inability to see comprehension as it happens, what we have referred to as the phenomenological "click" of comprehension. Instead, they have had to content themselves with "artifacts" and residual traces of the comprehension process—indirect indexes of its occurrence. Each of these indirect indexes carries with it a cost, one that can be measured by the inferential distance between the evidence and the phenomenon itself. Many of the advances in comprehension assessment have, at least in a virtual sense, narrowed the distance between evidence and the process, providing us with greater confidence in our measures.

Other hopes and disappointments have been particular to specific periods. Two examples stand out: (a) the great expectations built up around performance assessments in the early 1990s, followed by the disappointment at their failure to stand psychometric tests of generalizability and reliability, and (b) the short-lived exhilaration so prominent in the late 1980s, which held a promise that we might find assessments that would match the models of instruction built on the principles governing allegedly challenging constructivist curriculum. Although the disappointments and frustrations are real, there has also been genuine progress. That progress is probably best represented by NAEP and some of our other mixed model, wide-scale assessments

And, of course, there is still much more to learn about how to measure a phenomenon that is as elusive as it is important. We have tried to outline, in our suggestions for future research, some of the issues that merit our attention. It is our modest hope that this chapter will serve as a catalyst for both lively conversation and concentrated work to improve our capacity to assess what is assuredly most important about reading—our ability to marshal all of our resources to make sense of the texts we encounter.

REFERENCES

Allington, R. L. (1984). Oral reading. In P. D. Pearson, R. Barr, M. Kamil, & P. Mosenthal (Eds.), *Handbook of reading research* (pp. 829–864). New York: Longman.

Anderson, R. C., & Pearson, P. D. (1984). A schema-theoretic view of basic processes in reading comprehension. In P. D. Pearson, R. Barr, M. Kamil, & P. Mosenthal (Eds.), *Handbook of reading research* (pp. 255–291). New York: Longman.

Bachman, L. F. (1982). The trait structure of cloze test scores. *TESOL Quarterly, 16,* 61–70

Bachman, L. F. (2000). Modern language testing at the turn of the century: Assuring that what we count counts. *Language Testing, 17,* 1–42.

Baumann, J., Jones, L., & Seifert-Kessell, N. (1993). Using think alouds to enhance children's comprehension monitoring abilities. *The Reading Teacher, 47,* 184–193.

Betts, E. (1946). *Foundations of reading instruction.* New York: American Book.

Binet, A. (1895). Assessment in reading. In P. D. Pearson, R. Barr, M. Kamil, & P. Mosenthal (Eds.), *Handbook of reading research* (pp. 147–182). New York: Longman.

Bloom, B. S. (1956). Taxonomy of educational objectives. *Handbook 1: Cognitive domain.* New York: McKay.

Bloom, B. S. (1968). Learning for mastery. *Evaluation Comment, 1.*

Bloom, D., & Green, J. (1984). Directions in the sociolinguistic study of reading. In P. D. Pearson, R. Barr, M. Kamil, & P. Mosenthal (Eds.), *Handbook of reading research* (pp. 394–421). New York: Longman.

Board of Education, City of Chicago. (1984). *Chicago mastery learning reading.* Watertown, MA: Mastery Education Corporation.

Bock, R. D., Thissen, D., & Zimowski, M. F. (1997). IRT estimation of domain scores. *Journal of Educational Measurement, 34*(3), 197–211.

Bormuth, J. R. (1966). Reading: A new approach. *Reading Research Quarterly, 1*, 79–132.

Bormuth, J. R. (1970). *On the theory of achievement test items.* Chicago: University of Chicago Press.

California Learning Assessment System. (1994). *Elementary performance assessments: Integrated English-language arts illustrative material.* Sacramento: California Department of Education.

California Department of Education. (1987). *English language arts framework.* Sacramento, CA: Author.

Campell, J. R. (1999). Cognitive processes elicited by multiple-choice and constructed-response questions on an assessment of reading comprehension. Unpublished doctoral dissertation, Temple University, Philadelphia, PA.

Campell, J. R., Voelkl, K. E., & Donahue, P. L. (1998). *NAEP 1996 trends in academic progress: Achievement of U.S. students in science 1969 to 1996, mathematics , 1973 to 1996, reading, 1971 to 1996 and writing, 1984 to 1996* (NCES 97–985). Washington, DC: U.S. Department of Education.

Carroll, J. (1963). A model of school learning. *Teachers College Record, 64*, 723–732.

Chapman, J. C. (1924). *Chapman unspeeded reading-comprehension test.* Minneapolis, MN: Educational Test Bureau.

Courtis, S. A. (1914). Standard tests in English. *Elementary School Teacher, 14*, 374–392.

Davis, F. B. (1944). Fundamental factors of comprehension of reading. *Psychometrika, 9*, 185–197.

Davis, F. B. (1968). Research in comprehension in reading. *Reading Research Quarterly, 3*, 499–545.

Davis, F. B. (1972). Psychometric research on comprehension in reading. *Reading Research Quarterly, 7*, 628–678.

Derrik, C. (1953). *Three aspects of reading comprehension as measured by tests of different lengths* (Research Bulletin 53–8). Princeton, NJ: Educational Testing Service.

DeStefano, L., Pearson, P. D., & Afflerbach, P. (1997). Content validation of the 1994 NAEP in reading: Assessing the relationship between the 1994 assessment and the reading framework. In R. Linn, R. Glaser, & G. Bohrnstedt (Eds.), *Assessment in transition: 1994 Trial State Assessment Report on Reading: Background studies* (pp. 1–50). Stanford, CA: The National Academy of Education.

Dewey, J. (1938). *Experience and education.* New York: Collier Books.

Durrell, D. D. (1937). *Durrell analysis of reading difficulty.* New York: Harcourt Brace.

Ericsson, K. A., & Simon, H. A. (1984). *Protocol analysis: Verbal reports as data.* Cambridge, MA: MIT Press.

Farr, R., & Greene, B. G. (1992, February). *Using verbal and written think-alongs to assess metacognition in reading.* Paper presented at the 15th annual conference of the Eastern Education Research Association, Hilton Head, SC.

Feuerstein, R. R., Rand, Y., & Hoffman, M. B. (1979). *The dynamic assessment of retarded performance.* Baltimore: University Park Press.

Frederiksen, N. (1984). The real test bias: Influences of testing on teaching and learning. *American Psychologist, 39*, 193–202.

Freeman, F. N. (1926). *Mental tests: Their history, principles and applications.* Chicago: Houghton Mifflin.

Gagné, R. M. (1965). *The conditions of learning.* New York: Holt, Rinehart & Winston.

Garavaglia, D. (in press). *The impact of item format on depth of cognitive engagement.* Unpublished doctoral dissertation, Michigan State University, East Lansing.

Gates, A. I. (1937). The measurement and evaluation of achievement in reading. In *The teaching of reading: A second report*. Bloomington, IL.: Public School Publishing.

Gearhart, M., Herman, J., Baker, E., & Whittaker, A. K. (1993). *Whose work is it? A question for the validity of large-scale portfolio assessment* (CSE Tech. Rep. No. 363). Los Angeles: University of California, National Center for Research on Evaluation, Standards, and Student Testing.

Ginn & Company. (1982). *The Ginn reading program*. Lexington, MA: Author.

Ginsberg, H. (1997). *Entering the child's mind: The clinical interview of psychological research and practice*. New York: Cambridge University Press.

Glaser, R., Linn, R., & Bohrnstedt, G. (1997). *Assessment in transition: Monitoring the nation's educational progress*. Stanford, CA: National Academy of Education.

Goodman, K. S. (1968). *The psycholinguistic nature of the reading process*. Detroit, MI: Wayne State University Press.

Goodman, K. S. (1969). Analysis of oral reading miscues: Applied psycholinguistics. *Reading Research Quarterly, 5*, 1.

Goodman, Y. M., & Burke, C. L. (1970). *Reading miscue inventory manual procedure for diagnosis and evaluation*. New York: Macmillan.

Gray, W. S. (1916). *Standardized oral reading paragraphs*. Indianapolis, IN: Bobbs Merrill.

Gray, W. S. (1917). *Studies of elementary school reading through standardized tests* (Supplemental Educational Monograph No. 1). Chicago: University of Chicago Press.

Harris, C. W. (1948). Measurement of comprehension in literature. *The School Review, 56*, 280–289, 332–342.

Hartman, D. K. (1995). Eight readers reading: The intertextual links of proficient readers reading multiple passages. *Reading Research Quarterly, 30*(3), 520–561.

Hively, W. (1974). Introduction to domain-reference testing. *Educational Technology, 14*(6), 5–10.

Huey, E. (1908). *The psychology and pedagogy of reading*. Cambridge, MA: MIT Press.

Hunt, L. C. (1957). Can we measure specific factors associated with reading comprehension? *Journal of Educational Research, 51*, 161–171.

Illinois Goal Assessment Program. (1991). *The Illinois reading assessment: Classroom connections*. Springfield: Illinois State Board of Education.

Irwin, P. A., & Mitchell, J. N. (1983). A procedure for assessing the richness of retellings. *Journal of Reading, 26*, 391–396.

Johnson, D. D., & Pearson, P. D., (1975). Skills management systems: A critique. *The Reading Teacher, 28*, 757–764.

Johnston, P. H. (1984a). Assessment in reading. In P. D. Pearson, R. Barr, M. Kamil, & P. Mosenthal (Eds.), *Handbook of reading research* (pp. 147–182). New York: Longman.

Johnston, P. H. (1984b). *Reading comprehension assessment: A cognitive basis*. Newark, DE: International Reading Association.

Jones, L. V. (1996). A history of the National Assessment of Educational Progress and some questions about its future. *Educational Researcher, 25*(7), 15–22.

Kapinus, B., Collier, G. V., & Kruglanski, H. (1994). The Maryland school performance assessment program: A new wave of assessment. In S. Valencia, E. Hiebert, & P. Afflerbach (Eds.), *Authentic reading assessment: Practices and possibilities* (pp. 255–276). Newark, DE: International Reading Association.

Kelly, E. J. (1916). The Kansas silent reading tests. *Journal of Educational Psychology, 7*, 63–80.

Kelly, T. L. (1935). *Essential traits of mental life*. Cambridge, MA: Harvard University Press.

Kintsch, W. (1974). *The representation of meaning in memory.* Hillsdale, NJ: Lawrence Erlbaum Associates.

Kintsch, W., & van Dijk, T. A. (1978). Toward a model of text comprehension and production. *Psychological Review, 85,* 36–394.

Langer, J. (1995). *Envisioning literature: Literary understanding and literature instruction.* New York: Teachers College Press.

Linn, R. (1993). Educational assessment: Expanded expectations and challenges. *Educational Evaluation and Policy Analysis, 15,* 1–16.

Linn, R. (1999). Assessments and accountability. *Educational Researcher, 29*(2), 4–16.

Linn, R., DeStefano, L., Burton, E, & Hanson, M. (1995). Generalizability of New Standards Project 1993 pilot study tasks in mathematics. *Applied Measurement in Education, 9,* 33–45.

Mandler, J. M., & Johnson, N. S. (1977). Remembrance of things parsed: Story structure and recall. *Cognitive Psychology, 9,* 111–151.

Markman, E. M. (1977). Realizing that you don't understand: A preliminary investigation. *Child Development, 48,* 986–992.

Matthews, M. (1996). *Teaching to read.* Chicago: University of Chicago Press.

McNamara, T. P, Miller, D. L., & Bransford, J. D. (1991). Mental models and reading comprehension. In R. Barr, M. Kamil, P. Mosenthal, & P. D. Pearson (Eds.), *Handbook of reading research, Vol. 2* (pp. 490–511). New York: Longman.

Meyer, B. J. F. (1975). *The organization of prose and its effects on memory.* Amsterdam: North-Holland.

Meyer, B. J. F., & Rice, E. (1984). The structure of text. In P. D. Pearson, R. Barr, M. L. Kamil, & P. Mosenthal (Eds.), *The handbook of reading research* (pp. 319–352). New York: Longman.

Monroe, W. S. (1918). *Monroe's standardized silent reading tests.* Bloomington, IL: Public School Publishing.

Morrow, L. M. (1988). Retelling stories as a diagnostic tool. In S. M. Glazer, L. W. Searfoss, & L. M. Gentile (Eds.), *Reexamining reading diagnosis: New trends and procedures* (pp. 128–149). Newark, DE: International Reading Association.

National Assessment of Educational Progress (NAEP) Reading Consensus Project. (1992). *Reading framework for the 1992 national assessment of educational progress.* Washington, DC: U.S. Printing Office.

National Center for Education and the Economy. (n.d.). *New standards reference exams.* San Antonio, TX: Harcourt Educational Publishers.

Naylor, M. (1972). *Reading skill variability within and among fourth-grade, fifth-grad, and sixth-grade students attaining the same reading achievement score.* Unpublished doctoral dissertation, University of Minnesota, Minneapolis.

Olshavsky, J. E. (1976–1977). Reading as problem solving: An investigation of strategies. *Reading Research Quarterly, 12,* 654–674.

Olson, D. (1994). *The world on paper: The conceptual and cognitive implications of writing and reading.* New York: Cambridge University Press.

Otto, W. (1977). The Wisconsin design; A reading program for individually guided elementary education. In R. A. Klausmeier, R. A. Rossmiller, & M. Saily (Eds.), *Individually guided elementary education: Concepts and practices.* New York: Academic.

Otto, W. R., & Chester, R. D. (1976). *Objective-based reading.* Reading, MA: Addison-Wesley.

Pearson, P. D. (2000). Reading in the 20th century. In T. Good (Ed.), *American education: Yesterday, today, and tomorrow. Yearbook of the National Society for the Study of Education* (pp. 152–208). Chicago: University of Chicago Press.

Pearson, P. D., Calfee, R., Walker-Webb, T., & Fleischer, S. (2002). *The role of performance assessment in large scale accountability systems: Lessons learned from the inside.* Washington, DC: Council of Chief State School Officers.

Pearson, P. D., DeStefano, L., & Garcia, G. E. (1998). Ten dilemmas of performance assessment. In C. Harrison & T. Salinger (Eds.), *Assessing reading 1, theory and practice* (pp. 21–49). London: Routledge.

Pearson, P. D., Garavaglia, D., Danridge, J., Hamm, D., Lycke, K., Roberts, E., et al. (in press). *The impact of item format on the depth of students' cognitive engagement.* Washington, DC: American Institutes for Research.

Pearson, P. D., Greer, E. A., Commeyras, M., Stallman, A., Valencia, S. W., Krug, S. E., et al. (1990). *The validation of large scale reading assessment: Building tests for the twenty-first century.* Urbana, IL: University of Illinois, Center for the Study of Reading.

Pearson, P. D., & Johnson, D. D. (1978). *Teaching reading comprehension.* New York: Holt, Rinehart & Winston.

Pearson, P. D., Spalding, E., & Meyers, M. (1998). Literacy assessment in the New Standards Project. In M. Coles & R. Jenkins (Eds.), *Assessing Reading to Changing Practice in Classrooms* (pp. 54–97). London: Routledge.

Pearson, P. D., & Stephens, D. (1993). Learning about literacy: A 30-year journey. In C. J. Gordon, G. D. Labercane, & W. R. McEachern (Eds.), *Elementary reading: Process and practice* (pp. 4–18). Boston: Ginn.

Pressley, M., & Afflerbach, P. (1995). *Verbal protocols of reading: The nature of constructively responsive reading.* Hillsdale, NJ: Lawrence Erlbaum Associates.

RAND Reading Study Group (Catherine Snow Chair). (2001). *Reading for understanding: Towards an R&D program in reading comprehension.* Washington, DC: RAND.

Rankin, E. F. (1965). The cloze procedure: A survey of research. In E. Thurston & L. Hafner (Eds.), *Fourteenth yearbook of the National Reading Conference* (pp. 133–150). Clemson, SC: National Reading Conference.

Resnick, D. P. (1982). History of educational testing. In A. K. Wigdor & W. R. Garner (Eds.), *Ability testing: Uses, consequences, and controversies* (Part 2, p. 371). Washington, DC: National Academy Press.

Richards, I. A. (1929). *Practical criticism.* New York: Harcourt Brace.

Riddle Buly, M., & Valencia, S. W. (2002). Below the bar: Profiles of students who fail state reading assessments. *Educational Evaluation and Policy Analysis, 24*(3), 219–239.

Rosenblatt, L. M. (1978). *The reader, the text, the poem: The transactional theory of the literary work.* Carbondale: Southern Illinois University Press.

Royer, J. M. (1987). The sentence verification technique: A practical procedure for testing comprehension. *Journal of Reading, 30,* 14–22.

Royer, J. M., & Cunningham, D. J. (1981). On the theory and measurement of reading comprehension. *Contemporary Educational Psychology, 6,* 187–216.

Royer, J. M., & Hambleton, R. K. (1983). *Normative study of 50 reading comprehension passages that use the sentence verification technique.* Unpublished manuscript, University of Massachusetts at Amherst.

Royer, J. M., Hastings, N., & Hook, C. (1979). A sentence verification technique for measuring reading comprehension tests. *Journal of Reading Behavior, 11,* 355–363.

Royer, J. M., Lynch, D. J., Hambleton, R. K., & Bulgarelli, C. (1984). Using the sentence verification technique to assess the comprehension of technical text as a function of subject matter expertise. *American Educational Research Journal, 21*, 839–869.

Royer, J. M., Kulhavy, R. W., Lee, J. B., & Peterson, S. E. (1986). The sentence verification technique as a measure of listening and reading comprehension. *Educational and Psychological Research, 6,* 299–314.

Rumelhart, D. E. (1977). Understanding and summarizing brief stories. In D. LaBerge & J. Samuels (Eds.), *Basic processes in reading perception and comprehension.* Hillsdale, NJ: Lawrence Erlbaum Associates.

Rumelhart, D. E. (1981). Schemata: The building blocks of cognition. In J. T. Guthrie (Ed.), *Comprehension in teaching* (pp. 3–26). Newark, DE: International Reading Association.

Salinger, T., & Campbell, J. (1998). The national assessment of reading in the USA. In C. Harrison & T. Salinger (Eds.), *Assessing reading: Theory and practice* (pp. 96–109). London: Routledge.

Sarroub, L., & Pearson, P. D. (1998). Two steps forward, three steps back: The stormy history of reading comprehension assessment. *The Clearing House, 72,* 97–105.

Schreiner, R. L., Heironymus, A. N., & Forsyth, R. (1969). Differential measurement of reading abilities at the elementary school level. *Reading Research Quarterly, 5,* 1.

Shanahan, T., Kamil, M. L., & Tobin, A. W. (1982). Cloze as a measure of intersentential comprehension. *Reading Research Quarterly, 17,* 229–255.

Shavelson, R. J., Baxter, G. P., & Pine, J. (1992). Performance assessments: Political rhetoric and measurement reality. *Educational Researcher, 21*(4), 22–27.

Silver Burdett & Ginn. (1989). *World of reading.* Morristown, NJ: Author.

Smagorinsky, P. (2001). If meaning is constructed, what's it made from? Toward a cultural theory of reading. *Review of Educational Research, 71*(1), 133–169.

Smith, N. B. (1986). *American reading instruction.* Newark, DE: International Reading Association.

Spearitt, D. (1972). Identification of subskills of reading comprehension by maximum likelihood factor analysis. *Reading Research Quarterly, 8,* 92–111.

Spiro, R., & Jehng, J. (1990). Cognitive flexibility and hypertext: Theory and technology for the linear and nonlinear multidimensional traversal of complex subject matter. In D. Nix & R. Spiro (Eds.), *Cognition, education, and multimedia: Exploring ideas in high technology* (pp. 163–205). Hillsdale, NJ: Lawrence Erlbaum Associates.

Starch, D. (1915). The measurement of efficiency in reading. *Journal of Educational Psychology, 6,* 1–24.

Stein, N. L., & Glenn, C. G. (1977). An analysis of story comprehension in elementary school children. In R. O. Freedle (Ed.), *Discourse processing: Multidisciplinary perspective* (pp. 53–120). Norwood, NJ: Ablex.

Stenner, A. J., & Burdick, X. (1997). *The objective measurement of reading comprehension.* Durham, NC: MetaMetrics, Inc.

Stenner, A. J., Smith, D. R., Horabin, I., & Smith, M. (1987). *Fit of the Lexlie Theory to item difficulties on fourteen standardized reading comprehension tests.* Durham, NC: MetaMetrics Inc.

Taylor, W. (1953). Cloze procedure: A new tool for measuring readability. *Journalism Quarterly, 9,* 206–223.

Thorndike, E. L. (1917). Reading as reasoning: A study of mistakes in paragraph reading. *Journal of Educational Psychology, 8,* 323–332.

Thurstone, L. L. (n.d.). *Psychological examination* (Test 4). Stoelting.

Touchstone Applied Science Associates. (1995). *Degrees of reading power*. Benbrook, TX: Author.

Touton, F. C., & Berry, B. T. (1931). Reading comprehension at the junior college level. *California Quarterly of Secondary Education, 6*, 245–251.

Tuinman, J. J. (1974). Determining the passage-dependency of comprehension questions in 5 major tests. *Reading Research Quarterly, 9*, 207–223.

Tuinman, J. J. (1978). Criterion referenced measurement in a norm referenced context. In J. Samuels (Ed.), *What research has to say about reading instruction* (pp. 165–173). Newark, DE: International Reading Association.

Turner, A., & Greene, E. (1977). *The construction of a propositional text base* (Tech. Rep. No. 63). Boulder: University of Colorado Press.

Valencia, S., & Pearson, P. D. (1987a). *New models for reading assessment* (Reading Education Rep. No. 71). Urbana: University of Illinois Press, Center for the Study of Reading.

Valencia, S., & Pearson, P. D. (1987b). Reading assessment: Time for a change. *The Reading Teacher, 40*, 726–733.

Valencia, S., Pearson, P. D., Peters, C. W., & Wixson K. K. (1989). Theory and practice in statewide reading assessment: Closing the gap. *Educational Leadership, 47*, 57–63.

Valencia, S. V., Pearson, P. D., Reeve, R., Shanahan, T., Croll, V., Foertsch, D., et al. (1986). *Illinois assessment of educational progress: Reading*. Springfield: Illinois State Board of Education.

Vygotsky, L. (1978). *Mind in society: The development of higher psychological processes*. Cambridge, MA: Harvard University Press.

Wertsch, J. V. (1985). *Vygotsky and the social formation of mind*. Cambridge, MA: Harvard University Press.

White, E. B. (1952). *Charlotte's web*. New York: Harper & Row.

Winograd, P., & Johnston, P. (1980). *Comprehension monitoring and the error detection paradigm* (Tech. Rep. No. 153). Urbana: University of Illinois Press, Center for the Study of Reading.

Yepes-Bayara, M. (1996, April). *A cognitive study based on the National Assessment of Educational Progress (NAEP) science assessment*. Paper presented at the annual meeting of the National Council on Measurement in Education, New York.

3

Comprehension

Walter Kintsch
Eileen Kintsch
University of Colorado

What makes reading comprehension difficult, and how can we assess comprehension effectively? Before we attempt to answer such questions, we need to outline the nature and characteristics of comprehension processes, for comprehension is not a single unitary process. Instead, it requires the delicate interaction of several component processes that integrate information from the page that the student is reading with his or her background knowledge and experience, subject to a multitude of contextual constraints. Linguists and logicians have analyzed texts for a long time. Psychologists, on the other hand, have been less interested in the texts themselves and their structure and meaning, but in the processes involved to transform the meaning on the page into meaning in the mind. Although models of comprehension differ in many (important) details, we believe that there is an emerging consensus on a general framework. For concreteness, we focus here on our own work (Kintsch, 1998; Kintsch & van Dijk, 1978). The model we describe is a model of adult, fluent reading comprehension. Educators are primarily concerned with students who are learning to read; students, almost by definition, are not fluent readers. So why bother with a model of adult, fluent reading comprehension? There are two strong reasons for doing so. First, if we try to transform beginning readers into fluent readers, it is important to know the characteristics of the goal state that we want to achieve. Second, the striking contrast between the performance of fluent readers and the struggles of beginners must be the starting point for how instruction in reading comprehension should be conceptualized.

A MODEL OF READING COMPREHENSION

It is not possible to adequately discuss reading comprehension within the confines of this chapter. Readers who want the whole story should consult other sources, such as Kintsch (1998). Instead, what we shall do here is focus on two central issues in the theory of comprehension that are crucial for understanding the factors that make comprehension difficult. First, we focus on the complexity of the mental representations that are generated in reading. Then, we consider the inference processes that are required to construct the kind of mental representation that supports deep understanding, and hence learning, rather than shallow understanding and rote memory.

Levels of Comprehension

It is useful to distinguish three separable (although interacting) levels of comprehension processes in reading:

1. *Decoding processes* refer to the perceptual and conceptual processes involved in getting from the printed word on the page to word and sentence meanings in the mind of the reader. The mental representation resulting from decoding process consists of a sequence of idea units, usually referred to as propositions.

2. At the next level of analysis, propositions are interrelated in a complex network, called the *microstructure* of the text. In addition, the hierarchical relations among the various sections of a text are determined. This global structure of a text is called the *macrostructure*. Microstructure and macrostructure together form the *textbase*. A student who is asked to recall a text will rely both on the microstructure and macrostructure of the text. On the other hand, a good summary would reflect primarily the macrostructure. Of course, neither recall protocols nor summaries are usually complete. With longer texts, even good comprehenders do not include all text propositions in their mental representation, and they are not always able to retrieve all the propositions they have constructed. Good comprehension is indicated not so much by how many propositions are reproduced from a text, but which ones: insignificant detail can be neglected, but not important ideas.

The microstructure is constructed by forming propositional units according to the words of the text and their syntactic relations and by analyzing the coherence relations among these propositions. The relations among propositions are often, but not necessarily, signaled by cohesion markers in the text (e.g., sentence connectives such as "however" or "because"). However, inferences are necessary to bridge gaps in cohesion between propositions and to identify pronouns to arrive at a coherent microstructure.

(3.) Although inferences play a role in the construction of the textbase, the textbase (i.e., the mental representation that the reader constructs of the text) remains close to the text from which it was derived. Generally, however, the process of meaning construction proceeds beyond the text itself. To really understand a text, it is usually necessary that the reader integrate it with his or her prior knowledge and experience. That is, the reader must construct a situation model—a mental model of the situation described by the text. This requires the integration of information provided by the text with relevant prior knowledge and the goals of the comprehender. Going beyond the text also means going beyond the verbal domain. Texts consist of words, and the textbase is a propositional structure (that is, word meanings combined into idea units). The situation model, in contrast, is not necessarily purely propositional, but may contain other components, such as visual imagery, emotions, as well as personal experiences.

Consider a simple example to illustrate these concepts. Imagine a story about a Civil War battle. There might be a sentence like, "The soldiers passed some burning houses before they reached the river," which consists of two complex propositions, "soldiers passed (burning) houses" and "soldiers reach river," connected by "before." Note the inference that identifies "they" with "soldiers" rather than "houses." All the sentences of the story would similarly be analyzed into their constituent propositions and linked into a large network which forms the microstructure of the text. The macrostructure of our fictitious story would express the gist of the story. It would consist of a hierarchical structure of (macro) propositions—either propositions directly represented by the text or generalizations and constructions based on the text. It would have some conventional form (e.g., setting-complication-resolution). Let us assume it relates the experience of a young soldier who gets badly wounded in a battle at a river crossing.

Although the microstructure and macrostructure of the text are largely determined by what the author wrote (assuming a reasonably skilled and cooperative reader), the situation model of a particular reader is much less predictable. Consider a reader who knows very little about the Civil War; for him or her, the situation model would hardly be different from the text itself, because there is no background of knowledge to be added to the text. At the other extreme, imagine a Civil War buff, who might identify the battle by name, remember its date, its outcome, the generals involved, its consequences for the war at large, and so on. The mental representation of the story such a reader constructs would be much more elaborate than the text itself. Indeed, the unlucky soldier's experiences might be just a footnote to the war story that really was not at all related by the text, but of which the reader was reminded by the text. Thus, the situation model a reader constructs from a text depends on goals and background knowledge to a much greater extent than the textbase, which usually follows more or less faithfully the author's intentions. It also depends on the level of engagement of a reader with the text: even a knowledgeable reader is often satisfied with a superficial understanding. Indeed, as discussed in more detail later, a major pedagogical goal in comprehension instruction is to induce readers not to be satisfied with a superficial textbase, but to work for a situation model that links the text to their own knowledge base and goals.

We illustrate these concepts with a simple example. The text is an instructional text about the functioning of the heart, entitled "The circulatory system." In Fig. 3.1, the macrostructure of the text is diagrammed: it is signaled explicitly in the text by five subheadings; the last section, which is quite long, is further subdivided into three topical subsections.

Figure 3.2 shows an example of the microstructure of the text, specifically, the first three sentences of the macro-unit "The Valves." Note the hierarchical organization of the microstructure with the proposition introducing the concept "valves" at the top of the hierarchy. Not all relations among propositions are shown in the graph, for example, the repetition of "blood" in Propositions 1 and 9. The construction of the microstructure follows very closely the linguistic structure of the sentences. One inference is required to identify the referents of the pronoun "them" in the first sentence.

The situation model constructed on the basis of these two sentences is shown in Fig. 3.3. The situation model contains much more than the information expressed in the two sentences under discussion. To understand these sentences, the reader must retrieve prior knowledge about the heart and integrate it with the new information provided by the text. The prior information (for

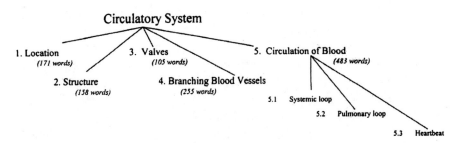

FIG. 3.1.   Macrostructure for the text "The Circulatory System."

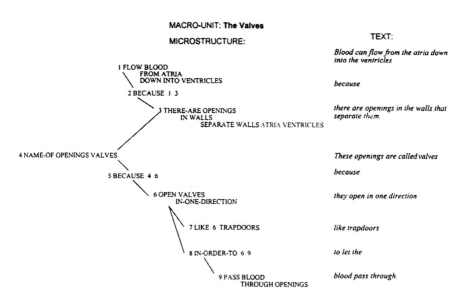

MACRO-UNIT: **The Valves**

MICROSTRUCTURE:

TEXT:

1 FLOW BLOOD
    FROM ATRIA
    DOWN INTO VENTRICLES

Blood can flow from the atria down
into the ventricles

2 BECAUSE 1 3

because

3 THERE-ARE OPENINGS
    IN WALLS
        SEPARATE WALLS ATRIA VENTRICLES

there are openings in the walls that
separate them.

4 NAME-OF OPENINGS VALVES

These openings are called valves

5 BECAUSE 4 6

because

6 OPEN VALVES
    IN-ONE-DIRECTION

they open in one direction

7 LIKE 6 TRAPDOORS

like trapdoors

8 IN-ORDER-TO 6 9

to let the

9 PASS BLOOD
    THROUGH OPENINGS

blood pass through.

FIG. 3.2.   Microstructure for two sentences from the macro-unit "Valves."

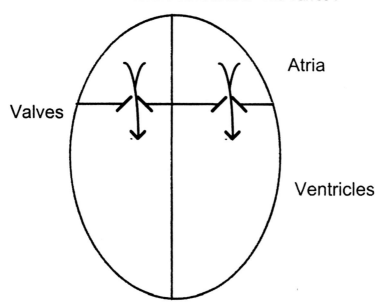

Situation Model
based on the first two sentences of "The Valves":

Atria

Valves

Ventricles

FIG. 3.3.   A possible situation model for the text "The Circulatory System."

some readers this might be prior knowledge about the heart, but in this case, it is also information presented earlier in the text) is printed in italics: it involves the spatial layout of the chambers of the heart, as well as their names. A reader who does not retrieve this information from his or her memory and integrate it with the new information provided by the text does not really understand the text, even if he or she had formed a correct textbase. Such a reader might be able to reproduce the text by rote, or even make some semantic judgments: for instance, on the basis of the hierarchical textbase shown in Fig. 3.2, the reader could say that the sentences were about valves. However, this reader could not make correct inferences about the functioning of the heart.

The goals of text comprehension vary widely. The reason for reading a manual might be to learn how to perform an action; one might read a detective story to be entertained for a while; one reads the newspaper to be informed, and so on. But in educational contexts, the goal is often to learn from a text, that is, to construct a situation model that will be remembered and can be used effectively when the information provided by that text is needed in some way at a later time. Thus, pedagogically, the question of interest is, how can one get students to construct good situation models from instructional texts. This is a difficult task, because it demands the use of prior knowledge and requires an active process of meaning construction—not just the passive registration of a textbase.

The Role of Working Memory

The limits of working memory put constraints on the processing of text. That we can process only a finite amount of information at any given moment has serious implications, not only for models of comprehension, but also for assessment of comprehension. For instance, if two concepts never co-occur in working memory during the processing of a text, no new associations between these concepts will be formed as a consequence of reading this text. Because the formation of both the textbase and the situation model depends on connections between concepts, lack of association would weaken both. This postulate sets severe limits on the comprehension process, especially because the capacity of short-term memory, on which working memory must rely, at least in part, is known to be quite small, only about four chunks.

If all processing depends on working memory, and working memory is so severely limited in terms of its capacity, variations of the capacity of working memory among individual readers ought to be closely related to comprehension. Daneman and Carpenter (1980) measured short-term memory capacity in the context of a reading task by asking participants to read a series of sentences and then recall the last word from each sentence. Working memory measured in this way (the Reading Span) correlates quite well with reading comprehension. Reading span differs among individuals, varying between about 2 and 6, and is a reliable predictor of performance on conventional reading comprehension tests (including the Scholastic Assessment Test or SAT), as well as inferencing (Singer et al., 1992).

Although the reading span is a good predictor of individual differences in reading comprehension, it can still be argued that estimates of working memory capacity arrived at in this way are still too low to be able to account for everything a good reader must maintain in working memory: crucial fragments of the prior text, including its macrostructure, linguistic knowledge, relevant world knowledge, and reading goals—a list much too long for even the highest reading span yet encountered. If Reading Span is limited to only 4 units or so, it would be difficult for a reader to make sense of even a simple text, not to mention texts as complex as those adults encounter every day.

An explanation for this apparent discrepancy was provided by Ericsson and Kintsch (1995) and Kintsch, Patel, and Ericsson (1999), who introduced the concept of long-term working memory. Working memory, when we are reading a text in a familiar domain, is composed not only of the capacity of limited short-term memory but also includes a long-term component.

We call this component "retrieval structures." Retrieval structures contain all items in the reader's long-term memory that are linked to the current contents of short-term memory (which, for this purpose, can be equated with consciousness or focus of attention). Rich retrieval structures are characteristic of experts in a domain, allowing the chess master to "see" the next move without having to figure it out; making it possible for the experienced physician to integrate patient data, medical knowledge, and prior experience to arrive at an intuitive diagnosis.

Retrieval structures are the basis for reading comprehension, for when we are reading texts in familiar domains, we are all experts, having practiced comprehension for many years. Retrieval structures exist only in domains where people have acquired expertise, which requires a great deal of practice. Thus, the chess master and the physician are not necessarily better readers than anyone else outside their domain of expertise. Most people reading a paper in theoretical physics do not readily comprehend it like they comprehend the daily newspaper, or as a physicist would comprehend the physics paper. Rather than fluent reading, their reading in the latter case would be an arduous and frustrating problem-solving activity. Thus, retrieval structures make available information stored in long-term memory that is directly relevant to the task at hand without the need for time- and resource-consuming retrieval processes.

The concept of long-term working memory allows us to understand how readers can juggle all the things they need for comprehension in working memory. It also suggests a reinterpretation of the reading span data. Thus, it is not the capacity of working memory that varies among individuals, but the skill with which they are using this capacity. High-span readers are readers who have a high level of reading expertise: they are fluent decoders who easily organize detailed information into a hierarchical macrostructure, and who possess rich, well-elaborated knowledge of word meanings. Their efficient processing allows them to effectively employ their retrieval structures as they comprehend and enables them to recall many words. In contrast, inefficient lower level reading processes are characteristic of readers with low reading spans.

If we regard reading comprehension as a kind of expert performance, certain pedagogic consequences are implied. Expert performance is based on very large amounts of practice, specifically, guided practice where an effort is made to continually push the envelope of performance (Ericsson & Charness, 1994). Mere mechanical repetition does not count. The beginning reader must be challenged, pushed, supported, and guided. Interests in particular domains should be exploited to allow the students to build up their expertise in these areas. Furthermore, a rich vocabulary and familiarity with a wide range of syntactic constructions are inherent components of the linguistic expertise that is required for skilled reading comprehension.

Inference

Going beyond the text requires inferences, not only of the gap-filling kind needed to construct a coherent text base, but also to construct a coherent situation model. Some inferences come easily; they are automatically activated during reading, especially if the topic is familiar. This automatic activation is dependent on rich and deep retrieval structures. However, at other times, readers may need to actively work to infer what is unsaid in the text, and what they need for their personal understanding. Texts are almost never fully explicit.

There are always gaps left to be filled in by the reader; the gaps may be local as in

(1)   *The river was broad. The water flowed swiftly.*

where the reader must realize that the water is

(2)   *river water.*

Or the gaps may be global, as when the topic of a story is not explicitly stated and left for the reader to construct, or when a reader must realize that a particular paragraph in an essay provides an example for a point made earlier. Such gap filling has traditionally been labeled *inference*. This terminology is somewhat unfortunate because it lumps together processes that are quite distinct psychologically and that differ dramatically in the demands they make on the reader (Kintsch, 1998). First, inferences vary along a dimension from automatic to controlled. Automatic inferences are made quickly and easily, such as the bridging inference linking river and water in (1). Controlled processes, on the other hand, can be highly resource demanding, as is the case, for instance, if a text requires syllogistic reasoning. A second dimension along which inferences in text comprehension vary is whether they are knowledge-based or text-based. (1) is a typical knowledge based inference—the reader knows that rivers have water. In contrast, if we conclude from

(3)   *Corporal Mitchell was a superb marksman, better than anyone in his unit, including Captain Jones, who could outshoot the legendary Lieutenant Franklin*

that

(4)   *Mitchell was a better marksman than Franklin*

we are not using what we already knew about the corporal and the lieutenant, but must employ the information provided by the text. In the literature, all these psychologically rather distinct processes are called "inferences"—but it is crucial that we keep in mind the important differences between various types of inference in text comprehension. (And it should go without saying that most of these inferences have nothing to do with what logicians call inference.)

The principal question about inferences in the text comprehension literature has been when what types of inferences are made and when they are not made. On the one hand, one can focus on all the inferences that can plausibly be made (e.g., Graesser, 1981). Of course, not all readers will actually generate all inferences at all times. So what do readers actually do? This simple question turns out not to have a simple answer. Whether a reader draws a particular inference depends on many factors. Under some conditions, readers are minimalists (McKoon & Ratcliff, 1992), making only those inferences that are absolutely necessary to understand the text. For instance, (1) cannot be understood without making the bridging inference linking river and water; but (2) can be understood perfectly well, and many readers will not bother to figure out whether the corporal shoots better than the lieutenant—unless asked to. On the other hand, it is easy to find conditions under which readers are far more active than minimally required (Graesser, Singer, & Trabasso, 1994). For instance, readers typically infer causal antecedents but not causal consequences (Magliano, Baggett, Johnson, & Graesser, 1993). Given

(5)   *The Confederate army attacked Cemetery Hill.*

(6)   *The battle lasted all day.*

readers infer

(7)   *The attack caused the battle.*

Given only (6), readers do not jump to the conclusion (7). However, under the right conditions, it is quite possible to get readers to make predictive inferences (e.g., Klin, Guzman, & Levine, 1999).

What happens when a reader "makes the inferences" (2) given (1), or (7), given (5) and (6), respectively? It is just that a piece of relevant knowledge is retrieved, namely, that rivers have water or that attacks are followed by a battle. It is not an active, controlled, resource demanding process, but instead happens quickly and automatically. The fact that antecedent causal inferences are more likely than predictive inferences does not mean that the knowledge does not become available in the latter case, only that it is more likely to be used when it is linked to two items—(5) and (6) in the earlier example—than when it is only linked to one (Kintsch, 1998; Schmalhofer, McDaniel, & Keefe, 2002).

Many inferences in text comprehension are straightforward cases of knowledge activation. That is, readers use their retrieval structures to propel themselves through the text. However, the importance of active, controlled, constructive inferencing in comprehension can hardly be overestimated, especially with instructional texts. Automatic knowledge activation will work well as long as the text is in a highly familiar domain. When we read a text to learn from it, by definition we are no longer on the kind of highly familiar ground where we can rely on well-practiced retrieval structures to activate relevant knowledge. It is still necessary, however, to retrieve whatever relevant prior knowledge and experience we have, which can be a very effortful process, requiring conscious control. Without this effort, no learning results—the textual information will remain, at best, inert knowledge, not linked up with existing knowledge structures and hence unusable, unavailable when needed in a slightly altered situation.

Resource demanding, controlled inference processes in text comprehension are not restricted to knowledge retrieval. The situation model for a literary text may require construction at more than one level of analysis; to understand a story, the reader may have to infer the protagonists' motivations; to understand an argument, the exact relations between its components may have to be analyzed. Deep understanding always goes beyond the text in nontrivial ways, requiring the construction of meaning, not just passive absorption of information.

Pedagogically, inferencing in text comprehension presents many problems. The basic problem is to get the reader to engage in the kind of deliberate processing that is necessary for deep understanding. Skilled readers adjust their inferencing to the requirements of specific text and specific situations. The metacognitive control of inferencing is something that must be learned. Readers must learn what inferences have to be made, and what inferences should be made in different contexts. That is not achieved by teaching them promiscuous inference strategies—irrelevant, excessive elaborations, for instance, can impede the construction of an appropriate situation model just as much as the failure to make required invited inferences. Thus, Gernsbacher and Faust (1991) and others have shown that readers who are unable to inhibit irrelevant associations during reading have comprehension problems. On the other hand, there is a great deal of evidence that teaching students to engage in relevant inferencing effectively promotes deep comprehension (Pressley, 1998).

Knowledge Representation

Comprehension requires inferences, and inferences require knowledge. Hence, to understand text comprehension, we must be able to understand how knowledge is used and how it is represented. Most psychological (and linguistic and artificial intelligence) models of knowledge representation are toy models that cannot deal with the sheer amount of information in human knowledge. Recently, however, Latent Semantic Analysis (LSA) has become available that provides psychologists at least with a tolerably good approximation to human knowledge representation (Landauer et al., 1998; Landauer & Dumais, 1997; see also the Web site http://lsa.colorado.edu).

LSA is a machine learning method that constructs a geometric representation of meaning that resembles the structure of human knowledge about words and texts. It constructs this representation simply from observing how words are used in a large number of texts. Formally, the problem faced by LSA might be characterized by an equation that expresses the meaning of a document as a function of its words, their order and interrelationships, as well as the (verbal and nonverbal) context (Landauer, 2001):

(8)   meaning (document) = f{ word$_1$, word$_2$, word$_3$, ... word$_n$, context

To solve this equation (for a large number of documents), LSA makes some sim-
plifying assumptions:

(9)   meaning(document$_1$) = meaning(word$_{11}$) + meaning(word$_{12}$) +
          ... meaning(word$_{1n}$)
       meaning(document$_2$) = meaning(word$_{21}$) + meaning(word$_{22}$) +
          ... meaning(word$_{2m}$)
       .
       .
       .
       meaning(document$_k$) = meaning(word$_{k1}$) + meaning(word$_{k2}$)
          + ... meaning(word$_{1k_z}$)

In other words, we disregard word order, syntax, as well as all context, and
take the meaning of a document to be just the meaning of a bag of words. These
may seem to be drastic simplifications, but, as we shall see, enough information
is retained in this way to produce useful results.

Consider a corpus of 11M word tokens, 90K word types, and 40K documents,
consisting of texts a typical high school graduate might have read. This corpus
clearly underspecifies word meanings and is furthermore inconsistent. What
LSA does is to extract from such a corpus a semantic representation that does
not attempt to specify "the meaning" of each word and document in absolute
terms (as would a dictionary or encyclopedia), but determines only the relations
 among all the words and documents. That is, LSA defines meaning as the relation of a word (or document) to all other words and documents in the corpus.
LSA does this by constructing a high-dimensional semantic space, using a standard mathematical technique called singular value decomposition for optimal
dimension reduction to eliminate noise in data.

Semantic relatedness in the LSA space is measured by the cosine between
words or documents, a statistic much like the familiar correlation coefficient.
The cosine between randomly chosen words is .02 +/– .04. Following are some
examples that show that the similarity measure calculated by LSA yields results
not unlike human intuition:

doctor—doctors	.79
doctor—physician	.61
go—went	.71
good—bad	.65
she—her	.98
blackbird—bird	.46
blackbird—black	.04

Note that in the original corpus, the correlation between the words *doctor* and *doctors* (or between singular and plural, in general) is quite low, because when one talks about a singular entity one rarely also mentions the plural, and vice versa. LSA, however, has inferred that these singulars and plurals are quite similar in meaning (not identical, however).

Many words have more than one meaning, and most have several senses, depending on context. In LSA, meaning is context free, but note that in a high-dimensional space, complex relations can be naturally represented. For instance, the homonym *mint* has (at least) three senses, as in leaves of a plant, flavored candy, and coin money. The cosines between the word *mint* and these three phrases are .20, .23, and .33, respectively. Thus, "mint" is strongly related to each of these phrases that involve different meanings, although these three phrases are not related to each other (the average cosine between the three phrases is only .05).[1]

LSA is not restricted to computing the semantic similarities among words. Sentences and whole texts can be represented in the same semantic space, and hence can be readily compared with each other. The similarity measures that LSA computes for texts correlate well with human judgments, as is most dramatically shown by the ability of LSA-based systems to grade essays as well as expert human graders (Landauer, Laham, & Foltz, 2000). LSA can be a valuable educational tool, in that it can provide feedback to students about the content of their writing, guiding their revisions until the essay they write achieves the content coverage teachers would like to see (E. Kintsch et al., 2000). LSA is not, however, a model of human comprehension processes; it is simply a representational system that allows researchers to represent the meaning of words and texts in such a way that the relations among the words and texts represented in LSA closely resemble human semantic judgments. It thus opens up numerous exciting possibilities for research and applications, only a few of which have so far been explored.

What Makes Reading Comprehension Difficult?

Reading is generally described as involving two skills: decoding and comprehension. Decoding is an isolable ability, which can be taught and assessed in straightforward ways (see Carpenter & Paris, this volume; Stahl & Hiebert, this volume). Comprehension, in contrast, is a complex skill that depends on a variety of factors, contexts, and reading goals. Both learner factors, text factors, as well as instruction, all play a role. For the purposes of this chapter, we discuss the first two.

---

[1] For a more detailed treatment of polysemy in Latent Semantic Analysis, see Kintsch (2001).

Learner Factors

Text comprehension depends first on adequate decoding skills. Thus, instruction must focus on developing these skills to an adequate level of accuracy and automaticity. Because reading comprehension and listening comprehension are closely related skills, instruction should include practice with both written and orally presented text. Multiple and continuous exposure to literacy experiences is essential to building the fluency and rich vocabulary knowledge that underlie successful comprehension.

The reader's background knowledge and motivation are further factors in comprehension: comprehension is easy when the domain knowledge is high. In addition, motivation and interest influence comprehension, both directly and indirectly (in that students are most likely to have good domain knowledge in areas in which they are interested).

Finally, there is an important set of factors associated with what readers do, namely, the strategies they employ in reading. Among the strategies that have been shown to be effective are the following (from E. Kintsch & W. Kintsch, 1996):

- Using words or imagery to elaborate the content.
- Rereading, paraphrasing, and summarizing in one's own words to clarify the content.
- Reorganizing the content into a hierarchical outline, diagram, or graph that shows the important relations between ideas.
- Consciously seeking relations between new content and existing knowledge (e.g., by self-explaining, forming analogies, hypothesizing, drawing conclusions and predictions, formulating questions, and evaluating the text for internal consistency and with respect to what one knows of the topic).
- Consciously monitoring one's ongoing comprehension, identifying the source for a breakdown in comprehension, and attempting to resolve the problem rather than passively reading on (for reviews of this literature, see Dansereau, 1985; Pressley et al., 1995).

All these strategies are variations on the same theme: the active construction of meaning during reading, and the deliberate linking of the text to be understood with prior knowledge and prior experience. Expert comprehenders are able to decide for themselves which particular activity is optimal in a given case. Novice comprehenders must acquire good metacognitive strategies to monitor ongoing comprehension and to choose appropriate strategies. This is where comprehension turns into problem solving. Normal, automatic, perception-like comprehension is no longer sufficient. When readers can no longer rely on their background knowledge for adequate comprehension, constructive problem solving must take its place.

Text Factors

There has been, and continues to be, a huge emphasis on the "readability" of texts. Primarily, this amounts to a requirement of short sentences and familiar words. There is very little in cognitive psychology that supports this widespread practice (e.g., Weaver & Kintsch, 1990). Obviously, using too many unfamiliar words and overly involved syntax will impede comprehension, but a text composed entirely of short sentences can easily become incoherent. Furthermore, students need to expand their vocabulary and familiarity with more complex syntactic structures—which they do mostly through reading.

Psychometric traditions (and requirements) clash with the laboratory study of reading when it comes to readability. If we take seriously what was said earlier about the complexity of the reading process, it makes no sense to talk about the readability of a text as if it were a single characteristic of the text, or about the reading ability of a student as if it were a single characteristic of the student. A text with short sentences and familiar words may lack coherence between sentences, or it may be disorganized globally, or it may fail to guide the student's knowledge activation, or it may bore the reader because it is too explicit and repetitive. Texts cannot be classified in a uni-dimensional manner, as readable or not; instead, they are differentiated qualitatively in many ways. Cognitive theory helps us to analyze the effectiveness of particular texts for particular readers. Similarly, the very concept of reading ability is questioned by the comprehension theory sketched here. Readers may have problems in many different areas—with decoding, establishing local or global coherence, using their prior knowledge to build a situation model, and so on. Lumping all of these differences into a single concept of reading ability may be useful for some gross statistical purposes, but not to guide instruction and diagnose comprehension problems.

One interesting way in which text characteristics affect comprehension is through their coherence at both the microstructure and macrostructure level. Texts that are coherent at the local level spell out what another text might leave implicit, requiring a bridging inference on the part of the reader (for example, making explicit that two words, such as *valves* and *openings*, refer to the same thing). Coherence is also maintained by using explicit linguistic markers to signal the relation between two clauses, rather than having it inferred by the reader (for example: Valves are like trap doors **because** they only open in one direction). At the global level, coherent texts are well organized and their structure is clearly signaled (e.g., by using section headings, topic introducers, order markers, and the like). Such texts are easier to read, and are generally recalled more successfully than less coherent texts (Beck, McKeown, Sinatra, & Loxterman, 1991; Britton & Gulgoz, 1991). Paradoxically, however, when comprehension is assessed differently, the less coherent texts turn out to be more effective. How easy it is to read a text and how well it can be reproduced yield a rather superficial measure of comprehension. Measuring whether the information in the text has been integrated with the reader's prior knowledge and whether it can be used to make inferences in new situations—to understand new texts and solve new problems—provides a better picture of how deeply a reader has understood a text. It has been shown that the less coherent text—the text that leaves unsaid what can be inferred by the reader with a little effort—results in better learning than reading a fully explicit text (e.g., McNamara, E. Kintsch, Songer, & W. Kintsch, 1996). The fully explicit text is easy to read because it does not require the reader to do much; the reader feels good about having understood the text, but in fact the level of understanding is a shallow one, because active inferencing and linking up with personal knowledge was never required. For the more difficult text, active inferencing and interpretation in terms of what the reader already knows is necessary, however, for the text cannot be understood without it. Hence, comprehension is more effortful, but the results are better: the reader has learned something from his or her work.

Pictures, graphs, and animations also facilitate text comprehension when they serve to illustrate and specify important ideas in the text. For instance, a simple diagram may help to clarify spatial relations among the various components described in the text. Levin and Mayer (1993) discussed the conditions under which illustrations are in fact helpful. Unfortunately, pictures are often misused in instructional texts—they are either irrelevant to the text and therefore distracting or they are deceptive because they oversimplify, or conversely, because they obscure essential relations with overelaborate detail (a useful review of the rich literature in this area is provided by Mayer, 2001).

ASSESSMENT OF COMPREHENSION

One of the most urgent implications of modern theories of comprehension concerns the assessment of comprehension. Current comprehension tests—the Nelson Denny, the comprehension subtest of the SAT and the like—were developed with a psychometric rationale and do not reflect our understanding of comprehension processes (for further discussion, see Shepard, 2000). There is no uniform comprehension process to be measured. Instead, comprehension involves different levels and a variety of skills: the extraction of meaning from the text, the construction of the situation model, and the integration of the reader's prior knowledge and goals with the information provided by the text. These separable components of comprehension need to be assessed separately, for, as we stressed earlier, how comprehension is assessed makes a great deal of difference. In several studies discussed earlier (e.g., McNamara et al., 1996), opposite conclusions are reached depending on whether superficial comprehension at the level of the textbase is measured, or deep comprehension at the level of the situation model is measured. For instance, if one looks only at how much students can recall, fully explicit, well-organized texts are better than texts that require the student to work harder. However, if one assesses deep comprehension, for example, by asking the student to apply the newly acquired knowledge to a novel problem, the exact opposite is the case. For a comprehension test to be useful it must be easy to use, and it must have a certain amount of face validity to ensure its acceptance by students, teachers, and parents. Current tests are easy to use, but pay a heavy price for that: the texts to be read are short and performance is measured by a few questions that can be objectively scored. However, some important comprehension skills do not come into play with such short texts, and deep understanding is not being assessed by most of the multiple-choice type questions used.

Efforts to correct this state of affairs are in the beginning stages. Hannon and Daneman (2001) have proposed and successfully evaluated a comprehension test that separates out the ability to reproduce a text from inferencing and knowledge use. Hannon and Daneman used (in one of their experiments) three-sentence texts that included (a) three nonsense words (e.g., jal, toc, and caz), (b) two real words (such as pony and beaver), and (c) a relation among them (e.g., larger than) specifying a linear ordering among the five terms. After studying such paragraphs, participants were given 18 true–false tests. Text memory statements simply tested what was stated in the paragraph. Text inference statements tested information that could be inferred from the paragraph. Knowledge access statements tested prior knowledge independent of the paragraph. Finally, knowledge integration statements tested the integration of prior knowledge with information from the paragraph. Individual differences among readers were well predicted by four components of comprehension: recall of new information, making inferences from information provided in the text, ability to access prior knowledge, and ability to integrate prior knowledge with information provided by the text.

Why do Hannon and Daneman (2001) find four factors, a result that flies in the face of a huge literature on readability, where one or two factors typically account for most or all of the individual difference variance? The answer seems to be that they looked for such differences, designing test items that were guided by their theory of reading comprehension. That made them design particular theoretically motivated test items—resulting in a complex picture of comprehension assessment, but in a picture whose complexity can be explained by comprehension theory. The use of test items directed at different levels or aspects of comprehension yields a more complex view of both comprehension ability and its assessment. As long as reading comprehension tests are composed of a theoretically unmotivated collection of test items—the criterion being whether an item discriminates good from poor readers—such a picture cannot emerge. Numerous studies, only a few of which were reviewed in the previous sections of this chapter, differentiate between various aspects of comprehension, such as gist comprehension, inferencing, and knowledge use. The readability literature disregards this important insight and would have us believe that comprehension is a unitary process, that people merely differ in the amount of their reading ability, not in qualitatively different ways. That is not what the laboratory research on comprehension in the last few decades has revealed. The importance of the Hannon and Daneman study is that it shows that tests can be developed that reflect the complexity of reading comprehension as we know it from the experimental work.

Nevertheless, one can find fault with the Hannon and Daneman (2001) procedure. All of their texts are quite short and involve nonwords. Indeed, what they ask their participants to do has more the feel of a problem solving task than normal reading. A test with better face validity, but equally easy to use and objective to score, would be desirable.

Research now in progress in our laboratory attempts to develop such a test. Our goal is to develop a test that is as easy to administer and score as current comprehension tests, but that is theoretically motivated and provides valid measures of the components of comprehension. Theoretically, we want to be able to differentiate between processing of the actual text, inferencing, and knowledge use—much like Hannon and Daneman (2001). However, our tests will use longer, more natural reading materials, and an unconstrained response format allows readers to express their understanding in a natural way. To make this practical, we relied on the essay-grading ability of LSA (for details, see Landauer & Dumais, 1997; Landauer, Foltz, & Laham, 1998). Using LSA, we can have our readers write essays about what they have read, inviting them to generate inferences that are implied by what they have read. Open-ended responses are more indicative of a person's real understanding than multiple-choice items (unless the latter are very carefully, and laboriously, constructed). LSA provides the capability for grading such essays as automatically as objective tests.

So far, we have only begun to contrast how well readers can reproduce a text versus their ability to make inferences about that text. The role of prior knowledge in these inferences has intentionally been minimized in these studies. In one study, we used 102 college students as participants. Each student read six texts, recalled each text, and wrote a short essay in answer to an inference question about each text. For instance, one text (292 words) described an episode in the history of Rome; the inference question was as follows: "Why were the threats of the plebeians effective in persuading the patricians to grant them a governmental assembly?" To answer this question, an inference had to be made based on three separate facts stated in the text. Thus, for each reader, we obtained six recall protocols and six inference essays.

All essays were graded by two graders and by LSA. LSA was able to score the memory protocols as well as the human graders, the correlation between two human graders being $r = .76$ and the correlation between human grades and LSA grades being $r = .77$. For inference protocols, the correlation between two human graders was $r = .81$, whereas the correlation between human grades and LSA grades was $r = .51$. Thus, automatic grading of these essays by LSA appears quite feasible.

The second question of interest in this study was whether the pattern of individual differences was the same for memory items and inference items. Performance on the six memory items and six inference items was reasonably consistent, Cronbach's alpha $\alpha = .88$ for the memory items and $\alpha = .53$ for the inference items. Memory and inference items were significantly but only moderately correlated, $r = .27$. Inspection of that correlation revealed an interesting pattern. Figure 3.4 plots the average performance on the six memory items against the average performance on the inference items for the 102 participants (a score of 1 means a participant received a passing grade on all six tests; a score of .33 means the participant passed two of the six tests, etc.). For most participants ($n = 73$), performance is approximately equal on memory and inference items (within 1.5 standard deviations), as shown in Fig. 3.4. However, there was a large group of participants ($n = 23$) who performed much worse on inference items than on memory items; their inference scores were more than 1.5 standard deviations below their memory scores, irrespective of whether their memory performance was good or poor. In contrast, there was only a single person who did better on inferences than on memory. Thus, it appears that the kind of textbase readers form, as indexed by their ability to reproduce the text, sets an upper limit to their ability to answer inference questions. Readers can only use text information for inferences if they have actually encoded that information. But having encoded the information in the text does not guarantee that a correct situation model could be formed.

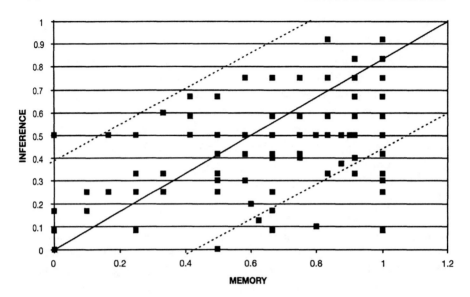

FIG. 3.4.   The correlation between memory and inference scores for 73 participants; the dotted lines indicate 1.5 standard deviations.

Indeed, as Fig. 3.4 shows, there were several readers who passed all memory tests, but failed the majority of the inference items.

This kind of information is potentially important. Memory and inference are correlated, and it does not look like there are separable memory and inference abilities. Instead, the ability to form a textbase sets an upper bound on inference performance: if readers do not remember the text content, their inference ability is impaired; if they do remember the text, that does not necessarily mean that they can answer inference questions. Readers who are poor on both the memory and inference tests will require different instructional interventions than readers who show by their good performance on the memory tests that they can comprehend the text at the level of the textbase, but who are either unable to construct a good situation model to support inferences, or merely fail to do so.

Our results are preliminary and incomplete, and many questions remain unanswered: Just what is wrong with college students who perform badly on the memory tests? Do they still have decoding problems? Would they perform equally poorly with shorter texts or with narratives? Why do readers fail on the inference tests when they are able to form a perfectly good textbase? How can we teach reading strategies that will support the construction of a situation model? In addition, we need to develop tests to diagnose knowledge deficits or failure to use available knowledge, which may be a major source of comprehension problems. It is not the case that comprehension theory has all the answers to guide educational practice. But thinking about instruction and assessment within the framework of a theory of comprehension can be useful and will be even more useful as that theory is further developed.

REFERENCES

Beck, I. L., McKeown, M. G., Sinatra, G. M., & Loxterman, J. A. (1991). Revising social studies texts from a text-processing perspective: Evidence of improved comprehensibility. *Reading Research Quarterly, 27,* 251–276.

Britton, B. K., & Gulgoz, S. (1991). Using Kintsch's model to improve instructional text: Effects of inference calls on recall and cognitive structures. *Journal of Educational Psychology, 83,* 329–345.

Daneman, M., & Carpenter, P. A. (1980). Individual differences in working memory and reading. *Journal of Verbal Learning and Verbal Behavior, 19,* 450–466.

Dansereau, D. F. (1985). Learning strategy research. In S. C. J. Segal & R. Glaser (Eds.), *Thinking and learning skills: Relating instruction to research* (Vol. 1, pp. 209–240). Hillsdale, NJ: Lawrence Erlbaum Associates.

Ericsson, K. A., & Charness, N. (1994). Expert performance: Its structure and acquisition. *American Psychologist, 49,* 727–747.

Ericsson, K. A., & Kintsch, W. (1995). Long-term working memory. *Psychological Review, 102,* 211–245.

Gernsbacher, M. A., & Faust, M. E. (1991). The mechanism of suppression: A component of general comprehension. *Journal of Experimental Psychology: Learning, Memory, and Cognition, 17,* 245–262.

Graesser, A. C. (1981). *Prose comprehension beyond the word.* New York: Springer.

Graesser, A. C., Singer, M., & Trabasso, T. (1994). Constructing inferences during narrative text comprehension. *Psychological Review, 101,* 375–395.

Hannon, N., & Daneman, M. (2001). A new tool for measuring and understanding individual differences in the component processes of reading comprehension. *Journal of Educational Psychology, 93,* 103–128.

Kintsch, E., & Kintsch, W. (1996). Learning from text. In E. DeCorte & F. Weinert (Eds.), *International encyclopedia of developmental and instructional psychology* (pp. 541–601). Amsterdam: Pergamon.

Kintsch, E., Steinhart, D., Stahl, G., Matthews, C., Lamb, R., & LSA Research Group. (2000). Developing summarization skills through the use of LSA-backed feedback. *Interactive Learning Environments, 8,* 87–109.

Kintsch, W. (1998). *Comprehension: A paradigm for cognition.* New York: Cambridge University Press.

Kintsch, W. (2001). Predication. *Cognitive Science.*

Kintsch, W., Patel, V. L., & Ericsson, K. A. (1999). The role of long-term working memory in text comprehension. *Psychologia, 42,* 186–198.

Kintsch, W., & van Dijk, T. A. (1978). Towards a model of text comprehension and production. *Psychological Review, 85*, 363–394.

Klin, C. M., Guzman, A. E., & Levine, W. H. (1999). Prevalence and persistence of predictive inferences. *Journal of Memory and Language, 40*, 593–604.

Landauer, T. K. (2001). Single representations of multiple meanings in Latent Semantic Analysis. In D. S. Gorfein (Ed.), *On the consequences of meaning selection.* Washington, DC: American Psychological Association.

Landauer, T. K., & Dumais, S. T. (1997). A solution to Plato's problem: The Latent Semantic Analysis theory of acquisition, induction and representation of knowledge. *Psychological Review, 104*, 211–240.

Landauer, T. K., Foltz, P., & Laham, D. (1998). An introduction to Latent Semantic Analysis. *Discourse Processes, 25*, 259–284.

Landauer, T. K., Laham, D., & Foltz, P. W. (2000). The Intelligent Essay Assessor. *IEEE Intelligent Systems*, 27–31.

Levin, J. R., & Mayer, R. E. (1993). Understanding illustrations in text. In B. K. Britton, A. Woodward, & M. Binkley (Eds.), *Learning from textbooks* (pp. 95–114). Hillsdale, NJ: Lawrence Erlbaum Associates.

Magliano, J. P., Baggett, W. B., Johnson, B. K., & Graesser, A. C. (1993). The time course of generating causal antecedent and causal consequence inferences. *Discourse Processes, 16*, 35–53.

Mayer, R. E. (2001). *Multimedia learning.* New York: Cambridge University Press.

McKoon, G., & Ratcliff, R. (1992). Inference during reading. *Psychological Review, 99*, 440–466.

McNamara, D. S., Kintsch, E., Songer, N. B., & Kintsch, W. (1996). Are good texts always better? Text coherence, background knowledge, and levels of understanding in learning from text. *Cognition and Instruction, 14*, 1–43.

Pressley, M. (1998). *Reading Instruction that works: The case for balanced teaching.* New York: Guilford.

Pressley, M., Woloshyn, V., & Associates. (1995). *Cognitive strategy instruction that really improves children's academic performance* (2nd ed.). Cambridge, MA: Brookline Books.

Schmalhofer, F., McDaniel, M. A., & Keefe, D. (2002). A unified model for predictive and bridging inferences. *Discourse Processes, 33*, 105–132.

Shepard, L. A. (2000). The role of assessment in a learning culture. *Educational Researcher, 29*(7), 4–14.

Singer, M., Halldorson, M., Lear, J. C., & Andrusiak, P. (1992). Validation of causal bridging inferences in discourse understanding. *Journal of Memory and Language, 31*, 507–524.

Weaver, C. A. I., & Kintsch, W. (1990). Expository text. In R. Barr, M. L. Kamil, P. B. Rosenthal, & P. D. Pearson (Eds.), *Handbook of reading* (Vol. II, pp. 230–245). New York: Longman.

4

Comprehension of What for What: Comprehension as a Nonunitary Construct

Nell K. Duke
Michigan State University

There is no uniform comprehension process to be measured.
—W. Kintsch & E. Kintsch (this volume, p. 84)

We often hear, read, and write discussions of terms including *comprehension processes, comprehension assessment, comprehension instruction*, even simply *comprehension*. For some situations, these broad-brush terms can be useful. But for many situations, and very often when we want to go in to some depth, such terms are not adequate. Comprehension is not a unitary construct. There are many different processes entailed in the broad thing called "comprehension," and "comprehension" proceeds very differently for different kinds of text, different topics, and different reading purposes. And this is not simply an interesting discussion point for researchers and theorists. It has real implications for comprehension assessment.

This commentary addresses three chapters well worth reading, and chapters very different in purpose, content, and stance. Despite these substantial differences, there are three important and interrelated themes regarding comprehension assessment that are salient in each of the chapters: the importance of theory in developing comprehension assessments, comprehension as a nonunitary construct, and the need for a system of comprehension assessment. I discuss the first two themes and then, in the context of discussing the third, highlight some challenges and opportunities for comprehension assessment.

THREE THEMES ACROSS CHAPTERS

The Importance of Theory in Developing Comprehension Assessments

All three of these chapters emphasize the importance of theory in developing comprehension assessments. Kintsch and Kintsch (this volume) wrote the following:

> One of the most urgent implications of modern theories of comprehension concerns the assessment of comprehension. Current comprehension tests—the Nelson Denny [e.g., 1993], the comprehension subtest of the SAT and the like—were developed with a psychometric rationale and do not reflect our understanding of comprehension processes (for further discussion, see Shepard, 2000). (p. 86)

Kintsch and Kintsch presented their theory of comprehension and its implications for comprehension assessment. They also described efforts underway to develop a comprehension assessment consistent with that theory.

Sweet (this volume) also stressed the importance of theory in the development of comprehension assessments. She wrote:

> The approach to assessment proposed here differs from current approaches to reading assessment in that it would both grow out of and contribute to the development of an appropriately rich and elaborated theory of reading comprehension. Assessment procedures generated by this approach are thus more likely to be influenced and changed by theoretically grounded reading research. (p. 7)

Note Sweet's view that comprehension theory is not a static entity but rather will continue to grow and evolve, in part through findings from research using assessments guided by the theory. Kintsch and Kintsch (this volume) also seem to hold that position: "... thinking about instruction and assessment within the framework of a theory of comprehension can be useful and will be even more useful as that theory is fully developed" (p. 91).

Pearson and Hamm's (this volume) discussion strongly illustrates the impact that theory and Theory with a capital T (that is, broad theoretical perspectives) have had on the development of comprehension assessment. They described comprehension assessments developed when underlying theoretical perspectives of behaviorism were dominant, then those developed when cognitive psychology came to the fore, and those developed from sociocultural and literary perspectives. They also described more specific

[handwritten annotations at top: "- P+H have more generous view because they discuss very wide range of assessment. - K+K focused on assessment more commonly used + referenced"]

theoretical perspectives, such as schema theory and constructivism, and their influences on assessment. In all cases, it easy to see relations between the T/theory and the assessments that were developed or in vogue. In this respect, Pearson and Hamm seem to have a more generous view of past comprehension assessment than Kintsch and Kintsch in that they do not represent past assessment as psychometrically-driven to the degree that Kintsch and Kintsch do. (In fact, they place the period of active psychometric work from 1955–1975.) However, this may be because Pearson and Hamm discussed a range of comprehension assessments developed over time whereas I believe Kintsch and Kintsch were focused on those assessments most commonly used and referenced, such as the Nelson Denny, (Brown, Fishco, & Hanna, 1993).

[handwritten margin notes: "P+H=over more comp. Ass", "K+K = more recent C.A."]

To some, the notion that theory must drive construction of assessments may seem to go without saying. However, some researchers emphasize the importance of psychometrics as a driving force for construction of comprehension assessments In its most extreme form, this may include not using assessments of anything we would even think of as "comprehension," but rather employing assessments of word recognition or fluency to measure comprehension with the rationale that those are well correlated (an approach critiqued later in this commentary).

Importantly, the authors of the three chapters that are the focus of this commentary were not suggesting that psychometric soundness is unnecessary. On the contrary, Pearson and Hamm (this volume) wrote repeatedly about issues of validity and reliability in assessments, in some cases noting that lack thereof was or should be the downfall of a particular assessment approach. Sweet (this volume) called repeatedly for psychometric quality in assessments to be developed. Kintsch and Kintsch (this volume) have made evaluating psychometric properties, most notably interrater agreement in scoring, a priority in their assessment development as well. In the view of these chapter authors, it seems to be not a matter of theory or psychometric soundness but theory and psychometric soundness. Or perhaps it is better to say that being consistent with theory is part of psychometric soundness for these authors, and in any case essential for construct validity.

[handwritten margin note: "balence of both"]

Finally, it is important to realize that how theory is actually enacted in assessments may well be more influential than the theory itself with respect to impact on classroom practices. For better and for worse, the nature of assessments does impact the nature of instruction in American classrooms (Shepard, 2000). As Pearson and Hamm (this volume) noted, "In the final analysis, a construct is judged as much by how it is operationalized as by how it is conceptualized" (p. 14).

Comprehension as a Nonunitary Construct

Each of these chapters espouses theory or cites evidence that comprehension is in fact not a unitary construct. I discuss this contention in four respects: subskills, type of text, topic, and purpose.

Subskills.   Pearson and Hamm (this volume) provided a review of a long line of research aimed at identifying subskills entailed in comprehension. It is clear that the number is not a resolved matter, but almost all studies converge on the point that there are several identifiable subskills or components of comprehension processes. I would add that these studies are conducted with a narrow range of texts, reading purposes, and, I suspect, a narrow range of readers. Greater diversity in texts, purposes, and readers included would very likely lead to identification of additional subskills. For example, including texts that carry substantial meaning in graphics may reveal subskills related to reading graphical devices. Studies of processing procedural texts (e.g., how to …) may reveal subskills related to comprehending spatial relations (entailed in many procedures).

Kintsch and Kintsch (this volume) also emphasized subskills. Consistent with their theory of comprehension, Kintsch and Kintsch identified as the subskills of reading comprehension extracting meaning from the text, constructing the situation model, and integrating the reader's prior knowledge and goals with information in the text. But their discussion suggests additional subskills within this. For example, they talked at some length about inference, noting in fact that "This terminology ["inference"] is somewhat unfortunate because it lumps together processes that are quite distinct psychologically and that differ dramatically in the demands they make on the reader" (Kintsch, 1998, p. 79). They went on to discuss a number of ways in which inferences differ and by extension, a number of ways in which comprehension processes are differentiated.

Sweet (this volume) did not address comprehension subskills as such. However, the notion that there are distinct components of the reading process does seem to undergird the discussion, for example, in the call for "Congruence between assessments and the process*es* [my emphasis] involved in comprehension" (p. 7). She went on to argue that

> Assessments that target particular operations involved in comprehension must be available, in the interest of revealing interindividual and intraindividual differences that might inform our understanding of the comprehension process and of outcome differences. The dimensionality of the instruments in relation to theory should be clearly apparent. (pp. 7–8)

That the term *subskill* is not used in Sweet's chapter may be deliberate. For some, the term connotes skills to be assessed in isolation of the larger context, in this case outside of actual comprehension of extended text. Assessments of this kind obviously pose formidable problems with respect to ecological validity and I doubt that Sweet or the authors of either of the other two chapters under discussion here would advocate such an approach.

It is worth noting that some view word recognition or fluency as, in essence, subskills of comprehension and, as noted earlier, some suggest measuring these as a proxy for comprehension. This is problematic. For example, several studies have demonstrated that there are children—and not just a few children but a good portion of struggling readers—who do well on measures of word recognition or fluency and poorly on measures of comprehension—even with the inadequate measures of comprehension that we currently have (Duke, Pressley, & Hilden, 2004). If we measure these subskills in lieu of comprehension, we miss, at the least, identifying those struggling readers who have strong word recognition and fluency but weak comprehension. A much more in-depth discussion of these issues is given by Stahl and Hiebert (this volume).

To talk of subskills of comprehension implies that there is, at least in broad terms, a single construct called "comprehension." However, it appears that this is true only in the broadest terms. Comprehension of different types of text, with different topics, and for different purposes, can be very different. It is therefore more appropriate to say subskills of comprehension *of what for what*, as discussed in the paragraphs that follow.

Type of Text.   Two of the three chapters emphasize differentiation of comprehension processes by type of text. Kintsch and Kintsch (this volume) do not emphasize issues of text type, although researchers influenced by their theoretical work have attended to text type effects on comprehension (e.g., van den Broek, Everson, Virtue, Sung, & Tzeng, 2002). Sweet's chapter (this volume) calls repeatedly for sensitivity to a variety of types of text in assessment. Pearson and Hamm (this volume) noted, among other things, the persistent problem of children being stronger readers of narrative than informational text, suggesting that we need to get a better handle on this discrepancy. Although notably, this discrepancy is not universal; a recent international comparative study found that although U.S. students have the highest gap in performance favoring literary reading over informational reading, in other countries, the gap is in the other direction, and in still others, relatively little gap, on average, exists (National Center for Education Statistics, 2003). This suggests that one of these types of text is not inherently more difficult than the other but rather than contextual factors such as schooling history and/or culture may explain discrepancies observed.

There probably are some factors, such as decoding and fluency, that have fairly consistent influences across different types of text. However, other factors, such as the ability to understand characters or to make use of headings, clearly apply to some types of text and not others (such as those with and without characters, those with and without headings). Consider some basic differences in reading practices for fictional narrative as compared to nonfiction informational text, for example. Fictional narrative texts are normally read from beginning to end, in their entirety, at a steady pace. Informational texts are often read nonlinearly (for example, beginning with the index, turning to a noted page in the middle of the book, then toward the beginning, then back toward the end), selectively (only for particular information needed), and at a pace that varies from that used in scanning, to that used in skimming, to that used when honing in on the particular information desired. It seems logical that comprehension processes with these different types of text would be different in important ways.

Evidence available thus far suggests that type of text or genre does have a profound influence on comprehension processes. It affects readers' use of comprehension strategies (see Kucan & Beck, 1997, for a review), their patterns of inference generation during reading (e.g., van den Broek et al., 2002), and their approach to text in general (e.g., Langer, 1985). Children show differential levels of comprehension with different types of text (e.g., Hidi & Hildyard, 1983; Langer, Applebee, Mullis, & Foertsch, 1990), with some children showing difficulties with some types of text and not others (Duke, Pressley, & Hilden, 2004). Indeed, some have argued that comprehension development is genre specific (Duke, 2000). That is, exposure to and instruction with one type of text does not necessarily transfer to another type of text. A child's ability to comprehend one type of text does not necessarily correspond to his or her ability to comprehend another type of text.

All of this has grand implications for comprehension assessment and assessment-instruction connections in classrooms. It means that we cannot simply extrapolate from results of an assessment of comprehension of one type of text to comprehension of another. We cannot really assess "comprehension," but "comprehension of ..." What follows the "of" should include not only text type but, as discussed in the following section, topic as well.

Topic.   Before reading these chapters we probably all already believed that the topic of a text, and the readers' knowledge of that topic, influences comprehension processes. The material in the Pearson and Hamm (this volume) and Kintsch and Kintsch (this volume) chapters dramatically underscores that belief. The most striking evidence in this area came from Pearson and Hamm's discussion of findings of the College Board. To reach a generalizability coefficient of .90, testing time ranged from 1.25 hr—for physics—to 13 hr—for European history. In fact, Pearson and Hamm discussed work by Pearson et al. (1990), concluding that "topical knowledge, not cognitive process, was a more salient factor in explaining variance in reading comprehension" (p. 36).

In Kintsch and Kintsch's (this volume) situation model, we again see emphasis on topic, and the reader's knowledge of the topic, as affecting comprehension processes:

> Although the microstructure and macrostructure of the text are largely determined by what the author wrote (assuming a reasonably skilled and cooperative reader) ... the situation model a reader constructs from a text depends on goals and background knowledge to a much greater extent than the textbase, which usually follows more or less faithfully the author's intentions. (p. 73)

Imagine an expert U.S. Civil War historian reading an excerpt from a social studies text on the subject and an immigrant who has never heard of the U.S. Civil War reading that same excerpt. The comprehension processes involved for those two readers may look much more different than alike. In Kintsch and Kintsch's (this volume) terms, the U.S. Civil War historian is likely to focus mostly on constructing the situation model whereas the reader without knowledge of the U.S. Civil War is probably expending more resources on the textbase. The U.S. Civil War historian may be overwhelmed by what he or she knows related to the text, with a chief challenge being to focus only on those aspects of prior knowledge most relevant to events reported in the text. The reader unfamiliar with the U.S. Civil War may be overwhelmed by how little he or she knows related to the text, with a chief challenge being to identify prior knowledge that will help him or her envision events reported in the text. The two readers are likely bringing different goals to the reading as well. Although in the basic sense both may be reading the text to find out what it reports about the U.S. Civil War, the U.S. Civil War historian is probably oriented toward comparing what the text says to what he or she believes to be true about the U.S. Civil War. The reader unfamiliar with that war, in contrast, is probably oriented toward understanding what the war was, what it was about, how it proceeded, and so on (information presumably already known by the historian). This last difference speaks not only to the topic of the text, but also to the reader's purpose, a subject considered in this next section.

Purpose. Although not as strong as with subskills, type of text, and topic, there is also a suggestion in these chapters that comprehension processes are differentiated by the purpose for comprehension. As quoted earlier, Kintsch and Kintsch (this volume) emphasized the impact of a reader's goals for reading. Pearson and Hamm (this volume), adapting from Valencia and Pearson (1987), emphasized the need to assess readers' ability to adapt strategies to the situation in which the reading is occurring. Sweet (this volume) also holds the position that purpose may significantly affect comprehension processes, listing this as an issue certain to arise in developing an assessment system. Indeed, past research suggests this issue in that readers' purpose for their reading does impact their comprehension of the text (e.g., Linderholm & van den Broek, 2002). So again we must talk not about assessment of comprehension, or even assessment of comprehension *of what ...*," but assessment of comprehension of what *for what*. We cannot talk meaningfully of comprehension outside the context of what that comprehension is for.

Despite substantial differences among these chapters, each contends or provides evidence that comprehension is not a unitary process. Comprehension processes involve a number of subskills, they vary by type and topic of text, and they may also differ by the purpose for reading. This has strong implications for comprehension assessment. As Kintsch and Kintsch (this volume) concluded with reference to some of these differences, "Lumping all of these differences into a single concept of reading ability may be useful for some gross statistical purposes, but not to guide instruction and diagnose comprehension problems" (p. 85).

The Need for a System of Comprehension Assessment

As would be expected given a view of comprehension as a nonunitary construct, these authors do not propose development of a single comprehension assessment. Pearson and Hamm (this volume) spent the last portion of their chapter suggesting an ambitious agenda of research on and related to comprehension assessment including, of course, development of comprehension assessments. Kintsch and Kintsch (this volume) discussed an instrument they are developing that would tap a number of different dimensions of comprehension and note the need for developing additional assessments as well. Sweet called for a system of comprehension assessment. This call seems to be grounded not only in the multidimensional, differentiated view of comprehension discussed earlier but also in a view of the developmental nature of comprehension and of the many audiences and purposes that comprehension assessments serve. She wrote:

> Clearly, no single assessment would meet all these criteria. Instead, we propose an
> integrated system of assessments, some of which may be particularly appropriate
> for particular groups (e.g., emergent or beginning readers, older struggling read-

ers, second-language readers, or readers with a particular interest in dinosaurs). Further, the various assessments included in the system would address different purposes, such as a portmanteau assessment for accountability or screening purposes, diagnostic assessments for guiding intervention, curriculum-linked assessments for guiding instruction, and so on. (p. 9)

In some sense, aiming not for a single assessment but for multiple assessments relieves some pressure on researchers. We are not, then, seeking the "holy grail" of comprehension assessment. That said, a multiple comprehension assessment system also introduces some pressure on researchers, and on practitioners as well, as discussed later in this section.

In many respects, the prospect of developing a comprehension assessment system is exciting. There is, as these authors have pointed out, the potential for such a system to not only be informed by but to inform development of more sophisticated theories of comprehension. There is the potential in such a system to help us learn more about subskills of comprehension and about influences on comprehension—text type, topic, and purpose, to name three—about which we know far too little. If the system is really integrated, as Sweet (this volume) requested, findings across different age groups, forms of comprehension, and instructional models can be brought together to form larger understandings about comprehension development, processes, and teaching and learning. If the system is all that is hoped, schools would, of course, have a coherent approach to assessment that would inform instruction and lead to higher achievement.

However, development of a system of comprehension certainly poses challenges as well. One very real challenge lies in the need to coordinate different assessments—how they map on and do not map on various constructs, how they are to be interpreted in light of one another, and so on. For example, for us to come to greater understandings about comprehension development, assessments for children at younger age groups and those for children at older age groups will have to be able to be placed on common scales and interpreted in light of one another.

There are also very real-time and monetary demands imposed by using an entire system of comprehension assessments. Consider the case of text type. Suppose additional research continues to bear out the conclusion that comprehension of different text types is indeed different, and that we cannot predict a child's comprehension of one type of text by his or her comprehension of another. Then we will need comprehension assessments for each type of text that we think is important. Suppose for a moment that we decide those types of text are as follows: fictional narrative text, nonfiction informational text, nonfiction informational hypertext, persuasive text, biographical text, poetry, and procedural text (see Duke & Tower, 2004, for further discussion of several of these

types; see Purcell-Gates, Duke, Hall, & Tower, 2003, for examples of two comprehension assessments for two different kinds of text—one for informational
text and the other for procedural text). Imagine the time and money required to
administer, score, and interpret assessments of these seven types of text. Then
multiply that by the number of different assessment formats, purposes (given to
the reader but also for which the assessment results would themselves be used),
and topics (e.g., if we assess comprehension separately in science and social
studies, or for particular domains or units) to be assessed. Imagine that these assessments were structured to give insights about particular comprehension subskills as identified by Kintsch and Kintsch (this volume), by the studies cited by
Pearson and Hamm (this volume), and in the lists provided by Sweet (this
volume). The prospect is formidable.

The practical challenges of developing an assessment system true to the
multifaceted and nonunitary character of comprehension does not excuse us
from the task. But we should be mindful that imperfection is inevitable. We
will not be able to measure, routinely, in schools, comprehension of all those
types of text we believe to be important. We will have to make hard decisions
about those types of text for which measurement of comprehension is most
important. We will not be able to assess comprehension for all the purposes,
domains, and situations that we believe are important; we will have to priori-
tize. Thus, at least one major challenge of developing a comprehension assessment system lies neither in developing better comprehension theory nor in
establishing psychometric quality, but in coming to agreement on our priorities, our values, the forms of comprehension that we most want to develop in
U.S. students.

CONCLUSION

I close by reminding us that the task of assessing comprehension of so many different forms mirrors very much what we ask classroom teachers to do every day.
In many senses, we expect classroom teachers to be knowledgeable about individual students' comprehension across a great range of texts, domains, and situations, and we expect them to provide instruction accordingly. Teachers
identified as exemplary have, in fact, as one of their characteristics, much more
extensive knowledge of individual students, their strengths and weaknesses in a
whole range of areas, than more typical teachers. For every imperfection in an
assessment system that we develop, it becomes the responsibility of the classroom teacher to make up for the shortcomings. For that reason, I contend that
the development of a comprehension assessment system must be accompanied
by an equally active program of research and development on teachers as asses-

sors. We need to learn not only how to help teachers be competent administers and interpreters of the assessments developed, but also how to help them be keen observers for those things our assessments fail to measure. Even if we are able to develop measures of comprehension of all the subskills, types of text, topics, and purposes that we ideally want, it is not practical to administer all of these assessments in school. The burden will fall on teachers to use informal means and everyday observation to supplement our measures in the many types of text, domains, and situations that our assessments fail to tap.

REFERENCES

Brown, J. I., Fishco, V. V., & Hanna, G. S. (1993). *Nelson–Denny Reading Test*. Itasca, IL: Riverside.

Duke, N. K. (2000). 3.6 minutes per day: The scarcity of informational texts in first grade. *Reading Research Quarterly, 35*, 202–224.

Duke, N. K., Pressley, G. M., & Hilden, K. (2004). Difficulties with reading comprehension. In C. A. Stone, E. R. Silliman, B. J. Ehren, & K. Apel (Eds.), *Handbook of language and literacy development and disorders* (pp. 501–520). New York: Guilford.

Duke, N. K., & Tower, C. (2004). Nonfiction texts for young readers. In J. V. Hoffman & D. L. Schallert (Eds.), *The texts in elementary classrooms* (pp. 125–144). Mahwah, NJ Lawrence Erlbaum Associates.

Hidi, S. E., & Hildyard, A. (1983). The comparison of oral and written productions in two discourse types. *Discourse Processes, 6*, 91–105.

Kintsch, W. (1998). *Comprehension: A paradigm for cognition*. New York: Cambridge University Press.

Kucan, L., & Beck, I. L. (1997). Thinking aloud and reading comprehension research: Inquiry, instruction and social interaction. *Review of Educational Research, 67*, 271–299.

Langer, J. (1985). The child's sense of genre: A study of performance on parallel reading and writing tasks. *Written Communication, 2*, 157–188.

Langer, J. A., Applebee, A. N., Mullis, I. V. S., & Foertsch, M. A. (1990). *Learning to read in our nation's schools: Instruction and achievement in 1988 in grades 4, 8, and 12*. Princeton, NJ: Educational Testing Service.

Linderholm, T., & van den Broek, P. (2002). The effects of reading purpose and working memory capacity on the processing of expository text. *Journal of Educational Psychology, 94*, 778–784.

National Center for Education Statistics. (2003). http://nces.ed.gov/pubsearch/pubsinfo.asp?pubid=2003026; http://nces.ed.gov/pubsearch/pubsinfo.asp?pubid=2003073.

Pearson, P. D., Greer, E. A., Commeyras, M., Stallman, A., Valencia, S. W., & Krug, S. E., et al. (1990). *The validation of large scale reading assessment: Building tests for the twenty-first century* (Reading Research and Education Center report, under grant number G 0087–C1001–90 with the Office of Educational Research and Improvement). Urbana, IL: Center for the Study of Reading.

Purcell-Gates, V., Duke, N. K., Hall, L., & Tower, C. (2003). *Explicit explanation of genre within authentic literacy activities in science: Does it facilitate development and achievement?* Symposium presented at the National Reading Conference, Scottsdale, AZ.

Shepard, L. A. (2000). The role of assessment in a learning culture. *Educational Researcher, 29*(7), 4–14.

Valencia, S., & Pearson, P. D. (1987). Reading assessment: Time for a change. *The Reading Teacher, 40,* 726–733.

van den Broek, P., Everson, M., Virtue, S., Sung, Y., & Tzeng, Y. (2002). Comprehension and memory of science texts: Inferential processes and the construction of a mental representation. In J. Otero, J. Leon, & A. C. Graesser (Eds.), *The psychology of science text comprehension* (pp. 131–154). Mahwah, NJ: Lawrence Erlbaum Associates.

Part II

Developmental and Motivational Factors in Reading Comprehension

5

Assessment of Comprehension Abilities in Young Children

Paul van den Broek
Panayiota Kendeou
University of Minnesota

Kathleen Kremer
Educational Testing Service

Julie Lynch
Saginaw Valley State University

Jason Butler
Mary Jane White
University of Minnesota

Elizabeth Pugzles Lorch
University of Kentucky

To grasp the meaning of a thing, an event or a situation is to see it in its relations to other things: to note how it operates or functions, what consequences follow from it; what causes it, what uses it can be put to.

—Dewey (1933/1963, p. 135)

The ability to read is essential for successful functioning in society and therefore is one of the most important "survival" skills to teach our children. In virtually all instances, the goal of reading is to identify the meaning or message of the text at hand. Doing so involves the execution and integration of many processes. These processes roughly fall into two main categories, those involved in translating the written code into meaningful language units and those involved in combining these units into a meaningful and coherent mental representation. In the context of teaching young children reading skills, the bulk of attention of researchers and educators has been on the first set of processes, those involved in *decoding* (e.g., Catts, Fey, Zhang, & Tomblin, 1999; Ehri, Nunes, Stahl, & Willows, 2001; Perfetti, 2003; Rayner, Foorman, Perfetti, Pesetsky, & Seidenberg, 2001; Whitehurst & Lonigan, 1998).

The second set of processes, those involved in *comprehension*, has received less attention. In this chapter, we focus on the development and assessment of comprehension skills in young children, from preschool into the early grades of elementary school. In the first section of the chapter, we discuss what it means to comprehend a text, drawing on research in psycholinguistics and cognitive sciences. In the second section, we summarize what is known about the development of comprehension skills in preschool and early grades. In the third section, we propose a methodology for assessing comprehension skills at these ages. In the fourth and final section, we provide validation for this methodology by summarizing findings on the relations between comprehension measures as well as between comprehension measures and decoding skills and on the relation between preschool comprehension skills and later reading comprehension.

Our aim in writing this chapter is to elucidate the development of comprehension skills in young children and to discuss possible ways of assessing such skills. Two recent developments make discussion of comprehension skills in young (i.e., preschool) children especially important. First, in educational and political circles there is a growing emphasis on early diagnosis and intervention, particularly at the preschool level (see, for example, No Child Left Behind Act of 2001). Second, the results of recent cognitive-developmental research has shown that comprehension skills relevant to reading comprehension start developing well before children reach elementary school age. In this context, it is crucial that we consider how comprehension skills develop in preschool children and how we can assess and instruct those skills.

WHAT DOES IT MEAN TO COMPREHEND?

Before discussing the development and assessment of comprehension in young children, we need to consider what it means to *comprehend*. Different researchers and educators use the term in different ways, emphasizing different skills and activities. For example, some define *comprehension* as the ability to remember what the text was about, others as the ability to apply the knowledge conveyed in the text to a concrete situation, to recognize the theme or moral of the text, to give a critical appraisal of the text, and so on (see Pearson

& Hamm, this volume, for an excellent historical overview of the varying views held in different approaches to comprehension instruction and assessment). To some extent, these different types of comprehension involve unique processes. This is important to recognize because it reflects the fact that comprehension is not a unitary phenomenon but rather a "family" of skills and activities.[1] As a result, comprehension in its different forms cannot be quantified and assessed easily along a single dimension—unlike phenomena such as height, weight, strength, and perhaps even basic reading skills such as vocabulary and phonological awareness.

At the same time, the different types of comprehension share a large common core of processes. Invariably, comprehension is assumed—explicitly or implicitly—to involve interpretation of the information in the text, the use of prior knowledge to do so and, ultimately, the construction of a coherent representation or picture of what the text is about in the reader's mind (e.g., Applebee, 1978; Gernsbacher, 1990; Graesser & Clark, 1985; Kintsch & van Dijk, 1978; Mandler & Johnson, 1977; Stein & Glenn, 1979; Trabasso, Secco, & van den Broek, 1984; this commonality is easy to discern in a review of different instructional approaches, for example, as in Pearson & Hamm, this volume). This mental representation is the foundation on which the reader can build for specific reading purposes and types of comprehension, to do things such as retelling the story, applying the knowledge gathered from the text, identifying the theme, critically appraising the text, and so on. In this fashion, comprehension can mean different things but it always involves a meaningful representation of the textual information in the reader's mind. Somewhat irreverently one can call this the "onion peel" nature of comprehension: a core of processes common to different types of comprehension with layers of additional, increasingly unique processes for each specific type. In this chapter, we focus on the core of comprehension, the construction of a representation of the text one is reading. Understanding how readers construct such a representation—and how they may fail to do so—may allow one to increase the effectiveness of instruction and assessment, regardless of one's particular view of comprehension. These core processes have been studied extensively in various areas of cognitive psychology and linguistics. Let us first consider how skilled, adult readers go about comprehending texts they read.

---

[1]An analogy illustrates this point: Consider how one would define someone being a good basketball player. Some players are considered good for different reasons: because they have strong shooting percentages, others because they are good passers, rebounders, defenders, and so forth. At the same time, these different skills and activities tend to covary to some degree within individuals and, moreover, tend to be built on a set of core skills such as eye–hand coordination, physical strength and agility, sense of direction, and so forth.

Identifying Meaningful Relations

Recent research in psycholinguistics and cognitive sciences has greatly increased our understanding of how a skilled reader constructs a coherent representation. Through a dynamic interplay of cognitive processes, the reader identifies meaningful relations between parts of the text. There are many different types of meaningful relations but two types have been found to be especially important: causal and referential relations. For example, imagine reading a text that contains the following sentence pair:

(1)   John dropped the banana peel on the floor.
        Mary fell on her back.

Most adult readers immediately connect the two sentences and assume that Mary fell *because* John dropped the banana peel. They make this causal connection by inferring that Mary slipped on the banana peel, although the text does not say so. This inference is supported by our world knowledge about the slippery nature of banana peels and about the fact that people usually do not fall without a cause. It is also supported by our knowledge about text conventions that considerate texts usually only juxtapose sentences if they are somehow connected. Consider a second example:

(2)   The lady gave the waiter $100.
        He returned to give her the change.

Again, most skilled, native readers connect the two sentences without problem and with minimal cognitive effort. As in example (1), the connection involves causal relations (e.g., the lady gave the waiter money because she was in a restaurant and had something to eat or drink, he returned because the $100 was more than the expense of the food or drink, etc.). It also involves a more basic type of connection, namely referential or anaphoric relations: We infer that the "he" in the second sentence refers to the waiter and that "her" refers to the lady. Again, these connections are not explicit in the text, yet skilled readers identify them without effort and often without even being aware of doing so.

Sometimes the identification of a meaningful connection requires more cognitive effort. Consider a third example:

(3)   The moon exerts gravitational pull on earth,
        thereby contributing to the development of life on earth.

Most of us have considerable difficulty identifying the causal relation between these two clauses. This is striking because, unlike in examples (1) and (2), the text in this example even helps us by explicitly stating that there *is* a causal relation to be identified. Of course, the difficulty arises because we do not have the background knowledge required for the relation readily available. As a result, readers (if motivated to comprehend) stop in their tracks and search their semantic memory for information that would allow the causal inference. For most readers, the associations to "moon," "pull on earth," and "life on earth" lead to some inference that tidal variations somehow provide the missing causal link (this inference is, in fact, incorrect; the correct answer is that the gravitational pull causes an electromagnetic field around the earth that protects it from lethal cosmic radiation).

Results of numerous studies show that readers indeed process texts as suggested in these examples (for reviews, see Singer, 1994, and van den Broek, 1994). For example, after reading the sentences about John dropping the banana peel and Mary falling (example 1) readers have been found to have the concept "slip" more active than after reading two neutral sentences or even two sentences with the same words as in (1) arranged in a different way. Likewise, notions such as "waiter," "restaurant," and "eat" are more active after reading the second sentence in example (2) than after reading control sentences. These examples illustrate several important principles concerning how successful, adult readers construct a coherent mental representation of a text. *First,* a crucial component of comprehension—common to all types of comprehension—is the identification of meaningful relations between different parts of the text. Of particular importance are causal and referential relations because they tend to lend coherence to many different types of text and across reading purposes, but other types of relations also may be inferred (for example, children's stories often contain associative and spatial relations in addition to causal and referential ones. Likewise, comprehension of expository texts often requires the additional identification of logical relations). Dewey (1933/1963) was correct: A crucial step in successful understanding is the identification of meaningful relations. *Second,* there are two basic types of processes by which readers can identify such relations, a quick, effortless, and automatic process that usually proceeds without the reader being aware of it, and a slow, effortful, and strategic process that requires conscious attention by the reader (e.g., Kintsch, 1988). Both of these types of processes take place during reading and, with practice, some strategic processes can become automatized. These two distinct types of processes are not only observed in reading, but exist in many arenas of cognition (e.g., Stanovich & West, 2000; for a particularly eloquent description of this distinction, see Kahneman, 2003, in his Nobel Prize acceptance speech).

A *third* principle is that for a complete text, the inferential processes are considerably more complex than for the sentence pairs described earlier. In a full text, individual events or facts have multiple connections to many other events and facts. Moreover, the connections themselves vary in their difficulty. As we see later in this chapter, for example, causal inferences vary in their abstractness, they may require extensive background knowledge, they may extend over long distances in the surface structure of the text, they may require coordination of multiple pieces of information, they differ in the amount of cognitive resources required, and so on.

A useful way to think of the outcome of these inferential processes, if all goes well, is as a *network* representation that includes the different parts of the text, relevant background knowledge, and the relations among these pieces of information (Graesser & Clark, 1985; Kintsch & van Dijk, 1978; Mandler & Johnson, 1977). An illustration of such a network representation for a simple story is provided in Table 5.1 and Fig. 5.1. For purposes of this illustration, we have rep-

TABLE 5.1
Epaminondas Story

1. Once there was a little boy,
2. who lived in a hot country.
3. One day his mother told him to take some cake to his grandmother.
4. She wanted him to hold it carefully
5. so it wouldn't break into crumbs.
6. The little boy put the cake in a leaf under his arm
7. and carried it to his grandmother's.
8. When he got there
9. the cake had crumbled into tiny pieces.
10. His grandmother told him he was a silly boy
11. and that he should have carried the cake on top of his head
12. so it wouldn't break.
13. Then she gave him a pat of butter to take back to his mother's house.
14. The little boy wanted to be very careful with the butter
15. so he put it on top of his head
16. and carried it home.
17. The sun was shining hard
18. and when he got home
19. the butter had melted.
20. His mother told him he was a silly boy
21. and that he should have put the butter in a leaf
22. so that it would have gotten home safe and sound.

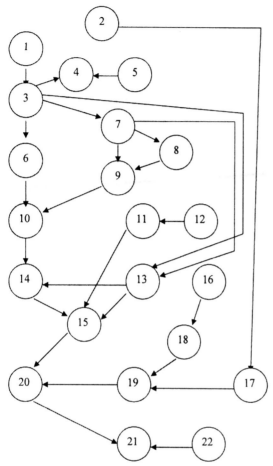

FIG. 5.1.   Epaminondas Story Network.

resented each event in the text (captured by the individual sentences) as a node, with the meaningful relations depicted as arcs between nodes. To keep things simple, we have only included the most basic, causal relations between the text elements themselves. The total number of relations that a reader identifies in a text depends on the complexity of the text and on the motivation and background knowledge of the reader. A reasonable estimate is that, on average, a skilled, adult reader infers between 200 and 300 semantic connections, causal ones as well as others, per page in a text of moderate difficulty. As illustrated earlier, good readers make the vast majority of these inferences without being aware of doing so. As we see later, beginning readers and readers with reading difficulty infer fewer relations and, moreover, the inferential process often requires much more (conscious) effort.

Evidence for Network Representations in Adult Readers

There is overwhelming evidence that proficient adult readers construct semantic networks of the texts they read. A full review of this evidence is beyond the
scope of this chapter, but three examples are worth mentioning. One important
property of these networks is that events and facts in a text vary in their number
of semantic connections to other parts of the text. This property has been found
to be a strong determiner of the psychological salience of the different parts of
the text. Readers perceive events or facts that have many connections to be
more important than those with fewer connections. Likewise, the more connections an event or fact has, the better it is remembered and the more often it is included in a summary of the text (Fletcher & Bloom, 1988; Goldman &
Varnhagen, 1986; Trabasso & van den Broek, 1985; van den Broek, 1988,
1989a, 1989b). A second property is that relations may span a considerable distance, connecting events or facts that are far apart in the text itself. There is
considerable evidence that reminding a reader of one part of the text activates
related other parts of the text more than unrelated parts even if the unrelated
parts are closer in the text itself (O'Brien & Myers, 1987). For example, readers
are both faster and more accurate in remembering related, distant items than
unrelated, but closer items. As a third example, the ability to identify semantic
relations between parts of a text has been found to be related to reading skills. In
particular, this ability distinguishes good from poor readers (Wolman, 1991;
Wolman, van den Broek, & Lorch, 1997). Moreover, providing readers with
training in identifying relations results in improved comprehension (Medo &
Ryder, 1993).

　　In summary, at the core of successful reading comprehension is the ability to
identify meaningful relations between the various parts of a text and between
these parts and the readers' background knowledge. To do so, readers engage in
inferential processes which, if all goes well, result in a coherent mental network
representation of the text.

COMPREHENSION IN YOUNG CHILDREN

Research on reading development in young preschool and early elementary
school children has focused largely on the role of basic literacy skills such as
phonological awareness, letter knowledge, vocabulary, and so on. In comparison, little reading research has been done on the development of reading comprehension skills at these ages. Fortunately, narrative comprehension in young
children has been investigated in other, non-reading contexts. The results of
this research provide important insights in the nature and development of com-

prehension skills at this early age (for reviews of research on developmental changes in comprehension skills, see, for example, Applebee, 1978; Bourg, Bauer, & van den Broek, 1997; van den Broek, 1997).

In considering the development of comprehension skills and processes, it is important to distinguish between age differences in the *type* of processes in which children engage during comprehension, in the *efficiency* of those processes, and in the *content* of those processes. To illustrate the importance of these distinctions, consider the role of a central aspect of cognitive development, the accumulation of experiences and background knowledge (e.g., Chi, Hutchinson, & Robin, 1989; Chi & Koeske, 1983). This accumulation results in increased knowledge of facts about the world, about how people interact, and so on, and hence, affects the content of whatever processes the child executes. Importantly, however, the accumulation also results in increased knowledge of strategies that work (in comprehension, as well as in every other aspect of a child's life). As a consequence, processes can be executed more efficiently. In the context of comprehension, for instance, experience plays an important role in more efficient use of one's limited attentional or working memory capacities (with another important role possible for maturation; see Case, 1992, 1995; Siegler, 1994, for discussions of the development of attention/working memory). Thus, observed developmental differences may appear to reflect the development of processes but in actuality be due to increases in background knowledge and corresponding processing efficiency. A classic example of this is found in the observation that very young children can create remarkably complex and abstract knowledge structures for domains in which they happen to have extensive knowledge (e.g., dinosaurs or chess; Chi et al., 1989; Chi & Koeske., 1983; Gobbo & Chi, 1986).

A similar situation has been found to apply to the development of reading comprehension skills. The research findings suggest that young children's comprehension is both remarkably similar and systematically different relative to that of adults. On the one hand, it is clear that children at an early age engage in very much the same inferential processes as do adults, identifying meaningful relations and establishing coherence. For example, when 4- and 6-year-old children watch television programs, they tend to recall events with many causal connections better than events with fewer causal connections (van den Broek, Lorch, & Thurlow, 1996). Likewise, when asked questions about events in the television program, they tend to answer them by following the connections in the network. Similar findings have been observed when 6-year-olds listened to aurally presented stories (Trabasso & Nickels, 1992). Thus, even at the age of 4, children make causal inferences and establish meaningful connections between elements of the events they experience, much as do proficient readers. With appropriate testing techniques and materials, these findings can be extended to even younger children (e.g., see Bauer, 1996, 1997; Wenner & Bauer, 2001, who demonstrated that 2-year-old children identify causal relations between events in a three-event sequence that they are shown). Thus, even very young children engage in causal-inferential processes to comprehend the events they experience.

On the other hand, there are systematic age differences in the ability to infer semantic relations. Some of these developmental differences are summarized in Table 5.2. For instance, whereas very young children are primarily able to identify relations between concrete events, older children increasingly become able to identify relations among abstract events as well (e.g., Goldman, 1985; van den Broek, 1989a). Likewise, young children readily recognize connections between external events whereas older children and adults routinely identify connections between internal events, such as the goals and feelings of characters, as well. Finally, young children limit their inference-making mostly to identifying relations between individual events; with age, children increasingly connect groups of events (e.g., episodes). These developmental trends reflect the different experiences that children at different ages have had as well as increasing efficiency of working memory and attention allocation.

It is important to note that even very young children *can* generate all of these types of inferences but they generally need the inferences involved to be less complex and more supported by text or background knowledge than do older children.[2] The trends described in Table 5.2 reflect dimensions of ease–difficulty of inference generation. Whether a child will be able to generate a particular type of inference in a particular comprehension situation is a function of the interaction between the child's inferential abilities and the difficulty of the inference involved; as his or her experience grows, comprehenders are able to negotiate more demanding inference-generating situations.

TABLE 5.2
Examples of Developmental Trends in Inference Making in Narrative Comprehension

Relations between Concrete Events	→	Relations between Abstract Events
Relations between External Events	→	Relations involving Internal Events
Relations between Individual Events	→	Relations between Clusters of Events

[2]Conversely, even experienced readers may fail to make types of inferences they ordinarily would make without a problem when the text materials are very challenging. Thus, many of us would have difficulty generating abstract inferences when reading technical articles about theoretical astrophysics.

Thus, children engage in the same types of inferential processes as do older readers but they develop in knowledge and efficiency. As a result, with age, they do so more routinely, with greater ease, and across texts of a wider range of difficulty. Conversely, even young children can engage in these processes, but they tend to need easier materials to do so. These findings are consistent with findings in other areas in cognitive development. For example, when asked to categorize concrete objects, even preschool children are able to draw relatively abstract inferences (e.g., Massey & Gelman, 1988). Likewise, preschool children have been shown to be able to make inferences about internal events, provided that the scenarios in which they encounter these events are concrete and familiar (e.g., Bartsch & Wellman, 1995; Stein & Liwag, 1997; Wellman, Harris, Banerjee, & Sinclair, 1995).

Together, these age trends result in a developmental sequence of relations that children can routinely identify. In the context of narrative comprehension, important steps in this development can be seen in Table 5.3 (e.g, Applebee, 1978; Bourg et al., 1997; Williams, 1993). As mentioned earlier, whether a particular type of inference is made in a particular situation depends on the interaction between the child's knowledge and experience and the complexity of the inference. For this reason, no definite ages for attaining each step are given. This is consistent with theoretical accounts of other cognitive-developmental sequences where age ranges are illustrative rather than definitive (e.g., Piaget, 1954).

The first type of relations that children usually are able to identify involves concrete, physical relations between events that occur close together in the text or narrative. The example of John dropping the banana peel and Mary slipping exemplifies such relations. The second type of relations that children are able to identify concerns relations between distant events. Third, they are able to identify causal relations involving characters' goals, emotions, and desires. For example, they understand how receiving a nice toy causes joy and how this joy

TABLE 5.3
Developmental Sequence of Inference Types
in Narrative Comprehension

Developmental Order	Inference Making
1	Concrete physical relations that occur close together
2	Concrete physical relations between distant events
3	Causal relations involving character's goals, emotions, and desires
4	Hierarchical and thematic relations between clusters of events
5	Translation of the story theme into moral or lesson

may, in turn, lead to laughing. Fourth, as children gain experience and deepen their cognitive abilities, they increasingly become able to recognize the hierarchical and thematic relations that exist between groups of events. They recognize, for example, that the narrative consists of several episodes, each revolving around a goal and connected by a theme. Finally, they will recognize that the theme of the episodes translates into an overall plot or point of the story. Examples of this plot or point are the moral or lesson of the narrative.

In summary, preschool children engage in very much the same comprehension processes as do their older counterparts. They make inferences and create network representations of the events they experience. They use these networks to remember or answer questions. However, their networks are less developed than those of older children or adults. They contain fewer relations and, in particular, fewer relations that are abstract, distant, or that involve groups of events. As their knowledge, comprehension skills, and processing efficiency expand, their networks become richer and richer, increasingly incorporating relations according to the developmental sequence described in Table 5.3.

These findings have important implications for understanding the development of reading skills and for educational practice. One implication is that comprehension skills begin developing at an early age, at the same time as do other features of children's competencies, including basic literacy skills, such as phonological awareness and letter-word identification. Thus, the commonly-held view that reading comprehension skills develop *after* basic literacy skills, depicted in Fig. 5.2, is incorrect. A more appropriate view highlights the parallel development of basic and comprehension skills, as depicted in Fig. 5.3. From an educational perspective, this means that instructional efforts at the preschool and early elementary school level should address comprehension as well as basic literacy skills, rather than focus only on the latter. As can be seen from the aforementioned description of comprehension, reading for meaning is a complex activity, consisting of the confluence of many skills and processes. These skills and processes develop over time and experience, starting at an early age—preschool and earlier. If we wait in teaching children these comprehension skills until they have mastered the basic literacy skills, we will have lost precious time—especially for children at risk.

The "old" model has guided educational practices. Phonological processing and other skills that are essential to word decoding are often the focus of early reading instruction. However, evidence of young children's rapidly developing comprehension skills suggests that preschool and early elementary school reading curricula should address comprehension as well. As part of this effort, we need comprehensive, authentic, and valid tools for assessing developing comprehension skills.

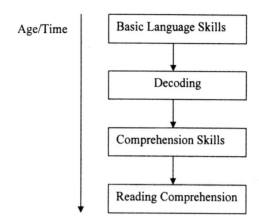

FIG. 5.2. Commonly-held view of comprehension developing after basic literacy skills.

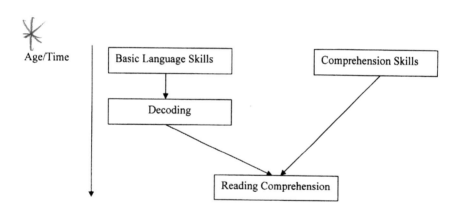

FIG. 5.3. Parallel development of comprehension and basic literacy skills.

THE ASSESSMENT OF COMPREHENSION SKILLS IN PRESCHOOL CHILDREN

Understanding what it means to comprehend and how comprehension skills develop in the preschool and early-school years provides a basis for the development of assessment tools of comprehension skills in these young children. The aforementioned review of theoretical models and empirical evidence suggests a set of principles that is useful in guiding assessment practices and tools.

Three Principles for Assessment

1. A Significant Development of Comprehension Skills Takes Place During the Preschool Years

Children as young as 4 engage in comprehension processes that are very similar to those that older children and adults use when reading—albeit perhaps with less efficiency and with less knowledge on which to draw. Comprehension skills and basic literacy skills such as phonological awareness and vocabulary develop in tandem rather than in sequence. As a consequence, comprehension instruction and assessment should start at the preschool level rather than be deferred to elementary school.

2. Preschool Comprehension Assessment Uses Nontextual Contexts

Comprehension assessment in preschool and beginning elementary students poses some practical challenges. One of these challenges is that children at this age are still developing basic written language skills such as letter and word identification. Fortunately, as the review of the research literature shows, children and adults use similar comprehension processes when comprehending events in different media. In all instances, they identify connections—causal, referential, and others—by making inferences. Further, in all cases, they have to negotiate limited attentional and working memory resources, use their background knowledge, search in their memory for the prior events, and so forth, to do so. This allows a solution to the practical problem of assessing comprehension without being able to do so in a textual context: to obtain a valid measure of comprehension skills, without contamination by basic skills, comprehension should be assessed in a nontextual context. Examples of such contexts are videos (discussed later) or picture books (e.g., Paris & Paris, 2003).

It is important to note that this does not mean, of course, that there are no differences in what children comprehend in different media. For example, video and text presentations of the same narrative will differ in the extent to which they draw attention to different aspects of the story, in the extent to which basic language skills are required, in the extent to which they draw on established strategies in the child, and so forth. Thus, the content of the resulting mental representation of the narrative will differ. The important point here is that the *processes* themselves are remarkably similar.

3. Assessment Focuses on the Developmental Sequence of Comprehension Skills Rather Than on a Single Dimension or Score

Comprehension skills develop in qualitative as well as in quantitative respects. As we have seen, the identification of connections is essential to comprehension, and with age, children come to recognize increasingly complex types of connections. Proper assessment of comprehension skills gauges not only the number of the connections in individuals' representations as a function of the informational structure but also of the types of connections included. Whereas one sign of improved comprehension is that a student identifies more relations of the same type in a text, another—and perhaps more telling—sign is that a student has advanced to include new, more complex types of relations.

A Methodology for Assessing Comprehension. In this section, we illustrate how what we know about the development of comprehension skills can be used to develop assessment tools by describing an assessment methodology that implements the three principles outlined earlier. In this methodology, children view television narratives and listen to aurally presented narratives. Consistent with principle 2, we use nontextual contexts to gauge children's comprehension skills. Two contexts—television and audiotape—are used to make sure that we measure comprehension as it generalizes across media rather than comprehension that is particular to one medium. The assessment method uses children's narratives because they contain relations at all levels of complexity and because the content tends to be familiar to children of a wide range of ages, thus reducing the likelihood of confounding of comprehension skills and background knowledge. In addition, the structure of narratives is relatively well understood (e.g., Mandler & Johnson, 1978; Trabasso et al., 1984) making the identification of inferences at different levels of complexity fairly straightforward. It is important to point out that the same method could, in principle, be applied to other text types as well.

Children's comprehension is measured by assessing the quality of their representation of the narratives, in terms of the extent to which their recall focuses on the events and facts that have many connections to other events and facts and in terms of their ability to answer comprehension questions at different levels of complexity. In principle, any authentic program could be used, as long as it contains both simple and complex relations. Here, the television narratives consist of 20-min episodes of "Blinky Bill," an Australian children's program, and of episodes of "Rugrats," a popular American children's television program. Both programs have a complex plot structure that includes the different types of relations. In addition, they are appealing to children of a wide age range. The audiotaped stories are fairy tales unfamiliar to the children. They too are structurally complex. They are aurally presented with an average length of about 8 min.

The relational structure of the narratives was determined using the methods developed by Trabasso and van den Broek (e.g., Trabasso, van den Broek, & Suh, 1989; Trabasso et al., 1984). On the basis of these structures, several important properties of the narratives were determined. First, we distinguished those elements in the narratives with many causal connections from those elements with few connections. Second, we identified types of connections of different levels of complexity, conformed to the distinctions made earlier (see Table 5.3). These connections formed the basis for comprehension questions. For the purposes of this study, we distinguished two levels of complexity. Basic coherence-building connections were those that establish causal relations between events that happened close together in the narrative. An example in the sample text in Table 5.1 and Fig. 5.1 is the causal relation between the boy carrying the cake under his arm (sentences 6 and 7) and it crumbling to pieces (sentence 9). Complex coherence-building connections were those that establish distant causal relations (e.g., the causal relation between the boy living in a hot country [sentence 2] and the sun shining hard [sentence 17]), internal relations to protagonists' goals (e.g., the relation between the boy wanting to be very careful [sentence 14] and his putting the butter on his head [sentence 15], or between the grandmother calling him silly [sentence 10] and his wanting to be careful [sentence 14]), and thematic relations (e.g., the fact that this boy tried hard to do the right thing but simply did not think through his actions well enough).

Both number of connections and the complexity of those connections can be used to assess the quality of individuals' comprehension and representation of the narratives. With regard to number of connections, more proficient comprehenders will tend to recall more elements from the narratives and, more importantly, their memory for the narratives will focus on those elements with many connections. With regard to the comprehension questions, good comprehenders are those who are particularly skilled at answering questions about the more complex relations.

To investigate the validity and usefulness of this assessment tool we asked preschool children to watch the television programs, listen to the audiotaped stories, and perform both memory and questioning tasks. Our first goal was to find out whether their performance was stable across the two media and whether their behavior was consistent with patterns reported in prior research.

Our second goal was to follow these children in a longitudinal study and see if their comprehension scores as a preschooler predicted their reading comprehension several years later.

Validating the Comprehension Assessment: Preschool Children's Comprehension Across Media. As a first step in determining whether the assessment tool is valid, we investigated the extent to which children's comprehension was determined by causal connections—as reported in prior research—and whether individual children's comprehension scores for the television narratives were related to their comprehension scores for the aurally presented narratives. With regard to the latter purpose, we also determined if any relation between the comprehension scores in the two domains simply was the result of basic literacy skills rather than of a common comprehension component. If this method of assessing comprehension in preschool children is valid, then their performance should be consistent across domains and, moreover, in general, should reflect factors that have been found to influence comprehension in prior studies. To do this, preschool (4-year-old) children received the aforementioned assessment as well as tests of basic language skills: The Peabody Picture Vocabulary Test–III (Dunn & Dunn, 1997), the letter and word identification subtests of the Woodcock Reading Mastery Test (Woodcock, 1987), and the Initial Sounds Frequency (phonological awareness) subset of the Dynamic Indicators of Basic Early Literacy Skills (Kaminski & Good, 1996).

First, with regard to memory for the narratives, the preschool children showed the pattern familiar from prior research with older children and adults: the more causal connections an element from the narrative had, the more often it was recalled. This was the case for both televised and audiotaped narratives, with the average $r = .74$. Thus, consistent with prior findings, the causal structure of these narratives was a strong determiner of the representations that the children constructed. Moreover, this pattern was observed for both media, supporting the notion that similar processes are involved in the comprehension in the two domains.

Second, individual differences between children proved stable across the two domains: the amount of information that the children remembered—and in particular the amount of causally central information—from the television narrative was strongly correlated with how much they remembered from the aural narrative, with a $r = .63$. Thus, children who are good comprehenders in one medium also tend to be good comprehenders in other media. These results indicate that a child's comprehension skills are not specific to a particular medium but generalize across comprehension contexts.

Third, children's comprehension of televised and aurally presented narratives were strongly related even after basic literacy skills were taken into account, residual $R = .59$. Thus, the similarity in comprehension in the different domains held independent of basic skills and, conversely, basic skills did not cause this similarity.

In summary, the proposed comprehension assessment tool appears to be a valid indicator of comprehension skills. In general, the patterns of findings with regard to recall for the narratives in the assessment tool are consistent with those reported in the research literature: Preschool children recalled events with many connections more often than events with fewer connections. Moreover, individual differences in comprehension performance were stable across the media: children who comprehended narratives well in one medium also remembered narratives well in the other medium. These findings are not explained by differences in basic language skills but instead appear to reflect comprehension skills. Analyses of the comprehension-question data showed similar patterns, thereby corroborating these conclusions.

Validating the Comprehension Assessment: Predicting Reading Comprehension. The second step in determining the validity and usefulness of the assessment is to test whether preschool children's performance on the comprehension tests predicts their later reading performance. If the assessment is valid and captures stable aspects of a child's comprehension ability, then we would expect that performance on the comprehension measures at preschool would predict reading comprehension in elementary school. To investigate the predictive validity of the assessment tool, we followed the preschoolers into second grade. At that time, they received the same tests as they had received as preschoolers, with two modifications: they saw new television and aurally presented narratives and they also read written narrative passages. They then performed recall and question-answering tests that were designed using the same principles as in preschool.

The results showed that the preschool comprehension assessment using television narratives predicted reading comprehension in second grade. The correlations were considerable, particularly considering what is usually found when predicting early reading: $r = .58$ for memory for causally central information and $r = .53$ for scores on the complex questions. Thus, a preschool child's comprehension skills—as measured in the context of TV viewing—strongly predicts the child's reading comprehension as a second-grade student.

In interpreting these results it is important to consider if they could be due to the common influence of basic literacy skills at both preschool and second-grade test points. After all, as described in the introduction to this chapter, there

5. ASSESSMENT OF COMPREHENSION ABILITIES   125

is ample evidence that basic skills predict reading scores on standardized tests. We considered this possibility by testing whether preschool comprehension scores predicted second-grade comprehension after differences in basic literacy skills were taken into account. The results of statistical regression techniques showed that the predictive power of early comprehension on later reading comprehension remained very strong even after the possible role of basic skills were factored in: residual $Rs = .53$ and $.46$ for memory and question-answering, respectively. Thus, the fact that early comprehension performance predicts later reading comprehension performance is not caused or mediated by basic literacy skills such as vocabulary, letter and word identification, and phonemic awareness. This provides further evidence for the validity and usefulness of an assessment tool like the one we outlined here. More generally, an important implication is that reading comprehension assessments based on a thorough understanding of the cognitive processes involved in comprehension have a powerful and unique role to play in determining whether our children learn the reading skills that they need to thrive in school and beyond.

CONCLUDING REMARKS

The comprehension processes that preschool children use when they try to comprehend the events and facts they encounter (e.g., on television or by listening to someone else read) are remarkably similar to those that older children and adults use when they read. At the heart of these processes is the identification of meaningful relations between the events and facts, in particular of referential and causal relations. Even preschool children engage in these processes and can be successful, particularly when the materials are about concrete, familiar events, and when they provide ample support for the necessary inferences.

Moreover, the ability of a child to engage in these processes at a young age is predictive of that child's ability to comprehend what he or she reads years later. Our findings show that an individual's ability to infer relations at the preschool level strongly predicts his or her later reading comprehension and that it does so over and above basic literacy skills such as vocabulary, letter and word identification, and phonemic awareness. Thus, comprehension skills develop at an early age, and to a large extent are independent from basics skills.

These results have important implications for comprehension assessment. First, they indicate the importance of developing tools for assessing comprehension in young children. Such comprehension assessment should go beyond the sheer assessment of basic skills. Our findings show that assessment of comprehension skills in very young children is possible by using nontextual materials. For example, television narratives provide a rich and intrinsically motivating context, often with a wide range of possible inferences. Other nontextual materials include picture tasks in which children are asked to relate a story about a series of pictures, thus allowing one to observe the child's inferential skills (for an excellent example, see Paris & Paris, 2003). These and other nontextual contexts provide an important window into the processes that children will later use to comprehend texts.

Second, comprehension assessment should focus on the structure of the mental representation of the text or narrative. As children grow older, they accumulate more knowledge, comprehension strategies, and increase the efficiency of their cognitive processes. As a result, they improve their ability to generate more challenging inferences, such as ones about relations that are abstract, span large distances in the text, and so forth. Accordingly, the emphasis in assessment should be on the quality of recall, question-answering, and so on, rather than on the sheer amount. Consider, for example, using memory as a measure of comprehension. As skills develop, the amount recalled may increase but, more importantly, the pattern of recall will change, focusing more and more on those events or facts that have complex connections. A simple count of the number of events or facts recalled gives an inadequate picture of an individual's skills. Similar considerations apply to using comprehension questions. As in the assessment tool outlined earlier, comprehension questions should span the range of different types of inferences. Development and individual differences are more likely to be captured by including questions about the more challenging relations, such as those in the latter half of the developmental sequence in Table 5.3, than by adding more questions about simpler relations. These implications are in contrast to established practice. The scores on many standardized tests are based on a single dimension—amount of recall, number of questions correct, and so forth. Moreover, they usually focus only on the lower levels of comprehension, as captured in the upper half of Table 5.3. Given the recent advances in our understanding of the complex nature of the reading process, it is time that tests start focusing on the rich and multifaceted aspects of comprehension. Thus, measures of individual differences in sensitivity to the causal connections in a text and in the extent to which one can detect adjacent versus distant relations, physical and concrete versus goal and theme relations, have strong psychological validity and good predictive power. Such measures can be based on sound cognitive theory and, as our results indicate, have tremendous predictive potential.

This does not mean that the measurement of basic literacy skills is superfluous. It is likely that the development of comprehension and of basic skills dynamically interact. As a child advances in comprehension skills, basic literacy skills are likely to develop as well. Conversely, with increases in basic literacy skills, a child gains new occasions to practice comprehension skills. Thus, comprehension and basic skills engage in a dynamic interaction resulting in distinct yet connected developments (Morris, Bloodgood, Lomax, & Perney, 2003). Moreover, both contribute to reading performance, especially in the beginning grades, when basic literacy skills are still developing and thus may limit a child's opportunity to exercise his or her comprehension skills (cf. Ehri et al., 2001).

The work presented here is only a first step toward constructing usable comprehension assessment tools. A broader range of materials needs to be developed and additional tests of reliability and validity need to be done. We are currently pursuing two lines of research to achieve this goal. The first involves following the children described in this chapter into higher elementary school grades with the goal of observing whether the predictive power of early comprehension tests remains strong. The second involves developing and validating curriculum-based assessment versions of our test that teachers can use to gauge the progress—or lack thereof—in their students (McConnell, Horst, Passe, Rodriguez, & van den Broek, 2003).

As mentioned at the outset of this chapter, "comprehension" means different things to different people. Each type of comprehension involves unique processes, but they also have a large common set of processes. At the core of comprehension—any type of comprehension—are the set of processes involved in identifying and inferring relations to build a coherent representation. Surrounding this core, as peels to an onion, are the processes unique to different types of comprehension. For example, to be able to apply the information in a text to a real-life situation, one needs to build on the coherent representation to connect the particulars of the situation to his or her relevant corollaries in the text. Or, to understand the theme or moral of a narrative, one can reflect on the coherent representation to identify more abstract relations (e.g., van den Broek, Lynch, Naslund, Levers-Landis, & Verduin, 2003; Williams, 1993). Ultimately, assessment should include all concentric layers, but a start should be— and, as the current chapter demonstrates, can be—made by assessing children's ability to detect meaningful relations between the events and facts they experience.

ACKNOWLEDGMENTS

We would like to thank Robert Calfee and Scott Paris for their insightful comments. This research was supported by funding from the Center for the Improvement of Early Reading Achievement and the National Science Foundation, TR R305 R7004, the Guy Bond Endowment in Reading and Literacy, and by grants from the Center for Early Education and Development, the Graduate School, and the Center for Cognitive Sciences, all at the University of

Minnesota, and from the National Institute of Child Health and Human Development (HD–07151). Correspondence concerning this article should be addressed to Paul van den Broek, Department of Educational Psychology, University of Minnesota, 178 Pillsbury Drive SE, Minneapolis, MN 55455 or at pvdbroek@umn.edu.

REFERENCES

Applebee, A. N. (1978). *The child's concept of a story: Ages two to seventeen.* Chicago: University of Chicago Press.

Bartsch, K., & Wellman, H. (1995). *Children talk about the mind.* Oxford: Oxford University Press.

Bauer, P. J. (1996). What do infants recall of their lives? Memory for specific events by 1- to 2-year-olds. *American Psychologist, 51,* 29–41.

Bauer, P. J. (1996). Development of memory in early childhood. In N. Cowan (Ed.), *The development of memory in childhood* (pp. 83–111). Sussex, England: Psychology Press.

Bourg, T., Bauer, P., & van den Broek, P. (1997). Building the bridges: The development of event comprehension and representation. In P. van den Broek, P. Bauer, & T. Bourg (Eds.), *Developmental spans in event comprehension and representation: Bridging fictional and actual events* (pp. 385–407). Hillsdale, NJ: Lawrence Erlbaum Associates.

Case, R. (1992). *The mind's staircase: Exploring the conceptual understanding of children's thought and knowledge.* Hillsdale, NJ: Lawrence Erlbaum Associates.

Case, R. (1995). Capacity-based explanations of working memory growth: A brief history and reevaluation. In F. E. Weinert & W. Schneider (Eds.), *Memory performance and competencies: Issues in growth and development* (pp. 23–44). Mahwah, NJ: Lawrence Erlbaum Associates.

Catts, H. W., Fey, M. E., Zhang, X., & Tomblin, B. J. (1999). Language basis of reading and reading disabilities: Evidence from a longitudinal investigation. *Scientific Studies of Reading, 3,* 331–361.

Chi, M. T. H., Hutchinson, J. E., & Robin, A. F. (1989). How inference about novel domain-related concepts can be constrained by structured knowledge. *Merrill-Palmer Quarterly, 35,* 27–62.

Chi, M. T. H., & Koeske, R. D. (1983). Network representations of a child's dinosaur knowledge. *Developmental Psychology, 19,* 29–39.

Dewey, J. (1963). How we think. Portions published in R. H. M. Hutchins & M. J. Adler (Eds.), *Gateway to the great books, 10.* Chicago: Encyclopaedia Britannica. (Original work published 1933)

Dunn, L. M., & Dunn, L. M. (1997). *Peabody Picture Vocabulary Test, 3rd edition (PPVT-III).* Circle Pines, MN: American Guidance Services.

Ehri, L. C., Nunes, S., Stahl, S., & Willows, D. (2001). Systematic phonics instruction helps students learn to read: Evidence from the national reading panel's meta-analysis. *Review of Educational Research, 71,* 393–447.

Fletcher, C. R., & Bloom, C. P. (1988). Causal reasoning and comprehension of simple narrative texts. *Journal of Memory and Language, 27,* 235–244.

Gernsbacher, M. A. (1990). *Language comprehension as a structure building.* Hillsdale, NJ: Lawrence Erlbaum Associates.

Gobbo, C., & Chi, M. T. H. (1986). How knowledge is structured and used by expert and novice children. *Cognitive Development, 1,* 221–237.

Goldman, S. R. (1985). Inferential reasoning in and about narrative texts. In A. C. Graesser & J. B. Black (Eds.), *The psychology of questions* (pp. 247–276). Hillsdale, NJ: Lawrence Erlbaum Associates.

Goldman, S. R., & Varnhagen, C. K. (1986). Memory for embedded and sequential story structures. *Journal of Memory and Language, 25,* 401–418.

Graesser, A. C., & Clark, L. F. (1985). *The structures and procedures of implicit knowledge.* Norwood, NJ: Ablex.

Kahneman, D. (2003). A perspective on judgment and choice: Mapping bounded rationality. *American Psychologist, 58,* 697–720.

Kaminski, R. A., & Good, R. H. (1996). Toward a technology for assessing basic early literacy skills. *School Psychology Review, 25,* 215–227.

Kintsch, W. (1988). The role of knowledge in discourse comprehension: A construction-integration model. *Psychological Review, 95*(2), 163–182.

Kintsch, W., & van Dijk, T. A. (1978). Towards a model of text comprehension and production. *Psychological Review, 85,* 363–394.

Mandler, J. M., & Johnson, N. S. (1977). Remembrance of things parsed: Story structure and recall. *Cognitive Psychology, 9,* 111–151.

Massey, C. M., & Gelman, R. (1988). Preschooler's ability to decide whether a photographed unfamiliar object can move itself. *Developmental Psychology, 24,* 307–317.

McConnell, S., Horst, K., Passe, A., Rodriguez, M. C., & van den Broek, P. (2003). Minnesota's early literacy training project report, Year 1. *U.S. Department of Education Early Childhood Educator Professional Development Project* (CFDA 84.349A). Minneapolis: Center for Early Education and Development, University of Minnesota.

Medo, M. A., & Ryder, R. J. (1993). The effects of vocabulary instruction on readers' ability to make causal connections. *Reading Research and Instruction, 33*(2), 119–134.

Morris, D., Bloodgood, J. W., Lomax, R. G., & Perney, J. (2003). Development steps in learning to read: A longitudinal study in kindergarten and first grade. *Reading Research Quarterly, 38,* 302–328.

No Child Left Behind Act of 2001, Pub. L. No. 107–110.

O'Brien, E. J., & Myers, J. L. (1987). The role of causal connections in the retrieval of text. *Memory and Cognition, 15,* 419–427.

Paris, A. H., & Paris, S. G. (2003). Assessing narrative comprehension in young children. *Reading Research Quarterly, 38,* 36–76.

Perfetti, C. A. (2003). The universal grammar of reading. *Scientific Studies of Reading, 7,* 3–24.

Piaget, J. (1954). *The construction of reality in the child.* New York: Basic Books.

Rayner, K., Foorman, B. R., Perfetti, C. A., Pesetsky, D., & Seidenberg, M. S. (2001). How psychological science inform the teaching of reading. *Psychological Science, 2*(Suppl. 2), 31–74.

Siegler, R. S. (1994). Cognitive variability: The key to understanding cognitive development. *Current Directions in Psychological Science, 3,* 1–5.

Singer, M. (1994). Discourse inference processes. In M. A. Gernsbacher (Ed.), *Handbook of Psycholinguistics* (pp. 479–515). London: Academic Press.

Stanovich, K. E., & West, R. F. (2000). Individual differences in reasoning: Implications for the rationality debate. *Behavioral and Brain Sciences, 23,* 645–665.

Stein, N. L., & Glenn, C. G. (1979). An analysis of story comprehension in elementary school children. In R. O. Freedle (Ed.), *New directions in discourse processing* (Vol. 2, pp. 53–120). Hillsdale, NJ: Lawrence Erlbaum Associates.

Stein, N. L., & Liwag, M. D. (1997). Children's understanding, evaluation, and memory for emotional events. In P. van den Broek, P. Bauer, & T. Bourg (Eds.), *Developmental spans in event comprehension and representation: Bridging fictional and actual events* (pp. 199–235). Hillsdale, NJ: Lawrence Erlbaum Associates.

Trabasso, T., & Nickels, M. (1992). The development of goal plans of action in the narration of a picture story. *Discourse Processes, 15,* 249–275.

Trabasso, T., Secco, T., & van den Broek, P. (1984). Causal cohesion and story coherence. In H. Mandl, N. L. Stein, & T. Trabasso (Eds.), *Learning and comprehension of text* (pp. 83–111). Hillsdale, NJ: Lawrence Erlbaum Associates.

Trabasso, T., & van den Broek, P. (1985). Causal thinking and the representation of narrative events. *Journal of Memory and Language, 24,* 612–630.

Trabasso, T., van den Broek, P., & Suh, S. Y. (1989). Logical necessity and transitivity of causal relations in stories. *Discourse Processes, 12,* 1–25.

van den Broek, P. W. (1988). The effects of causal relations and hierarchical position on the importance of story statements. *Journal of Memory and Language, 27,* 1–22.

van den Broek, P. W. (1989a). Causal reasoning and inference making in judging the importance of story statements. *Child Development, 60,* 286–297.

van den Broek, P. W. (1989b). The effects of causal structure on the comprehension of narratives: Implications for education. *Reading Psychology: An International Quarterly, 10,* 19–44.

van den Broek, P. (1994). Comprehension and memory of narrative texts. In M. A. Gernsbacher (Ed.), *Handbook of Psycholinguistics* (pp. 539–588). London: Academic Press.

van den Broek, P. (1997). Discovering the cements of the universe: The development of event comprehension from childhood to adulthood. In P. van den Broek, P. Bauer, & T. Bourg (Eds.), *Developmental spans in event comprehension: Bridging fictional and actual events* (pp. 321–342). Mahwah, NJ: Lawrence Erlbaum Associates.

van den Broek, P., Lorch, E. P., & Thurlow, R. (1996). Children's and adult's memory for television stories: The role of causal factors, story-grammar categories, and hierarchical level. *Child Development, 67,* 3010–3028.

van den Broek, P., Lynch, J. S., Naslund, J., Ievers-Landis, C. E., & Verduin, K. (2003). The development of main ideas in narratives: Evidence from the selection of titles. *Journal of Educational Psychology, 95,* 707–718.

Wellman, H. M., Harris, P., Banerjee, M., Sinclair, A. (1995). Early understanding of emotion. Evidence from natural language. *Cognition and Emotion, 9,* 117–149.

Wenner, J., & Bauer, P. J. (2001). Bringing order to the arbitrary: One to two-year olds' recall of event sequences. *Infant Behavior and Development, 22,* 585–590.

Whitehurst, G. J., & Lonigan, C. J. (1998). Child development and emergent literacy. *Child Development, 69,* 848–872.

Williams, J. P. (1993). Comprehension of students with and without learning disabilities: Identification of narrative themes and idiosyncratic text representations. *Journal of Educational Psychology, 85,* 631–642.

Wolman, C. (1991). Sensitivity to causal cohesion in stories by children with mild mental retardation, children with learning disabilities, and children without disabilities. *Journal of Special Education, 25,* 135–154.

Wolman, C., van den Broek, P., & Lorch, R. F. (1997). Effects of causal structure on immediate and delayed story recall by children with mild mental retardation, children with learning disabilities, and children without disabilities. *Journal of Special Education, 30,* 439–455.

Woodcock, R. W. (1987). *Woodcock Reading Mastery Test (WRMT).* Circle Pines, MN: American Guidance Service.

6

Spurious and Genuine Correlates of Children's Reading Comprehension

Scott G. Paris
Robert D. Carpenter
Alison H. Paris
Ellen E. Hamilton
University of Michigan

The ability to comprehend text is a fundamental requirement for education, and it is the renewed focus of American educational research and policy (RAND Reading Study Group, 2002). Yet, reading comprehension is difficult to define, isolate, and measure because it includes multiple processes. Developmental changes confound these problems because how and what beginning readers understand differs from comprehension among more expert readers (Kintsch, 1998). Teachers generally regard reading comprehension in terms of classroom practices such as the ways that students answer questions about text, retell important ideas, and discuss text from different perspectives. In contrast, researchers measure comprehension using a variety of assessments that range from microprocesses to global processes. However, the de facto definition and public benchmarks of reading comprehension are standardized test scores usually derived from reading text silently and responding to multiple-choice questions (Pearson & Hamm, this volume). The wide variation in the definitions, assessments, and standards of reading comprehension is where educational practices, theories, and policies may converge and conflict.

The pressing needs for better definitions and assessments of reading comprehension have been accompanied by greater reliance on scientific research, so that state and federal policymakers can provide clear guidelines for allocating funds, rewarding success, and sanctioning failure—three clear consequences of educational accountability (Linn, Baker, & Betebenner, 2002; National Reading Panel, 2000). The climate of educational accountability through high-stakes testing in the 1990s escalated into more federal control under the No Child Left Behind Act of 2001 (NCLB). The "Reading First" part of NCLB provided Federal funding for every state to improve the reading achievement of children from kindergarten through third grade (K–3), but the plans had to be made on scientifically based reading research (SBRR). Although we are encouraged by the increased reliance on scientific evidence, we worry that policies may be established prematurely on contested and inconclusive research. Evidence can be seductive when it appears to deliver quick and clear answers to complex questions about reading, learning, and development—issues that academics, researchers, and educators continue to debate long after the policies have been established. Equivocal and contrary research findings and prolonged academic debates are shifting sands on which to build policies, yet that may be the case today in recent Federal legislation regarding reading education.

The purpose of this chapter is to examine SBRR on children's reading comprehension in an effort to create better policies for reading instruction and assessment. The focus of our analyses is on correlational evidence that is used to establish predictive and concurrent validity of reading assessments because these claims are used to substantiate the importance of specific reading processes and the usefulness of specific assessments. We examine several correlates of children's reading comprehension to expose warranted and unwarranted claims about the skills and knowledge that contribute to reading development. We rely on conventional outcome measures of reading comprehension, such as informal reading inventories and standardized tests, in our discussion because the focus of our analyses is on the skills that are correlated with traditional measures of comprehension. The correlational evidence and the statistical features of the data are scrutinized rather than the measures of comprehension.

DEVELOPMENTAL DISJUNCTION BETWEEN FLUENT ORAL READING AND COMPREHENSION

It seems intuitively obvious that children who read text accurately and quickly and with appropriate intonation also comprehend what they are reading. It is the foundation of stage theories of reading development (e.g., Chall, 1967), and it is typical of "bottom-up" processing views in which reading proceeds from identification of letters to words to meaning (Adams, 1990; LaBerge & Samuels, 1974). Fluent reading includes the components of reading rate, accuracy, and intonation, and fluency is generally considered essential for comprehension (see Stahl & Hiebert, this volume). For example, informal reading inventories generally suggest that children should be able to read 95% of the words in text accurately to read and understand a text independently. Thus, very high levels of word recognition and decoding are required as prerequisites for comprehension of text. Researchers have found that rate measures based on the numbers of words that children read correctly per minute are often correlated with reading comprehension and achievement (Hasbrouck, Ihnot, & Rogers, 1999; Koshkinen et al., 2000; Kranzler, Brownell, & Miller, 1998; Samuels, 1979). The ability to read with intonation is also related to children's reading comprehension (e.g., Pinnell et al., 1995).

Instruction that promotes fluent reading appears to increase automatic word recognition and sometimes comprehension (Carver & Hoffman, 1981; Kuhn & Stahl, 2003). For example, Dowhower (1987) found that reading accuracy, rate, prosody, and comprehension increased over repeated readings of the same text. Roller (1994) worked with six children intensively to increase their oral reading fluency, but their comprehension did not display corresponding improvement. Kuhn and Stahl (2003) found that many different instructional programs, including assisted and unassisted repeated reading, have been used successfully to increase children's oral reading fluency and accurate word recognition. However, the results regarding comprehension are more ambivalent and the findings vary across the ages of the students. For example, 14 of 20 repeated reading studies led to improved microprocessing of comprehension but only two of eight studies led to better general comprehension (Kuhn & Stahl, 2003). Thus, intervention research on fluency provides modest support for the correlation between oral reading fluency and comprehension.

We became interested in the relation between children's oral reading fluency and comprehension while conducting an evaluation of the effects of K–3 summer reading programs in Michigan (Paris et al., 2004). In the first study, we used the Qualitative Reading Inventory II (QRI) designed by Leslie and Caldwell (1995) to assess children's oral reading, comprehension, and retelling both before and after summer school. In the second study the following summer, we used the Basic Reading Inventory (BRI) developed by Johns (1997) to assess more than 400 children who either did or did not attend summer reading programs. The key finding from those two studies was that attending summer reading programs had positive benefits for children, but the issue for this chapter concerns the correlation between oral reading fluency and comprehension.

In the first study, we performed a factor analysis and identified a fluency factor based on accuracy, acceptability, rate, and a comprehension factor that included measures of the percentage of questions answered correctly, percentage of text propositions recalled, and percentage of key ideas (6 per

passage) recalled (Carpenter & Paris, submitted). There was no overall correlation between the oral reading factor and the comprehension factor at pretest ($r = -.01$) or posttest ($r = -.01$). However, there were differences when
the data were disaggregated by passage level. Figure 6.1 shows the
correlational pattern between the two factors by passage level at pretest.
The correlations were moderate but not significant for the preprimer passage ($r = .34, p = .06$) and generally declined as passage difficulty increased,
.23, .19, .32, –.42, and –.38. The third-grade correlation ($r = -.42, p < .01$)
was the only significant correlation for a passage level. The correlations also
declined with increasing grade level: grade 1 = .05, grade 2 = –.17, and grade
3 = –.38. It is clear that accurate oral reading and comprehension were more
highly correlated for beginning readers, by both age and skill, than accomplished readers.

The same pattern was evident for each component of the comprehension factor, that is, questions answered correctly about each passage, percentage of propositions recalled, and the number of key ideas recalled.
We then examined the correlations between fluency and comprehension
at posttest and found strong positive correlations between the oral reading
factor and the comprehension factor at the lowest passage levels
(preprimer, $r = .56, p < .001$) and strong negative correlations for the highest passages (third grade, $r = -.64, p < .01$; fourth grade, $r = -.69, p < .01$).
The grade level analyses confirmed the declining pattern: grade 1 = .19,
grade 2 = –.43, and grade 3 = –.41. Analyses of the accuracy and comprehension raw scores confirmed the same pattern as the factor scores. At
posttest, the overall correlation between accuracy and comprehension was

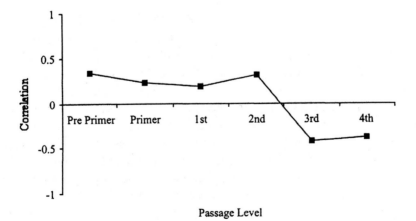

FIG. 6.1.   Correlations between comprehension and fluency factors at pretest with the QRI.

$r = .18$. The passage level correlations from preprimer to fourth grade levels were $rs = .55, .31, .11, .14, -.47$, and $-.07$. The grade level correlations declined from $.12$ to $.08$ to $-.07$ from first to third grade. The relation between reading rate and comprehension also declined at posttest.

The results were similar but not as clear in the second study with the BRI (where a measure of prosody was included with accuracy and semantic acceptability in the fluency factor). The correlational pattern between oral reading and comprehension measures was more variable than in the first study with the QRI. The oral reading factor (accuracy, acceptability, prosody, and rate) was not significantly related to the comprehension factor (propositions recalled, ideas recalled, and comprehension questions) at pretest ($r = .00$) or posttest ($r = .00$). However, when we examined passage level correlations, we found a declining pattern like in Study 1. The pretest correlations between the oral reading factor and the comprehension factor are shown in Fig. 6.2. The only positive significant correlation was for the first-grade passage ($r = .34, p < .01$) and stronger correlations are evident for the primer ($r = .21$), first- and second-grade ($r = .20$) passages than for the third- ($r = -.02$), fourth- ($r = .02$), fifth- ($r = -.01$), and sixth-grade ($r = .09$) passages.

At both testing times, the majority of significant relations between oral reading measures and comprehension measures (72.7% at pretest and 78.9% at posttest) were on passages below the third-grade level. The disjunction between fluency and comprehension increased from beginning to advanced readers in both studies on both informal reading inventories. This suggests that the assumed simple correlation between oral reading fluency and comprehension may be intuitively appealing, but it is wrong.

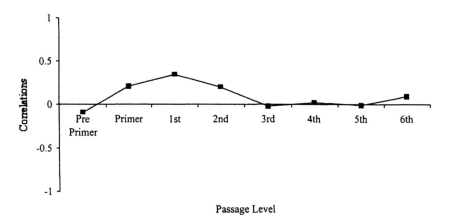

FIG. 6.2.   Correlation between comprehension and fluency factors at pretest with the BRI.

Why Oral Reading Fluency Is a Spurious Correlate
of Reading Comprehension

There are conceptual and statistical reasons why oral reading fluency is not uniformly related to children's reading comprehension. Conceptually, it is clear that children may be able to say all the words in a passage without understanding much of the meanings of sentences and text. (Reading rate and intonation may also be high.) Such readers are often labeled as "word callers." Conversely, other children, sometimes labeled "gap fillers," may be able to construct meaning from text without being able to read all the words or without reading quickly or with few errors. Riddle-Buly and Valencia (2002) found a wide variety of patterns of reading skills among fourth graders with many children exhibiting little relation between fluency components and reading comprehension. These bottom-up and top-down processes, identifying words and constructing meaning, may operate together, as Stanovich (1980) hypothesized in his interactive-compensatory model of reading. Conceptually, it is evident that fast and accurate word recognition does not always lead to high levels of comprehension, and neither does slow, less accurate word recognition necessarily imply poor comprehension.

There are several other reasons why fluency and comprehension may not be related. For example, beginning readers may focus all their attention on pronouncing words correctly at the expense of comprehension so there are few resources or time left to think about text meaning. Young readers may not have as many comprehension strategies as older readers or may not be able to access and them use while reading orally. Older readers might be more unfamiliar or more anxious with reading aloud which may reduce comprehension. Of course, there is the general speed-accuracy trade-off whereby faster reading may generate more miscues.

Some of the reasons for disjunction between fluency and comprehension are characteristics of readers, but others are characteristics of situations or texts. For example, when a person is asked to read aloud in front of an audience, there is more attention placed on oral reading accuracy and prosody than comprehension. In contrast, when a reader is privately rereading a text, poem, or lyrics for pleasure, attention is most likely devoted to comprehension and enjoyment rather than word-for-word accuracy or speed. Likewise, texts that are difficult, boring, or written in an unfamiliar language may evoke more gap filling than fluent reading compared to easy and familiar text. Therefore, fluency and comprehension may or may not be related for some readers, some texts, and some situations. Indeed, it may be the special case of young children who are learning to read (in classroom and research situations where they read aloud in front of others) who exhibit the strongest relation between oral reading fluency and comprehension.

There are even more compelling statistical reasons why fluency and comprehension may be related on only some occasions. The argument rests on the statistical distributions of oral reading accuracy (and acceptability) scores because they are not normally distributed. Teachers know that readers cannot make sense of text unless they can identify nearly all the words. Usually, teachers define 95% to 100% accurate oral reading as an independent level of reading, 90% to 94% as an instructional level, and below 90% as a frustration level (Lipson & Wixson, 2003). Quite simply, there is little variance in the top 10% of a distribution, even a highly skewed distribution like oral reading accuracy, to yield strong correlations with any other variables. It is a ceiling effect that threatens the validity of parametric statistics such as Pearson correlations. In fact, it makes no sense to conceptualize oral reading accuracy scores as normally distributed because a reader who can only identify 50% of the words in a text has little hope of understanding it.

There are also strong floor and ceiling effects that operate in all measures of oral reading accuracy and fluency. That is why teachers and researchers select different levels of texts for children to read, and those levels are nearly always defined according to ease of word recognition. The rules for using oral reading fluency assessments ensure that the distributions of accuracy scores are always skewed, although few researchers report the skew statistics or the effects of children who have low scores. Correlations between fluency and comprehension for highly accurate oral readers have little variance to begin with in the fluency data so modest correlations are the most that can be expected. Maybe that is why Taft and Leslie (1985) found no comprehension differences among children who had oral reading accuracy scores at instructional versus independent levels.

Floor effects, however, are paradoxical. Although there is little variance in very low scores on fluency and comprehension, they will covary by necessity because decoding and fluency enable comprehension, that is, there can be no comprehension if the words cannot be read. It makes no sense to assess the relation between fluency and comprehension when oral reading accuracy is at floor (or even 20% or 50%) levels because the relation will always reveal the obvious and spurious positive correlations. It should not be surprising that children who cannot recognize many words in a passage also cannot comprehend it. The non-independence of the variables at low levels of decoding certainly confounds and inflates the positive relation, and it may invalidate correlational analyses.

It is tempting to say that decoding and fluent oral reading are necessary but not sufficient for comprehension, but there are occasions when fluency may not even be necessary. Clearly, when students can answer the comprehension questions without reading the passage, there is a negative relation between fluency and comprehension scores. This occurs when guessing or prior knowledge contribute to correct answers (Tuinman, 1973–1974). This alarming confound may contaminate correlations between fluency and comprehension on a variety of assessments.

So, why do so many studies find modest positive correlations between oral reading fluency and comprehension? Sometimes the studies include data from many readers who are reading below 90% accuracy, so the data include spurious cases of readers who cannot decode or comprehend the text. The variance in scores between 0% to 90% accuracy is huge and yields positive correlations with comprehension because both scores are so low for poor readers (see Kibby, 1979). Even when the majority of participants have accuracy scores above 90%, the correlations with comprehension are unduly influenced by the few cases with the most variance, outliers in a statistical sense, because there is little variance in fluency scores among the best readers. Consider which readers are likely to exhibit oral reading accuracy below 90%. It will be beginning readers who have not mastered decoding skills, children with less automatic word recognition skills, and anyone who is reading unfamiliar words and text. These characteristics probably overlap with many other characteristics of struggling readers so the simple correlation between accuracy and comprehension may be misleading.

A second reason why researchers have found positive correlations between fluency and comprehension is that both skills are correlated with many other intellectual skills. Readers who have poor oral reading fluency or who struggle to understand text may also exhibit inadequate prior knowledge, poor vocabulary, unfamiliarity with standard English, unfamiliarity with the passage genre and test format, and motivational obstacles such as low self-efficacy and self-handicapping strategies (Paris & Paris, 2001). Simple canonical correlations between fluency scores and comprehension may disguise the importance of these other constructs and the multiple correlations among variables. Put another way, oral reading fluency may only be a proxy measure for other influences on reading development. This makes oral reading fluency a positive predictor of reading difficulties, but it does not mean that fluency is the cause of the difficulty. When causal status is erroneously inferred from the predictive relation, remedial intervention may be prescribed for the predictor variable. This reasoning is unscientific and inaccurate, but it is evident in programs such as DIBELS (Good & Kaminski, 2002) that make oral reading fluency an instructional priority.

A third reason for the frequently reported correlation between fluency and comprehension is due to a methodological error in testing the relation. Researchers often assess fluency on one task and comprehension on another. For example, curriculum-based measurement (CBM) was popularized in special education as a quick assessment with strong predictive power (Deno, 1985). CBM involves 1-min samples of children's reading rate and the words read correctly per minute (wcpm) are the main scores derived from the assessment and correlated with other measures of comprehension. Fuchs, Fuchs, Hosp, and Jenkins (2001) reported that criterion-related validity of oral reading fluency with comprehension on the Stanford Achievement Test is stronger than criterion-related validity of direct measures of reading comprehension including answering questions, passage recall, and cloze performance. This counterintuitive claim rests on assessing fluency and comprehension in different tasks. Conceptually, the claim contradicts the necessary within-text and within-subject relations while reading, and methodologically, it presumes that fluency is a stable individual difference. Perhaps this is why Fuchs et al. (2001) claimed, "These findings are consistent with the idea that oral reading fluency appears to reflect individual differences in overall reading competence" (p. 247).

A fourth problem concerns the degree of variance within each measure and in the covariance matrix of the two measures. (We assume that the comprehension measure is normally distributed and interacts equally with skewed data to simplify the argument here.) Fluency measures are highly skewed so the variance in fluency measures is usually greatest among those who have low scores on accuracy, rate, and prosody. This will affect the covariance of the two outcome measures in different ways depending on the distribution of scores in the particular sample. Covariance is also affected in subtle ways because of the logical necessity of covariation when fluency and comprehension are measured on the same passage. Regardless of whether fluency and comprehension are measured on the same or separate reading tasks, the LACK of fluency carries the most variance in the correlations, and it may be a proxy for low scores on a host of factors. It leads to spurious interpretations of the correlation between the constructs. For example, many people assert that (a) fluency is correlated with good comprehension and therefore (b) children should develop fast, accurate, fluent reading in order to understand. Both the premise and implication are wrong. The data actually show that low fluency is correlated with low comprehension, a relation that is obvious and necessary, but it is certainly not causally true for high fluency and high comprehension. Indeed, our data show modestly negative or no correlations between high fluency and high comprehension, and the positive relation may be limited to young or beginning readers.

Interpreting Constrained Variables

Our claim is that oral reading accuracy is not correlated usually or generally or simply with reading comprehension, and to assert so is spurious conceptually and statistically. Instead, it is the lack of accurate oral reading that is correlated with the lack of comprehension. Likewise, the lack of oral reading accuracy may be correlated with the low scores on many other variables. For example, lack of preschool reading experiences, lack of rich vocabularies, lack of high socioeconomic status (SES), lack of high achievement scores, and so forth, might all be correlated positively with low fluency and low comprehension scores. However, a positive correlation does not imply that high fluency is correlated with high scores on these other constructs. There is simply not enough variance in high accuracy scores because the variance and explanatory power rest in the 0% to 90% range of unskilled readers who cannot read many of the words in the text. That is quite a different conclusion than is usually made from simple demonstrations that oral reading accuracy and comprehension are correlated, and it has very different implications for practices and policies.

The constrained variance argument also applies to other skewed data derived from oral reading assessments, but they are only mentioned briefly here. Rubrics that are used to assess prosody (or retellings) can be severely skewed if the sample of readers has little or great difficulty with the texts. Easy or hard texts should yield constrained scores, and on typical 4-point rubrics, this means that most children score in a 2-point range. Consequently, there is little variance to discriminate among readers or to correlate the rubric scores with other data (especially using Pearson correlations that do not handle tied scores well).

Reading rates are also constrained if most readers in the sample are given texts at their independent levels because, for a given age, there is not much variation in rate. Indeed, across grades 2 to 5, most children (i.e., mean wcpm for the 25th–75th percentiles) read between 23 to 151 words per minute (Hasbrouck & Tindal, 1992), a modestly constrained range that is usually large enough for statistical correlations. However, among the top 25% of readers at Grades 2, 3, 4, and 5, respectively, the differences in reading rates from fall to spring are confined to 42, 35, 18, and 25 wcpm. This indicates (a) limited growth in annual reading speed within grades, (b) more constrained reading rates among older and better readers, and (c) greater variance in reading rates among less skilled readers. Again, the variance and derived correlations are due to statistical artifacts in the distributions of scores for poor readers, not necessarily the positive association of rapid reading with good comprehension. It is clear that many other measures of children's early reading skills may also be constrained by skewed distributions, floor and ceiling effects, and greater variability among poor readers.

One implication of the constrained skill interpretation is that all studies using oral reading accuracy or fluency variables must examine and report the skew of the distributions. It may be necessary to eliminate all cases below a certain level, perhaps 80% accuracy, to attenuate the spurious effects of the skewed distributions. Second, parametric statistics such as Pearson's r may prove to be inappropriate for examining relations among constrained variables and new techniques may be warranted. Third, conceptually, it may make more sense to consider oral reading fluency components as mastered skills that are measured against standards of text difficulty and rates. For example, if children read several passages at their grade level with 95% accuracy, they may be considered proficient oral readers.

A fourth implication concerns how we map the relation between fluency and comprehension. Comprehension skills can be assessed in many ways, but the data cannot be correlated simply with fluency scores. Instead, contingency or conditional probability analyses may be used to report attained levels of comprehension given a threshold of proficient oral reading. Perhaps we should simply chart progress on fluent reading by percentages, rates, and categories as dichotomous data, that is, mastered versus not mastered, so there is no mistaking assessments of the skills as normally distributed data. This is consistent with the original intent of informal reading inventories, and it allows both fluency and comprehension to be assessed and reported. The crucial difference is that oral reading fluency is treated as a highly constrained skill that yields a skewed distribution and needs to be mastered with progressively difficult text.

A fifth implication is the conceptual recognition that oral reading fluency and 90% to 100% accuracy are neither necessary nor sufficient for comprehension, although the lack of fluency can impede many aspects of reading including comprehension. Sixth, classroom instruction can and should still emphasize the importance of oral reading fluency, but it should not be presumed that fluency causes comprehension or that comprehension must wait until fluency is achieved. These spurious interpretations have led to classroom instruction and assessment policies that privilege oral reading fluency over comprehension. Whether the skills are treated together, sequentially, or independently, may depend on the proficiency of the readers, difficulty of the text, and purpose of reading in a given situation. However, there is no statistical or conceptual evidence that indicates that reading comprehension instruction should be delayed until children become fluent oral readers. Seventh, all policies for assessing oral reading fluency and accuracy should reconsider how the data are reported and used so that the scores are not mistaken for normally distributed variables, traits of beginning readers, or underlying simple causes of reading comprehension.

LONGITUDINAL RELATIONS BETWEEN PRINT
KNOWLEDGE AND READING COMPREHENSION

Many early skills predict later reading development and reading comprehension, and researchers have tried to identify which skills are the best early predictors (e.g. Share, Jorm, Maclean, & Matthews, 1984). One of the most frequent claims is that children's knowledge about letters and letter-sound relations predicts subsequent reading. Gates (1940) and Wilson and Flemming (1940) were perhaps the first to describe strong positive correlations between children's early abilities to name letters and later reading achievement. The same claim has since been made by many other researchers (e.g., Adams, 1990; Johnston, Anderson, & Holligan, 1996; Stevenson & Newman, 1986). Recently, Lonigan, Burgess, and Anthony (2000) said, "… knowledge of the alphabet (i.e., knowing the names of letters and the sounds they represent) at entry into school is one of the strongest single predictors of short- and long-term success in learning to read …" (p. 597). We think this is a spurious claim for many of the same reasons that fluency is a misleading correlate of comprehension. First, we examine empirical evidence for the claims to illuminate the sources of misinterpretation, and then we analyze the conceptual and statistical problems with traditional claims about the positive relation. Longitudinal studies of literacy often include multiple measures of early reading and related skills (e.g., Wagner et al., 1997). These multivariate studies use various statistical methods to identify correlations, factors, and causal paths among the variables. In particular, there is a growing body of research on letter naming, letter-sound identification, and related measures of graphophonic knowledge. For example, McBride-Chang (1999) collected data on children's letter knowledge at four time-points and correlated the data with measures of word identification and phonological awareness. At time 1, letter knowledge had a mean of 12.4 (SD = 8.8). By time-point 4, the variable lost 60% of its variance and had a mean of 24.5 (SD = 3.4), near ceiling on the task. The effects of ceiling performance on the correlations with other variables were consistent and dramatic.

Correlations between letter knowledge and the "Word Attack" test decreased from r = .54 at time 1 to r = .23 at the final time point. Similarly, correlations between letter knowledge and phoneme elision decreased from r = .51 to r = .18. The same decreasing pattern was found for correlations between letter knowledge and every other predictor. Other researchers have described similar patterns of decreasing strength of letter knowledge in predictions of reading proficiency with increasing age (e.g., Johnston et al., 1996). Although some researchers describe this pattern as a consequence of the developmental trajectory of letter knowledge, it seems more prudent to interpret the changing correlations as artifacts of increasing skew in the variable as ceiling levels are approached. Stated differently, the constrained developmental trajectories of skills such as letter recognition and letter-sound correspondence necessarily reduce the strength of correlations as growth reaches asymptote and the variance diminishes.

A similar pattern of variable correlations is evident in other longitudinal investigations of print knowledge. Hecht, Burgess, Torgeson, Wagner, and Rashotte (2000) analyzed the effects of SES on children's early reading skills from kindergarten to fourth grade with a subset of the data used in previous research by Wagner et al. (1997). Among the 20 measures were three tasks used to assess Print Knowledge. Print Concepts included 13 items derived from Clay's (1979) "Concepts About Print" task, Letter Names required children to name all 26 uppercase letters, and Letter Sounds required children to provide sounds for letters shown on cards. These tasks were given to 197 children in the beginning of kindergarten and the data were correlated with other variables collected in the beginning of first, second, third, and fourth grades.

The canonical correlations of the three Print Knowledge tasks with the other 17 variables ranged from $rs = .24$ to .60, all significant at levels similar to previous research. The researchers used a measurement model based on factor analyses and created a latent factor for Print Knowledge composed of an aggregate of the three tasks. This factor was highly correlated with other latent factors across years. For example, Print Knowledge was correlated with Reading Comprehension at Grades 2, 3, and 4, respectively, with $rs = .74, .60,$ and $.53$. These are impressive correlations, but note the decline with age. Next, Hierarchical Linear Modeling (HLM) procedures were used to determine the amount of variance that each factor accounted for in the longitudinal predictions. The authors found that Print Knowledge scores at kindergarten accounted for significant variance in reading comprehension scores at Grade 2 (33%), Grade 3 (16%), and Grade 4 (9%), again a declining pattern. It should be noted that all other variables accounted for significant variance in reading comprehension across years with a general decline with increasing grade level. However, the variance accounted for ranged only between 2% to 19%. Print Knowledge was the strongest predictor of reading comprehension at grades 2 and 3.

Why Print Knowledge Is a Spurious Correlate of Reading Comprehension

Many researchers have used longitudinal data derived from assessments of children's Print Knowledge, Concepts About Print, Letter Naming, and Letter-Sound Identification to claim that these basic skills and knowledge are valid and reliable predictors of reading development (e.g., Muter, Hulme, Snowling, & Taylor, 1998). Unfortunately, the claims are spurious. The fundamental error in this kind of research is treating Print Knowledge variables as normally distributed. They are not, and all the subsequent statistical tests with these data that require normally distributed variables are wrong. Conceptually, it is obvious that recognizing and naming the 26 letters in the English alphabet is a highly constrained skill in two ways. First, the set of letters and knowledge to be mastered is finitely bound and small. Furthermore, all (or nearly all) the letter names and sounds must be mastered for proficient reading to develop. Second, Print Knowledge, alphabet recognition, and letter naming are skills that are constrained by a relatively brief age range of development. Few 4-year-olds know many letters and their sounds whereas most 7-year-olds know them all. In other words, for most children, they either know very few or nearly all the letters of the alphabet so floor and ceiling effects should be expected among children on all tasks involving Print Knowledge except for children in the 4- to 7-year-old range who are mastering the skills.

Of course, this is exactly the age range where the assessments are given, and some might say, it is the developmentally appropriate age. However, we think it is clear that Print Knowledge variables will only be normally distributed as a special case, when the task is given to children who know some but not all letter names and sounds. When the sample includes a large number of children with either little or great knowledge, the data exhibit floor and ceiling effects that minimize the variance in the measure and attenuate any correlations with other variables. Actually, there is zero predictive power for reading comprehension (or any other variable) when there are ceiling effects in the Print Knowledge data. Hecht et al. (2000) minimized the problem of ceiling effects by testing children at the beginning of kindergarten. Their data indicate mean scores on Print Concepts of 11.4 (maximum $= 18$; $SD = 4.1$), Letter Names of 21.2 (maximum $= 26$; $SD = 7.5$), and Letter Sounds of 10.4 (maximum $= 36$; $SD = 10.4$). It is not clear why the first measure has a maximum score of 18 on 13 items or why the Letter Sounds has a maximum of 36, but it is clear that the researchers avoided ceiling effects and there was adequate variability among the children. Those two features underlie the positive correlations they found in the data.

However, floor effects of constrained variables may exhibit strong correlations because low scores on one variable are associated with low scores on other reading variables. Like fluency measures, the low scores may reflect two different types of confounds: (a) interdependence between the skills, and (b) proxies for lack of other developmental skills and experiences. These factors influence the interpretations of correlations based on constrained variables such as Print

Knowledge. Three problems seem fundamentally important. First, Print Knowledge variables are correlated with many other features of children and their development so they may be serving only as proxies for other relations. This is the problem of multicolinearity that confounds all multivariate longitudinal studies, but it is often overlooked in the interpretations of canonical correlations. For example, Hecht et al. (2000) noted that the effects of SES were severely attenuated by 30% to 50% when Print Knowledge scores were controlled, so they concluded that, "… most of the SES related variance in growth of reading skills was accounted for by beginning kindergarten levels of print knowledge" (p. 119). These results led the authors to conclude the following:

> A practical consequence of the present results is that measures of reading related abilities should be included in test batteries used to identify beginning kindergarten children, particularly those from lower social class backgrounds, at risk for later reading failure …. In addition, the results suggest that preschool and kindergarten interventions involving intensive training in print knowledge, phonological awareness, and/or rate of access skills may help reduce the incidence of later reading failure among children from lower SES families …. (Hecht et al., 2000, p. 122)

In the Hecht et al. (2000) data, the researchers found that composite scores for SES and Print Knowledge were correlated at $r = .41$, and that when they controlled the effects of Print Knowledge on SES, the effects of SES were attenuated. This led them to conclude that kindergarten Print Knowledge mediated reading scores at Grades 3 and 4. However, we think it is more plausible to interpret Print Knowledge scores at kindergarten as measures of parental assistance and involvement in helping their children learn to read. Those kindergarten children who scored highly on Print Concepts, Letter Names, and Letter Sounds were most likely to have had more social supports and opportunities for reading, learning, and education than those kindergarten children who scored lower on these tasks. That should be expected by the strong correlation with SES and might be evident if other data were available, such as preschool experiences, parental education, parental time spent with children, or quality of children's literacy materials in the home. Therefore, knowing letter names in kindergarten is probably not the mediator of reading comprehension at Grades 3 and 4. Instead, home environment, SES, and many variables associated with parent–child interactions probably account for better comprehension in later grades, especially if those same factors continued to be influential several years later.

Aggregated Data Confound Constrained and Unconstrained Skills

Simplistic interpretations of correlations are easy to recognize, but the relations can be obscured in sophisticated statistical analyses. For example, researchers can aggregate data from different tasks to minimize floor and ceiling effects. The Hecht et al. (2000) data have highly skewed data for Letter Names that are aggregated with less skewed data on Print Concepts and Letter Sounds. When composite scores are created based on factor analyses or HLM or Item Response Theory (IRT), the result may be an artificially normalized distribution that is more influenced by scores on one measure than another. This problem is exacerbated when researchers aggregate data from highly constrained and less constrained variables. It is also evident when the data are transformed to normalize the distributions, when the sample size is so large that it includes many participants with floor and ceiling effects, and when the skewed data are blocked to create categorical data. For example, The Early Childhood Longitudinal Study—Kindergarten Class of 1998–99, confounds early reading measures with these practices and the aggregated variables obscure developmental differences among the component knowledge and skills (U.S. Department of Education, National Center for Education Statistics, 2000). These problems are rarely acknowledged. The underlying distributions are rarely described. Alternative explanations based on developmental proxies are rarely offered.

Transitory Relations Between Constrained Skills and Comprehension Are Unstable

Another interpretive problem is the transitory nature of the purported relation between Print Knowledge and reading comprehension. The only time that constrained variables provide distributions that approximate normal distributions and therefore include enough variance to exhibit relations with other variables is in the intermediate phase of learning. This is the time when children develop letter knowledge and naming that goes from a few to most letters. Most children learn the alphabet within a year or two, although there are large individual differences in the age of onset, rate of learning, and time of mastery. Thus, the predictive power of Letter Naming and Print Knowledge is restricted to a period of approximately a year or less when children know about half of the alphabet, or at least score near the midpoints on the reading assessments. These are transitory and changing relations, statistically as well as cognitively, and they only yield significant relations during a brief period of growth.

Walsh, Price, and Gillingham (1988) described the transitory relation problem as one of diminishing returns. They examined the longitudinal relations between letter naming accuracy and letter naming speed at kindergarten with reading development at Grade 2 on a multileveled reading inventory and the Gates-MacGinitie Reading test. The effects of speed and accuracy could be separated. Accuracy of Letter Naming improved from a mean of 67% correct at kindergarten to 100% correct at second grade. The correlation with later read-ing achievement was zero for the kindergarten data and meaningless for the sec-ond graders. The researchers found that letter-naming speed was a significant predictor of reading development and comprehension at kindergarten but not Grade 2. This interaction with grade suggests that Letter Naming has transitory importance. They hypothesized that there is a speed threshold for Letter Nam-ing and once the threshold is exceeded, there is little benefit of further increases in letter-naming speed. We think the analogous argument can be made about constrained skills. Once a skill exceeds a certain threshold, which is usually close to the mastery level, there is no further variance or predictive power in the variable. The diminishing returns hypothesis reflects (a) mastery of a con-strained skill, (b) within a narrow age range, (c) and nonlinear growth that reaches asymptotic levels. It appears to describe the case for Print Concepts, Letter Naming, and Letter-Sound correspondence variables.

The developmental changes in the relations between constrained variables and other reading skills are evident in a study by Hamilton and Paris (in prepa-ration). They analyzed data from 802 children in a 3-year longitudinal study (Christian, Morrison, & Bryant, 1998). Children's alphabet knowledge scores were correlated with vocabulary and reading scores within and across grade lev-els from kindergarten to Grade 3. Alphabet knowledge scores at kindergarten were correlated about $r = .5$ with vocabulary and reading growth scores at all grade levels, but the correlations dropped to zero when alphabet knowledge scores from Grades 1 and 2 were used. Why? It was because the alphabet knowl-edge scores were at ceiling levels after kindergarten and there was little variance left. In contrast, vocabulary scores were less constrained and exhibited correla-tions with other vocabulary and reading scores in the $r = .5$ to .7 range at all time-points in the longitudinal study.

Sampling Influences the Patterns of Relations Among Skills

A third interpretive problem concerns the sample of children used in a research study. Researchers choose participants who are unlikely to exhibit floor and ceiling effects on their tasks. For Print Concepts, Letter Names, and Letter Sounds, this usually implies a sample of kindergarten children, but it is clear that individual differences are important. If the sample includes many children with learning difficulties or children from lower SES homes or homes where English is not the first language, then floor effects in the data are likely. (Ironi-cally, these floor effects may actually inflate the artificial correlation between variables if the lack of one is associated with the lack of the other.) The degree of learning and mastery reflected in the scores on Print Knowledge variables will depend on the characteristics of the sample. Because the distribution of constrained variables is influenced so much by the characteristics of the sample, such as age and SES, it is the initial participant selection that determines the degree of relations observed among variables in the study. If a researcher samples kindergarten children in a university lab school, there may be ceiling effects and little variance in Print Knowledge. If the researcher samples randomly on a variable such as SES, there will be more variation in the sample on both SES and the constrained variable so there will be more chance of finding a significant correlation. Clearly, the underlying problem is that constrained variables are not normally distributed, and extreme bias and skewed data can be influenced by participant selection.

SUMMARY OF KEY POINTS ABOUT SPURIOUS CLAIMS

It may be worthwhile to summarize the main points in our challenges to conventional interpretations of early correlates of reading comprehension.

1. Many early reading skills are enabling skills that must be mastered in order for children to read.

2. Mastered skills are constrained in many ways, including the size of the set of elements or knowledge to be mastered, the prototypical or essential elements that must be mastered, the time period required for mastery, and the thresholds of performance required for reading and mastery.

3. Constrained skills are not normally distributed and yield normal distributions only in special cases when the sample of participants includes children who have learned only some of the knowledge or skills. Thus, constrained skills are skewed variables with floor and ceiling effects, but the degree of skew depends on characteristics of the particular sample.

4. Parametric statistics cannot be applied to data derived from constrained skills, even if the data are normally distributed in the particular sample, because normality assumptions violate the construct validity of the skills.

5. When data from constrained skills approximate normal distributions and are analyzed with conventional parametric statistics, the results indicate relations that are both spurious and transitory.

6. The empirical finding that lack of fluency or lack of mastery (i.e., threshold not attained) for a constrained skill is associated with a lack of progress on another skill or dimension may imply that the emergence or operation of the skills is interdependent. However, it does not imply a causal relation between an abundance of one skill and the abundance of another skill.

7. Constrained skills develop early in childhood or in the early phases of complex skill development and thus may be necessary precursors to expertise, but that does not make them sufficient enablers of later development.

8. Mastered skills are likely to be susceptible to multicolinearity so they may be proxies for many other variables and developmental changes.

9. It is important to help children master many constrained skills because they enable further development, but once the skills are mastered, they lose predictive power. Correlations with other variables decrease dramatically with increasing skill mastery because there is little variability left in the constrained skill assessments.

10. Skills with greater variability and normal distributions may exhibit stronger and more stable correlations with reading comprehension and achievement over time, but the statistical power of the relation is not necessarily the best guide for making decisions about what should be assessed or instructed. In other words, predictive validity should not be overemphasized when deciding instructional priorities.

GENUINE CORRELATES OF READING COMPREHENSION

In contrast to reading skills and knowledge that are limited in scope or duration of acquisition, other linguistic and cognitive skills contribute to reading development with more enduring longitudinal impact. These skills may begin to develop in young children, they may continue to develop into adulthood, and they may influence reading comprehension at all ages. Length limits of this chapter do not permit an exhaustive discussion of these skills, but we describe some longitudinal research on three related abilities: language skills, vocabulary, and narrative reasoning.

Language Skills

Storch and Whitehurst (2002) used structural equation modeling to map the relations among early code-related skills, language ability, and later reading skills of children from low-income families. A total of 626 4-year-olds who attended Head Start were assessed at six time-points, once per year from the spring of preschool through the spring of fourth grade. Children received a variety of oral language tasks in the spring of Head Start and kindergarten including tests of receptive and expressive vocabulary, narrative recall, conceptual knowledge, and syntactic ability. Children also received in preschool and kindergarten a battery of school readiness tasks from the Developing Skills Checklist (e.g., naming pictured letters, identifying sounds and letters, print concepts, printing first name, drawing a person).

After children began reading instruction, standardized tests were administered to assess reading achievement. In first grade, children received three tests of decoding skills, the Word Reading subscale from the Stanford Achievement Test (SAT), the Reading subscale of the Wide Range Achievement Test, and the Word Attack subscale of the Woodcock Reading Mastery Tests (WRMT). In second grade, students received Word Reading from the SAT, Word Attack from the WRMT, a Reading Comprehension subtest from the SAT, and Word Study Skills from the SAT. Decoding and comprehension scores were combined into a single factor in path model analyses. In third and fourth grade, children received Word Attack, Word Study Skills, and Reading Comprehension as well as the Reading Vocabulary subtest of the SAT; code-related and comprehension measures were analyzed separately at third and fourth grade.

High longitudinal continuity was shown within the oral language domain. Approximately 90% of the variance in children's oral language ability in kindergarten was accounted for by preschool language ability, 96% of the variance of oral language in Grades 1 to 2 was accounted for by kindergarten ability, and 88% of the variance of oral language in Grades 3 to 4 was accounted for by Grades 1 to 2 ability. In contrast, the continuity of code-related skills was much weaker—only 38% of the variance in kindergarten code-related skills was accounted for by preschool code-related skills. These results highlight the long-term stability of language as an individual difference characteristic in contrast to the temporary differences in constrained, code-related skills. Additionally, indirect influences were found between early language skills and later reading achievement. Oral language skills in Head Start had a significant indirect effect on kindergarten code-related skills (standardized coefficient for indirect effect = .72), Grade 1 reading ability (.55), Grade 2 reading ability (.58), Grades 3 to 4 Reading Accuracy (.43), and Grades 3 to 4 Reading Comprehension (.65). Oral language skills in kindergarten had a significant but weaker indirect effect on Grade 1 reading ability (.24), Grade 2 reading ability (.25), Grades 3 to 4 Reading Accuracy (.19), and Grades 3 to 4 Reading Comprehension (.43).

Butler, Marsh, Sheppard, and Sheppard (1985) examined the predictive relations between a battery of tests administered in kindergarten and various reading achievement tests administered at the end of the academic years in Grades 1, 2, 3, and 6. Multiple regressions with a set of eight predictor variables (psycholinguistic abilities, figure drawing, language, rhythm, perceptual motor skills, spatial/form perception, sex, and parent's language) showed that the language skills factor was the single most important predictor of reading achievement. It should be noted that six of the eight predictive variables represented factors, most of them comprised of a variety of skills. For example, the language factor included a nonsense syllables task, a semantic differentiation task, several narrative discourse tasks, and a task that assessed comprehension of spoken language. Such a factor might mask the unique contributions of different types of language and comprehension skills. For example, Speece, Roth, Cooper, and de la Paz (1999) found that oral language skills where more predictive of reading achievement for children who demonstrated high overall language ability.

In a short-term longitudinal study, Scarborough (1989) also examined the relations between a set of variables collected at age 5 and reading achievement at Grade 2. Predictor variables collected from the 5-year-olds included the General Cognitive Index from the McCarthy Scales of Children's Abilities, a measure of syntax, a measure of vocabulary, and several sections of readiness tests: the Visual Discrimination test from the California Achievement Test and three sections of the Stanford Early School Achievement Test (Story Comprehension, Word Reading, and Sounds and Letters). Information was also collected from parents about their children's reading and television viewing habits as well as their preschool experiences, and parents were asked to provide information about their own reading abilities and history of reading problems.

Correlations were examined between individual and familial measures and both Grade 2 reading performance on the Woodcock–Johnson Psycho-Educational Battery (WJP) and Grade 2 intelligence (as assessed by the Wechsler Intelligence Scale for Children–Revised). The WJP score is a composite based on three subtests: word recognition, pronunciation of pseudonyms, and comprehension of short prose passages. The only scores at age 5 that were correlated significantly with Grade 2 reading achievement were vocabulary ($r = .42$) and phonemic awareness ($r = .36$). In contrast, all scores at age 5 were significantly correlated with grade 2 intelligence, with syntax ($r = .45$), vocabulary ($r = .48$), and story comprehension ($r = .44$) being the most strongly correlated. This study used a reading ability score that combined decoding and comprehension skills, perhaps confounding the relations among early code-related, language, and comprehension skills with subsequent reading achievement

Vocabulary Skills

A second genuine predictor of reading comprehension is vocabulary, but it is embedded in children's early experiences and language development so the effects are not easily separated. Hart and Risley (1995) studied the early language experiences of 42 families from distinctly different social and educational backgrounds. They documented profound differences in the frequencies and uses of language among families. For example, they calculated that by age 4, children in professional families were exposed to 45 million words compared to only 13 million words heard by children in welfare families. Indeed, vocabulary growth at age 3 was correlated with family SES at $r = .65$. Exposure was significantly related to several features of children's cognitive and linguistic growth. For example, vocabulary use at age 3 correlated with scores at ages 9 to 10 years on the Peabody Picture Vocabulary Test (PPVT; $r = .57$), the Test of Language Development ($r = .74$), and the reading comprehension score on the Comprehensive Test of Basic Skills ($r = .56$). The quality and sheer quantity of language in children's early experiences can profoundly influence vocabulary development and may be part of the reason that it becomes a genuine predictor of IQ scores, academic achievement, and reading comprehension.

Other studies of vocabulary growth with older children confirm the importance of word learning and background knowledge for reading comprehension. For example, Cunningham and Stanovich (1997) examined the predictive relations of 27 students' receptive vocabulary skills as measured by the PPVT in first grade and their reading comprehension and vocabulary skills 10 years later, when the students were in the 11th grade. They found that receptive vocabulary skills at Grade 1 correlated modestly yet significantly with vocabulary scores in the 11th grade on both the PPVT ($r = .22, p < .05$) and the written vocabulary subtest of the Nelson–Denny Reading Test ($r = .19, p < .05$). Furthermore, first-grade vocabulary predicted 11th-grade comprehension scores on the Comprehension subtest of the Nelson–Denny Reading Test ($r = .33, p < .01$).

Tabors, Snow, and Dickenson (2001) examined the predictive relations between kindergartners' narrative production and receptive vocabulary skills as assessed by the PPVT-revised and their subsequent receptive vocabulary and reading comprehension skills in the fourth and seventh grades. The kindergarten narrative productive task, called the "Bear Story," required children to look at a sequence of three colored slides and then tell a story about them. Children's stories were coded for structure, story elements (e.g., conventional expressions, problem, outcome resolution), and syntactic complexity, so the score was an aggregate measure that included both language and narrative skills. Significant correlations were found between kindergartners' narrative production skills and both their reading comprehension and receptive vocabulary skills at fourth and seventh grades. Receptive vocabulary scores at kindergarten were also correlated significantly with comprehension and vocabulary scores at fourth and seventh grades. Emergent literacy at kindergarten was also strongly correlated with receptive vocabulary and reading comprehension at both grades. However, the aggregated measure of emergent literacy included scores for writing concepts, letter recognition, story and print concepts, sounds in the words, and environmental print, so it may be a confounded correlation.

Other studies of vocabulary growth with older children confirm the importance of word learning and background knowledge for reading comprehension. Stahl, Chou-Hare, Sinatra, and Gregory (1991) studied the impact of vocabulary and prior knowledge with high school students and found that strong vocabulary knowledge predicted the recall of more story elements. Prior knowledge influenced the type of information recalled; students with greater knowledge recalled more details regardless of their vocabulary knowledge.

Narrative Reasoning Skills

A third genuine predictor of reading comprehension is children's narrative reasoning, the ability to understand the elements and relations in goal-directed narratives typically found in children's literature, fables, films, and stories. Children's earliest socialization experiences promote the development of their narrative comprehension skills long before they begin to read. Narratives surround children from their earliest language experiences (Dickenson & Snow, 1987; Heath, 1982). Children as young as 2 to 3 years old develop a rich repertoire of knowledge about narrative (Stein & Albro, 1996), and they use their knowledge to communicate their needs, desires, plans, and frustrations. Young children become increasingly skilled at understanding and producing complex narrative stories (Dickenson & Tabors, 1991). Narratives become important for communication between adults and children because they are interwoven in daily experience. Parents model the construction of narrative for their children by telling personal and family stories in their presence (Fiese et al., 1999; McCabe & Peterson, 1991). Parents also co-narrate events with their children by providing scaffolding with questions and assisting them in "learning how to narrativize" (Pressley, 1996; Wiley, Rose, Burger, & Miller, 1998). Joint book-reading experiences help children learn to understand and produce narrative as they talk with parents about characters, actions, intentions, and endings (Dickenson & Smith, 1994; Morrow, 1985; Teale, 1986).

Not only does narrative reasoning develop before and independently from decoding, it can also be assessed without the demands of printed text. Children can be shown pictures, TV, films, or video displays, or they can listen to oral stories, before subsequent assessments of their comprehension of narrative elements and relations. In a series of three studies, Paris and Paris (2003) found that children in kindergarten through second grade exhibited progressively better narrative comprehension with increasing age and reading skills. The narrative comprehension (NC) assessment task is conducted in several phases (e.g., Picture Walk, Retelling, Prompted Comprehension) with a picture book with a clear story line but no words except the title. In the Prompted Comprehension phase, children are asked a series of 10 questions (half explicit and half implicit) about the setting, the characters' feelings, the plot, and so forth. Children's abilities to identify, infer, and understand the narrative elements and relations were consistently related to other measures of reading comprehension. Total comprehension scores on the NC task correlated significantly with the Gates–MacGinitie Reading Test Comprehension score ($r = .53, p < .01$), the Gates–MacGinitie Reading Test Vocabulary score ($r = .39, p < .05$), the QRI comprehension scores ($r = .26, p < .05$), and the QRI retelling ($r = .30, p < .01$). The NC task also was correlated with reading comprehension scores 1 year later. Children's NC Prompted Comprehension scores were correlated significantly with the Iowa Test of Basic Skills (ITBS) comprehension ($r = .52, p < .01$) and vocabulary ($r = .41, p < .01$) subscores. A similar predictive relation was reported by van Kraayenoord and Paris (1996) who found that Australian children's comprehension of wordless picture books at age 5 to 6 was related significantly to their standardized reading scores 2 years later.

Faegans and Appelbaum (1986) performed cluster analyses on language variables collected from 55 6- and 7-year-old learning disabled (LD) children and examined the relations between the different clusters and academic performance 1, 2, and 3 years later. It was hypothesized that children characterized by deficits in narrative skills, relative to other language skills, would be most at risk for general academic problems, especially in reading comprehension. Six variables were derived from a set of language measures that were collected from the children in the first year that they entered the study. The measures included assessments of children's syntactic skills, semantic skills based on a vocabulary test, narrative comprehension, narrative paraphrase, and two language output measures, the number of words in children's paraphrased stories, and the complexity of the language in the paraphrased stories.

Cluster analyses with these variables revealed a six-cluster solution. The LD children's scores were compared to scores from 66 non-LD children on the six clustering variables. The "Syntax" cluster included nine children who demonstrated normal ability in producing and understanding syntactic structures yet were below normal on all other skills, and the "Semantic" cluster included nine children who had superior vocabulary but had poor skills in all other areas. The "Hyperverbal" cluster included eight children who talked abundantly but the meaning and substance of their words were poor. The "Narrative" cluster included 15 children whose narrative skills exceeded their syntactic and semantic skills which were below normal, so they could understand and paraphrase narratives adequately with relatively little vocabulary and syntax. The "Superior Narrative" group included nine children whose narrative and language output skills were at superior levels. Cluster six, "Superior Syntax and Semantic," contained five children whose syntax and semantic skills were very high relative to average narrative and output skills.

Multivariate analyses of variance (MANOVAs) were then performed on the Reading Recognition, Reading Comprehension, and Math subtests of the Peabody Individualized Achievement Test over the next 3 consecutive years. The MANOVAs showed that the two narrative clusters had significantly stronger reading comprehension scores at year 1 and year 3 as well as significantly higher math achievement at all 3 years. The narrative clusters also had significantly higher reading recognition scores after 1 year, but no group differences between the clusters were found in reading recognition scores at years 2 and 3. Conversely, the three clusters showing the poorest academic performance were the "Syntax," "Semantics," and "Superior Syntax and Semantic" clusters. This study suggests that narrative skills are critically important in predicting reading outcomes, especially reading comprehension.

In a related series of studies, van den Broek et al. (in press) examined preschool children's comprehension of televised narratives. They showed 20-min episodes of children's television programs and presented 13-min audiotaped stories to children to compare the children's viewing and listening comprehension. Children recalled causally related events in the narratives better than other kinds of text relations, and their recall in viewing and listening conditions were highly correlated. Furthermore, preschoolers' comprehension of TV episodes predicted their standardized reading comprehension test scores in second grade. The predictive strength remained even when vocabulary and word identification skills were controlled in a regression analysis. Thus, narrative comprehension skills of preschoolers can be assessed with TV and picture books and has significant predictive validity for later reading comprehension. We think that narrative comprehension viewing and listening tasks can help teachers to focus on comprehension skills of young children even if the children have limited decoding skills, limited experience with books, or limited skills in speaking English.

CONCLUSIONS

For many years, researchers and educators have asserted that some early reading skills and knowledge are significant correlates of reading comprehension, that is, correlated concurrently at the same measurement time and correlated over time to show predictive validity. Fluent oral reading, letter naming, and letter-sound correspondence have abundant empirical evidence that they are correlated with children's reading comprehension, so our contention that these are spurious claims may be met with disbelief and resistance. Indeed, the implications of constrained skill theory may be even more controversial because the reach can be extended to many other measures of early reading and learning. For example, Concepts About Print (Clay, 1979) are constrained by the number of items in the assessment set, the number of core concepts that are required for beginning reading, the brief duration of mastery, and the floor and ceiling effects associated with the non-normal distribution of the skill. Measures of phonological awareness may also be subject to constraints that influence the distribution of the data that in turn influence the kinds of correlations that are possible among other variables. If these challenges to conventional views of early reading skills are upheld, it will require fundamental changes in the ways that children's reading is assessed, interpreted, and instructed. We identify some of those implications briefly in the following list.

First, we think that reading comprehension and the functional uses of reading should be the primary focus of educators. This means that instruction and assessment should give priority to benchmarks of appropriate understanding of text and the subsequent uses of the derived knowledge. The emphasis on meaning-making and text-using should occur from children's earliest encounters with print, wherever they occur.

Second, enabling or basic skills should still be taught early and thoroughly to children, but the focus should be on mastery rather than measurement. Letter names and sounds need to be mastered in kindergarten if not before to enable children to decode words. Print knowledge and book handling skills should also be among the earliest knowledge and skills mastered in kindergarten. Key features of phonological awareness and skills should be taught and mastered in the primary grades.

Third, assessments of early reading should identify constrained skills and knowledge as non-normally distributed data. Educators, parents, and policymakers should chart progress toward mastery, and clear expectations for mastery of various skills should be established. The use of parametric statistics with constrained skills to assess reliability and validity should be avoided.

Fourth, reading researchers should reexamine longitudinal data sets to assess skewed data, sample characteristics, and the effects of constrained variables on their statistics and interpretations. Revised data analyses and interpretations should be published, especially for cases that have been used to establish policies for reading instruction and assessment.

Fifth, publishers of commercial assessments and state educational agencies should reconsider the ways that constrained skills are assessed, analyzed, reported, and interpreted. All tests that purport to measure letter naming, letter-sound correspondence, print concepts, oral reading accuracy, reading rate, and similar constrained skills as normally distributed skills should be revised to show expected rates of learning and mastery.

REFERENCES

Adams, M. J. (1990). *Beginning to read: Thinking and learning about print*. Cambridge, MA: MIT Press.

Butler, S., Marsh, H., Sheppard, M., & Sheppard, J. (1985). Seven-year longitudinal study of the early prediction of reading achievement. *Journal of Educational Psychology, 77*, 349–361.

Carpenter, R. D., & Paris, S. G. (2004). *Developmental disjunction between oral reading fluency and reading comprehension*. Manuscript submitted for publication.

Carver, R. P., & Hoffman, J. V. (1981). The effect of practice through repeated reading on gain in reading ability using a computer-based instructional system. *Reading Research Quarterly, 16*, 374–390.

Chall, J. S. (1967). *Learning to read: The great debate*. New York: McGraw-Hill.

Christian, K., Morrison, F. J., & Bryant, F. B. (1998). Predicting kindergarten academic skills: Interactions among childcare, maternal education, and family literacy environments. *Early Childhood Research Quarterly, 13*, 501–521.

Clay, M. M. (1979). *An observation survey of early literacy achievement*. Portsmouth, NH: Heinemann.

Cunningham, A. E., & Stanovich, K. E. (1997). Early reading acquisition and its relation to reading experience and ability 10 years later. *Developmental Psychology, 33*, 934–945.

Deno, S. L. (1985). Curriculum-based measurement: The emerging alternative. *Exceptional Children, 52*, 219–232.

Dickenson, D. K., & Smith, M. W. (1994). Long-term effects of preschool teachers' book readings on low-income children's vocabulary and story comprehension. *Reading Research Quarterly, 29*, 105–121.

Dickenson, D. K., & Snow, C. E. (1987). Interrelationships among prereading and oral language skills in kindergartners from two social classes. *Early Childhood Research Quarterly, 2*, 1–26.

Dickenson, D. K., & Tabors, P. O. (1991). Early literacy: Linkages between home, school, and literacy achievement at age five. *Journal of Research in Childhood Education, 6*, 30–46.

Dowhower, S. L. (1987). Effects of repeated reading on second-grade transitional readers' fluency and comprehension. *Reading Research Quarterly, 22*, 389–406.

Faegans, L., & Appelbaum, M. (1986). Validation of language subtypes in learning disabled children. *Journal of Educational Psychology, 78*, 358–364.

Fiese, B. H., Sameroff, A. J., Grotevant, H. D., Wamboldt, F. S., Dickstein, S., & Fravel, D. L. (1999). The stories that families tell: Narrative coherence, narrative interaction, and relationship beliefs. *Monographs of the Society for Research in Child Development, 64*(2), 1–162.

Fuchs, L. S., Fuchs, D., Hosp, M. K., & Jenkins, J. R. (2001). Oral reading fluency as an indicator of reading competence: A theoretical, empirical, and historical analysis. *Scientific Studies of Reading, 5*, 241–258.

Gates, A. I. (1940). A further evaluation of reading readiness tests. *Elementary School Journal, 40*, 577–591.

Good, R. H., & Kaminski, R. A. (Eds.). (2002). *Dynamic indicators of basic early literacy skills* (6th ed.). Eugene, OR: Institute for the Development of Educational Achievement.

Hamilton, E. E., & Paris, S. G. (2004). *Why alphabet knowledge is not an appropriate predictor of reading development*. Manuscript in preparation.

Hart, B., & Risley, T. R. (1995). *Meaningful differences in the everyday experience of young American children*. Baltimore: Brookes.

Hasbrouck, J. E., Ihnot, C., & Rogers, G. H. (1999). "Read Naturally": A strategy to increase oral reading fluency. *Reading Research and Instruction, 39*(1), 27–37.

Hasbrouck, J. E., & Tindal, G. (1992). Curriculum-based oral reading fluency norms for students in grades 2 through 5. *TEACHING Exceptional Children, 24*(3), 41–44.

Heath, S. B. (1982). What no bedtime story means: Narrative skills at home and school. *Language in Society, 11*, 49–76.

Hecht, S. A., Burgess, S. R., Torgeson, J. K., Wagner, R. K., & Rashotte, C. A. (2000). Explaining social class differences in growth of reading skills from beginning kindergarten through fourth-grade: The role of phonological awareness, rate of access, and print knowledge. *Reading and Writing: An Interdisciplinary Journal, 12*, 99–127.

Johns, J. L. (1997). *Basic reading inventory* (7th ed.). Dubuque, IA: Kendall/Hunt.

Johnston, R. S., Anderson, M., & Holligan, C. (1996). Knowledge of the alphabet and explicit awareness of phonemes in pre-readers: The nature of the relationship. *Reading and Writing: An Interdisciplinary Journal, 8*, 217–234.

Kibby, M. W. (1979). Passage readability affects the oral reading strategies of disabled readers. *The Reading Teacher, 32*, 390–396.

Kintsch, W. (1998). *Comprehension: A paradigm for cognition*. New York: Cambridge University Press.

Koshkinen, P. S., Blum, I. H., Bisson, S. A., Phillips, S. M., Creamer, T. S., & Baker, T. K. (2000). Book access, shared reading, and audio models: The effects of supporting the literacy learning of linguistically diverse students in school and at home. *Journal of Educational Psychology, 92*, 23–36.

Kranzler, J. H., Brownell, M. T., & Miller, M. D. (1998). The construct validity of curriculum-based measurement of reading: An empirical test of a plausible rival hypothesis. *Journal of School Psychology, 36*, 399–415.

Kuhn, M. R., & Stahl, S. A. (2003). Fluency: A review of developmental and remedial practices. *Journal of Educational Psychology, 95*, 3–21.

LaBerge, D., & Samuels, S. J. (1974). Toward a theory of automatic information processing in reading. *Cognitive Psychology, 6*, 293–323.

Leslie, L., & Caldwell, J. (1995). *The Qualitative Reading Inventory–II*. Glenview, IL: Scott, Foresman.

Linn, R. L., Baker, E. L., & Betebenner, D. W. (2002). Accountability systems: Implications of requirements of the No Child Left Behind Act of 2001. *Educational Researcher, 31*(6), 3–16.

Lipson, M. Y., & Wixson, K. K. (2003). *Assessment and instruction of reading and writing difficulty*. Boston: Allyn & Bacon.

Lonigan, C. J., Burgess, S. R., & Anthony, J. L. (2000). Development of emergent literacy and early reading skills in preschool children: Evidence from a latent-variable longitudinal study. *Developmental Psychology, 36*, 596–613.

McBride-Chang, C. (1999). The ABCs of the ABCs: The development of letter-name and letter-sound knowledge. *Merrill-Palmer Quarterly, 45*, 285–308.

McCabe, A., & Peterson, C. (1991). *Developing narrative structure*. Hillsdale, NJ: Lawrence Erlbaum Associates.

Morrow, L. M. (1985). Reading and retelling stories: Strategies for emergent readers. *The Reading Teacher, 38*(9), 870–875.

Muter, V., Hulme, C., Snowling, M., & Taylor, S. (1998). Segmentation, not rhyming, predicts early progress in learning to read. *Journal of Experimental Child Psychology, 71,* 3–27.

National Reading Panel. (2000). *Teaching children to read: An evidence-based assessment of the scientific research literature on reading and its implications for reading instruction: Reports of the subgroups.* Bethesda, MD: National Institute of Child Health and Human Development.

No Child Left Behind Act of 2001, Pub. L. No. 107–110, paragraph 115, Stat. 1425.

Paris, S. G., & Paris, A. H. (2001). Classroom applications of research on self-regulated learning. *Educational Psychologist, 36,* 89–101.

Paris, A. H., & Paris, S. G. (2003). Assessing narrative comprehension in young children. *Reading Research Quarterly, 38,* 36–76.

Paris, S. G., Pearson, P. D., Cervetti, G., Carpenter, R., Paris, A. H., DeGroot, J., Mercer, M., Schnabel, K., Martineau, J., Papanastasiou, E., Flukes, J., Humphrey, K., & Bashore-Berg, T. (2004). Assessing the effectiveness of summer reading programs. In G. Borman & M. Boulay (Eds.), *Summer learning: Research, policies, and programs* (pp. 121–161). Mahwah, NJ: Lawrence Erlbaum Associates.

Pinnell, G. S., Pikulski, J. J., Wixson, K. K., Campbell, J. R., Gough, P. B., & Beatty, A. S. (1995). *Listening to children read aloud: Data from NAEP's Integrated Reading Performance Record (IRPR) at grade 4* (Report No. 23-FR-04). Washington DC: U.S. Department of Education, Office of Educational Research and Improvement.

Pressley, M. (1996). More about the development of narrative skills. *Issues in Education, 2,* 69–72.

RAND Reading Study Group. (2002). *Reading for understanding: Toward an R&D program in reading comprehension.* Santa Monica, CA: RAND.

Riddle-Buly, M., & Valencia, S. W. (2002). Below the bar: Profiles of students who fail state reading assessments. *Educational Evaluation and Policy Analysis, 24,* 219–239.

Roller, C. M. (1994). Teacher–student interaction during oral reading and rereading. *Journal of Reading Behavior, 26,* 191–209.

Samuels, S. J. (1979). The method of repeated reading. *The Reading Teacher, 32,* 403–408.

Scarborough, H. (1989). Prediction of reading disability from familial and individual differences. *Journal of Educational Psychology, 81,* 101–108.

Share, D. L., Jorm, A. F., Maclean, R., & Matthews, R. (1984). Sources of individual differences in reading acquisition. *Journal of Educational Psychology, 76,* 1309–1324.

Speece, D. L., Roth, F. P., Cooper, D. H., & de la Paz, S. (1999). The relevance of oral language skills to early literacy: A multivariate analysis. *Applied Psycholinguistics, 20,* 167–190.

Stahl, S. A., Chou-Hare, V., Sinatra, R., & Gregory, J. F. (1991). Defining the role of prior knowledge and vocabulary in reading comprehension: The retiring of Number 41. *Journal of Reading Behavior, 23,* 487–508.

Stanovich, K. E. (1980). Toward an interactive-compensatory model of individual differences in the development of reading fluency. *Reading Research Quarterly, 16,* 32–71.

Stein, N. L., & Albro, E. R. (1996). The emergence of narrative understanding: Evidence for rapid learning in personally relevant contexts. *Issues in Education, 2,* 83–98.

Stevenson, H. W., & Newman, R. S. (1986). Long-term prediction of achievement and attitudes in mathematics and reading. *Child Development, 57,* 646–659.

Storch, S., & Whitehurst, G. (2002). Oral language and code-related precursors to reading: Evidence from a longitudinal structural model. *Developmental Psychology*, 38, 934–947.

Tabors, P., Snow, S., & Dickenson, D. (2001). Homes and schools together: Supporting language and literacy development. In D. Dickenson & P. Tabors (Eds.), *Beginning literacy with language* (pp. 313–334). Baltimore: Brookes.

Taft, M. L., & Leslie, L. (1985). The effects of prior knowledge and oral reading accuracy on miscues and comprehension. *Journal of Reading Behavior*, 17, 163–179.

Teale, W. H. (1986). Home background and young children's literacy development. In W. H. Teale & E. Sulzby (Eds.), *Emergent literacy: Writing and reading*. Norwood, NJ: Ablex.

Tuinman, J. J. (1973–1974). Determining the passage dependency of comprehension questions in 5 major tests. *Reading Research Quarterly*, 9(2), 206–223.

U.S. Department of Education, National Center for Education Statistics. (2000). *Early Childhood Longitudinal Study, Kindergarten Class of 1998–99*. Washington, DC: U.S. Department of Education, Office of Educational Research and Improvement.

van Kraayenoord, C. E., & Paris, S. G. (1996). Story construction from a picture book: An assessment activity for young learners. *Early Childhood Research Quarterly*, 11, 41–61.

Wagner, R. K., Torgeson, J. K., Rashotte, C. A., Hecht, S. A., Barker, T. A., & Burgess, S. R., et al. (1997). Changing relations between phonological processing abilities and word-level reading as children develop from beginning to skilled readers: A 5-year longitudinal study. *Developmental Psychology*, 33, 468–479.

Walsh, D. J., Price, G. G., & Gillingham, M. G. (1988). The critical but transitory importance of letter naming. *Reading Research Quarterly*, 23, 108–122.

Wiley, A. R., Rose, A. J., Burger, L. K., & Miller, P. J. (1998). Constructing autonomous selves through narrative practices: A comparative study of working-class and middle-class families. *Child Development*, 69, 833–847.

Wilson, F., & Flemming, C. (1940). Grade trends in reading progress in kindergarten and primary grades. *Journal of Educational Psychology*, 31, 1–13.

7

The "Word Factors": A Problem for Reading Comprehension Assessment

Steven A. Stahl
University of Illinois, Urbana-Champaign

Elfrieda H. Hiebert
University of California, Berkeley

If we were to ask experts on reading comprehension, such as the contributors to this volume, how they define "reading comprehension," answers might range from making meaning from text to thinking critically about the text. Our guess would be that none of these scholars would mention word recognition, even in elaborated definitions. Many models of reading comprehension, such as those of Kintsch (1998) and Anderson and Pearson (1984), begin once words are recognized, as in "supposing the reader recognizes the words in the text, here is how comprehension proceeds ..."

Yet, from a psychometric perspective, word recognition plays an important role in reading comprehension. Studies that include both measures of word recognition and reading comprehension (which were surprisingly difficult to find) find strong correlations between the two variables, not only in the primary grades, but also through the higher grades (e.g., Carver, 2000). This was found for both word recognition in and out of context, in paragraphs and in lists.

Word meaning also plays an important role both in word recognition and in reading comprehension. Some (e.g., Carver, 2000; Thorndike, 1972), in fact, have suggested that a person's knowledge of word meanings is so closely correlated to their ability to comprehend text that the two constructs are almost identical. We do not want to make as strong a claim here, but the consistently high correlations between vocabulary and reading comprehension need to be taken into account in any theory of comprehension assessment. Word meaning is also related to word recognition. Words that are meaningful to a reader are recognized faster and more accurately than words whose meaning is unknown, including nonwords (e.g., Adams, 1990).

We present this as a problem to theories of reading comprehension assessment. If these word factors account for significant proportions of variance in reading comprehension, as they seem to do, then this leaves less variance that can be accounted for by differences in higher order processes. It becomes increasingly possible to suggest, as some have, that comprehension will take care of itself after accounting for fluent and automatic word recognition. This position has profound implications for both assessment and instruction. The strong position of this relation is not just a "straw man" argument. This argument has been used to make a number of claims including calls for more phonics instruction, even in the middle grades. We believe that the strong version of this position is wrong. However, to understand why is it wrong, one must understand how fluent word recognition, vocabulary, and reading comprehension relate to each other. Instead, we suggest that words do matter in reading comprehension, but that word knowledge, both word recognition and knowledge of word meanings, interact with other sources of knowledge to affect reading comprehension.

ASSUMPTIONS, SPOKEN AND UNSPOKEN

A Simple View of Reading

There is an assumption about the nature of reading that supports this strong view of the relation between fluent word recognition and comprehension. This assumption is exemplified by the "Simple View of Reading" (Gough & Tumner, 1986). Gough and Tumner (1986) suggested that Reading (or reading comprehension; R) can be discussed in terms of two factors—the ability of children to decode words quickly (D) and efficiently and their language comprehension (C). This view can be expressed in the equation:

$$R = D \times C$$

If we think of these variables as ranging from zero (or complete inability) to 1 (or complete ability), reading comprehension skill can be thought of as the product of a person's decoding and language comprehension. People who cannot decode a text will not be able to comprehend a written version, regardless of their knowledge of the language of the text. Similarly, people with perfect decoding ability will not comprehend a text if they do not understand the language of the text. This is true of hyperlexics reading in their native language or people reading phonetically regular foreign languages without knowledge of that language. The "Simple View" has been tested by Carver (1993, 2000) and Hoover and Gough (1990), who found that, as a metaphor if not as an equation, it captures quite well the importance of both word recognition and language comprehension. Both studies found that, once word recognition and language variables were entered into a regression equation, the only remaining variance was test error. In this view, once a child can read fluently (or that $D = 1$), then any variation in comprehension is due to his or her language understanding. That is, once the written text is transparent, the reader can look through the words to the meaning of the language contained within.

The Simple View is an extension of LaBerge and Samuels's (1974) classic model of reading. In this theory, the mind is seen as a limited capacity information processor, capable of paying attention to only a limited number of operations at any given time. LaBerge and Samuels suggested that some operations are nonautomatic or demand attention and others are automatic or do not demand attention. Processes involved in comprehension, especially those involving certain inferences or critical judgment, will always demand attention. If word recognition is automatic, then the reader can devote a larger proportion of cognitive resources to comprehension, especially the attention-demanding aspects of comprehension. If word recognition is nonautomatic, as in younger children who have to concentrate on decoding, then less attention is available for comprehension.

That this theory is still cited in discussions of fluency is a testament to its classic nature. We know of only one theorist who has extended LaBerge and Samuels' (1974) model—Logan and colleagues (Logan, Taylor, & Etherton, 1999). Logan et al. (1999) suggested that automaticity can be thought of in terms of speed, obligatoriness, and availability of resources. As a response moves toward automaticity, it follows a power curve. That is, increases in speed will be greater at the beginning of learning than they will be as the response becomes close to automatic, or that gains in speed will move toward an asymptote. Once a response is automatic, a person cannot not perform it. An example would be the Stroop Task, in which the child is asked to identify a particular color or picture while ignoring a printed label as when the word "green" is presented in blue ink. Identification of the color ("blue") would be hampered by obligatory processing of the word ("green"). Thus, automatic responses are also obligatory. Similar to the LaBerge and Samuels' model, the result of automatic processing in Logan et al.'s model means that the reader has more resources available for nonautomatic or thoughtful processes.

Being Fluent is More Than Being Fast

One problem with the Simple View is that word recognition is not independent of a person's language knowledge. Gough and Tumner (1986) seemed to imply that their decoding factor is a measure of the reader's automaticity of word recognition. First, word recognition is affected by the word's semantic properties. When the recognition of words in isolation has been studied, it has been found that known words are recognized more quickly and accurately than unknown words and nonsense words (Adams, 1990). Further, semantic properties of words, such as their concreteness and abstractness (Schwanenflugel & Akin, 1994), affect both children's and adults' recognition of words. A model such as that of Adams (1990) posits that word knowledge is connected to lexical knowledge, so that semantic factors will affect readers' recognition of words. Recognizing words is more than a function of quickly executing decoding algorithms. Knowledge of the word's meaning affects even activities such as finding a letter embedded in a word, as unsemantic a task as one could find (Gibson & Levin, 1975).

Second, and more important, recognizing words in context is more than simply serial recognition of words in isolation. We prefer to discuss "fluent reading" rather than automatic word recognition. Fluent reading is when a reader's recognition of words in context is so transparent that readers are able to move from the text to comprehension without conscious attention to words. When we hear such a reader read orally, it seems natural and "language-like." Of course, fluent reading does not have to be oral. In fact, fluent readers spend more of their time reading silently. This involves more than just recognizing words quickly in isolation. It also involves prosody (Kuhn & Stahl, 2003; Schwanenflugel, Hamilton, Kuhn, Wisenbaker, & Stahl, in press). Prosody refers to the language-like quality of the reading, including the preservation of suprasegmental features that signal syntactic relations (Schwanenflugel et al., in press). This includes the drop in pitch at the end of a declarative sentence and the rise in pitch at the end of a question.

We discuss these three components of fluent reading—accuracy, rate, and prosody—and their contributions to comprehension in turn.

ACCURACY AND COMPREHENSION

The relations between reading accuracy, usually oral, and comprehension have traditionally been studied through informal reading inventories and the use of oral reading accuracy to establish appropriate levels for instruction. This body of research dates back at least to the work of Betts (1946), and probably before that. We examine, first, evidence for the word recognition levels established for instructional, independent, and frustration designations on informal reading inventories (IRIs) and oral reading measures.

Word Recognition Levels and Comprehension on Informal Reading Inventories

Traditionally, an "instructional level," or the level at which a child can benefit from instruction, is that level at which the child can read with 95% to 98% accuracy (Betts, 1946). This level is used in most IRIs (Johns, 1997, pp. 87–96). There are other views of the appropriate level of accuracy. Clay (1993) suggested that first graders in Reading Recovery programs read material that they can read with 90% accuracy. Stahl, Heubach, and Cramond (1997) found that children could benefit from instruction in texts that they could originally read with an 85% accuracy level in a program—Fluency Oriented Reading Instruction (FORI)—that involved repeated reading and other instructional support. In programs such as Reading Recovery or FORI, where substantial support is provided to readers, children might be able to benefit from more difficult texts. Taft and Leslie (1985) found no difference in comprehension as measured by free recall or questions whether students read with 95% to 99% accuracy or with 90% to 94% accuracy.

Using standardized measures of word recognition and comprehension, Kendall and Hood (1979) identified struggling readers with good comprehension but poor word recognition and those with poor comprehension but adequate word recognition. Those students with good comprehension but poor word recognition were found to make more use of contextual information in oral reading of two short stories. In addition, their rate was significantly slower than that of the children with adequate word recognition, suggesting that their gains in comprehension came at a cost of slower reading.

Paris, Carpenter, Paris, and Hamilton (this volume) found similar groupings with both struggling and normally achieving readers. They found a greater tendency for older readers (fourth-, fifth- and sixth-graders in their study) to be in the low comprehension and high accuracy group, suggesting that there is a separation between comprehension and accuracy, especially as children get past the third grade. Paris and Carpenter (2003) presented two studies, each with a different set of children, given different IRIs at two different time points apiece. They found the same pattern of correlations across each replication. Basically, accuracy on the IRI correlated significantly with passage comprehension only at the achievement levels below third grade. Above third grade, the correlations were nonsignificant and some were even negative.

A similar developmental trend was found by Willson and Rupley (1997). Using structural equation modeling, they found that phonemic knowledge (the ability to decode words) appeared to drive comprehension in Grades 2 and 3, but its effects diminished in the upper grades. By third grade, background knowledge and strategy knowledge became more important (see also Rupley & Willson, 1997).

Similarly, the Oral Reading Special Study, conducted as part of the National Assessment of Educational Progress (NAEP; Pinnell, Pikulski, Wixson, Campbell, Gough, & Beatty, 1995), found no significant relations between oral reading accuracy of the fourth-graders they examined and their fluency rating scale. Fluency, in turn, was significantly related to comprehension. In their sample, the majority of children read the test passage at an accuracy rate above 94%, possibly restricting the range of possible correlations. However, similar to Kendall and Hood (1979) and Paris and Carpenter (2003), Pinnell et al. (1995) found sizable numbers of children who were accurate, but nonfluent.

Pinnell et al. (1995) divided students into one of four fluency groups based on ratings of experimenters: 1 = word-by-word reading; 2 = mostly two-word phrases; 3 = 3- or 4-word phrase groups; and 4 = larger, meaningful phrase groups. The accuracy percentages of the two less fluent groups (1 and 2) did not differ much from those of the two more fluent groups (3 and 4): 94 for each of the former and 96 and 97 for the two latter groups. However, the average words-per-minute rates were substantially different: 65, 89, 126, and 162, respectively, for fluency groups 1, 2, 3, and 4.

In a follow-up analysis, Pinnell et al. (1995) examined the distribution of students in the four fluency groups according to five accuracy groups: 99%, 97%, 96%, and less than 94%. The majority (about two thirds) of students in the two less fluent groups were in the two lowest accuracy groups. However, approximately one third of the less fluent students had accuracy levels of 96% or higher. These data indicate that there are students who were rated as nonfluent but who read relatively accurately. Because Pinnell et al. (1995) did not simultaneously present data for rate and accuracy, it is not possible to determine whether these fourth-graders had the same rate or accuracy trade-off as in the Kendall and Hood (1979) study, but it is possible to speculate that they did. Thus, it appears that accuracy alone (at least in Grades three and higher) does not seem to be sufficient for comprehension, at least within a certain band.

Miscue Analysis

A widely held view in the field of reading suggests that oral reading accuracy reflects children's construction of meaning during reading, as much as it reflects
their word recognition skill. Goodman (1968) suggested that readers use a variety of types of knowledge when reading words in context, including knowledge
of syntax, prior knowledge of the topic of the text, ongoing information gained
from context, as well as knowledge of grapheme-phoneme relations (see Clay,
1993). When confronted with challenging texts, readers' ongoing construction
of meaning is evidenced by miscues that reflect the meaning of the text, as evidenced by both semantic and syntactic similarity, and, when a miscue does not
make sense, that miscue is corrected.

Goodman and Goodman (1977; Goodman, Watson, & Burke, 1987) have developed an extensive system of miscue analysis in which miscues, or deviations from
the text in oral reading, are analyzed by asking a series of questions about the miscues and self-corrections. The question areas include syntactic acceptability (presence of miscue in same grammatical form class as the text word); semantic
acceptability (whether the miscue makes sense in the passage or sentence or part of
the sentence); meaning change (the degree of meaning change related to what the
teacher or researcher expects the meaning to be); correction (whether the reader
self-corrected); and graphic similarity and sound similarity (the degree to which the
graphophonic system is being used during reading). Questions about the type of acceptability can be asked at the passage, sentence, partial sentence, and word levels.

Goodman (1968, Goodman & Goodman, 1977) considered grapheme-phoneme knowledge the least important of these knowledge sources, arguing that efficient reading requires the reader to orchestrate the knowledge of the topic and
ongoing context with knowledge of the syntactic structure of the language to predict possible meanings for each word encountered, using a minimal amount of visual information to confirm the predictions. There is ample evidence to
disconfirm the strong version of his theory, that readers proceed through text actively predicting the identity of each word in turn, relying heavily on context (see
Nicholson, 1991; Stanovich, 2000). However, there is also ample evidence that
readers are somewhat better at reading words in context than they are in isolation, although this effect is smaller than Goodman suggested (Nicholson, 1991)
and may be more important for struggling readers than for proficient readers (e.g.,
Stanovich, 2000). For example, Adams (1998) found that children read irregu-
larly spelled words better in sentences than in lists.

There have been a number of criticisms of this model (see Allington, 1984,
for a review), but its influence is undeniable. The presence of meaning-accept-

able miscues suggests that if proficient readers perceive miscues as semantically acceptable, they will proceed through the text, believing that they are understanding the text. If the miscue is not acceptable, they will correct it. Clay (1991) has taken this pattern as evidence that beginning readers have developed a "self-extending system." That is, they are able to orchestrate the various cues in the text to learn words. From this model, the pattern of miscues described by Goodman (1983) and Clay has been used as evidence that beginning readers are comprehending the text. Consequently, for some educators (e.g., Fountas & Pinnell, 1996), the pattern of miscues is used as a measure of comprehension, in addition to oral reading.

Within the extensive research on readers' miscues (see Allington, 1984, for a review), researchers have found the most variation in behavior among beginning readers, usually first graders, but also with older, struggling readers. For example, Biemiller (1970) found three stages in children's miscues. The miscues of very beginning readers produced words that made sense in the story, but had little graphical relation to the text word. After this emergent phase, Biemiller found that children would not respond to words they did not know. After this period of nonresponse, children would produce miscues that were both semantically acceptable and graphically similar to the text word. Similar developmental patterns were found by Sulzby (1985) in her observations of young children's attempts at storybook reading.

The children Biemiller (1970) studied were in "meaning-oriented" programs, in which the emphasis was on constructing meaning during reading. Barr (1974) found different patterns in the initial miscues of children in meaning-emphasis and code-emphasis programs (see also Cohen, 1974). Barr found that children generally adhered to the approach they were taught, with phonics-taught children sounding words out more often and sight word-taught children using more visual strategies. Barr and Cohen both found that children in code-emphasis programs gave nonsense words for between 15% and 28% of their substitutions in oral reading. Connelly, Johnston, and Thompson (1999) found that 38% of the oral reading errors made by children involved in intensive phonics instruction were nonsense words. Similarly, in Cohen's study of children in phonics instruction, 30% of all substitutions made by good readers and 2% of those made by poor readers were self-corrected. Similar patterns were found more recently by Johnston and Watson (1997), who examined reading instruction in Scotland in which strong phonic emphasis programs were contrasted with whole language programs. This suggests that, in these older programs, children taught with a phonics emphasis were not viewing reading as a meaningful act.

However, in current reading instruction, even the most explicit phonics instruction stresses the importance of meaning. Stahl, McCartney, and Montero

(2004) found that children's miscues did not vary as a result of programs which all emphasized decoding and some degree of comprehension. Children in that study self-corrected a high percentage of miscues and rarely produced nonsense words. Even these program differences seem to wash out by the time students' proficiency reaches late first-grade or second-grade levels (Allington, 1984). The vast majority of children who have reached that proficiency make semantically acceptable miscues and self correct those which are not. Although this brief review necessarily oversimplifies a rich literature, a conclusion that can be drawn is that children's reading miscues seem to be due to initial differences in instruction and to lack of proficiency at the initial stages of reading in orchestrating various cues to maintain ongoing meaning during reading.

What Do We Mean by "Comprehension"?

The preceding discussion assumes that comprehension is unitary; that is, one can comprehend more or less. Instead, we feel that it is important that we think about comprehension as a set of interacting processes, and that word recognition difficulties will impact comprehension in different ways.

Kintsch's (1998; Kintsch & Kintsch, this volume) construction-integration (CI) model suggests that representational models, or the mental models of the information learned from the text, are mediated in interactions with written texts. Kintsch's model supports the notion that representation of texts is cyclical and ongoing and that lower and higher systems inform and extend each other. All of Kintsch's work has been done with adults and "developed" readers. Basically, CI is a bottom-up constraint-satisfaction theory. It addresses two stages of psychological processing that occur during reading. During construction, concepts from the text are activated to produce a network of activated mental concepts. This may be represented as a set of propositions in a hierarchy, with some propositions being higher (more important) in the hierarchy and others lower (Kintsch & van Dijk, 1978) or as a network of propositions. In the second stage, integration, the network concepts that are compatible with the context enhance the activation of one another, whereas concepts that are not compatible with the context lose activation. "Thus, comprehension arises from an interaction and fusion between text information and knowledge activated by the comprehender" (McNamara & Kintsch, 1996, p. 251). The product of the CI process is a unitary mental representation structured from the text-based and situation model. The textbase consists of elements directly derived from the text. According to Kintsch (this volume, McNamara & Kintsch, 1996), this is a propositional network that would yield an impoverished and incoherent network without the addition of the links brought by the reader based on his or her prior knowledge and experience.

Without adequate background knowledge, the textbase will predominate in the comprehension process. That is, the representation might appear fragmented or as a list of "facts" without much coherence. Without an adequate textbase, the representation would rely more heavily on the reader's knowledge and experience. The reader's previous knowledge might intrude into their representation for the text, even when that information was not in the text or was contradicted by text information. The more knowledge and experience brought to the text, the greater the influence of the situation model. This influence can take the form of elaborations and cognitive integration of the text or a disregard for the text. Ideally, we are striving for a balance of text-derived and situation model contributions to comprehension.

Miscues and Microprocesses. Even if substantial variations in miscues occurred after the initial stages of reading, what would they tell us about the relation between oral reading and comprehension? Consider the following sets of miscues for the text line:

(IS A, DAY, WARM)
　　(DAY, SUMMER)

If we were to analyze the original sentence in terms of propositional analysis (Kintsch, 1974), we would have two propositions, the second subordinate to the first:

Text:　It was a warm summer day.
Child$_1$:　It was a warm *spring* day.
Child$_2$:　It was a warm *winter* day.
Child$_3$:　It was a warm *simmer* day.

The first of these miscues, "spring" for "summer," would be considered as acceptable because the substituted word is of the same semantic class, "seasons," as the text word and is similarly a warm season, so it does not violate the constraints of context. Further, it contains the same initial sound as the text word. This would suggest that the reader is integrating context, semantic, and grapho-phonemic cues. However, "spring" is not "summer." In most ordinary situations, this difference would not impair comprehension, but it is possible to think of scenarios where it would. The second miscue, "winter" for "summer," is less acceptable, because it would seem to violate the constraint, "warm." It is, however, a season, and may not represent a serious problem with comprehension. In both cases, the reader has correctly parsed the sentence, so that it read that it was a "warm day," regardless of the season.

The last miscue, "simmer" for "summer," is more problematic because it violates all constraints, except some phonics elements. Even with the anomalous word included, the basic parts of the sentence are intact. The reader still produced that it was a warm day, the major part of the sentence.

In all cases, the reader correctly identified the first proposition. Because we would not expect readers to remember all the propositions, especially those lower in the text hierarchy (Kintsch, 1974), we might not expect proposition 2 to be remembered, unless some subsequent information highlighted its importance. Thus, even a miscue that would be judged as in violation of the semantic cues in the text might preserve enough of the meaning so that the reader can get a main point. In fact, the reader making this miscue might remember as much as a reader who did not, because it is likely that the subordinate proposition would not be remembered anyway. (It also may be that the reader may process miscue 3 as a typo.)

A miscue such as "It was a warm summer dog" creates a different problem because this involves a misunderstanding of the key proposition, that it was a "day" that is being described. Such a major change might impact comprehension. In our experience, we see such miscues rarely, usually when there is a picture, which distracts a child. In other words, if there was a picture of a dog with this sentence, the child might say "dog" in place of the "d" word by overrelying on the picture.

In the first three miscues, the violation would have impaired the child's ability to develop a fully realized textbase. However, even if such a textbase were developed, the detail of "season" would have been forgotten, unless it tied to something else in the text, such as fireworks on July 4. Thus, the miscue would impact the child's comprehension of a detail, which might have been forgotten in ordinary comprehension. In the fourth case, the violation was at the macrolevel. This would not integrate well with prior knowledge and with information from the rest of the text, thus impairing the development of the situation model. In our experience, a child making such a miscue would either (a) make other changes in the text compatible with the "dog" idea, or (b) have their comprehension fall apart. As predicted earlier, such a reader might be able to remember facts or fragments, but have difficulty putting together a coherent account of the text. In practice, most of the miscues we see are at the microlevel, especially with children beyond the initial stages, but we know of no study which has made that distinction.

Our experience is that children's miscues overwhelmingly preserve the syntactic functions of the text. Schlieper (1977) found a developmental pattern in the oral reading of first, second, and third graders with third graders making a significantly higher proportion of syntactically acceptable miscues (70.4%) than first (42.3%) or second graders (49.4%). This echoes still earlier work by Goodman (1965) and Ilg and Ames (1950).

Meaning changing miscues, such as "dog" for "day," are related to comprehension. Pinnell et al. (1995) found that the number of meaning-changing miscues was significantly related to children's overall comprehension level. One explanation for this finding is that meaning-changing miscues disrupted the comprehension of the passage. However, because this data is correlational, it is possible that impairments in children's ongoing comprehension may have led to a higher proportion of meaning-changing miscues. Taft and Leslie (1985) found that children who had high knowledge of the text topic made significantly fewer meaning-changing miscues than children who had low topic knowledge. This suggests that their topic knowledge influenced their ongoing processing of the words in the text. The influence may be at the word recognition level or at a somewhat higher level (Adams, 1990).

Our reading of the research leads us to conclude that most miscues will disrupt the development of a textbase, forcing children to over-rely on background knowledge. A less than coherent textbase would impair the development of an integrated representation of the information in the text. Thus, when a reader misses a sizeable proportion of words, comprehension will suffer. A critical question for instruction as well as assessment pertains to the size of the corpus of words that are recognized incorrectly, before comprehension breaks down.

RATE AND COMPREHENSION

Because this research shows that conventional word recognition levels do not predict comprehension particularly well at all grades, we need to examine the aspect that Gray (1919) suggested as part of his original oral reading assessment but has often not been part of the designation of reading levels from IRIs in decades since—rate of reading. In the NAEP study (Pinnell et al., 1995), accuracy was not related to comprehension, but rate was related. Similarly, Rasinski (1999; Rasinski & Padak, 1998) examined the oral reading accuracy and rate of fifth graders involved in remedial reading programs. He found that the average accuracy of his remedial readers was near the instructional level, as was their general comprehension, similar to the findings of the NAEP study (Pinnell et al., 1995). However, the remedial readers in his studies had significantly lower reading rates. This suggests that, at least for children receiving instruction in decoding, accuracy levels may be generally high, because children are using decoding skills to compensate for a lack of automatic word recognition. However, this involves a trade-off, which would be reflected in a slow reading rate. If the rate is too slow, it is likely that comprehension might be very difficult.

The relations between rate and comprehension, then, reflect a trade-off between word identification and comprehension. If word recognition is not automatic, as reflected in slower rates, then the reader is presumed to be devoting resources to decoding. Under LaBerge and Samuels's (1974) and Logan et al.'s (1999) models, this would mean that there are fewer resources available for comprehension. This does not mean that comprehension cannot occur; only that it is more difficult. This trade-off would also explain the success of Curriculum-Based Measurements (CBMs) in measuring comprehension. CBMs are short passages, either taken from children's texts (Deno, 1985; Shinn, 1988) or from standard passages (Good, Wallin, Simmons, Kame–enui, & Kaminski, 2003), which children read aloud. Scoring is based on the number of correct words read in 1 minute. Typically, a child will read three passages at a level to get a score. These CBM-based scores also have high concurrent validity when compared to reading comprehension measures. Hintze, Shapiro, Conte, and Basile (1997) found correlations between 0.64 and 0.69 for CBM and the Degrees of Reading Power test in Grades 1 to 5. Shinn, Good, Knutson, Tilley, and Collins (1992) found correlations between CBMs and the Stanford Diagnostic Reading Test Literal and Inferential comprehension subtests of 0.55 for fifth graders, and correlations between CBMs and cloze measures of 0.75 for third graders and 0.62 for fifth graders.

One would expect that word recognition accuracy would have a strong effect in first grade, tapering off as children develop decoding skills that would enable them to read reasonably accurately. One would expect rate to affect reading comprehension strongly at first. As children improve as readers, rate should hit an asymptote, following the power curve (Logan et al., 1999), where possible improvements in rate are slight.

We have found some indication of this developmental effect in our data. Schwanenflugel, Strauss, Sieczko, Kuhn, Morris, and Stahl (2004) examined 195 first, second, and third graders on a variety of measures of single word reading, text reading, orthographic knowledge, obligatory processing (as evidenced by variations of the Stroop test), and reading comprehension. Using LISREL modeling, they found that the measures of isolated word recognition, including phonemic decoding and orthographic knowledge, as well as recognition of irregular words, loaded on the same factor as a measure of text reading (the Gray Oral Reading Test) and that this factor was strongly related to the comprehension measure (from the Wechsler Individual Achievement Test) at all three grades tested. However, this relation diminished between first and second and between second and third, suggesting that, as children become more automatic in their decoding abilities, other factors account for more variance in comprehension than word recognition factors.

The Schwanenflugel et al. (in press) study also established that single word decoding and recognition loaded on the same factor as text reading. Although studies have differed in the size of the effect, children have been found to read words better in context than in isolation (e.g., Adams & Huggins, 1985; Goodman, 1965; Nicholson, 1991). Regardless of the size of the effect, measures of children's reading words in isolation and in context are bound to be highly correlated with each other. Koolstra, van der Voort, and van der Kamp (1997) reported correlations between measures of decoding and comprehension in Dutch as part of a 3-year study of the effects of television on reading comprehension and decoding. For third graders, they reported correlations of 0.53, 0.49, and 0.41 for each of the 3 years of the study. For fifth graders, the corresponding correlations are 0.32, 0.33, and 0.27, a sizable drop.

The preponderance of research presented so far is correlational. The results of the instructional research is mixed. On one hand, Fleisher, Jenkins, and Pany (1979), working with fourth and fifth graders, found that speeded practice in reading words did not significantly improve comprehension. On the other hand, Blanchard (1980), working with sixth graders, and Tan and Nicholson (1997), working with 7- to 10-year-olds, found that training in automatic word recognition did improve comprehension. It is unclear why there were such differences between studies. Tan and Nicholson taught 20 difficult words from a 200-word story. Both Blanchard and Fleisher et al. taught all the words in the to-be-read passages. Blanchard found that only "very poor" readers and not the "poor" readers in his study benefited from the training. The poor readers were from a half-year to 2 years below grade placement. The very poor readers were students who more than 3 years behind grade placement on a standardized test—some as much as 4 years. Thus, the children that Tan and Nicholson and Blanchard worked with may have had lower reading abilities than those in Fleisher et al.'s study.

The general picture from these studies is that, as children become more automatic in word recognition, the relation between word recognition and comprehension drops. As the process of word recognition demands fewer resources, comprehension of written language would become more like comprehension of oral language. This would confirm the predictions of both the Simple View (Gough & Tumner, 1986; Hoover & Gough, 1990) and Chall's (1996) stage model. Chall's model assumes that automatic word recognition is achieved by the end of grade 3. Our data (Schwanenflugel, Kuhn, Meisinger, Bradley, Stahl, & Wisenbaker, 2003) as well as that of others suggest that automaticity is not attained by the end of that grade.

PROSODY AND COMPREHENSION

The third aspect of fluency—prosody—has not been as well researched as accuracy and rate. It is commonly observed that children who are not fluent read choppily, or in ways that diverge from naturally sounding language (e.g., Clay & Imlach, 1971). Dowhower (1987) found good and poor reader differences on several measures of prosody. Such differences could reflect that differences in prosody are caused by differences in reading ability or that differences in reading ability and prosody are caused by common factors, such as differences in comprehension or word recognition. Schreiber (1991) suggested that prosody is related to syntactic processing. In oral language, children seem to rely more heavily on prosody in syntactic processing (Read & Schreiber, 1982). However, it is not clear whether the use of prosody reflects children's understanding of the syntax of what they read or whether the understanding of syntax comes from the ability to assign prosodic cues.

Our data (Schwanenflugel et al., in press) suggest that prosody's link to comprehension goes indirectly through automatic word recognition. Digitized recordings of second- and third-grade children reading a passage from the Gray Oral Reading Test–3 were made as part of a larger study on the development of reading fluency. The children were assessed on reading comprehension. In LISREL models, we found that differences in automatic word recognition accounted for significantly more variance than nearly all the prosody variables. The exception was the overall resemblance of the child's reading to that of adults from the child's community. In addition, based on the features we have sampled from the recordings, we found that poor readers have longer and more variable intersentential pause lengths than good readers. The drop in pitch of poor readers showed smaller declinations at the end of declarative sentences than that of good readers, and poor readers were somewhat less likely to consistently drop in pitch.

In this study, we used simple declarative and question structures. These are prosody features which emerge early in children's language development. Prosody-comprehension relations may be seen in more complex constructions. We are currently testing these relations using other syntactic patterns.

FLUENCY AND COMPREHENSION

Reviewing the research concerning all three aspects of fluent reading behavior—rate, accuracy, and prosody—it seems that at least two (accuracy and prosody) seem directly connected to the ability of the reader to create a textbase or an ordered list of propositions (Kintsch, 1998). A fragmented textbase would entail a reader over-relying on prior knowledge to construct a representation of the meaning of the text.

When we measure comprehension in broad forms, we might be missing the specific knowledge used to develop a textbase. There is a trend toward including "response" questions, for example, such as "How do you think [a character] felt about [an action]?" Such questions may be important, not only because they measure an important aspect of reading, but also because they encourage teachers to include response to literature in their teaching. However, an over-reliance on such questions may inflate the measurement of comprehension because they would allow a reader who has not developed a textbase representation to appear to have understood. The answers to these questions could be derived largely from the readers' prior knowledge and general world knowledge, rather than specific items from the text. Other items vary in terms of their text dependency (Tuinman, 1974).

The relation between comprehension and fluency appears to be developmental. There seems to be a stronger relation between word recognition accuracy, rate, and prosody and comprehension in the first and second grades. This relation appears to diminish in the third and fourth grades (Paris et al., this volume). There are several possible explanations for this. First, as word recognition becomes more automatic, there is less variation in word recognition itself, so that there is less potential correlation. Although we (Schwanenflugel et al., 2003; see also Pinnell et al., 1995) have been finding that children do not seem to reach automaticity by the end of third grade as assumed by Chall (1996), there certainly is less variation in fluent reading behaviors by third grade. Second, as the texts children read become more complex, higher level factors, such as those involved in reasoning and inference, become more important. The simple texts used in first and second grade, if the words are recognized, may present few higher-level comprehension problems. The more complex texts read in later grades, however, may require both more involved background knowledge and more involved reasoning about the text to understand them.

A third explanation for the diminishing relation between word recognition and comprehension may be that another word factor, vocabulary knowledge, becomes more important by third grade and that variations in children's store of word meanings becomes more important as children progress through school. Vocabulary knowledge is an important correlate with reading comprehension throughout the grades (Anderson & Freebody, 1981). Tests of knowledge of word meaning correlate so highly with measures of reading comprehension that some have suggested that they are close to 1.0, given the error inherent in both measures (Carver, 2000; Thorndike, 1972). Evidence from correlational studies, readability research, and experimental studies all found strong and reliable relations between the difficulty in a text and text comprehension (Anderson & Freebody, 1981).

But why is there such a relationship? The most obvious notion is that knowing word meanings causes comprehension of a text containing those words. The cause of this correlational relation is unclear, however. Anderson and Freebody (1981) suggested three hypotheses that might explain these strong correlations. The instrumentalist hypothesis suggests that knowledge of word meanings directly causes comprehension. Although Stahl and Fairbanks (1986) found that teaching word meanings directly improved comprehension, there might be more to the relation than this hypothesis predicts. Two other of Anderson and Freebody's hypotheses, a general knowledge hypothesis and a general aptitude hypothesis, suggest that vocabulary knowledge's relation to a third factor, either a person's overall knowledge store or his or her general cognitive abilities, underlies the correlations between vocabulary knowledge and comprehension. Knowledge of certain words certainly does imply that a person has knowledge of a general cognitive domain, such as knowledge of the meaning of *jib* implies that a person knows about sailing or knowledge of the word *dharma* suggests a familiarity with Hinduism. For this reason, vocabulary tests have been used as tests of domain knowledge (Johnston, 1984). Vocabulary knowledge is also strongly related to a person's overall cognitive aptitude, as evidenced by high correlations between vocabulary tests and overall intelligence tests.

It is important to make a distinction between recognition of written words that a person knows the meaning of (the child learning to decode a word like "sun") and knowledge of word meanings themselves (words like "corona," "solar flare," and so on). It is not unreasonable to suggest that there is a shift in the "word factor" in comprehension from a recognition factor to a word-meaning factor. Observing common reading measures such as the Wide Range Achievement Test (WRAT; Jastask & Wilkinson, 1995), for example, shows high correlations between the Reading subtest, which is mostly a list of words to be read aloud, and passage comprehension measures. In the technical manual, correlations between the WRAT and the Comprehensive Test of Basic Skills (CTBS), California Achievement Test (CAT), and Stanford Achievement Tests (SAT) all respected passage comprehension measures, are reported as between 0.69 and 0.87. They do not present the correlations broken down by grade level, but, assuming that they are consistent across grade, these are substantial correlations, suggesting a strong relation between word knowledge and passage comprehension. The nature of the words, however, changes on the measure. The first three words on one form of the WRAT are "see," "red," and "milk," which most English-speaking first graders will know. Items 10 to 12 are "cliff," "stalk," and "grunt," words of moderate difficulty. Items 20 to 22 are "rancid," "conspiracy," and "deny," which are difficult words and have somewhat irregular spell-ing-sound correspondences that probably have to be known to be pronounced. The test goes up to "epithalamium," "inefficacious," and "synecdoche," which are not known by many college-educated adults and are difficult to pronounce for those who know them.

Although we have been talking about accuracy of word recognition, it is im-possible to separate this factor from word knowledge. Words are easier to pro-nounce if one knows their meaning, even words whose pronunciations can be derived from basic decoding rules (Adams, 1990).

Richness of Language

Related to the issue of vocabulary and word recognition is the issue of richness of language. In recent years, under the influence of "Guided Reading" (Fountas & Pinnell, 1996), there has been a growth in the use of leveled texts, or primary grade texts designed to be readable for early readers. These texts are designed to become increasingly less predictable in terms of syntactic pat-terns, less reliant on picture information, more complex in topic, longer and more complex page layouts, and to depend more on children's increasing ca-pabilities in knowledge of the alphabetic system (Peterson, 1991). Decodable texts, or texts tightly controlled for use of taught sound-symbol correspon-dence, may be useful for supporting children in knowledge of decoding (e.g., Stahl, Stahl, & McKenna, 1999). However, the richness of the language that children read suffers.

Consider the following three texts—the first a leveled text, the second a decodable, and the third a literary text—all intended for the early second-grade level.

Example 1:   *Wet Grass*
Ned and Lottie were playing inside. Mom looked out of the window. "The rain's stopped," she said. "Come for a walk." They walked down the road. Lottie climbed over a fence. "Come and walk in the wet grass," she said. Mom climbed over the fence. "Come on, Ned," she said. (Wright Group, 1996).

Example 2:   *Big Hog's House Hunt*
Big Hog was looking for a new home when he met Hot Dog. "It's my job to help pals look for new homes," said Hot Dog. "It just so happens that at the present time, I have seven homes for sale. I bet I can sell you a home!" (Coo-per et al., 2003).

Example 3: *Julius*
Maya's granddaddy lived in Alabama, but wintered in Alaska. He told Maya that was the reason he liked ice cubes in his coffee. On one of Granddaddy's visits from Alaska, he brought a crate. A surprise for Maya! "Something that will teach you fun and sharing." Granddaddy smiled. "Something for my special you." (Johnson, 1993).

Although similar in their word recognition demands, texts of these three types may create different expectations about the nature of texts. Such expectations may affect children's processing of text on comprehension assessments. With excessive exposure to leveled or decodable texts, children may attend to decoding the texts, not devoting attention to comprehension (LaBerge & Samuels, 1974). We are not saying that texts used in instruction should be of one type or another, but that there be a "balanced diet" of texts, so that children will develop varied expectations and flexible processing of texts.

Words and Comprehension Assessment

Although, as we suggested at the beginning of this chapter, the majority of attention in comprehension assessment research is devoted to "higher level" aspects of comprehension, including metacognition, the use of cognitive strategies, and inferencing, the arguments in this chapter suggest that one ignores word level factors, both fluent reading and vocabulary knowledge, at one's risk. Children whose reading is not fluent tend to either fail to create a coherent textbase or read slowly to compensate for their difficulties. Either of these strategies would impact comprehension assessment.

Our observations of comprehension testing suggest that developers do ignore word level factors. Consider the following excerpt from the 2000 NAEP (Donahue, Finnegan, Lutkus, Allen, & Campbell, 2001), a measure used to develop the "Report Card for the Nation":

Excerpt 1: The meeting houses had no heat of their own until the 1800s. At home, colonial families huddled close to the fireplace, or hearth. The fireplace was wide and high enough to hold a large fire, but its chimney was large, too. That caused a problem: Gusts of cold air blew into the house. (Donahue et al., 2001, p. 98)

Then peruse an excerpt of similar length from the Basic Reading Inventory (BRI; Johns, 1997), a typical IRI:

Excerpt 2: Martha and Johnny traveled in a covered wagon pulled by horses. As time passed, the weather became colder. One night when they stopped to sleep, it

was six degrees below zero. The next night they were caught in a blizzard. Martha
and Johnny stopped at a house to ask for directions. (Johns, 1997, p. 271)

Both passages are intended for fourth graders. If a criterion for a word that could
challenge a fourth grader who is not reading with rapidity is one that is infre-
quent and multisyllabic, about 6 unique words in every 100 running words of
text in the Johns text will be difficult. In the NAEP text, approximately 9 unique
words out of every 100 running words of text will be difficult. If these words give
students the greatest difficulty, we might expect students to read with approximately 94% to 95% accuracy on the Johns and at 90% to 91% accuracy on the
NAEP. The 95% accuracy level would conventionally be considered a child's instructional level; the 90% to 91% level would be considered as a "Frustration"
level, especially without any instructional preparation (Betts, 1946).

Although it is unlikely that all challenged students will struggle with precisely the words that we would predict to be difficult, a consideration of some of
the words in the two excerpts illustrate the task that confronts them. The
NAEP passage contains words like "hearth" or "meeting house" that, even if
they do not represent decoding problems (and "hearth" probably does), represent concepts that may not be known by fourth graders. The BRI passage contains fewer difficult concepts, although the general topic (olden times) is
similar. Among the group of difficult words in the NAEP passage, 45% had a
standard frequency index on Zeno's word list (Zeno, Ivens, Millard, & Duvvuri,
1995) that indicates frequency of appearance less than once per 1 million
words. None of the difficult words on the Johns passage had frequency levels below three appearances per 1 million words. For students who do not read much,
such differences may not seem great but the difference between words such as
"huddled" and "hearth" when attempting to make sense of text on an assessment, and words such as "degrees," "zero," and "blizzard" (on the Johns assessment), is a substantial one. This is not to say that passages such as the one from
the NAEP are not appropriate for learning and instruction. Questions of
whether passages with a substantial number of rare words are appropriate for a
national assessment or for large-scale state assessments need to be addressed in
light of policies and perceptions that follow such assessments.

This review has shown that word recognition is central in defining the reading performances of beginning readers. For challenged readers, word recognition accounts for a significant portion of the variance in student performance
beyond the beginning levels as well. Although an empirical and theoretical
foundation exists for identifying the end of third grade as the point where processes other than speed and accuracy in identifying words should dominate, this
is not the case for many children. A substantial portion of a grade-level cohort

has developed a grasp of the alphabetic principle but this knowledge has not moved to an automatic level (Schwanenflugel et al., 2003).

These findings call for the inclusion of fluency as a task that is part of reading assessment at least through the third grade and possibly through the elementary grades. We are certain that this proposal will meet with less argument for beginning reading batteries than with students in the middle grades. However, we think it is as critical for the middle-grade students who are not attaining standards. We hasten to emphasize that we are not suggesting more assessment of word recognition. What we are arguing for is attention to fluency.

As well as assessment of fluency, attention is required to the difficulty of the words within texts. For beginning readers, texts in which high-frequency and phonetically regular words dominate are read with more speed than texts where a sizable number of the words fall into the category of rare words (Hiebert & Fisher, 2002). We expect that is also the case with challenged readers in the middle grades. At the macrolevel of selecting grade-appropriate texts, consideration is given to texts on assessments. For example, a selection from *Charlotte's Web* (White, 1952) does not appear in an assessment for first graders, just as excerpts from Minarik's (1957) *Little Bear* do not appear in an assessment for fifth graders. But we are arguing for more than attention to genre and the cohesiveness of ideas within texts. We are suggesting that, in assessing beginning and challenged readers, the words in texts matter.

Strong and Weak Views of Fluency and Comprehension

Thus, the strong view, that automaticity of word recognition enables children to comprehend text at the ability predicted by their level of language development, is clearly inadequate. First of all, children's ability to recognize words is related to their knowledge of word meanings, so that language knowledge and word recognition are not independent. This is true for words in isolation (e.g., Adams, 1990; Schwanenflugel & Akins, 1994) and in context (Goodman, 1965; Nicholson, 1991). Second, word recognition in context reflects children's perceptions of the syntax and meaning of the text they are reading. This has been found in studies of miscue analysis as well as studies of the relations of prosody to comprehension. Third, the relation between word recognition and comprehension seems to be developmental, in that the relations seem stronger in first and second grade than in third grade and beyond. As children develop as readers, the variations in their word recognition ability diminish because they are moving toward automaticity, and other aspects of reading such as text complexity and reasoning skills become more important, both of which may reduce the correlations.

The strong view that word recognition causes children to be able to comprehend would suggest that older children need more intense instruction in word
recognition to be better readers. In fact, a follow-up analysis of the studies used
by the National Reading Panel's (2000) subgroup on alphabetics (Ehri, Nunes,
Stahl, & Willow, 2001) found that phonics instruction was not effective for
children in Grades 2 through 6 for improving comprehension, although it was
significantly effective in Grade 1.

There are important entanglements between word recognition, vocabulary, and reading comprehension. Misreading of individual words can have an
impact on ongoing comprehension. This impact might show up in measures of
a coherent representation, but might be missed on questions that ask for a literary response or in which the reader can use prior knowledge to infer an answer. Further, vocabulary knowledge impacts children's text reading, a factor
that may influence scores of children on measures such as the NAEP that require a great deal of specialized knowledge. In short, comprehension is built
on a foundation of words.

REFERENCES

Adams, M. J. (1990). *Beginning to read: Thinking and learning about print*. Cambridge,
    MA: MIT Press.
Adams, M. J. (1998). The three-cuing systems. In J. Osborn & F. Lehr (Eds.), *Literacy for
    all: Issues in teaching and learning* (pp. 73–99). New York: Guilford.
Adams, M. J., & Huggins, A. W. F. (1985). The growth of children's sight vocabulary: A
    quick test with educational and theoretical implications. *Reading Research Quarterly,
    20*, 262–281.
Allington, R. L. (1984). Oral reading. In P. D. Pearson, R. Barr, M. L. Kamil, & P.
    Mosenthal (Eds.), *Handbook of reading research* (Vol. 1, pp. 829–864). White Plains,
    NY: Longman.
Anderson, R. C., & Freebody, P. (1981). Vocabulary knowledge. In J. T. Guthrie (Ed.),
    Comprehension and teaching: Research reviews (pp. 77–117). Newark, DE: Interna-
    tional Reading Association.
Anderson, R. C., & Pearson, P. D. (1984). A schema-theoretic view of basic processes
    in reading comprehension. In P. D. Pearson, R. Barr, M. L. Kamil, & P. Mosenthal
    (Eds.), *Handbook of reading research* (Vol. 1, pp. 255–291). White Plains, NY:
    Longman.
Barr, R. (1974). The effect of instruction on pupil reading strategies. *Reading Research
    Quarterly, 10*, 555–582.
Betts, E. (1946). *Foundations of reading instruction*. New York: American Book.
Biemiller, A. (1970). The development of the use of graphic and contextual information
    as children learn to read. *Reading Research Quarterly, 6*, 75–96.
Blanchard, J. (1980). A preliminary investigation of the transfer effect between single
    word decoding ability and contextual reading comprehension in poor reading sixth
    graders. *Perceptual and Motor Skills, 51*, 1271–1281.

Carver, R. P. (1993). Merging the simple view of reading with rauding theory. *Journal of Reading Behavior, 25*, 439–455.

Carver, R. P. (2000). *The causes of high and low reading achievement.* Mahwah, NJ: Lawrence Erlbaum Associates.

Chall, J. S. (1996). *Stages of reading development* (2nd ed.). Fort Worth, TX: Harcourt Brace.

Clay, M. M. (1991). *Becoming literate: The construction of inner control.* Portsmouth, NH: Heinemann.

Clay, M. M. (1993). *Reading recovery : A guidebook for teachers in training.* Portsmouth, NH: Heinemann.

Clay, M. M., & Imlach, R. H. (1971). Juncture, pitch, and stress as reading behavior variables. *Journal of Verbal Behavior and Verbal Learning, 10*, 133–139.

Cohen, A. S. (1974). Oral reading errors of first grade children taught by a code emphasis approach. *Reading Research Quarterly, 10*, 616–650.

Connelly, V., Johnston, R. S., & Thompson, G. B. (1999). The influence of instructional approach on reading procedure. In G. B. Thompson & T. Nicholson (Eds.), *Learning to read: Beyond phonics and whole language* (pp. 103–123). New York: Teachers College Press.

Cooper, J. D., Pikulski, J. J., Ackerman, P. A., Au, K. H., Chard, D. J., Garcia, G. G., et al. (2003). *Houghton Mifflin reading: The nation's choice.* Boston: Houghton Mifflin.

Deno, S. L. (1985). Curriculum-based measurement: The emerging alternative. *Exceptional Children, 52*, 219–232.

Donahue, P. L., Finnegan, R. J., Lutkus, A. D., Allen, N. L., & Campbell, J. R. (2001). *The nation's report card for reading: Fourth grade.* Washington, DC: National Center for Education Statistics.

Dowhower, S. L. (1987). Effects of repeated reading on second-grade transitional readers' fluency and comprehension. *Reading Research Quarterly, 22*, 389–406.

Ehri, L., Nunes, S., Stahl., S. A., & Willows, D. M. (2001). Systematic phonics instruction helps students learn to read: Evidence from the National Reading Panel's meta-analysis. *Review of Educational Research, 71*, 393–447.

Fleisher, L. S., Jenkins, J. R., & Pany, D. (1979). Effects on poor readers' comprehension of training in rapid decoding. *Reading Research Quarterly, 15*, 30–48.

Fountas, I. C., & Pinnell, G. S. (1996). *Guided reading: Good first teaching for all children.* Portsmouth, NH: Heinemann.

Gibson, E. J., & Levin, H. (1975). *The psychology of reading.* Cambridge, MA: MIT Press.

Good, R. H., Wallin, J. U., Simmons, D. C., Kame–enui, E. J., & Kaminski, R. A. (2003). *System-wide percentile ranks for DIBELS benchmark assessment* (Tech. Report No. 9). Eugene: University of Oregon.

Goodman, K. S. (1965). A linguistic study of cues and miscues in reading. *Elementary English, 42*, 853–860.

Goodman, K. S. (1968). The psycholinguistic nature of the reading process. In K. S. Goodman (Ed.), *The psycholinguistic nature of the reading process* (pp. 13–26). Detroit, MI: Wayne State University.

Goodman, K. S. (1983). A linguistic study of cues and miscues in reading. In L. M. Gentile, M. L. Kamil, & J. S. Blanchard (Eds.), *Reading research revisited* (pp. 187–192). Columbus, OH: Charles E. Merrill.

Goodman, K. S., & Goodman, Y. M. (1977). Learning about psycholinguistic processes by analyzing oral reading. *Harvard Educational Review, 47*, 317–333.

Goodman, Y. M., Watson, D., & Burke, C. (1987). *Reading miscue inventory: Alternative procedures.* New York: Owen.

Gough, P. B., & Tumner, W. E. (1986). Decoding, reading, and reading disability. *Remedial and Special Education, 7*(1), 6–10.

Gray, W. S. (1919). *Standard passages for oral reading.* Bloomington, IN: Public School Publishing.

Hiebert, E., & Fisher, C. W. (2002, April). *Describing the difficulty of texts for beginning readers: A curriculum-based measure.* Paper presented at the annual meeting of the American Educational Research Association. New Orleans, LA.

Hintze, J. M., Shapiro, E. S., Conte, K. L., & Basile, I. M. (1997). Oral reading fluency and authentic reading material: Criterion validity of the technical features of CBM survey-level assessment. *School Psychology Review, 26*, 535–553.

Hoover, W. A., & Gough, P. B. (1990). The simple view of reading. *Reading and Writing: An Interdisciplinary Journal, 2*, 127–160.

Ilg, F. L., & Ames, L. B. (1950). Developmental trends in reading behavior. *Journal of Genetic Psychology, 76*, 291–312.

Jastask, J., & Wilkinson, G. (1995). *Wide Range Achievement Test (3).* Wilmington, DE: Wide Range, Inc.

Johns, J. (1997). *Basic reading inventory.* Dubuque, IA: Kendall, Hunt.

Johnson, A. (1993). *Julius.* New York: Orchard Books.

Johnston, P. (1984). Prior knowledge and reading comprehension test bias. *Reading Research Quarterly, 19*, 219–239.

Johnston, R. S., & Watson, J. (1997). Developing reading, spelling, and phonemic awareness skills in primary school children. *Reading, 31*, 37–40.

Kendall, J. R., & Hood, J. (1979). Investigating the relationship between comprehension and word recognition: Oral reading analysis of children with comprehension or word recognition disabilities. *Journal of Reading Behavior, 11*, 41–48.

Kintsch, W. (1974). *The representation of meaning in memory.* Hillsdale, NJ: Lawrence Erlbaum Associates.

Kintsch, W. (1998). *Comprehension: A paradigm for cognition.* Cambridge, England: Cambridge University Press.

Kintsch, W., & van Dijk, T. (1978). Toward a model of text comprehension and production. *Psychological Review, 85*, 363–394.

Koolstra, C. M., van der Voort, T. H. A., & van der Kamp, L. J. (1997). Television's impact on children's reading comprehension and decoding skills: A 3-year panel study. *Reading Research Quarterly, 32*, 128–152.

Kuhn, M. R., & Stahl, S. A. (2003). Fluency: A review of developmental and remedial practices. *Journal of Educational Psychology, 95*, 3–21.

LaBerge, D., & Samuels, S. J. (1974). Toward a theory of automatic information processing in reading. *Cognitive Psychology, 6*, 293–323.

Logan, G. D., Taylor, S. E., & Etherton, J. L. (1999). Attention and automaticity: Toward a theoretical integration. *Psychological Research, 62*, 165–181.

McNamara, D. S., & Kintsch, W. (1996). Learning from text: Effects of prior knowledge and text coherence. *Discourse Processes, 22*, 247–287.

Minarik, E. (1957). *Little bear.* New York: Harper.

National Reading Panel. (2000). *Report of the subgroups: National Reading Panel.* Washington, DC: National Institute of Child Health and Development.

Nicholson, T. (1991). Do children read words better in context or in lists: A classic study revisited. *Journal of Educational Psychology, 83*, 444–450.

Paris, S. G., & Carpenter, R. D. (2003). FAQs about IRIs. *The Reading Teacher, 56*, 578–580.

Paris, S. G., Carpenter, R. D., Paris, A. H., & Hamilton, E. E. (in press). Spurious and genuine correlates of children's reading comprehension. In S. G. Paris & S. A. Stahl (Eds.), *Children's reading comprehension and assessment.* Mahwah, NJ: Lawrence Erlbaum Associates.

Peterson, B. (1991). Children's literature in Reading Recovery. In D. E. DeFord, C. A. Lyons, & G. S. Pinnell (Eds.), *Bridges to literacy: Learning from Reading Recovery.* Portsmouth, NH: Heinemann.

Pinnell, G. S., Pikulski, J. J., Wixson, K. K., Campbell, J. R., Gough, P. B., & Beatty, A. S. (1995). *Listening to children read aloud: Data from NAEPs Integrated Reading Performance Record (IRPR) at grade 4.* Washington, DC: National Center for Education Statistics.

Rasinski, T. V. (1999). Exploring a method for estimating independent, instructional, and frustration reading rates. *Reading Psychology, 20*, 61–69.

Rasinski, T. V., & Padak, N. (1998). How elementary students referred for compensatory reading instruction perform on school-based measures of word recognition, fluency, and comprehension. *Reading Psychology: An International Quarterly, 19*, 185–216.

Read, C., & Schreiber, P. A. (1982). Why short subjects are harder to find than long ones. In E. Wanner & L. Gleitman (Eds.), *Language acquisition: The state of the art* (pp. 78–101). Cambridge, England: Cambridge University Press.

Rupley, W. H., & Willson, V. L. (1997). Relationship between reading comprehension and components of word recognition: Support for developmental shifts. *Journal of Research and Development in Education, 30*(4), 255–260.

Schlieper, A. (1977). Oral reading errors in relation to grade and level of skill. *The Reading Teacher, 31*, 283–287.

Schreiber, P. A. (1991). Understanding prosody's role in reading acquisition. *Theory into Practice, 30*, 158–164.

Schwanenflugel, P. J., & Akins, C. E. (1994). Developmental trends in lexical decisions for abstract and concrete words. *Reading Research Quarterly, 29*, 96–104.

Schwanenflugel, P. J., Hamilton, A. M., Kuhn, M. R., Wisenbaker, J., & Stahl, S. A. (in press). Becoming a fluent reader: Reading skill and prosodic features in the oral reading of young readers. *Journal of Educational Psychology.*

Schwanenflugel, P. J., Kuhn, M., Meisinger, E., Bradley, B., Stahl, S., & Wisenbaker, J. (2003, April). *An examination of the attentional resource model and the development of reading fluency.* Paper presented at the biennial meeting of the Society for Research in Child Development, Tampa, FL.

Schwanenflugel, P. J., Strauss, G., Sieczko, J., Kuhn, M. R., Morris, R. K., & Stahl, S. A. (2004). *The influence of word unit size on the development of Stroop interference in early word decoding.* Athens: University of Georgia Press.

Shinn, M. R. (1988). Development of curriculum-based local norms for use in special education decision making. *School Psychology Review, 17*, 61–80.

Shinn, M. R., Good, I. R. H., Knutson, N., Tilley, W. D., & Collins, V. L. (1992). Curriculum based measure of oral reading fluency: A confirmatory analysis of its relation to reading. *School Psychology Review, 21*, 459–478.

Stahl, K. A. D., Stahl, S. A., & McKenna, M. C. (1999). The development of phonological awareness and orthographic processing in Reading Recovery. *Literacy, Teaching and Learning, 4*, 27–42.

Stahl, S., Heubach, K., & Cramond, B. (1997). *Fluency-oriented reading instruction*. Athens, GA: National Reading Research Center, U.S. Department of Education, Office of Educational Research and Improvement, Educational Resources Information Center.

Stahl, S. A., & Fairbanks, M. M. (1986). The effects of vocabulary instruction: A model-based meta-analysis. *Review of Educational Research, 56*, 72–110.

Stahl, S. A., McCartney, A. A., & Montero, M. K. (2004). *Reading first: An extensive investigation of intensive phonics instruction* (CIERA technical report). Ann Arbor: University of Michigan Press, Center for the Improvement of Early Reading Achievement.

Stanovich, K. E. (2000). *Progress in understanding reading: Scientific foundations and new frontiers*. New York: Guilford.

Sulzby, E. (1985). Children's emergent reading of favorite storybooks: A developmental study. *Reading Research Quarterly, 20*, 458–481.

Taft, M. L., & Leslie, L. (1985). The effects of prior knowledge and oral reading accuracy on miscues and comprehension. *Journal of Reading Behavior, 17*, 163–179.

Tan, A., & Nicholson, T. (1997). Flashcards revisited: Training poor readers to read words faster improves their comprehension of text. *Journal of Educational Psychology, 89*, 276–288.

Thorndike, R. L. (1972). Reading as reasoning. *Reading Research Quarterly, 9*, 135–147.

Tuinman, J. J. (1974). Determining the passage-dependency of comprehension questions in five major tests. *Reading Research Quarterly, 9*, 207–223.

White, E. B. (1952). *Charlotte's Web*. New York: HarperTrophy.

Willson, V. L., & Rupley, W. H. (1997). A structural equation model for reading comprehension based on background, phonemic, and strategy knowledge. *Scientific Studies in Reading, 1*, 45–63.

Wright Group. (1996). *Sunshine Reading Program*. Bothell, WA: Author.

Zeno, S. M., Ivens, S. H., Millard, R. T., & Duvvuri, R. (1995). *The educator's word frequency guide*. Brewster, NY: Touchstone Applied Science Associates, Inc.

8

Roles of Motivation and Engagement in Reading Comprehension Assessment

John T. Guthrie
Allan Wigfield
University of Maryland

It is rare in discussions of reading assessment that motivation should be introduced as a topic. Historically, the debate about reading comprehension assessment has centered on such issues as what cognitive skills should be assessed and what formats should be incorporated. When the dimensionality of reading has been discussed by psychometricians, the major factors on the table for discussion were such topics as word knowledge, reasoning, inference, passage comprehension, and, more recently, the relations of background knowledge to text comprehension.

Yet, motivation and engagement in reading are now rightfully considered issues in assessment because they are increasingly understood as contributors to students' measurable levels of reading comprehension. In this chapter, our rationale for raising issues of motivation is expressed as three questions that begin with "what if":

1. What if a nontrivial percentage of students are failing or performing poorly on reading comprehension tests due primarily to their relatively low levels of motivation for reading, rather than their inadequacy on reading comprehension skills?

2. What if reading comprehension tests, by virtue of their structural and content characteristics, were decreasing students' engagement with the text, thereby, decreasing the observed level of students' achievement, as indicated by the test?

3. What if one of our highest priorities in education, that students become not only competent but committed to reading and writing as avenues for learning, goes unfulfilled because we have unsatisfactory indicators for students' success in attaining this goal?

This chapter is organized to address these "what if" questions. First, we examine the empirical evidence that reading motivation predicts and causally influences reading comprehension assessment scores of students in the kindergarten through 12th-grade range. Two kinds of motivation are explored: (a) general motivation that endures across time, types of reading situations, and student contexts; and (b) situational motivation that is more temporary, task specific, and locally conditioned. We argue that situational motivation may be especially relevant to performance on assessments. Second, we describe several characteristics of reading comprehension assessment tasks that influence processes of motivation and engagement during the assessment. We discuss features of the assessment situation such as text interest, learner control, learner goals, difficulty sequence, task complexity, and accompanying activities. These are manipulable features of assessments and may influence assessment outcomes.

One of the areas that does not receive our attention here, due to lack of space, is the broad role of testing as it may influence motivation and engagement in schooling. We defer from treating the problem of whether accountability systems with testing as the centerpiece are likely to engender positive or negative affects on students' motivation and learning. Others in the motivation field have discussed this issue in detail; for instance, Hill and Wigfield (1984) discussed how testing increases many students' anxiety, thereby lowering their performance, and Deci & Ryan (2002) discussed how testing and accountability may increase students' extrinsic motivation at the expense of their intrinsic motivation. Another area that we do not examine refers to teaching practices related to testing programs. It is not our purpose to examine whether certain teaching practices increase students' preparedness for tests or change their motivation to succeed on them, although we have addressed this elsewhere (Guthrie, 2002). Finally, we do not tackle the political challenge of whether high-stakes testing systems are advantageous for students' motivational development and reading achievement. Our purposes are more restricted to the following: (a) reviewing the extent to which students' motivations and engagement in reading contribute to success on existing tests, and (b) examining whether the tests themselves have features that influence students' engagement in reading during assessment.

MOTIVATIONAL AND COGNITIVE PROCESSES INFLUENCING READING COMPREHENSION

Our model of how cognitive and motivational processes influence reading comprehension is presented in Fig. 8.1. There are four cognitive processes contributing to text comprehension represented here, including the following: (a) activating background knowledge, (b) forming text representation, (c) constructing causal inferences, and (d) integrating prior knowledge and text representations (Guthrie & Wigfield, 1999). This schematic is intended to be consistent with the text-based integration model of Kintsch (1998) and the recent findings regarding inferencing during reading (Graesser & Bertus, 1998). That is, we assume that the reader proceeds by the following: (a) forming a representation of text based on its prepositional information and structure, (b) using prior knowledge related to the representation, and (c) constructing a situation model that integrates prior knowledge and new text-based information. Further, we assume that the reader constructs inferences based on lexical or semantic information in words, and also builds causal representations (e.g., why the lead character performed an action) based on use of prior world knowledge.

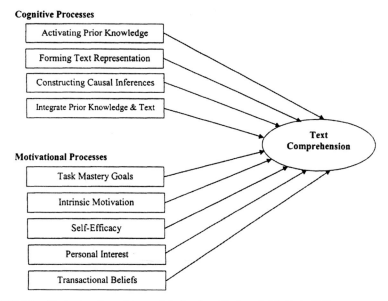

FIG. 8.1.   Motivational-cognitive model of reading (Guthrie & Wigfiled, 1999).

Motivational processes appear in parallel to these cognitive processes as contributors to text comprehension. Like the cognitive processes, these multiple motivational attributes of learners are related to each other, but can be measured and manipulated independently to influence text comprehension. These processes include the following:

1. Task mastery goals, which refer to the nature of the reader's intentions for a given reader-text interaction. Students with high task mastery goals seek to understand texts fully, comprehend them completely, and build a well-integrated situated model (Anderman, Austin, & Johnson, 2002; Pintrich, 2000). Students with low task mastery goals have weaker intentions to construct knowledge and lower goals of commitment to comprehending.

2. Intrinsic motivation, which refers to an individual's participation in reading for its own sake, and positive disposition toward engaging in reading activity (see Ryan & Deci, 2000, and Sansone & Harackiewicz, 2000, for further discussion of intrinsic motivation). Individuals high in intrinsic motivation are likely to read more frequently and report higher amounts of reading than other students (Wigfield & Guthrie, 1997).

3. Self-efficacy, which refers to the reader's belief in one's own capacity to read effectively, compete well, and attain high recognition for reading success (Schunk & Zimmerman, 1997). Self-efficacy beliefs relate to reading effort, persistence, and choice of more difficult reading materials.

4. Personal interest, which refers to an individual's positive affect associated with topics that are contained in text. A personal interest relates to the reader's identification with the content and leads to deep conceptual processing during reading activities (Schiefele, 1999).

5. Beliefs about reading, which refers to students' values relevant to a text. Students with high beliefs and values expect that reading will be useful and important to them and place a premium on being an effective reader (Wigfield & Eccles, 1992).

These motivational processes do not include all of the constructs in the theoretical or empirical literature on motivation. However, we selected them because they all correlate with text comprehension and some of them have been examined experimentally to show causal contributions to text comprehension. In addition, some of these motivational attributes (e.g., interest) influence text comprehension indirectly by influencing cognitive processes (e.g., depth of processing) during reading (Schiefele, 1999).

In presenting these motivation constructs, we distinguish between general and situational motivation. Some motivation theorists define and measure the constructs they are interested in at relatively general levels. Intrinsic motivation is an example of a construct often defined broadly, and measured in terms of intrinsic motivation for school rather than for particular activities (see Deci & Ryan, 1985; Harter, 1981; Ryan & Deci, 2000). When measured more specifically, it is measured at the domain or subject area level, such as intrinsic motivation for math and reading, which is still a relatively general level of measurement (Gottfried, 1990; Gottfried, Fleming, & Gottfried, 2001). Mastery goal orientation is another example; this construct often is used to refer to a broad orientation or approach to learning, rather than a response to a specific situation, and usually is measured either at the general school level, or at the level of an achievement domain such as math or reading.

Motivation theorists have recently articulated a situational perspective on motivation which can be applied to reading comprehension assessment. In this perspective, a distinction is drawn between general motivation, which is pervasive and enduring across contexts and time, as described in the previous paragraph, and situational motivation, which refers to immediate affective responses prompted by particular characteristics of a task or a text (Paris & Turner, 1994; Urdan, 1999). One particular example of a situated motivation construct is situational interest, or interest sparked by a particular task or activity (Schiefele, 1999). Self-efficacy also is often measured quite specifically, such as efficacy for a particular reading passage or set of math problems.

Several of the constructs in Fig. 8.1 have characteristics that make them relevant to both general motivation and situational motivation. For example, both mastery goals and self-efficacy can possess task specific and situational characteristics. However, as just noted, students can also have a mastery orientation, which is general. Self-efficacy theorists (e.g., Bandura, 1997; Pajares, 1996) often define self-efficacy in specific terms, referring to efficacy for a particular task or activity. However, self-efficacy can develop into a generalized characteristic of the individual with respect to a domain, such as academic endeavors. Many of these constructs are used to discuss and study both general and situational motivation.

The model in Fig. 8.1 shows a situational representation of the cognitive factors in comprehension. That is, activating background knowledge is a process specific to an individual text and circumstance of reading. A particular text will be better understood if particular, text-relevant background knowledge is activated in the immediate moment of reading. Analogously, the motivational processes are situational. That is, task mastery goals will influence text comprehension for a particular text, in a specific situation of reading. We propose at present that both the cognitive factors, such as activating background knowledge, and the motivational factors, such as holding task mastery goals, are processes that will facilitate text comprehension in specific situations, such as an assessment. It should be acknowledged, however, that many of the motivation processes are also studied as generalized factors in reading and learning. We next review work on how general aspects of motivation relate to children's reading comprehension. In a subsequent section, we discuss situational motivation's role.

CONTRIBUTIONS OF GENERAL READING MOTIVATION TO MEASURED READING COMPREHENSION

Relations Between Reading Motivation and Reading Comprehension

A substantial body of evidence across grade levels, from Grade 3 through high school, has been generated to show how motivational attributes measured at a relatively general level relate to measured reading comprehension. We briefly present this evidence as it appears across elementary and secondary school populations. Gottfried (1985) showed that a measure of academic intrinsic motivation predicted students' academic achievement at Grade 4. Her findings support the view that academic intrinsic motivation is differentiated into school-subject areas, such that measures of motivation for reading more highly predict achievement in reading than achievement in math. Confirming this result, Guthrie, Wigfield, Metsala, and Cox (1999) found that reading motivation predicted measured reading comprehension on two tests for students in Grades 3 and 5, when prior knowledge of the topic, past achievement, and amount of reading were controlled statistically. Indicators of achievement in these investigations have included both grades and test scores. Although correlations between academic intrinsic motivation and reading achievement were statistically significant according to Gottfried (1990), she also reported that the correlations were higher between grades and motivation than between test scores and motivation. Corroborating this result, Sweet, Guthrie, and Ng (1998) found that grades in reading for 10-year-olds were substantially correlated with teachers' perceptions of students' intrinsic reading motivation.

Studies have found that Harter's (1981) scale of intrinsic versus extrinsic motivation in the classroom correlated with students' achievement in reading across Grades 3 to 6 (Hoffman, 1995). Consistent with these findings, Baker and Wigfield (1999) found that aspects of urban fifth- and sixth-grade students' reading motivation was related to their achievement on the Gates MacGinitie Reading Test and the Comprehensive Test of Basic Skills (CTBS). The aspects of reading motivation measured included intrinsic and extrinsic motivation, and reading self-efficacy.

The contribution of general motivation to achievement in reading has been observed for middle and high school students, as well as elementary students. Gottfried (1985) reported that her academic intrinsic motivation measure predicted students' school achievement in reading, and perceptions of competence in reading, for seventh- and eighth-grade students. Confirming this result, Lehrer and Hieronymus (1977) reported that eighth-grade students' reading achievement on the Iowa Test of Basic Skills was predicted by a reading motivation measure. Finally, Raymond Cattell (1972) reported that a school motivation measure predicted performance on a reading achievement test published by Educational Testing Service (ETS) for sixth and seventh graders. He found that motivation for schooling predicted reading achievement, independently from personality and ability variables.

One of the important characteristics of academic intrinsic motivation, as it is differentiated into subject areas such as reading, is its growing stability over time. You may want to identify developmental trends explicitly and note increasing stability with age. The developmental aspects of the motivation-reading link are not clear for children younger than ages 9 to 10. Wigfield and Guthrie (1997) assessed children's enjoyment of reading over 3 years, in a sample of children who began the study in Grades 1, 2, and 4. They found that the stability correlations in children's interest increased over time. For instance, the stability correlation for first- and second-grade children was .18, and for fifth- and sixth-grade children .58. Gottfried, Fleming, and Gottfried (2001) reported a longitudinal investigation of students ages 9 to 17. They observed that academic intrinsic motivation was stable throughout these years with stability increasing over time, and moderate stability observed for both boys and girls. As the construct has a certain degree of permanence and durability throughout the schooling years, its influence on tested comprehension will have some level of consistency, particularly after second or third grade.

In addition, reading motivation has been observed to predict aspects of reading that are correlated to achievement, such as students' amount and breadth of reading (Baker & Wigfield, 1999; Wigfield & Guthrie, 1997). Cox and Guthrie (2001) showed that students' amount of reading in Grades 3 and 5 was predicted by motivation when previous reading achievement and measured use of comprehension strategies were controlled statistically. Because it is known that amount of reading predicts levels of reading achievement (Baker & Wigfield, 1999), it is important to consider the possibility that reading motivation has an indirect effect on achievement through increasing students' amount and breadth of reading, as well as a direct effect on achievement.

Because the variables of reading achievement, reading motivation, amount of reading, and previous reading achievement are all correlated, it is sensible to examine the unique effects of reading motivation controlling other variables. Wang and Guthrie (2004) used the International Association for the Evaluation of Educational Achievement (IEA) Narrative Reading Comprehension Test as the dependent variable in a study with 187 American and 197 Chinese Grade 4 students. This measure has four narrative texts, 20 multiple-choice questions, and was found to be reliable within a cross-cultural study in 32 countries. The scale of intrinsic motivation consisted of 19 items regarding students' curiosity, involvement, and preference for challenge in reading, such as the following:

I like to read about new things. (*curiosity*)

I feel like I make friends with people in good books. (*involvement*)

I like hard, challenging books. (*challenge*)

Extrinsic motivation was measured with items on recognition, grades, social, competition, and compliance, such as the following:

I like having the teacher say I read well. (*recognition*)

I look forward to finding out my reading grade. (*grades*)

I like to tell my family about what I am reading. (*social*)

I like being the best at reading. (*competition*)

I read because I have to. (*compliance*)

Children responded as follows on a 4-point Likert-type scale: *very different from me, a little different from me, a little like me,* and *a lot like me.* Students' amount of reading was measured with the Reading Activity Inventory (RAI), consisting of 20 items that included school reading and reading for enjoyment. Items consisted of questions such as, "How often do you read a major book for your own interest?" with a response mode 1 to 4 from *almost never* to *almost everyday.* The data were subjected to structural equation modeling. The optimal model revealed that intrinsic motivation was highly predictive of text comprehension when past reading achievement, extrinsic motivation, amount of reading for enjoyment, and amount of reading for school, were statistically controlled (see Fig. 8.2). Under these conditions, past reading achievement positively predicted text comprehension and extrinsic motivation negatively predicted text comprehension. It is interesting that the optimal model for the American and Chinese populations was substantially similar. The two models did not differ in a statistical test of their distinctiveness. Thus, within the limits of this statistical modeling approach for both American and Chinese students, intrinsic motiva-

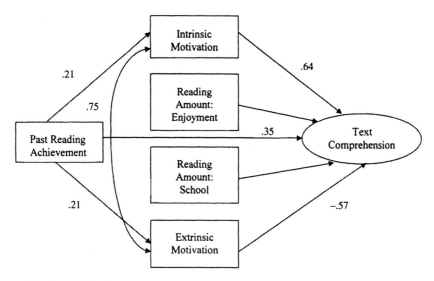

FIG. 8.2. Model of reading motivation, comprehension, and achievement.
Note: All weights are significant at $p < .05$; CFI = .95; RMSEA = .05.

tion for reading was highly predictive of reading comprehension test
performance, with statistical controls for potentially confounding variables.

It is reasonable to ask whether there are certain mechanisms that are relatively more important for transmitting motivation to measured reading
achievement. Several investigators have emphasized students' use of complex
comprehension strategies in this regard. For example, Paris, Lipson, and Wixson
(1983) proposed that to become strategic readers, students depend partly on
their intentions, perceptions, and motivations. In a review of literature, Carr,
Mizelle, and Charak (1998) argued that there is a causal pathway from reading
motivation to comprehension strategy use to reading achievement. In this proposed casual chain, the links between strategy use, self-regulation, and achievement, have been confirmed by many investigations, some of which are reported
in the National Reading Panel Report. The association between reading motivation and strategy use has been shown by such investigators as Pintrich and
DeGroot (1990) and Cox and Guthrie (2001) for elementary students in reading (see Pintrich, 2000, for a review). However, the plausible hypothesis that
the effects of motivation on achievement are mediated through strategy-use
has not been subjected to such approaches as path analysis.

Motivation's effects on performance are not always positive. Indeed, some
aspects of motivation can act as barriers to successful reading. Low self-efficacy

is one example (Bandura, 1997; Schunk & Zimmerman, 1997). Children's self-efficacy is determined by a number of factors, the most important being their previous performance. When students do well they gain confidence in their reading; when they do poorly their confidence wanes. The early elementary years are a crucial time for the development of reading self-efficacy, because there is such a strong focus on learning various skills related to reading. Students who struggle with reading early on are likely to develop low self-efficacy for reading. Confronted with a challenging (although manageable) text, such students in the intermediate grades (3–8) simply say, "I can't do it." Due to text characteristics, such as the amount of print, small font size, presence of unfamiliar words, and so on, they withdraw from the text and do not attempt to read. Such students will likely struggle with complex reading assessments.

Children who experience repeated failure in reading and develop low self-efficacy for reading are at risk for becoming helpless in learning situations. Learned helplessness refers to the belief that no matter how hard one tries, success will not be possible (see Dweck, 1975, 2002). Helplessness has its roots in low efficacy. When children have little or no confidence in their abilities, they come to believe success in school, and at activities like reading, is not possible for them. Such children seek to avoid challenging reading activities and attempt to withdraw (either literally or figuratively) when they perceive a task or activity as too difficult. As we discuss later, such children likely will have great difficulty completing challenging reading comprehension tests.

Anxiety is an equally debilitating negative motivation (Hill & Wigfield, 1984; Wigfield & Eccles, 1989). Like learned helplessness, anxiety can arise when children do poorly in school. Excessively critical parents with overly high expectations can also produce anxiety in children. Children's anxiety often increases over the school years, and strongly influences their performance in school. Hill and Sarason (1966) found that by the end of elementary school, the most anxious children were 2 years behind low anxious children in reading and math performance.

With respect to reading, anxious readers are nervous, fearful, and distracted when they are confronted with reading tasks (Gottfried, 1982). Stemming from myriad unpleasant experiences with reading activities, this anxiety is maintained, even if the anxious student has adequate reading ability. Because anxiety correlates negatively with intrinsic reading motivation (Gottfried, 1990), there are often many challenges for the teacher or test administrator in initiating reading with these students. However, researchers have shown that changing testing conditions can improve anxious children's performance on different kinds of assessments (Hill & Wigfield, 1984). For instance, giving students instructions about how to handle difficult items, and reducing test time pressure, facilitate anxious students' performance.

THE SITUATIONAL PERSPECTIVE
ON READING MOTIVATION

As noted earlier, motivation for reading is often very specific to a particular type of reading in a certain context. For example, some people are intrinsically motivated to read mystery novels on vacation, but do not read mystery novels at other times. For these individuals, the particular motivation is situated in this genre and this occasion. By situated motivation, we mean motivation that occurs for certain tasks or activities, in particular contexts (see Hickey, 1997; Paris & Turner, 1994; Urdan, 1999, for discussion of situated models of motivation). These responses may be favorable values or positive affects, such as enjoyment, but they are transitory and are not a permanent characteristic of the individual.

This distinction has been studied primarily with reference to interest, although as discussed earlier, mastery goals and self-efficacy have both task-specific and general characteristics. The terms used for these distinctions, by theorists such as Schiefele (1999), are personal interest for general motivation and situational interest for situational motivation. Concomitantly, Hidi and Harackiewicz (2000) used the terms individual interest (related to general motivation) and situational interest (related to situational motivation). Interest researchers concur that situational motivation is an affective reaction that is likely to be temporary. It can be positive or negative, in the sense that one may be interested in a text on snakes without liking snakes. When a person is situationally motivated, he or she is in "an emotional state of concentration and enjoyment that accompanies an activity" (Schiefele, 1999). Under these conditions of situational motivation, individuals are likely to experience enjoyment, pleasure, and effortless attention. Their values for the activity are likely to be positive, with the sense that they are worthy, important, and relevant. These responses are "elicited by specific situational cues" (e.g., text features; Schiefele, 1999, p. 264) and are "generated by certain conditions and/or stimuli in the environment that focus attention" (Hidi & Harackiewicz, 2000, p. 152).

We believe that situational motivation is particularly important for reading comprehension assessment because it is likely that tests involve temporary, affective states that may be important to students' cognitive functioning during the testing process. A student's more general motivation, such as overall self-efficacy and intrinsic motivation, likely influences his or her general approach to an assessment. A student high in self-efficacy for reading, for instance, approaches reading assessments with more confidence that he or she will do well than does a student low in efficacy. However, once the assessment begins, the student's situational motivation likely becomes the crucial motivational driving force, as each assessment has unique characteristics that influence a student's motivation.

A reading comprehension assessment may be considered a task in which the individual may have high or low situational motivation. Under conditions of high situational motivation, there is evidence that students perform relatively deep processing of text and they sustain their attention to cognitive performance. Schiefele (1999) reported that a review of 14 studies on situational motivation and text learning yielded an average correlation of .33 ($p < .05$) between situational interest and text learning. This positive relation between situational motivation and task performance in reading was independent of text length, readability, importance of text, unit of analysis, nature of text (narrative versus expositional), method of learning, age of student, and reading ability. Note that reading time was not controlled in most of these studies, and the extent to which the interest effect was mediated by time spent in concentrated reading effort is relatively unknown at present. How might situational motivation be influenced by different reading comprehension assessments? We consider this issue next.

Characteristics That Influence Situational Motivation in Reading Comprehension Assessments

The main purpose of this chapter is to investigate the roles of reading motivation to students' performance on reading comprehension assessments. To examine the contributions of situational motivation to reading comprehension assessment we can view an assessment as a task embedded in a particular context. There are characteristics of the assessment setting that can influence student motivation and performance in that setting. These include characteristics of the text, student choice and control in the setting, student goals, difficulty sequence of the items, complexity of the task, response opportunities, and accompanying activities that may influence the situational motivation of students during an assessment, and thereby influence performance on the assessment. We examine each of these in turn.

Text Interest.   Situational motivation for reading has usually been measured with ratings of interestingness. For example, students are given a text on a specific topic, such as falcons, and asked to rate questions such as, "How interesting is this to you?" on a scale of 1 to 10, from *totally boring* to *extremely fascinating*. In other measures, students may be requested to rate individual segments of a three-page passage on a topic, such as grasslands, and their situational interest for the different aspects of grasslands (grasses, zebras, cheetahs) is related to their comprehension of the text segments. Such ratings of interestingness are consistently correlated with text comprehension (for a review, see Schiefele,

1999). However, prior knowledge may be a confounding variable correlated with both situational interest and reading achievement. To examine this, Schiefele (1999) has measured prior knowledge with three response questions on multiple-choice tests and correlated the findings to the effect of interest on achievement. His studies showed that the interest effect is independent of prior knowledge or intelligence in the form of verbal ability. In addition, students' interest in a text will influence some of their cognitive processes more than others. Deep processing strategies, such as activating prior knowledge, linking knowledge with new information in text, monitoring comprehension, and drawing inferences during reading, are consistently more highly correlated with situational motivation than strategies for surface processing, such as rehearsing individual words, memorizing sentences, or completing tasks as quickly as possible. Therefore, text interest is important by virtue of its effect on deep processing, which is likely to foster measured comprehension.

Several aspects of text are known to influence perceived interest by students. Schraw, Bruning, and Svoboda (1995) showed that students' ratings of ease of reading, presence of vivid details, attractiveness of illustrations, text length, and relevance, were predictive of interestingness (Fransson, 1977; Schraw, Bruning, & Svoboda, 1995). Wade, Buxton, and Kelly (1991) reported that students' interest was related to their perceived importance, surprise, and familiarity with the content. It is possible that text interest is more important for lower achievers than higher achieving students. deSousa and Oakhill (1996) showed that for elementary school students, text interest had a greater influence on reading comprehension for poor comprehenders than for good ones. They attributed this finding to lower levels of comprehension monitoring during the reading assessment, which was measured directly in the investigation. It is possible that higher achievers spontaneously perform comprehension monitoring during reading, irrespective of text interest, whereas lower achievers are more likely to self-monitor if they find the text interesting. Further work on this issue seems to be needed. In particular, analyses of different assessments to determine the interest level of the text passages included in the assessment should be done.

Student Choice and Control.   In most reading assessments, students are given a series of passages to read and a sequence of questions to answer. Usually there is little or no choice for the learner within the task. Yet, one of the most strongly supported principles of motivation theory is that students' control and perceived autonomy are associated with motivation and interest in learning and performance (Ryan & Deci, 2000). This has been demonstrated in studies in which choice is measured generally and specifically. For example, in a study of students' perceptions of general levels of student choice, Skinner and Belmont (1993) showed that when teachers afford students choices of specific classroom tasks, students become invested, commit effort, and persevere in their attempts to succeed. In a study of elementary school children's specific choices of reading activities, Reynolds and Symons (2001) showed that when students were given a choice of which text to use in a reading comprehension and search task, they invested more time and effort, and had more correct responses, than a condition in which students were not provided a choice. Therefore, the prediction from self-determination theory, that support for students' autonomy increases intrinsic motivation and fosters academic achievement, is confirmed in specific reading activities for elementary school children, as well as college students (Benware & Deci, 1984). Even when the choices given to students are irrelevant to the task, students' interest and perseverance in the task are increased (Cordova & Lepper, 1996). Under some conditions, learner control in computer-assisted instruction increases achievement more highly than program control (Kinzie, Sullivan, & Berdel, 1988). By making their own choices during a complex task, students may feel more intrinsically motivated, which ultimately results in better performance.

Certainly, most tests place students in a "low-control" position. Although this may be difficult to change in some assessments, this lack of choice or control in the assessment task is likely to decrease situational motivation, which may decrease students' attention and lead them to withdraw from attempting items or minimize the use of their best cognitive skills.

Task Goals.   Currently in motivation theory, three types of goal orientation are distinguishable. With a *mastery goal orientation*, students seek to understand the material, gain command of the content, and bring new information into their existing knowledge. With a *performance-approach goal orientation*, students attempt to succeed on tasks because they are seeking recognition, competitive advantage, or high grades. Finally, with a *performance-avoidance goal orientation*, students act to prevent their parents or friends from perceiving them as incompetent, to preclude the shame of failure, and to avoid looking foolish.

A substantial number of correlational and experimental studies have found that mastery goals enable students to perform better on tests, and recall more knowledge, than do situations in which performance-avoidance goals are activated. Performance-approach goals also can facilitate motivation and performance, although there is some debate about this (Bergin, 1995; Harackiewicz, Baron, Pintrich, Elliot, & Thrash, 2002; Midgley, Kaplan, & Middleton, 2001; Pintrich, 2000). Within a specific circumstance, such as reading a two-page text or taking an exam, mastery goals and performance goals can be induced in students (Elliot & Harackiewicz, 1996; Graham & Golan, 1990). Whether goals can be manipulated within authentic testing situations is unknown, but it should be recognized that these motivational goals are highly likely to influence students' performance in reading comprehension tests. Testing situations eliciting performance-avoidance goals will be the ones most likely to lower many students' performance.

Difficulty Sequence.   One situational motivational construct that is likely to be operational in testing situations is self-efficacy, referring to students' belief in their capacity to do a specific task. In a review of research on self-efficacy in reading, Schunk and Zimmerman (1997) found that students' level of accuracy in responding to comprehension questions grew with increasing self-efficacy during a task and fell with decreasing self-efficacy. In many assessments, the items are sequenced from relatively easy to relatively more difficult. It is possible, although unknown empirically, that this sequence increases students' self-efficacy for performing the items. This expectation is based on the assumption that students accurately recognize their success on relatively easier items and that they set short-term goals for doing well in subsequent items. These assumptions seem plausible for Grade 3 students and above. The body of evidence for the effects of self-efficacy in reading achievement tasks, involving relatively brief texts and questions with short response formats, is clear and affirmative. Investigation on whether these relations should occur with actual testing materials is merited.

Task Complexity.   Reading comprehension assessments vary substantially in their complexity. Higher complexity occurs with the use of longer tests, extended written response requirements, integration across multiple texts as a requirement for success, and multiple formats in responding. We formed the hypothesis that reading comprehension assessments with high complexity would be more sensitive to reading motivation than reading comprehension assessments that were less complex. Our rationale is that motivational constructs, such as intrinsic motivation to read, self-efficacy for reading tasks, and interest in text, are all known to increase students' effort, concentration, and perseverance in reading tasks. Thus, if a reading assessment has a high level of complexity, students' sustained effort, avoidance of distractions, and commitment to completing tasks successfully, are likely to contribute to successful performance. In contrast, in a simpler reading comprehension task, which may consist of a short passage, a brief selected response to a few items in a relatively short amount of time would be less likely to be influenced by motivational attributes.

We examined this hypothesis with 400 Grade 3 students in December 2001. A test was given in three parallel forms on the topics of (a) ponds and deserts, (b) rivers and grasslands, and (c) oceans and forests. The assessments consisted of the following:

1. Prior knowledge, in which students wrote on a blank sheet of paper, everything they knew about the biomes and animals' survival within those biomes for the form to which they had been assigned.

2. Questioning, in which students wrote, for 15 min, questions they had about living in those biomes.

3. Searching for information in a 75-page packet with 22 sections, including a table of contents and index that simulated multiple trade books, occurring for 50 min in two sessions.

4. Writing what they knew about living in the biomes assigned to them in an open-response essay after reading for 30 min. These written statements were coded to a rubric on a scale 1 (*low knowledge*) to 6 (*high knowledge*) with 85% interrater agreement for exact coding and 100% interrater agreement for adjacent coding.

5. Computer-based assessment consisting of reading a 300-word passage and rating the relatedness of pairs of words drawn from the passage. Nine words were selected for 36 ratings, which required 7 min for reading and 15 min for rating. Proximity data were analyzed by Pathfinder to provide a score of 0 to 1, indicating similarity of the students' knowledge structure to the experts' knowledge structure for this text.

6. Students completed a questionnaire on motivations for reading (MRQ) that tapped intrinsic motivation, self-efficacy, and extrinsic motivation.

7. Students completed a reading activity inventory (RAI) that measured the amount and breadth of their in-school and out-of-school reading.

The students' reading comprehension on the complex assessment task, for example, the score on writing about what they learned from the packet, was the dependent variable in a multiple regression with students' prior knowledge, passage comprehension (performance on the short passages on the computer-based assessment), and motivation (score on the motivation questionnaire) as independent variables. In this analysis, the passage comprehension on the short passage contributed to comprehension scores on the complex task, with a beta weight of .39 ($p < .001$). Importantly, motivation contributed significantly to performance on the complex comprehension task, after the other variables of prior knowledge and passage comprehension had been accounted for, with a beta of .26 ($p < .01$). Increasing levels of motivation were clearly as-

sociated with increasing levels of reading comprehension on the complex reading task. The same benefit of motivation for success on the complex reading
assessment task appeared for students who were low on passage comprehension
as students who were high on passage comprehension. In conclusion, when the
reading comprehension assessment was complex, students' levels of motivation
consistently influenced task performance, even when prior knowledge for that
content and passage comprehension for texts relevant to those topics in the
complex assessment were statistically controlled (see Fig. 8.3).

To further examine this interpretation, we used the same measures in a different multiple regression analysis. The less complex passage comprehension
task was the dependent variable, and the same motivation, prior knowledge,
and complex comprehension task scores were included as independent variables. The result was that motivation did not contribute significantly to comprehension on the simpler task, when students' prior knowledge and
performance on the more complex task were statistically accounted for. Taking
the findings of these two regression analyses together, we conclude that students' reading motivation contributed significantly to their success on a complex reading comprehension assessment task, but motivation did not predict
performance on the simpler passage comprehension task. This suggests that
task complexity within reading comprehension assessments influenced the extent to which motivation had an impact on the outcomes. Also, see Paris (1998)
for more benefits of task complexity in reading assessment.

Classroom Activities Accompanying a Reading Comprehension Assessment.
In most classrooms, tests are given in isolation from other activities. However, it
is possible to link a brief accompanying activity to a reading comprehension assessment, thereby influencing motivation on the assessment. This might be especially valuable if accompanying activities could induce positive influences on
motivation to perform well on assessments. There is evidence to suggest that an
activity that is situationally motivating will increase students' motivation for

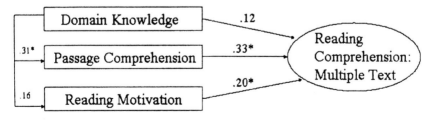

FIG. 8.3.   Contributions to reading comprehension assessment performance.
Note: * = $p < .05$; R = .51; CFI = .95.

performing another highly related activity. In an extensive review, Hidi and Harackiewicz (2000) stated the following: "We agree with Mitchell (1993) that creating situational interest may work to enhance individual interest in some students" (p. 157). Swan and Guthrie (in press) examined this hypothesis with a two × two factorial experiment with fifth graders. Half of the students participated in a situationally motivating activity, consisting of observing live crabs in the classroom, whereas the other half did not perform this observation. Immediately following, half of the students read texts related to the crabs they observed and half of the students did not. Then, students rated the interestingness of their activities. Following their reading, students wrote what they had learned from the text about survival of crabs and other animals. Results showed a statistically significant interaction, such that the students with the highest test scores on the reading comprehension assessment had participated in both the observational activity and read the interesting texts. We conclude that accompanying a text with a situationally motivating activity leads to higher comprehension of the text than simply presenting the text in isolation.

This interpretation was embellished by the finding that when the ratings of interestingness of the accompanying activity were entered as a controlling variable, the effect of the accompanying activity and interesting text on comprehension was not significant. In other words, the effect of combining a situationally motivating activity with interesting text on reading comprehension was mediated by the level of situational motivation for the activity. Students who did not find the activity to be motivating were not higher in their reading comprehension performance than students who did not participate in the motivating activity (Swan & Guthrie, 2000).

This principle of accompanying activity has been shown in inverse form. When students were deprived from doing an attractive activity, consisting of coloring pictures, and were required to replace it with the less attractive activity of reading, their later interest in reading was undermined. We interpret this to mean that when reading is viewed as a replacement of a situationally motivating activity, rather than an extension of one, reading interest may be reduced (Higgins, Lee, Kwon, & Trope, 1995). To summarize, because reading is never totally isolated in the classroom, the relation of reading assessment to the classroom activity structure might be considered an issue related to motivation for assessment.

Extrinsic Motivations for Reading Assessment Performance.   It is possible that performance on reading comprehension assessments can be increased with extrinsic incentives, such as rewards and recognition. Motivation theory contains substantial evidence that under certain conditions, these constructs increase academic achievement (Cameron & Pierce, 1994; Lepper & Henderlong, 2000). The National Assessment of Educational Progress (NAEP) is an important assessment for Federal policymaking, but student performance may be reduced by lack of motivation and effort because it is a "low stakes" measure for individuals and schools. To address this, O'Neil, Sugrue, and Baker (1995) found that an extrinsic incentive, consisting of money, increased the performance of 8th and 12th graders on the mathematics section of NAEP. This finding suggests that there is a motivational element in NAEP math scores. However, this solution to the problem may not be easy to scale up for widespread application.

In another attempt to motivate students extrinsically to perform well on the NAEP, Kiplinger and Linn (1993) embedded the NAEP into the curriculum-based assessments of the state of Georgia. Mixed results were found with facilitation for one set of data, but no facilitation for another data set. In this case, it may be that performance-avoidance goals (e.g., fear of failure) rather than performance-approach goals (e.g., desire for recognition) were evoked, and it is well established that performance-avoidance goals can readily undermine, rather than enhance, achievement (Midgley, Kaplan, & Middleton, 2001; Pintrich, 2000). If extrinsic incentives lead students to seek recognition and success, they may be valuable, but if such incentives cause teachers or students to try to avoid failure, or minimize publicity for their incompetence, extrinsic incentives may, in fact, be counterproductive for reading comprehension assessments.

RESEARCH AGENDA: WHAT DO WE NEED TO KNOW REGARDING MOTIVATION AND READING COMPREHENSION ASSESSMENT?

We have reviewed evidence that reading motivation influences children's performance on different kinds of reading assessments. We conclude the chapter with recommendations for further research needed on the topics we addressed. We also provide some policy recommendations regarding motivation and reading assessment.

First, we believe it is desirable to conceptualize motivation as a component of reading comprehension and reading comprehension assessment should be explored more fully. If we believe that reading comprehension should be defined to include motivation, then valid assessment should include a motivational dimension. This may consist of an explicit motivation assessment, or the inclusion of tasks known to be highly correlated with one or more motivation constructs.

The definition of reading comprehension offered from the RAND panel is "reading comprehension is the process of simultaneously extracting and constructing meaning through interaction and involvement with written language" (Snow, 2002, p. 11). This includes the phrase *involvement with written language*, which refers to motivational processes. Following this definition, a valid reading comprehension assessment should be sensitive to students' motivations, language, and cognitive capabilities. Of course, it could be argued that reading comprehension is primarily a language-cognitive process and that assessments should tap language and cognitive competencies, holding motivation as a separate construct whose impact on the outcomes of assessments should be minimized. This is a policy issue about desired attributes in the definition of reading comprehension and the validity of assessments.

Our belief is that motivational processes are integral to reading comprehension. As we have discussed in this chapter, evidence suggests that motivation is correlated to comprehension. Further, motivation is causally related to comprehension in the sense that classroom conditions that increase reading motivation also increase reading comprehension and recall of text that is read. Consequently, we suggest that a measure of reading should be sensitive to motivation, just as it is sensitive to language and cognitive characteristics of students. As we reported in this chapter, one method to accomplish sensitivity to motivation is to have relatively long, complex tasks. Student effort, persistence, desire for success, and self-efficacy for reading will then be reflected in students' cognitive performance on the assessment.

One possibility is to use open-ended response formats that require extended writing. Although effort-demanding, these formats may not be feasible for widespread testing practices. However, longer texts, with complex writing requirements, could be used as criteria for judging the validity of briefer measures. In that case, a short (and usable) test that correlated better with the complex, motivationally sensitive test would be more valid than a short test that correlated less well with this criterion. If the definition of reading comprehension is rightly incorporating motivation, then tests of reading comprehension should meet the standard of correlating with motivation measures.

Second, it would be valuable to assess the relations of children's reading motivation to their performance on currently widely-used reading tests. Such research would tell us the extent to which measures such as the Iowa Test of Basic Skills, the Gates–MacGinitie Reading Test, or NAEP, are loaded with general motivation and situational motivation, as well as cognitive and language competencies.

To examine this issue, measures of motivations for reading, including intrinsic motivation, extrinsic motivation, self-efficacy for reading, and reading attitude, should be correlated with these tests. Age and demographic factors should be considered. There are a variety of measures of these constructs available in the literature that could be used in such research, and many of them have been mentioned in this chapter. However, these measures were designed primarily to inform us about the nature of a particular aspect of reading motivation, such as reading self-efficacy, rather than to inform us about children's motivation on reading comprehension tests. Further, as discussed earlier, many of these measures are relatively general, not providing a clear indication of children's situated reading motivation.

In addition, there are measurement issues with these different motivation scales. It is a challenge to give group-administered, self-report assessments of motivation to students who are 4 to 7 years old, due to their limitations in reading proficiency. Such constraints also occur for low achieving readers who are older (e.g., a 10-year-old reading at a 7-year-old level). The developmental consistency of the measure across ages 8 to 18 should be examined.

Self-report measures of motivation are subject to social desirability, as are all self-report measures, and this may be especially problematic with younger children. Students will sometimes give answers they think the teacher or administrator expects, rather than "authentic" ones. This problem can be minimized with high caliber items, response-formats, directions, and monitoring during administration. Regrettably, few measures of reading motivation have been constructed and fully validated. One strong criterion for a paper-and-pencil, self-report measure of reading motivation is an individual interview. A high correlation between a paper-and-pencil measure and a 30-min interview on reading motivation for 100 students would provide initial evidence of validity for the paper-and-pencil measure.

Third, we need to address whether reading comprehension assessments should be designed to increase rather than decrease students' motivation during the assessment. It is quite possible to redesign assessment measures to increase motivation by attending to the task characteristics that influence motivation, as described in this chapter. A test redesign endeavor could identify means to improve scores on tests by enabling students to purposefully use their cognitive competencies in the testing situation. It will be valuable to investigate whether such effects occur equally for all students, or whether they facilitate performance of traditionally low achieving populations.

One possible redesign includes the characteristics described in this chapter as relevant to motivation. It was shown that text interest and choice are motivational constructs. For example, an assessment for 9-year-old students could have five sections. In each section, students choose between three texts on different topics. Students are given 2 min to choose in each section, and then the test for that section begins. Time in testing per se should not be squandered with choice making. Item difficulties should proceed from low (easy) to high (difficult) to lend students a sense of efficacy for success at the beginning. Complexity of the text and response requirements should be high in some portions of the test to reflect effort, perseverance, and task completion. Finally, the goals announced to the students and the reporting of the test should emphasize the positive attributes of text understanding and display of competencies, rather than the negative attributes of embarrassment and humiliation for low scores. An assessment with these characteristics should be compared to a traditional test in terms of students' motivations for reading and performing during the assessment. There are many other redesigns that could be constructed.

Fourth, there is a strong need to design assessment instruments that are indicative of an actively literate individual. This point ties directly to our third "what if" question that opened this chapter: What if the goal of students not only being competent at reading but committed to reading goes unfulfilled because we do not have measures of commitment to reading? In reviewing the short list of high priority goals in education, and especially reading education, we encounter the following: (a) high achievement in valid measures; (b) equity in achievement across ethnicity, gender, and geographical location; and (c) use of reading for productive employment, continuing education, and personal enjoyment. The last goal is motivational. Although this educational aim is widely shared publicly and professionally at Federal, state, and local levels, we do not know whether we are attaining it, because we have not seriously attempted to measure this outcome of schooling. Yet, substantial evidence suggests that young adults' beliefs about literacy, uses of reading, and reading behaviors influence their income, employment, further education, and community participation (Guthrie, Schafer, & Hutchinson, 1991). It would facilitate this educational objective to develop indicators of students' motivation and engagement in reading to complement our current measures of achievement in reading comprehension.

This aspect of reading motivation assessment is most speculative. A research endeavor here should begin with brainstorming, and follow with careful investigation. For example, it is possible to imagine different kinds of measures of how widely and frequently students read. We have measured this by giving a reading activity inventory to children which asks them to indicate whether they read different kinds of books, and how often (Guthrie, McGough, &Wigfield, 1994). As noted earlier, we have found that this measure relates to reading achievement (Baker & Wigfield, 1999; Wigfield & Guthrie, 1997).

Another such measure is the Title Recognition Test, in which a list of book titles and nontitles are presented and students distinguish among them. For example, students rate whether the following are books: *War and Peace* (yes or no), and *War and Victory* (yes or no). Also, Author Recognition Tests are used in which students distinguish between authors and nonauthors. Stanovich and Cunningham (1993) reported that these indicators of wide and frequent reading predict many competencies such as world knowledge, vocabulary, and reading proficiency skills. Such an indicator could also be used to gauge students' overall involvement with reading.

It is also possible to imagine an assessment in which students analyze vignettes of adults engaged in reading activities to identify characteristics of "effective readers." Of course, students could write an essay on their book reading, but coding it would be laborious. All of these measures would be validated against individual interviews, and probably knowledge measures, because individuals should be knowledgeable in their chosen domain(s) of reading. Other factors being equal, students who show higher predisposition to read widely and frequently have better prospects for continuing education and productive work than students who prefer not to read. Therefore, such measures of "reading engagement" should be considered as a complement to the standardized reading achievement test scores and grade point averages of students as indicators of their currently existing qualities and their potentials for future productivity.

In conclusion, we have reviewed research relevant to three questions concerning possible relations of students' motivation to their performance on reading comprehension assessments. This research provides preliminary evidence that motivation indeed does influence students' performance on such assessments. Although more research is needed to document these relations more specifically, we believe assessments of reading motivation should become a part of assessments of children's reading comprehension.

REFERENCES

Anderman, E. M., Austin, C. C., & Johnson, D. M. (2002). The development of goal orientation. In A. Wigfield & J. S. Eccles (Eds.), *Development of achievement motivation* (pp. 197–220). San Diego, CA: Academic Press.

Baker, L., & Wigfield, A. (1999). Dimensions of children's motivation for reading and their relations to reading activity and reading achievement. *Reading Research Quarterly, 34,* 452–477.

Bandura, A. (1997). *Self-efficacy: The exercise of control.* New York: Freeman.

Benware, C. A., & Deci, E. (1984). Quality of learning with an active versus passive motivational set. *American Educational Research Journal, 21,* 755–765.

Bergin, D. A. (1995). Effects of a mastery versus competitive motivation situation on learning. *Journal of Experimental Education, 63,* 303–314.

Cameron, J., & Pierce, W. D. (1994). Reinforcement, reward, and intrinsic motivation: A meta-analysis. *Review of Educational Research, 64,* 363–423.

Carr, M., Mizelle, N. B., & Charak, D. (1998). Motivation to read and learn from text. In C. R. Hynd & S. A. Stahl (Eds.), *Learning from text across conceptual domains* (pp. 45–70). Mahwah, NJ: Lawrence Erlbaum Associates.

Cattell, R. B. (1972). Prediction of school achievement from motivation, personality, and ability measures. *Psychological Reports, 30,* 35–43.

Cordova, D. I., & Lepper, M. R. (1996). Intrinsic motivation and the process of learning: Beneficial effects of contextualization, personalization, and choice. *Journal of Educational Psychology, 88,* 715–730.

Cox, K. E., & Guthrie, J. T. (2001). Motivational and cognitive contributions to students' amount of reading. *Contemporary Educational Psychology, 26,* 116–131.

Deci, E., & Ryan, R. (2002). The paradox of achievement: The harder you push, the worse it gets. In C. Dweck (Ed.), *Improving academic achievement* (pp. 61–87). New York: Elsevier.

Deci, E. L., & Ryan, R. M. (1985). *Intrinsic motivation and self-determination in human behavior.* New York: Plenum.

deSousa, I., & Oakhill, J. (1996). Do levels of interest have an effect on children's comprehension monitoring performance? *British Journal of Educational Psychology, 66,* 471–482.

Dweck, C. S. (1975). The role of expectations and attributions in the alleviation of learned helplessness. *Journal of Personality and Social Psychology, 31,* 674–685.

Dweck, C. S. (2002). The development of ability conceptions. In A. Wigfield & J. S. Eccles (Eds.), *Development of achievement motivation* (pp. 57–88). San Diego, CA: Academic.

Elliot, A. J., & Harackiewicz, J. M. (1996). Approach and avoidance goals and intrinsic motivation: A mediational analysis. *Journal of Personality and Social Psychology, 70,* 461–475.

Fransson, A. (1977). On qualitative differences in learning: IV. Effects of intrinsic motivation and extrinsic test anxiety on process and outcome. *British Journal of Educational Psychology, 47,* 244–257.

Gottfried, A. E. (1982). Relationships between academic intrinsic motivation and anxiety in children and young adolescents. *Journal of School Psychology, 20,* 205–215.

Gottfried, A. E. (1985). Academic intrinsic motivation in elementary and junior high school students. *Journal of Educational Psychology, 77,* 631–645.

Gottfried, A. E. (1990). Academic intrinsic motivation in young elementary school children. *Journal of Educational Psychology, 82,* 525–538.

Gottfried, A. E., Fleming, J. S., & Gottfried, A. W. (2001). Continuity of academic intrinsic motivation from childhood through late adolescence: A longitudinal study. *Journal of Educational Psychology, 93,* 3–13.

Graesser, A. C., & Bertus, E. L. (1998). The construction of causal inferences while reading expository texts on science and technology. *Scientific Studies of Reading, 2,* 247–271.

Graham, S., & Golan, S. (1990). Motivational influences on cognition: Task involvement, ego involvement, and depth of information processing. *Journal of Educational Psychology, 83,* 187–194.

Guthrie, J. T. (2002). Preparing students for high-stakes test taking in reading. In A. Farstrup & S. J. Samuels (Eds.), *What research has to say about reading instruction* (pp. 370–391). Newark, DE: International Reading Association.

Guthrie, J. T., McGough, K., & Wigfield, A. (1994). *Measuring reading activity: An inventory* (Instructional Resource No. 4). Athens, GA: National Reading Research Center.

Guthrie, J. T., Schafer, W. D., & Hutchinson, S. R. (1991). Relationships of document literacy and prose literacy to occupational and societal characteristics of young Black and White adults. *Reading Research Quarterly, 25,* 31–48.

Guthrie J. T., & Wigfield, A. (1999). How motivation fits into a science of reading. *Scientific Studies of Reading, 3,* 199–205.

Guthrie, J. T., Wigfield, A., Metsala, J. L., & Cox, K. E. (1999). Motivational and cognitive predictors of text comprehension and reading amount. *Scientific Studies of Reading, 3,* 231–256.

Harackiewicz, J. M., Baron, K. E., Pintrich, P. R., Elliot, A. J., & Thrash, T. M. (2002). Revision of achievement goal theory: Necessary and illuminating. *Journal of Educational Psychology, 94,* 638–645.

Harter, S. (1981). New self-report scale of intrinsic versus extrinsic orientation in the classroom: Motivation and informational components. *Developmental Psychology, 117,* 300–312.

Hickey, D. T. (1997). Motivation and contemporary socio-constructivist instructional perspectives. *Educational Psychologist, 32,* 175–193.

Hidi, S., & Harackiewicz, J. M. (2000). Motivating the academically unmotivated: A critical issue for the 21st century. *Review of Educational Research, 70,* 151–179.

Higgins, E. T., Lee, J., Kwon, J., & Trope, Y. (1995). When combining intrinsic motivations undermines interest: A test of activity engagement theory. *Journal of Personality & Social Psychology, 68,* 749–767.

Hill, K. T., & Sarason, S. B. (1966). The relation of test anxiety and defensiveness to test and school performance over the elementary school years: A further longitudinal study. *Monographs of the Society for Research in Child Development, 31*(2, Serial No. 104).

Hill, K. T., & Wigfield, A. (1984). Test anxiety: A major educational problem and what can be done about it. *Elementary School Journal, 85,* 105–126.

Hoffman, R. A. (1995). A study of the effect of intrinsic and extrinsic motivation on achievement in grades three, four, five, and six. *Dissertation Abstracts International Section A: Humanities & Social Sciences, 55*(9-A), 2698.

Kintsch, W. (1998). *Comprehension: A paradigm for cognition.* Cambridge, England: Cambridge University Press.

Kinzie, M. B., Sullivan, H. J., & Berdel, R. L. (1988). Learner control and achievement in science computer-assisted instruction. *Journal of Educational Psychology, 80,* 299–303.

Kiplinger, V. L., & Linn, R. L. (1993). Raising the stakes of test administration: The impact on student performance on NAEP. *Education Assessment, 3,* 111–133.

Lehrer, B. E., & Hieronymus, A. N. (1977). Predicting achievement using intellectual, academic-motivational, and selected non-intellectual factors. *Journal of Experimental Education, 45,* 44–51.

Lepper, M. R., & Henderlong, J. (2000). Turning "play" into "work" and "work" into "play": Twenty-five years of research on intrinsic versus extrinsic motivation. In C. Sansone & J. M. Harackiewicz (Eds.), *Intrinsic and extrinsic motivation: The search for optimal motivation and performance* (pp. 257–307). San Diego, CA: Academic.

Midgley, C., Kaplan, A., & Middleton, M. (2001). Performance-approach goals: Good for what, for whom, under what circumstances, and at what cost? *Journal of Educational Psychology, 93,* 77–86.

Mitchell, M. (1993). Situational interest: Its multifaceted structure in the secondary school mathematics classroom. *Journal of Educational Psychology, 85,* 424–436.

O'Neil, H. F., Sugrue, B., & Baker, E. L. (1995). Effects of motivational interventions on the national assessment of educational progress mathematics performance. *Educational Assessment, 3,* 135–157.

Pajares, F. (1996). Self-efficacy beliefs in achievement settings. *Review of Educational Research, 66,* 543–578.

Paris, S. G. (1998). Why learner-centered assessment is better than high-stakes testing. In N. M. Lambert & B. L. McCombs (Eds.), *How students learn: Reforming schools through learner-centered education* (pp. 189–209). Washington, DC: American Psychological Association.

Paris, S. G., Lipson, M. Y., & Wixson, K. K. (1983). Becoming a strategic reader. *Contemporary Educational Psychology, 8,* 293–316.

Paris, S. G., & Turner, J. C. (1994). Situated motivation. In P. R. Pintrich, D. R. Brown, & C. E. Weinstein (Eds.), *Student motivation, cognition, and learning* (pp. 213–237). Hillsdale, NJ: Lawrence Erlbaum Associates.

Pintrich, P. (2000). An achievement goal perspective on issues in motivation terminology, theory and research. *Contemporary Educational Psychology, 25,* 92–104.

Pintrich, P., & DeGroot, E. (1990). Motivational and self-regulated learning components of classroom academic performance. *Journal of Educational Psychology, 82,* 33–40.

Reynolds, P. L., & Symons, S. (2001). Motivational variables and children's text search. *Journal of Educational Psychology, 93,* 14–23.

Ryan, R. M., & Deci, E. L. (2000). Intrinsic and extrinsic motivations: Classic definitions and new directions. *Contemporary Educational Psychology, 25,* 54–67.

Sansone, C., & Harackiewicz, J. M. (Eds.). (2000). *Intrinsic and extrinsic motivation: The search for optimal motivation and performance.* San Diego, CA: Academic.

Schiefele, U. (1999). Interest and learning from text. *Scientific Studies of Reading, 3,* 257–279.

Schraw, G., Bruning, R., & Svoboda, C. (1995). Sources of situational interest. *Journal of Reading Behavior, 27,* 1–19.

Schunk D., & Zimmerman, B. (1997). Developing self-efficacious readers and writers: The role of social and self-regulatory processes. In J. Guthrie & A. Wigfield (Eds.), *Reading engagement: Motivating readers through integrated instruction* (pp. 34–51). Newark, DE: International Reading Association.

Skinner, E., & Belmont, M. J. (1993). Motivation in the classroom: Reciprocal effects of teacher behavior and students' engagement across the school year. *Journal of Educational Psychology, 85,* 571–581.

Snow, C. (2002). *Reading for understanding: Toward a research and development program in reading comprehension.* Arlington, VA: RAND.

Stanovich, K. E., & Cunningham, A. E. (1993). Where does knowledge come from? Specific associations between print exposure and information acquisition. *Journal of Educational Psychology, 85,* 211–229.

Swan, E. A., & Guthrie, J. T. (in press). *Benefits of science observation and science trade books on learning conceptual knowledge.*

Sweet, A. P., Guthrie, J. T., & Ng, M. (1998). Teacher perceptions and student reading motivation. *Journal of Educational Psychology, 90,* 210–224.

Urdan, T. (Ed.). (1999). *The role of context (Advances in motivation and achievement, Vol. 11).* Stamford, CT: JAI.

Urdan, T. (Ed.). (1999). *Advances in motivation and achievement, Volume II: Motivation in context.* Stamford, CT: JAI.

Wade, S., Buxton, W., & Kelly, M. (1991). Using think-alouds to examine reader-text interest. *Reading Research Quarterly, 34,* 194–216.

Wang, J. H. Y., & Guthrie, J. T. (2004). Modeling the effects of intrinsic motivation, extrinsic motivation, amount of reading, and past reading achievement on text comprehension between U.S. and Chinese students. *Reading Research Quarterly, 39,* 162–186.

Wigfield, A., & Eccles, J. (1989). Test anxiety in elementary and secondary school students. *Educational Psychologist, 24,* 159–183.

Wigfield, A., & Eccles, J. (1992). The development of achievement task values: A theoretical analysis. *Developmental Review, 12,* 265–310.

Wigfield, A., & Guthrie, J. T. (1997). Relations of children's motivation for reading to the amount and breadth of their reading. *Journal of Educational Psychology, 89,* 420–432.

9

Comprehending Through Composing: Reflections on Reading Assessment Strategies

Robert Calfee
Roxanne Greitz Miller
University of California, Riverside

The assignment to comment on the four chapters in this section, which present interestingly distinctive perspectives on the conference topic, is both engaging and challenging. The engagement springs from the depth of the ideas, the challenge from the task of molding the ideas into a coherent image. To address this task, we rely on three relatively standard lenses, and introduce a fourth that is less typical. Three constructs spring from the conference focus and the recent history of comprehension assessment: comprehension, (re)construction, and assessment. The fourth theme, composition, reflects our recent research, but, somewhat to our surprise, also emerged during the conference. Toward the end of the conference, for instance, Dick Anderson suggested that researchers might consider shifting attention from reading comprehension to literacy comprehension. Such a move is consonant with our thinking about the issues, and meshes with the increasingly important concept of academic language (Fillmore-Wong & Snow, 2000). Our chapter begins with brief reflections on the four lenses, continues with comments on the four chapters, and concludes by illustrating our recent efforts to engineer the reading-writing connection.

FOUR LENSES

Discussions of comprehension assessment arouse memories of "Rashomon" (Kurosawa, 1950), the Japanese movie classic demonstrating that any given situation can be perceived and construed in different ways. The articles presented at this conference are no exception, with varying construals of the two key terms. There was also frequent reference to a (re)constructivist stance toward these terms, and to the Rand Report (Snow, 2002). "Constructivist" denotes the active connection between text and reader, "re" to the reflective, metacognitive overlay. Composition is our addition to the mix, suggesting that one of the most trustworthy indicators of comprehension is the individual's capacity to compose a response to a text. Note that we did not say "write," which entails the mechanics of print. We must forego the temptation to compare the origins of comprehend and compose, although a story is to be found in the morphology.

COMPREHENSION

To comprehend a message is to understand or "get" it—right? Hence, the simple model of reading, which proposes that once the young child is taught to translate print into sound, then the existing natural language system kicks in and the child has learned to read. In "Understanding and Comprehending," Freedman and Calfee (1984) described the contrast between natural and formal language, the former referring to the variety of existing language registers that young children bring to school, and the latter to the academic register that serves as a standard for communication in educational settings, business, and government, and other middle-class exercises. From this perspective, the acquisition of literacy is the acquisition of a formal register with specific features, including an emphasis on explicitness, coherence, and attention to stylistic conventions. The argument, with wellsprings in discussions of the impact of literacy on thinking (Goody, 1977), was that literacy instruction for modern times should influence the way in which students think and communicate.

All kindergartners can understand a variety of linguistic messages, including those found in printed texts. They vary considerably in their experiences with words, sentences, and discourse patterns. Nevertheless, almost all children respond to language in a casual and nonstrategic manner. To be sure, some children have learned something about the "school game" (Heath, 1983), and know when and how to answer questions about the obvious: "How did the wolf feel when he fell down the chimney into the boiling water?"

ASSESSMENT

A decade ago, this construct would have required further explanation; only at the end of the conference, however, did Wixson suggest that this term required attention. For this chapter, three elements capture the contrast between testing and assessment (Calfee & Hiebert, 1988): purpose, method, and context.

Purpose is captured in several contrasts, most notably the difference between summative and formative evaluations of student performance, between growth and accomplishment. A related distinction is information that can be used to guide instruction versus indicators that predict later performance. External authorities increasingly strive to move summative operations into the classroom, suggesting, for instance, that externally mandated tests serve for "diagnosis."

Method encompasses variations, such as recognition versus production, multiple-choice versus short (or long) answers. "Testing," with the emphasis on cost-effectiveness, moves toward less expensive alternatives, generally with caveats about appropriate limitations on the results of such exercises. "Classroom assessment"—and the conjoined term has a meaning of its own—typically emphasizes the validity of the information for instructional decision making, and when integrated with instruction need not entail substantial increases in time. To be sure, this comment assumes a decision-making approach to instruction, which is not especially common. The most recent version of a cost-effective test is DIBELS (Dynamic Indicators of Basic Early Literacy; Kaminski & Good, 1998), a 1-min "production" task, where the job is to do as many simple things as possible within 1 min, including oral reading.

Context refers to the situation that surrounds the collection of evidence about comprehension. The testing mindset envisions the individual working in isolation, and distrusts any product that comes through social interaction—"Whose work is it?" The complement is direct instruction, wherein the teacher treats the class as a collection of individual learners. A different view places students within problem-solving groups, where comprehension is part of the process needed to obtain and use information required to complete a project. The teacher's assessment roles are complex in such settings, both for supporting group activities and for gathering and evaluating information about individual student growth and accomplishment.

(RE)CONSTRUCTION

The notion of comprehension as a constructive activity has been with us for a while. More recently, the idea has been grown in two interrelated ways. First, from Vygotskian sources comes the notion of the social dimension of constructivist activities. Second, the "meta" label speaks to the importance of reflection. For these purposes, we propose three significant elements in reconstructive comprehension: (a) passive versus active, in which the reader can take in the words and sentences as they appear, compiling a collection of "propositions," or can approach the task more strategically, formulating hypotheses and instantiating schemata; (b) part versus whole, in which comprehension spans a continuum from the memorization of textual details toward deeper engagement in the macrostructural ideas that constitute a well-written passage; and (c), absorb versus transform, which on the surface is related to the active-passive contrast, but with different implications. A reader can rework the ideas in a passage, call on previous experience, integrate, summarize, and expand, all without attempting any major reshaping of the ideas. Transforming entails the use of comprehension outcomes to achieve results that transcend the original activity. The construct appears most obviously when the task is to combine two or more passages to create an entirely different product.

COMPOSITION

The fourth lens might seem a natural extension of the three previous ones, but as an alternative lens, it brings distinctive features to bear on the issues. Moreover, current practice suggests that more is involved than a "natural extension." For various reasons, reading and writing have become largely disconnected in present practice (Nelson & Calfee, 1998).

Like comprehension, composition encompasses a variety of meanings: spoken versus written, natural versus formal, formative versus summative. Kindergartners can neither "read" nor "write," but they can comprehend and compose in either natural or formal language registers. The third grader's journal contains a rich array of written material, typically casual accounts of personal experiences. District or state tests include a written composition, often to a decontextualized prompt providing students with limited guidance about purpose and audience.

To expand on this lens, consider the following scenarios springing from contemporary practice. First is the contrast from kindergarten "show and tell" activities to the research paper required from the late elementary grades onward. These two tasks differ in "medium," in the sense that kindergartners do not need to write, but also in the reliance on comprehension, in the sense that kindergartners can rely on personal experience, whereas a research paper typically builds on external texts.

Second is the way in which external texts serve as the basis for a composition. Reproduction is the classic requirement; the student answers questions about propositional specifics. Summarization is a slightly higher-level task; write an abbreviated version of a passage presenting major elements in relation to one another. A variation on this theme is the integrated summary, in which two or more passages are combined. A third level is the critical review, wherein the writer is asked to analyze and evaluate one or more texts. Quite different from any of the previous is the task that occurs when a passage serves as a basis for transformation, which requires comprehension, but more importantly, calls on the writer to use the passage for the creation of a new product (Bereiter & Scardamalia, 1987; Flower & Hayes, 1984). The nature of comprehension required for such tasks would seem to go beyond the notions underlying most conference discussions.

A third point centers around the role of integrated reading–writing activities within the classroom. As noted earlier, standard practice separates these domains. Connecting them poses various challenges: curriculum schedules, textbook materials, and the management of time during and across days and weeks. On the other hand, project-based learning, another label for this concept, offers the potential to enhance student motivation and support broad-based transfer of skills and knowledge.

THE FOUR PAPERS

This segment summarizes the four chapters in this section, reviewing each contribution through the four lenses. Other issues emerged during our review: The lenses entail implications for the value assigned to various educational outcomes. The developmental dimension pervades the discussion; what can (and should) children learn as they progress through the elementary grades? How do we deal with individual differences? Should conceptual and practical models emphasize the mean or the variance?

van den Broek

This chapter directly addresses the two conference themes: comprehension and assessment. The comprehension focus is on the early grades and stories, using a causal-network model as the foundation. Assessment is broadly construed as the capacity to "retell, apply, identify theme, critically appraise," with varying emphasis on these four elements. A developmental theme pervades the chapter; what are the varied ways in which young children process textual information (spoken or written, but primarily narrative) as they move from kindergarten into the mid-elementary grades? In particular, in what ways do the causal networks that appear to underlie student responses change across these early years?

The research team created an assessment instrument around three principles: sensitivity to developmental changes, reliance on speech rather than print, and examination of profiles as well as single scores. Practically speaking, children viewed audio and video presentations of two popular narratives, "Blinky Bill" and "Rugrats," and were interviewed about their memories. The students generated more complete and complex responses across the years, but the changes were quantitative more than qualitative: "Preschool children engage in very much the same comprehension processes as do their older counterparts" (van den Broek, this volume). For instance, at all ages, children were more likely to recall the central story elements. In addition, relative standings remained much the same across the years; children who displayed higher levels of performance in kindergarten were still at the top of the heap at the end of second grade, even after factoring in differences in decoding skill. In this sense, the assessment exhibited predictive validity.

This chapter touches all four "lenses," including an assessment of students' capacity to reconstruct the essential elements of a passage. The particulars of "Blinky Bill" and "Rugrats" notwithstanding, the model offers interesting views about how the teachers of young children might delve into their charges' understandings of engaging passages. The presentation relies mainly on statistics to portray what also offers a rich qualitative image. The team seemed somewhat disappointed at the lack of more clear-cut developmental transitions; the Piagetian search for stages has a fascination that will not wane.

Neglected in this search is the potential of schooling to influence language and thought. That is, rather than concluding that development proceeds quantitatively more than qualitatively, another interpretation is that contemporary instruction may not typically produce fundamental changes in how children comprehend. More specifically, those children who enter kindergarten whose experiences align with the academic register are more likely to benefit from standards-based curriculum offerings, whereas those lacking these experiences may puzzle over what is going on. This hypothesis would account for the lack of developmental changes and the high levels of predictive validity, the basis for the "Matthew" effect.

What if teachers were to instruct youngsters in the secrets of the causal model, introducing such arcane terms as *character*, *plot*, and *theme*, and leading students to explore the role of motivation in the evolution of a narrative? What if students were provided a toolbox that they could use to "unbuild" a passage, or to build their own works? To be sure, such a strategy might undermine predictive validity by opening the way for all children to do rather remarkable things regardless of their background. The conference focused on assessment, and so instruction remained in the background.

Paris and Colleagues

This contribution extends the previous one by inquiring into genuine and spurious correlates of comprehension. The challenge at the outset, of course, is to establish a standard—will the "real" comprehension indexes please stand up? The authors rely on the existing literature, which depends for the most part on "conventional outcome measures such as IRIs [informal reading inventories] and SATs [standardized achievement tests]" (Paris, this volume). Although the chapter offers a substantial variety of meaty findings and observations, it finesses the challenge of establishing a standard. The bottom line seems to be that the task of conceptualizing and operationalizing comprehension remains in such a primitive state that it is relatively easy to identify serious problems, even in the absence of a clear-cut standard.

The chapter critiques two spurious correlates: fluency and alphabet knowledge. Fluency refers mostly to the 1-min samples like those found in the DIBELS (Kaminski & Good, 1998) technique, mentioned throughout the conference. The researchers do not question the correlations; in a variety of settings, fluency correlates with comprehension. To be sure, the magnitude of the correlations depends on the particular comprehension measure and the developmental-achievement level of the students. Performance on surface-level measures (multiple-choice and cloze tests) are more likely to match with fluency indicators (interestingly, the "stimulus" does not seem to matter very much), and the relation is strongest in the earliest developmental stages, diminishing substantially by the midelementary grades.

What do the correlations mean, and how should they be used? The chapter reminds that correlation is not causality, and hence the researchers question the validity of claims that such instruments "assess" comprehension. Perhaps more significant are cautions about the instructional implications based on performance on such measures. The third grader who struggles to read a word list is probably going to have trouble comprehending a complex passage. Is the remedy to teach the student to read word lists more quickly? Perhaps not.

Alphabet knowledge offers another perspective on similar issues, with some additional fillips. For more than a half-century, research has shown a strong and persistent correlation between an entering kindergartner's knowledge of the ABCs, measured in various ways, and reading performance in later elementary grades, measured in a variety of ways. The chapter argues that the correlation is spurious for several reasons. For instance, although the correlation is strong

when ABC knowledge is measured on school entry, the relation quickly diminishes when ABC knowledge is measured later, for obvious reasons—by the end
of kindergarten, virtually all children have been taught their ABCs.

"Spurious" has a negative connotation, from the Latin *spurius*; false or illegiti-
mate. Is the kindergarten teacher mistaken in assessing alphabet knowledge and
acting on it? Probably not, depending on the action and the interpretive basis for
action. Preschool children acquire the ABCs for a variety of reasons, which, in
combination, make alphabet knowledge a useful proxy for previous experience.
Kindergartners are likely to learn their ABCs because they will be taught. However, the previous experiences continue to impact children's capacity to benefit
from instructional activities, and in this sense, the initial assessment might provide useful information. The initial assessment can be predictive much like a
blood pressure reading; a high reading calls for action. The pressure can be reduced in a variety of ways, but some are more effective than others in addressing
the more fundamental problem. Likewise, teaching the ABCs is probably a good
thing, but a "letter a week" is not necessarily the most effective way to introduce
kindergartners to the full range of academic language competence.

Another interesting facet of ABC knowledge on kindergarten entry is statistical in character. The chapter notes that the distribution of ABC scores is sel-
dom normal, in the sense of following the typical bell-shaped curve. In fact, at
any given time a child either knows most or virtually none of his or her ABCs,
producing a bimodal distribution, which actually enhances the potential of this
simple indicator for decision making (Calfee, 1976). Spuriousness springs from
misinterpretation and overuse.

Now to the lenses: this chapter addresses both comprehension and assessment, primarily focusing on methodological issues. At the end, the authors hint
at some "genuine correlates"—language skills, receptive and productive vocabulary skills, and narrative reasoning, all pointing to the importance of construction and composition. They mention assessment procedures that might offer
greater insight into underlying processes that would enhance both screening
and diagnosis, which would seem to open the way for constructivist and compositional elements.

Stahl and Hiebert

"In the beginning was [and is] the word." Comprehension implies a passage, a
collection of words, including the complex relations among these words—actually, among the constructs that they represent. What if the process stalls or fails
at the word level? This question is of central concern in this chapter.

How does one think about the "word" as a starting point? At one level, translating a string of letters into a spoken response is important; "word recognition"

is one label for this construct. At a second level, connecting a string of letters to a semantic network is equally important; "word meaning" may reflect this assemblage. To be sure, these two interpretations of "word" carry quite different implications, cognitively and instructionally. This chapter starts with the "simple model," in which reading rests on decoding and oral language, with decoding essentially a word-level task. However, decoding without meaning is unlikely to promote comprehension, and so the authors explore three facets of "oral word reading": accuracy, rate, and prosody.

The authors' review of the literature in these areas is thorough and helpful, not because it resolves all of the issues, but by bringing attention to the relation between oral reading performance and comprehension. In brief, the conclusions are that (a) beyond third grade, accuracy does not seem sufficient to guarantee comprehension; (b) reading rate is correlated with comprehension on standardized measures, perhaps reflecting the impact of processing automaticity; and (c) prosody is difficult to pin down, is potentially important, and is not well researched.

Now to the lenses—at the outset, the authors' insistence that comprehension include a semantic component meshes with other contributions in this section. Their success in conceptualizing and operationalizing this component is less clear-cut, especially in the assessment arena. How might one design a vocabulary component to a comprehension exercise that illuminates specific and generic contributions at the "word" level? Oral reading in the early grades is common practice toward this end, and offers some insights into "word recognition." But which facets of this complex array of tasks best reveal the semantic and comprehension elements as separable entities, and in combination with one another?

This chapter does not directly address either constructive or compositional issues, but both offer openings to the role of word knowledge in comprehension assessment. We argue later for the critical importance of establishing the semantic basis for compositional activities. More to the point, it is probably unreasonable to ask anyone to "write" without an explicit textual base, either a specific passage or a well-defined set of experiences. In either instance, the resource will include words in one form or another. At a practical level, students are best positioned to compose when they have ready access to a collection of words, ideas, concepts, and relations. Assessments that do not provide this undergirding are likely to underestimate student competence.

Guthrie and Wigfield

The introduction of motivation into this section fills an often-overlooked gap. Paris suggested some time ago that achievement depended on both "skill" and "will" (Paris & Oka, 1986), and we would add "thrill" to the list. The impact of the "age of accountability" appears in a parent's comment during a PTA meeting on reading programs: "I want my kid to learn to read, and I don't care if he wants to or not." Guthrie and Wigfield (this volume) focus on assessment more than comprehension, hypothesizing that low performance levels may reflect lack of effort more than competence. Their comprehension model includes several key facets, including background knowledge, text structure, causal networks, and integrative schema; the motivation model also covers several bases, including task mastery, intrinsic motivation, self efficacy, personal interest, and transactional beliefs. The review of relevant studies, including an investigation by the authors, shows that many facets in the two-part model correlate with one another. The most productive part of the chapter inquires into the influence on performance of situational characteristics, including both task conditions and inherent interest. Again, most studies are correlational, but the possibilities for experimental investigations appear obvious. A concluding research agenda suggests exploration of "relatively long, complex tasks ... [with] open-ended response formats that require extended writing" (Guthrie & Wigfield, p. 206, this volume) as situations that are more likely than brief decontextualized multiple-choice or short-answer tasks to engage and motivate students. In addition, the recommendation is routinely to inquire of students how interesting they found the task, and how hard they tried to do well.

Looking at the chapter through the four lenses speaks to the importance of motivational elements as essential components of effective comprehension assessment. The domain is largely ignored in policy and practice, and the chapter reveals the rather thin research base for making substantial claims. The (re)constructivist perspective offers conceptual (or at least metaphorical) support for considering motivation as part of the equation. Building is hard work, and will garner students' best efforts only when they are either pressured (a frequent strategy) or intrinsically engaged (relatively rare, especially for students with reading problems). Long, complex tasks requiring extended writing would seem to pose unwelcome challenges to many students, further hindering genuine engagement. In the next section, we describe a scenario that addresses some of these issues.

A motivational ingredient not mentioned by Guthrie and Wigfield (this volume) is the social context for the comprehension-composition task. As noted earlier, assessment often carries the connotation of individual efforts, and group tasks are suspect. To be sure, most "outside and beyond school" tasks involve cooperative activities, and techniques are available for sorting out individual and collective contributions. We do not attempt to review the literature on the motivational concomitants of social versus group activities, but the positive conse-quences of working together would seem to warrant further consideration.

A Conceptual and Practical Example

Constructing a conceptual framework that joins comprehension, composition, and assessment, and then translates this concept into successful practice, has been a major focus of our work over recent years (Calfee & Miller, 2003; Miller & Calfee, 2004a; Miller & Calfee, 2004b). The basis for the framework rests on the Vygotskian theories already mentioned, and relies extensively on the con-structs of "schema theory" (Anderson, Spiro, & Anderson, 1978). The schema construct provides a unifying framework for linking comprehension, composi-tion, and assessment; understanding a text requires connecting with an existing memory framework that contains "slots" for incoming information, and that es-tablishes prospective relations among these elements. A similar conceptualiza-tion applies to composition; the author chooses a framework to guide the assembly of known and new elements during composition.

Schema theory applies with particular force to the design of constructivist as-sessment tasks. The challenge here is to tap into both processes and products as students reconstruct and "transconstruct" textual materials. The challenge is to delve into students' thinking to evaluate and—more importantly—to shape their capacities to work with ideas and communicate with others. Elsewhere we have presented the "Read–Write Cycle" as a conceptual bridge for connecting schema constructs with the practicalities of the "research paper" assignment, the classroom commonplace where comprehension, composition, and assess-ment are most frequently juxtaposed (see Calfee, 1998; Miller & Calfee, 2004a). We conclude this review with a practical analogue to the Read–Write Cycle, which we offer partly as a concrete example of the potential for valid reading comprehension assessment through appropriately designed composi-tion activities, and partly to suggest the potential for enhancing composition as-sessment through appropriately designed comprehension activities. Moreover, this combination provides a model for effective integrated literacy activities across a broad range of content areas, and across the span of formative and summative assessments.

The example, which might seem mischievous on our part, builds on CLAS, the California Learning Assessment System, which for 2 years served as the primary vehicle for California's statewide evaluation of literacy achievement. Following a rough start because of implementation shortcomings, CLAS al-most immediately captured the attention and commitment of classroom teachers across the state as the type of assessment that warranted their investment; it was a test worth teaching to. The demise of CLAS is a story in its own right, reflecting a variety of concerns including (a) the feasibility of performance-based assessment, (b) technical concerns about reliability and SEM (standard error of measurement), and (c) choices of reading materials and performance tasks (Underwood, 1999). CLAS-Plus builds on the constructivist framework that undergirded CLAS, with modifications reflecting the opportunities available in a nonstandardized environment. As shown in Fig. 9.1, students (a) read and respond to a passage, (b) meet in small groups to discuss their responses in preparation for (c) a writing composition based on the text. The augmentations in CLAS-Plus include (a) introductory scaffolding of the topic, facilitated by the teacher through "webbing" activities; (b) posting of the products of student discussions throughout the classroom (practically speaking, lots of words presented on public display); (c) provision of graphic organizers for both comprehension and composition; (d) explicit discussion of performance criteria or rubrics; and (e) inclusion of a social component of the activity, including project presentations at the end of the exercise. Teachers praised CLAS because it appeared to be valid, the tasks were interesting and engaging, and it offered a workable classroom model. The writing assignments (compositions) attended to audience, purpose, and voice. The cooperative phases, wherein students shared their knowledge and views on the topic, enhanced students' reflective and critical stance during their writing and enhanced motivation.

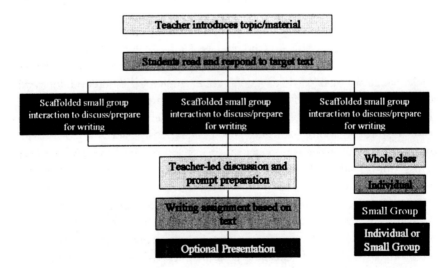

FIG. 9.1.   California Learning Assessment System-Plus Sequence of Activities (Calfee & Wilson, 2004). Reprinted with permission.

The "Reading and Writing About Science Project" (RWS) has employed the CLAS-Plus design as both an instructional and assessment model within the Read–Write Cycle framework. The aim in RWS was to evaluate the impact of content-area-embedded literacy activities to enhance mid-elementary grade students' comprehension of expository passages of the sort found in science, and to improve their competence in composing research reports. The project has been based in California, where the accountability emphasis in recent years has focused on reading and math—finding a niche for science in "low-performing" schools has proven a challenge.

During RWS, students were exposed to curriculum "blocks" based on a single science theme (e.g., the rock cycle or plate tectonics). Each block introduced three different reading samples using the CLAS-Plus format, following the sequence of steps illustrated in Fig. 9.1. The subsequent example from the rock cycle block illustrates how schema theory was interwoven through comprehension, composition, and assessment.

During an introductory lesson on the rock cycle, the teacher first identifies for students what will be studied (in this case, different kinds of rocks and how they are formed). Teachers activate students' prior topic knowledge (Alexander, Schallert, & Hare, 1991) and preexisting schema by having them actively reflect, share with others, and use prewriting and other reflective techniques as brainstorming methods (see Miller & Calfee, 2004a, 2004b). Students write down and share their knowledge and experience in whole class and small groups about different kinds of rocks and their origins, and make predictions about the content of the upcoming reading sample.

Students then (a) read a reading sample on the stages of the rock cycle (igneous, sedimentary, metamorphic), use "think-aloud" strategies while reading individually, and conduct analysis of text structure, purpose, and audience; (b) organize prereading and postreading concepts using graphical structures; and (c) use contextual clues in the text to translate new and unfamiliar vocabulary. Graphic organizers are not given to the students; instead, students, with teacher guidance, actively construct an organizer appropriate to the context, justifying their organization of the content matter into particular graphic structures. Defense of the organizer undergirds students' metacognitive and reasoning ability and engages them in creating the structure that works best for them (Chambliss & Calfee, 1998).

The think-aloud procedure (Davey, 1983), voicing and writing down thoughts as the text is read, either as teacher modeling or student self-monitoring, appears effective in raising students' reading comprehension. RWS teachers are encouraged to model think-aloud procedures with students prior to reading. As they read, students are instructed to write both their observations and questions onto the reading sample copies, and to monitor their own comprehension. Written comments from think-aloud exercises also serve as a bridge to the composition phase.

Vocabulary development through context clues is also incorporated in the read-and-respond portion of instruction. We agree with arguments that comprehension depends on word-level processing. Acquisition of context strategies for vocabulary development provides students a transferable method that applies to all subject areas (again, creating a "slot" for students to rely on across other multiple subject matters). In RWS, teachers developed vocabulary exercises from the assigned readings so that students derived word meanings from the text itself rather than simply looking up words in the dictionary. For example, *metamorphic* was a key term in the rock cycle unit (referring to both a rock type and a stage in the rock cycle). Many students had heard of *metamorphosis*, but only considered this term in relation to living things like caterpillars and butterflies. The application to describe changes in rocks was not obvious to them, and had to be explored in the full context of the target texts to reveal the meaning, and to construct new schemata.

After reading the text sample, students examine the structure and content of their graphic organizer, facilitated by the teacher. Students may discard, reorder, or restructure their ideas, which may be incorrect, inaccurate, or simply irrelevant. The costs of changes at this stage are relatively modest—nothing has been "written." Students share their reflections on the reading in small groups and with the teacher, again serving to further externalize and shape students' reflections on the content knowledge transmitted through the reading.

The teacher introduces the writing prompt and students proceed to reflect on the task. Writing prompts used for assessment in the Read–Write Cycle follow specific guidelines developed by Miller and Calfee (2004), which also teaches students to "dissect" the prompt into its constituent elements, to locate ideas from the reading, and to translate the information into a writing plan. The frequent use of defined "prompt elements" creates a schema for students to use when faced with an assessment task, extending schema theory to encompass the full assessment spectrum. Students understand the purpose of their writing, the intended audience for the writing, the form that the writing is to take, and the type of supporting details to use in their writing. When faced with subsequent assessments, they have access to a packet of methods for prompt and passage deconstruction and composition construction.

The final task is writing the individual compositions. The writing task provides an opportunity for students to synthesize, transform, and apply knowledge. This extension is performed individually, with no assistance from peers or the teacher. After composing, students share their compositions with peers in small groups or whole class interactions. Opportunities for students to literally "compare notes" expose them to different interpretations and points of view, and to varying levels of writing expertise. The "Writing to Models" approach is subtly at work here; good examples of student writing delivered to students by students provide a standard for future compositions. The final drafts are scored using multiple rubrics (Miller & Calfee, 2004a), reflecting both standard writing gauges (e.g., grammar, mechanics, vocabulary) and transmission of content knowledge. The specific attention to content knowledge makes this assessment strategy a more comprehensive representation of student comprehension.

FINAL THOUGHTS

Comprehension may arguably be viewed as a definitive cognitive achievement in its own right. Unfortunately, this accomplishment can be fully appreciated only when made public in some fashion. To be sure, the individual may experience great internal delight after struggling with a message and finally "getting it." But how can external observers (teachers and researchers) tap into this experience, assuming a good reason for such an attempt? The most direct and comprehensive approach is to ask the individual to present the results of the activity, by retelling, summarizing, applying, critiquing, extending, transforming, and so on—in brief, by composing some sort of response. A range of indirect tactics is also available: multiple-choice and short-answer queries, surveys of "feeling of knowing," and other less direct indicators.

In reviewing the chapters in this section, we have emphasized a direct approach in which comprehension is connected with composition, the latter a definitive cognitive achievement in its own right. We offer three arguments in support of this proposal. First, it builds on a defensible pedagogical model for promoting the growth of formal language and literacy. The model has a long history stretching back to the Greek rhetoricians; in today's world, it is increasingly important that these "secrets" to effective communication become available to all of our citizens.

Second, the read–write model embodied in the Read–Write Cycle and CLAS-Plus turns out to be practically workable in classroom settings, both for assessment and instruction within literacy programs, but also readily extendable to other content domains. Moreover, the model provides a foundation for teachers' professional development in literacy as the basis for integrated projects that support students' thinking and communication skills in the elementary grades. Rather amazingly, given various snafus in California's initial implementation of CLAS, teachers' memories of the program remain generally positive, rather uniformly evoking the response that CLAS tested what teachers ought to be teaching (Underwood, 1999).

The third point addresses the question of the validity of assessing comprehension through composition. The concern is that the composing task presents barriers to adequate assessment of student understanding; students may "know" much more than they can express in writing. Our response to such concerns is twofold. We would suggest that first, students may also "know" much more (or less) than is likely to be revealed by other means of assessment. This suggestion has instructional implications as well. The most effective tactics for enhancing performance on multiple-choice comprehension tests, for instance, have more to do with test taking than with passage comprehension. In the age of accountability, teachers are well advised to consider "what works" for the privileged indicators, which means teaching directly to the test. Our second claim, based on achievement patterns emerging from the RWS, is that effectively scaffolded reading–writing experiences enhance both comprehension and composition. Students taught that reading is reading and writing is writing are unlikely to be able to demonstrate either comprehension or composition skills in a CLAS-like situation; instructional experiences that integrate the two domains are essential to our argument.

Several counterarguments to the proposal also warrant consideration. The first is the pressure springing from the current accountability systems, which emphasize reading and efficient correlates of reading comprehension to the neglect of writing. Related to this point is the inertia embodied in instructional materials, which determine both curriculum and pedagogy, and which today privilege reading. The reading–writing model requires support that is generally not available in today's materials.

Second is the implicit assumption in our argument that the classroom teacher is capable of the professional judgments required to manage complex projects, which call for ongoing adaptations in the original instructional plan in response to emerging needs and opportunities. For the proposed model to work, control would spring more from classrooms than statehouses.

A third problem arises from "grain size"—over the past half-century, textbook publishers and test makers have created templates that emphasize the reading "lesson," a set of activities lasting for an hour or so, during which a series of objectives are covered by the teacher, in accord with the checklist format of the typical standards-based scope-and-sequence chart. Objectives are introduced, reviewed, and tested across a series of lessons. The integrity across lessons rests on a passage that students will encounter for a week or so, depending on holidays and other less predictable events. In the read–write model, integrity builds on a series of interrelated activities all aimed toward completion of a "construction" of substantial dimensions, a grain size measured more in weeks than in minutes. An aside—the challenges for instructional design arise not from the concept of educational standards, but from the grain size used to create and implement the standards. In general, most national and state standards begin with laudable outcomes at the highest level of the design, but then are overwhelmed by the steady accumulation of lower-level objectives that serve as the operational basis for textbook and test materials.

Finally, the No Child Left Behind act emphasis on the "children left behind" undermines any suggestion that demanding tasks should be the actual basis for assessing the achievement of students from at-risk backgrounds. High standards are operationalized as (arbitrarily) high scores on low-level tests. Relying on complex projects that call for both comprehension and composition as a way of judging the achievements of students from at-risk backgrounds is an idea that evokes disbelief and derision in many quarters. And yet, that is our proposal.

How do we achieve the proposed outcomes, especially for those students most in need? Instruction would seem to be the answer. The conference and the chapters in this section centered on assessment, for understandable reasons. However, the integration of instruction and assessment makes sense both conceptually and practically. A quarter-century ago, Durkin (1978) suggested that something was amiss with comprehension instruction in the elementary grades. We are not aware of any recent reports demonstrating any substantial change in this state of affairs. We also have not encountered any parallel investigations of the situation for composition instruction. Perhaps worth consideration as a research agenda ...

ACKNOWLEDGMENTS

Support for this chapter was provided by Interagency Educational Research Initiative (IERI) grant 9979834.

Correspondence concerning this article should be addressed to Robert Calfee, Graduate School of Education, University of California, Riverside, CA 92521. E-mail: robert.calfee@ucr.edu

REFERENCES

Alexander, P. A., Schallert, D. L., & Hare, V. C. (1991). Coming to terms: How researchers in learning and literacy talk about knowledge. *Review of Educational Research, 61,* 315–343.

Anderson, R. C., Spiro, R. J., & Anderson, M. C. (1978). Schemata as scaffolding for the representation of information in connected discourse. *American Educational Research Journal, 15,* 433–440

Bereiter, C., & Scardamalia, M. (1987). *The psychology of written composition.* Hillsdale, NJ: Lawrence Erlbaum Associates.

Calfee, R. C. (1976). Sources of dependency in cognitive processes. In D. Klahr (Ed.), *Cognition and instruction: 10th Annual Carnegie-Mellon Symposium on Cognition.* Hillsdale, NJ: Lawrence Erlbaum Associates.

Calfee, R. C. (1998). Leading middle-grade students from reading to writing: Conceptual and practical aspects. In R. C. Calfee & N. N. Nelson (Eds.), *The reading–writing connection: The ninety-seventh yearbook of the National Society for the Study of Education* (pp. 203–228). Chicago: University of Chicago Press.

Calfee, R. C., & Hiebert, E. (1988). The teacher's role in using assessment to improve learning. In C. V. Bunderson (Ed.), *Assessment in the service of learning* (pp. 45–61). Princeton, NJ: Educational Testing Service.

Calfee, R. C., & Miller, R. G. (2003, April). *Embedding reading and writing instruction in the content area.* Paper presented at AERA National Convention, Chicago.

Calfee, R. C., & Wilson, K. M. (2004). A classroom-based writing assessment framework. In C. A. Stone, E. R. Silliman, B. J. Ehren, & K. Apel (Eds.), *Handbook of language and literacy: Development and disorders* (p. 590). New York: Guilford.

Chambliss, M. J., & Calfee, R. C. (1998). *Textbooks for learning: Nurturing children's minds.* Malden, MA: Blackwell.

Davey, B. (1983). Think-aloud modeling cognitive process of reading comprehension. *Journal of Reading, 27,* 44–47.

Durkin, D. (1978). What classroom observations reveal about reading comprehension instruction. *Reading Research Quarterly, 14,* 481–533.

Fillmore-Wong, L., & Snow, C. E. (2000). *What teachers need to know about language.* Washington, DC: Center for Applied Linguistics.

Flower, L. S., & Hayes, J. R. (1984). Images, plans, and prose: The representation of meaning in writing. *Written Communication, 1,* 120–160.

Freedman, S. W., & Calfee, R. C. (1984). Understanding and comprehending. *Written Communication, 1,* 459–490.

Goody, J. (1977). *The domestication of the savage mind.* Cambridge, England: Cambridge University Press.

Heath, S. B. (1983). *Ways with words.* Cambridge, England: Cambridge University Press.

Kurosawa, A. (Director). (1950). *Rashomon* [Motion picture]. Japan: RKO Pictures.

Kaminski, R. A., & Good, R. H., III. (1998). Assessing early literacy skills in a problem-solving model: Dynamic indicators of basic early literacy skills. In M. R. Shinn (Ed.), *Advanced applications of curriculum-based measurement* (pp. 113–142). New York: Guilford.

Miller, R. G., & Calfee, R. C. (2004a). Building a better reading/writing assessment: Bridging cognitive theory, instruction, and assessment. *English Leadership Quarterly, 26,* 6–13.

Miller, R. G., & Calfee, R. C. (2004b). *Breaking ground: Creating opportunities for authentic literacy instruction in the upper elementary content areas.* Manuscript submitted for publication.

Miller, R. G., & Calfee, R. C. (2004c). Making thinking visible: A method to encourage science writing in upper elementary grades. *Science and Childen, VV*(N), 20–25.

Nelson, N. N., & Calfee, R. C. (Eds.). (1998). *The reading–writing connection: The yearbook of the National Society for the Study of Education.* Chicago: University of Chicago Press.

Paris, S. G., & Oka, E. R. (1986). Self-regulated learning among exceptional children. *Exceptional Children Special Issue: Competence and Instruction, 53,* 103–108.

Snow, C. (2002). *Reading for understanding: Toward an R&D program for reading comprehension.* Washington: RAND.

Underwood, T. (1999). *The portfolio project: A study of assessment, instruction, and middle school reform.* Urbana, IL: National Council of Teachers of English.

Part III

Assessment in School Contexts

10

Using Study Groups and Reading Assessment Data to Improve Reading Instruction Within a School

Barbara M. Taylor
University of Minnesota

P. David Pearson
University of California, Berkeley

This chapter investigates one approach to using students' comprehension and fluency scores as a tool to help schools evaluate the effectiveness of their classroom reading instruction. This chapter was prompted by the findings from a recent study we conducted on school improvement in reading. With respect to reading comprehension, as both a goal and an outcome, we found that when coupled with strong professional development effort, in the form of a study group process to improve instruction, reading comprehension assessment data that is benchmarked against a national database can serve as a tool to help teachers within a building modify their classroom reading instruction and, in turn, increase students' growth in reading achievement (Taylor, Pearson, Peterson, & Rodriguez, in press).

The purpose of the Center for the Improvement of Early Reading Achievement (CIERA) School Change Project (Taylor et al., in press), from which the data for this chapter were drawn, was to investigate the effectiveness of a grass roots reading reform effort in which elementary (kindergarten through Grade 5) teachers within a building participated in weekly study groups to improve their classroom reading instruction with the ultimate goal of accelerating students' reading growth. The reform effort was data-driven in that teachers and schools received reports benchmarking their instruction activities and their students' performance against other teachers and students in a national database of 13 schools, all of which were a part of the project. The goal was to encourage teachers, in concert with their principal and a project facilitator, to use these data, along with recommendations from national reviews of best practices in teaching reading, to design professional development activities to encourage changes in classroom practices that would, in turn, lead to changes in student achievement. In each year of the study, we used the data from the previous year to determine significant relations between classroom practices and students' reading growth. In the third and final year of the study, looking across the 13 high poverty schools in the national sample, we conducted three-level Hierarchical Linear Modeling (HLM; Raudenbush, Bryk, & Congdon, 2000) analyses to determine which classroom instructional practices had an impact on students' growth on a variety of reading measures; we also evaluated, across the 13 schools, the degree to which adherence to the principles in the reform effort accounted for students' reading growth. In this iteration of these analyses, we have reexamined our data with an eye toward examining the role of comprehension, both as an important instructional goal and as an outcome.

BACKGROUND

The CIERA School Change Framework was designed by consulting the research related to improving performance, particularly in low-performing (and usually high-poverty) schools. The corpus of work we examined included research on effective schools (e.g., Knapp, 1995; Taylor, 2002; Taylor, Pressley, & Pearson, 2002), effective reading instruction and effective teachers of reading (e.g., National Reading Panel, 2000; Pressley, 2000; Taylor, 2002; Taylor, Peterson, Pearson, & Rodriguez, 2002; Taylor, Pearson, Peterson, & Rodriguez, 2003b), and effective school improvement (e.g., Fullan, 1999; Hawley, 2002). The emphasis of the project was improving classroom practice through reflective professional development. The professional development had both an inward-looking facet (teachers were asked to examine the practices within their classrooms and the school as a whole) and an outward-looking face (examining the literature on effective teachers and teaching and benchmarking one's own practices against the national sample of schools in the study).

From the research on effective schools, we know that teachers within effective schools collaborate to develop a collective sense of responsibility for improving students' reading achievement, collaborate in their teaching of reading, and engage in collaborative professional development to improve their reading instruction (Taylor, 2002). We also know that effective reading instruction includes explicit instruction in phonemic awareness, phonics, vocabulary, and comprehension strategies, as well as guided oral reading practice (National Reading Panel, 2000), and that effective reading teachers emphasize higher-level thinking, provide motivating instruction, use a coaching focus to develop students' self-regulation and independence as a learner, and maintain high expectations (Pressley, 2002; Taylor, 2002).

Teachers who want to improve reading instruction within their building to significantly improve students' reading achievement must collectively adopt an attitude of continuous improvement within their school (Fullan, 2002) and a sense of shared commitment to the process (Newmann, 2002). To transform reading instruction within a school, teachers must come together as a learning community (Lieberman & Miller, 2002) to engage in professional development activities that are school-based, ongoing, and tied directly to the teachers' efforts to implement new or revised strategies within their classrooms (Valli & Hawley, 2002). Professional development has to be situated within the building, making use of data on student work and outcome measures as well as on teachers' instruction. Furthermore, the process selected by a school must help the school community solve problems and continue to move forward toward its specific goals (Valli & Hawley, 2002).

In this chapter, we particularly focus on the use of school level data, especially data on reading comprehension outcomes, to drive the professional development cycle of activities designed to improve instruction and, thereby, student achievement. In the CIERA School Change Project, this cycle involved the teachers in several iterative steps: (a) looking at data, (b) making choices for professional development based on data, (c) using collaborative study groups as a vehicle for reflection on and changes in teaching practices, and (d) revisiting sources of data to evaluate the success of their individual and collective efforts.

IMPLEMENTING THE CIERA SCHOOL CHANGE FRAMEWORK

Nine schools participated in the CIERA School Change Project in 2000 and 2001. Two of these schools had been in the project the previous year as well. The schools were in Connecticut, North Carolina, Michigan, Iowa, Minnesota, and California. Six of the nine schools continued with the project in 2001 and 2002, and four new schools joined the project. Consequently, a total of eight schools were in their second year and five schools were in their first year during the 2001 to 2002 school year. Across these high-poverty schools, 70% to 95% of the students qualified for subsidized lunch, with an average of 81%. Just over 20% were English language learners.

To be a part of the effort, at least 75% of the teachers in a building had to agree to participate. Two teachers per grade were randomly selected for classroom observations. Within these classrooms, nine children were randomly selected as students to be assessed, three each from the high, middle, and low thirds of the classroom in terms of reading achievement.

Schools were asked to meet for a minimum of 1 hr a month as a large group and 1 hr three times a month in study groups. Each school selected a leadership team made up of a literacy coordinator, teachers, the principal, and an external facilitator (who spent a minimum of 8 hr a week in the school supporting the reform effort.) The leadership team members were expected to keep the reform effort moving forward, to solve problems, and to provide support to all of the teachers in the building as they engaged in the school change activities. Large group activities were to include discussion of and action directed toward the school-wide reading program, conversations about school change and professional development, reports from study groups, and cross-grade dialogue about reading instruction and curriculum. Study groups had action plans and in study group meetings teachers were to discuss research-based articles of effective reading instruction practices, watch and discuss video clips of effective practice, video share one's own practice, problem solve, and share expertise. Additionally, teachers were to try out new instructional techniques in the classroom between study group meetings.

At the beginning of a school's participation in the project, it received a report that highlighted the research on effective teachers of reading and the findings from the previous year's analyses of the impact of various classroom practices on students' reading achievement. In the year from which the data for this chapter are included, the report suggested strengths and possible weaknesses in the classroom reading instruction within the school. The analyses that were shared with teachers (Taylor et al., 2003; Taylor, Peterson, Pearson, & Rodriguez, 2002) revealed relations of this sort, for example, with respect to reading comprehension:

- The more a teacher was coded as asking higher-level questions, the more students grew in reading comprehension and fluency in Grade 1 and comprehension, fluency, and writing in Grades 2 to 5.
- In Grades 2 to 5, high levels of rote comprehension skill practice were negatively related to growth in reading comprehension.
- In Grade 1, the teacher practice of teaching comprehension strategies was positively related to students' growth in writing.

The school report also revealed other findings not directly related to comprehension practices. For example, in kindergarten, the teaching of word-level skills was positively related to growth in letter name scores, but in Grades 2 to 5, a high level of teaching of phonics was negatively related to fluency growth. A high level of telling was negatively related to growth in letter-name scores, phonemic awareness, word dictation, and concepts of print in kindergarten. Active responding was positively related to growth in fluency in Grade 1 and passive responding was negatively related to growth in comprehension in Grades 2 to 5. On the other hand, coaching and active reading practice were positively related to growth in fluency in Grades 2 to 5.

DATA SOURCES

The children randomly selected for participation were assessed in the fall and spring on a number of literacy measures including the Gates-MacGinitie standardized reading comprehension test, an oral reading task to determine fluency (as measured by words correct per minute), and a writing task. Because the topic of this volume is reading comprehension assessment, this chapter is limited to growth in comprehension and fluency of students in Grades 2 to 5.

Teachers' use of data on classroom level practices was an important part of this reform effort. On three occasions (fall, winter, spring), each teacher randomly selected for data collection purposes was observed for a scheduled hour during reading instruction to document his or her classroom practices in the teaching of reading. The observers took detailed field notes to capture teacher and student talk and activities. At the end of each 5-min note-taking period, the observer (a) scanned the room to record the number of children productively engaged, and (b) coded practices in the following categories: grouping patterns, reading and writing activities, materials, teacher interaction styles, and students' modes of responding to the lesson. The observation system has been used with good reliability (see Taylor et al., 2003, for a detailed description of the observation system).

Teachers received copies of their observations along with information on the research behind the practices that were coded. They were also encouraged to get help from their external facilitator or literacy coordinator on how to interpret their observations. Research on effective reading instruction that was shared with the teachers of Grades 2 to 5 included the following: the value of (a) systematic phonics instruction and phonemic awareness instruction, especially in Grades kindergarten through first; (b) the application of phonics to reading through use of word recognition strategies; (c) comprehension strategies instruction; (d) higher level questioning; (e) vocabulary instruction; (f) active reading practice; (g) coaching and modeling; and (h) active pupil responding (National Reading Panel, 2000; Pressley et al., 2001; Snow, Burns, & Griffin, 1998; Taylor, Pearson, Clark, & Walpole, 2000; Taylor et al., 2003).

The reform effort at a school was documented through study group meeting notes and action plans, facilitator logs, facilitator end-of-year reports, teacher and principal interviews, and notes from site visits made by the project director. Based on items related to the reform effort, (e.g., teachers met regularly in study groups, reflected on their practice in study groups, focused on substantive topics over time, met regularly as a whole group on the reform effort, and had an effective internal leadership team), a school received a reform effort rating ranging from 1 to 10.

FINDINGS

These findings are reported elsewhere (Taylor et al., in press) but are summarized here, with a special focus on comprehension, both as an instructional goal and a performance outcome. From three-level HLM analysis (Raudenbush, Bryk, & Congdon, 2000) on Gates comprehension normal curve equivalent (NCE) scores ($n = 722$), after accounting for fall scores, we found that 24% of the variance was between teachers and 10% of the variance was between schools. Reform effort rating was positively related to students' spring standardized reading comprehension scores, accounting for 17% of the between-school variance. At the classroom level, we found that grade and the coding of comprehension skill instruction, both negatively related, accounted for 29% of the between-teacher variance.

The finding on the impact of the reform effort on growth in comprehension scores was corroborated through growth curve analysis that was performed on the comprehension scores of students who had been in the project for 2 years ($n = 240$). These students came from eight schools. Again, results are reported elsewhere, but are summarized here (Taylor et al., in press). Eleven percent of the variance in comprehension growth was between schools, and 65% of this variance was accounted for by reform effort. Mean growth between data points was .19 NCEs, but there was an increase of .59 NCEs per data point for every additional point a school received on the reform effort rating.

We found similar results for the effect of the reform effort when considering fluency scores. Reform effort significantly contributed to the between-school variance, and high-level questioning (positively related) and comprehension skill instruction (negatively related) significantly contributed to the between-teacher variance (Taylor et al., in press). Furthermore, reform effort significantly contributed to the school-level variance in the growth curve analysis.

To investigate the impact of reform effort more fully, schools were categorized as high, medium, or low reform effort schools. Five schools with a reform effort rating score of 5, 6, or 7 were designated as high reform effort schools. Three schools with a reform effort rating of 4 were designated as moderate reform effort schools. Five schools with a reform effort rating of 1, 2, or 3 were designated as low reform effort schools. Most relevant to this chapter are changes in teacher practices in high reform effort schools that are discussed later. More detail about the impact of the reform effort can be found in Taylor et al. (in press).

Based on the observations from schools in the project for 2 years, a number of mean scores for teaching practices changed from year 1 to year 2 in high reform effort schools (n = four schools) in the directions suggested by the research, whereas the mean scores in low reform effort schools (n = three schools) did not (Taylor et al., in press). Averaging across high reform effort schools, the mean score for higher-level questions increased whereas in low reform effort schools it did not. Furthermore, the teachers in the high reform effort schools were observed asking higher-level questions about twice as often as teachers in the low reform effort schools. The mean scores for use of coaching, modeling, and active pupil responding increased from year 1 to year 2 in high reform effort schools, whereas in low reform effort schools it did not. However, in neither high nor low reform effort schools did the incidence of observed comprehension strategies instruction increase.

A DESCRIPTION OF ONE HIGH REFORM EFFORT SCHOOL

In this section of the chapter (in part adapted from Taylor et al., in press), we describe the professional development and outcomes at Howard Elementary School (Howard), one high reform effort school that had been in the project for 2 years. At Howard, a school situated in a large urban area, 81% of the students qualified for subsidized lunch and 78% of the students were English language learners. We present this description to illustrate how the use of data on teaching, along with the study group process, led to changes in classroom teaching practices.

Data from Howard also suggested increases in students' reading growth from the first year of the project to the second. Based on the national sample of 13 schools in the spring of 2002, students at Howard were achieving well at each grade level in terms of Gates comprehension scores and fluency scores (See Table 10.1) Also, students at Howard in the spring of 2002 had higher Gates comprehension scores and fluency scores at each grade level in the second year than students at Howard in the spring of 2001 (see Table 10.2).

TABLE 10.1

Mean Comprehension and Fluency Scores Across All Schools and at Howard in Spring of 2002

Grade	N	Spring Gates NCE	N	Spring Wcpm
2 All	149	44.14 17.98	149	84.40 (32.86)
2 Howard	16	46.75 (9.12)	16	109.00 (36.50)
3 All	166	42.35 (17.54)	170	104.70 (33.96)
3 Howard	16	42.25 (16.11)	16	122.73 (48.22)
4 All	155	35.53 (19.08)	161	128.03 (39.66)
4 Howard	18	44.17 (17.57)	18	152.83 (42.59)
5 All	152	38.46 (18.13)	154	134.43 (36.75)
5 Howard	17	43.59 (14.69)	17	145.18 (22.82)

Note. NCE = normal curve equivalent; Wcpm = words correct per minute.

The Study Group Process at Howard

During the first year in the project, the teachers at Howard selected topics for study groups that were influenced by the research report on effective reading instruction shared with the school at the beginning of the year. Groups focused on the following topics: higher-level thinking, reading comprehension, reading assessment, reading interventions within the classroom, and approaches to coaching and modeling. In spite of teachers' enthusiasm for study groups, learning how to be productive in study groups took up a fair amount of teachers' energy in the first half of their first year in the project.

During the second year of the project, teachers at Howard were more focused on specific instructional strategies in study groups than they had been in the first year. They spent the fall of the second year in cross-grade study groups in which they learned how to teach children to use thinking maps to summarize what they had read. During the winter and spring of the second year, the teachers met in study groups that focused on strategies to improve students' compre-

TABLE 10.2
Mean Comprehension and Fluency Scores at Howard
in Spring of 2001 and 2002

Grade	N	Spring Gates NCE 2002	N	Spring Wcpm 2002
2 Howard 2002	16	46.75 (9.12)	16	109.00 (36.50)
2 Howard 2001	15	40.73 (14.17)	11	110.91 (25.54)
3 Howard 2002	16	42.25 (16.11)	16	122.73 (48.22)
3 Howard 2001	24	36.58 (16.20)	23	101.39 (27.83)
4 Howard 2002	18	44.17 (17.57)	18	152.83 (42.59)
4 Howard 2001	22	32.18 (18.03)	24	137.04 (35.88)
5 Howard 2002	17	43.59 (14.69)	17	145.18 (22.82)
5 Howard 2001	16	37.56 (12.73)	16	123.25 (23.89)

Note.   NCE = normal curve equivalent; Wcpm = words correct per minute.

hension. For example, one group refined its use of the Directed Reading Thinking Activity (DRTA) routine (Blachowicz & Ogle, 2001). Another group learned how to teach students to use Students Achieve Independence in Learning (SAIL; Brown, Pressley, Van Meter, & Schuder, 1996). One group worked on developing challenging independent seatwork activities to foster reading comprehension whereas another group focused on vocabulary instruction to improve reading comprehension.

Changes in Observation Data

Our investigation of classroom teaching practices revealed that collectively from year 1 to year 2, teachers at Howard made changes in their teaching practices in the directions suggested by the research. However, not all of the teachers who were observed at Howard were the same in year 1 and year 2. Fortunately, five of the eight teachers observed each year were the same across the 2 years of the project. When considering these five teachers, we found that, in general, they were observed doing more high-level questioning, more comprehension strategies instruction, more coaching and modeling, and had their students engaged in more active responding in year 2 as compared to year 1 (see Table 10.3).

Looking at Two Teachers

To illustrate teachers' changes in teaching practices at Howard, we describe two of the five teachers who were observed in each year of the project. Ms. Lopez (Teacher B) was a second-grade teacher in a study group focusing on higher-level thinking in the first year in the project. In the second year, she was in one of the thinking map study groups and a study group learning how to implement a study strategy called SAIL (Bergman, 1992) during the second year.

In fall of the first year, as Ms. Lopez was reading with a group of four students, she stopped at predetermined places in the story that she had marked for each child with "sticky" notes. Her questioning at these stopping places was at a fairly low level. "Why is Joe so surprised? How do you know that? What else was he surprised about? What happened at night? Then the teacher had the students continue reading until they came to the next "sticky" note.

In spring of the second year, Ms. Lopez's questioning with a small group was at a higher level of thinking and focused on reading strategies. Also, the students were doing more of the work for themselves than in the previous year. Ms. Lopez was no longer using "sticky" notes to mark stopping points for questioning, and she was doing less recitation and more coaching than in the previous year In Year 2, as Ms. Lopez was working with a small group, she had students start their reading of a new story about spiders by doing a picture walk on their own. Then, after they chorally read the first page, they each completed the portion of a story map that dealt with characters and setting. Then the students continued reading on their own, and as a group they identified the problem of the story which they added to their story map. At the end of the lesson, the teacher reminded students that a story map helped them remember the important parts of a story and that they could use the strategy when they were reading on their own.

Also, Ms. Lopez had found a new use for "sticky" notes. Instead of using them herself to make stopping points for questioning, she now had students use "sticky" notes when reading on their own to mark places where they had used strategies. For example, at the end of the small group lesson on using story maps, a child who had been working on his own proudly showed the teachers a "sticky" note in a book on which he had written down a strategy he had used. Clearly, Ms. Lopez's students were learning how to use comprehension strategies when reading.

TABLE 10.3
Percentage of Segments in Which Teaching Practice Is Observed

Teacher	Grade	Year	Low Level Questioning[a]	High Level Questioning[a]	Comp Skills[a]	Comp Strategies[a]	Coaching[a]	Active Responding[b]
A	2	1	85	15	0	11	21	39
		2	17	83	50	0	38	52
B	2	1	57	29	14	19	33	49
		2	54	8	0	40	54	51
C	3	1	73	9	9	9	0	15
		2	69	9	18	0	6	19
D	3	1	38	0	18	27	13	40
		2	55	63	0	13	38	41
E	5	1	83	28	0	0	0	27
		2	79	47	26	5	13	40

[a]Out of all reading segments coded; [b]Out of all level 7 responses coded.

Ms. Gray (Teacher D) was a third grade teacher in the reading comprehension study group in the first year and the thinking map and SAIL study groups in the second year. During the beginning of the first year, Ms. Gray's lessons were fairly teacher-directed and engaged students in low-level thinking. For example, as a small group was reading *Goldilocks and the Three Bears*, Ms. Gray asked low-level questions abut the story such as, "What happened to the rocking chair? How did Mama feel when the rocking chair broke." In the winter, Ms. Gray and a group of students were reading a nonfiction story about penguins. The teacher listed things the students told her they had learned about penguins as she went around to every student to offer an idea. At the end she asked students to review with her what they had learned that day. They responded as follows: "We worked on finding the meaning of a word. We read the table of contents. We learned about reading nonfiction books."

During the spring of the second year, Ms. Gray's small group lessons looked very different. One small group interpreted characters in a story they were reading. Ms. Gray asked the following, "What does Mrs. Gorf think of kids?" A student replied, "She thinks they are a bother." She had the student elaborate and then she asked, "What do you think is the theme of the story?" After students took turns sharing about the importance of being nice to people, Ms. Gray asked, "How does the author's message affect your life?" Students talked about things that someone might do that might hurt other kids. As in the first year, Ms. Gray ended her lesson by having students summarize what they had learned that day. They responded as followed: "We learned about theme. We learned about being nice to other people." They then went to their seats to complete the story map for the story they had just discussed with the teacher.

Teachers' Perceptions of Important School Factors

An analysis of grade kindergarten through fifth-grade teachers' comments on interviews revealed striking consistencies across teachers at Howard. Specifically, four types of responses are addressed: teachers' focus on reading comprehension, the usefulness of teacher observation as a comprehension assessment tool, the value of the study group process, and the usefulness of the observation data.

Teachers at Howard saw improved reading comprehension for students as a personal and school wide goal, and clearly, reading comprehension instruction was a major focus in the classroom of Grades 1 to 5. Ten of ten teachers interviewed in Grades 1 to 5 talked about some aspect of reading comprehension when asked to describe three critical components of their reading program. Comments included the following:

- "Improve comprehension skills and critical thinking."
- "Focus on higher level thinking."
- "Focus on comprehension strategies."
- "Work on my questioning skills and help my students learn how to think."
- "Help students go beyond literal comprehension, thinking at a higher level."
- "Help students locate information and engage in higher-level thinking."
- "Work on oral and written response to literature."
- "Focus on writing and basic comprehension."
- "Focus on responding to text in writing."

Across Grades kindergarten through fifth, 10 of 12 teachers interviewed also mentioned that improved reading comprehension was a school wide goal. Most mentioned the fact that there was consistency in their practices. They were all using thinking maps and writing in response to reading. They were using guided reading consistently, with a focus on higher-level questions and use of comprehension strategies.

In response to the question, "What kinds of literacy assessments do you use and why?" and "Which do you find most valuable to make instructional decisions?" 12 of 12 teachers in kindergarten through fifth grade mentioned the value of teacher observations. Many of their comments pertained to reading comprehension assessment:

- "Observations help me see what strategies my students are using."
- "I use observations to assess and reassess strategies and skills students need help with."
- "Teacher observation and anecdotal notes are most helpful in guiding my instruction."
- "Teacher observation is best. It helps me change during a lesson, focus on something specific students are having trouble with."
- "I look at students' work progress."
- "My students use a self-assessment rubric on their work and I go over that with them."
- "Informal assessment helps me focus more, be more student-oriented. Kids tell me through assessment what to teach and how to teach. If I see a drop in scores, I see it as my fault."

Teachers mentioned many different kinds of informal assessment as helpful. Most mentioned teacher observation. Others mentioned looking at written work, asking questions, listening to verbal summaries, taking anecdotal records, and looking at the questions students create for one another.

Interestingly, 8 of 12 teachers in Grades kindergarten through fifth pointedly claimed that required tests, within the building or by the district, were not useful:

- "It takes so much time to do required assessments and they don't give us the best information."
- "Required basal assessments—we use them because we have to, but they don't really impact instruction."
- "The district assessments are overwhelming. We have to give them one-on-one in kindergarten which takes so much time away from working with the children."

When asked about helpful opportunities for learning about literacy instruction, 12 of 12 teachers in Grades kindergarten through fifth made positive comments about the CIERA study group process. The model was helping to provide consistency in instruction:

- "It keeps us focused."
- "We are more consistent as a school."

Teachers were clear about the study group's process:

- "We read about new ideas in the research, try things out, come back and share how it is going."

Teachers uniformly commented on the value of reflection:

- "We are more reflective as a school."
- "Reflection on instruction is important."

Teachers valued learning from one another:

- "I'm open to learning from others."
- "When we share and discuss, it expands my understanding."
- "Teachers need to see modeling of lessons."

Teachers talked about the value of change:

- "We all need to change, or we are dead."
- "The study groups help us to be always changing."

Importantly, 12 of 12 teachers in kindergarten through fifth grade reported that their teaching had changed in positive ways:

- "In the beginning I did literacy centers, but I reflected on my program, and saw the need to include more independent reading "
- "I used to just follow the teacher's guide, but now I am guided by standards and use what I have learned to teach well."

Many teachers mentioned that they were now more confident about their teaching of reading. As one teacher commented, "I now see more clearly how to help kids, how to meet their individual needs."

Six of twelve teachers mentioned the value of the collegiality the study group process provided:

- "It helped with communication and collaboration."
- "The study group process helped people know each other better. It was good for the school."
- "It helped us develop more relationships with teachers at other grade levels."

One teacher summed it up well: "At first I thought study groups were a waste of time. But it's been very positive. It has helped us use similar approaches. We have more unity. I hope we can continue with study groups. As teachers, we need time to reflect on the effectiveness of our lessons."

Seven of twelve teachers interviewed mentioned the usefulness of the observation data.

- "The data gives the school and teachers important feedback."
- "The observation feedback has been useful in that it provides another pair of eyes."
- "The observations and student data make you reflect more on your program and your students."
- "The observation feedback helped me be more aware of the instructional strategies I used and to what extent my students were actively involved."
- "At first I was hesitant, but I'm glad for the observations. They helped me to see myself and analyze my teaching strategies."

In her interview, the principal echoed many of the comments of the teachers. She said that it was important to stay focused as a school on literacy, and that a major challenge was developing the reading comprehension of English Language Learner (ELL) students. She mentioned that guided reading, thinking maps, and writing in response to reading, were consistent approaches being used at the school to focus on comprehension. She reported that the school was working on using the analysis of multiple assessments and that data was important to use to inform classroom instructional planning. She valued the collaboration developed through the study group process, the collaborative dialogue about reading, the discussion about assessment and lesson planning, and the importance of using research. Howard was fortunate to have a principal who was informed about the teachers' classroom instructional practices and professional growth through study group activities. Also, she shared the same goals as the teachers.

Finally, teachers consistently mentioned the valuable assistance they received from the CIERA literacy coordinator, dubbing her their "CIERA guru." Teachers appreciated that she was well-informed about the latest research, organized, and enthusiastic. They also valued the other members of the leadership team, commenting, "I know there is always help out there to listen. If you had a question, someone will gladly come up to model." Finally, teachers saw teacher leadership as a shared responsibility, commenting that, "Teachers also take on leadership by talking to each other."

In summary, the teachers at Howard were focusing on improved reading comprehension as a school wide goal. In study groups, they were learning new approaches to teach reading comprehension. They were reflecting on their reading comprehension instruction as part of the study group process. They were honing their observation skills as an assessment tool to better understand students' growth and needs, especially as related to higher-level talk and writing about text and use of comprehension strategies. They were using the observation data as one more tool to give them feedback on their teaching. The teachers, teacher leaders, and principal at Howard were working together as a collaborative, learning community, and they were observing the growth they were hoping to see in their students' reading comprehension.

DISCUSSION

Our findings suggest that in the high reform schools, the CIERA School Change Framework was effective in helping teachers change their practices from year 1 to year 2 in the directions suggested by the research on effective reading instruction and effective teachers of reading. Further, in the most effective of the schools, Howard, a major professional development focus on various aspects of teaching comprehension, including comprehension strategies such as in SAIL and higher-level questions, led to major changes in instructional practices and student performance. Furthermore, across all the schools, the reform effort made a significant contribution to spring reading comprehension and fluency scores, after accounting for fall scores.

A teaching staff is complex, with individual members operating from different perspectives. Therefore, it is encouraging to see that an organization as complex as a school teaching staff can come together as a community and use data on teaching practices along with focused study group activities to improve reading instruction. It is also important to point out, however, that such change takes time, and growth in students' reading scores as well as in classroom teaching practices generally comes in small increments from year to year, with no quick fixes and no magic bullets.

The high reform effort schools typically had a supportive principal and one strong, respected teacher leader who made sure that teachers looked at the data linking students' reading growth to classroom reading practices. For the most part, this leader also steered teachers into study group topics that would make a difference—topics such as increasing higher-level questioning or teaching comprehension as a strategy, not a skill. In most of the high reform effort schools, the teacher leader received support and assistance from a group of teachers who served with her on the school's leadership team.

Unfortunately, about a third of the schools in the project were not very successful in implementing the components of the CIERA School Change Framework although they had voted to implement the model. These schools generally lacked principal support, and no teacher leader emerged to keep the reform effort moving forward.

CONCLUSIONS

Five components come to mind when thinking about essential elements of a school change framework for reading improvement, such as the one described in this chapter. First, a flexible but specific structure, whether it is the CIERA School Change Framework or a school-developed blueprint for change, once agreed to, needs to be in place and followed. Reading reform is slow, challenging work that can as easily fail as succeed. In the CIERA School Change Project, this structure included teachers meeting regularly in study groups, trying out new research-validated teaching techniques, and reflecting on this practice. Looking at data on teaching at the beginning, during, and at the end of a year was an important part of this reflection.

Second, teachers need to "buy in" to whatever school improvement structure is implemented. However, initial teacher buy-in to a concept may not be as strong once the concrete activities of change effort actually begin.

Third, and related to the aforementioned point, a leadership team is needed to keep the reform effort moving forward successfully. Maintaining school commitment, providing structure without taking away teachers' voice, and reminding others of the necessity of perseverance, are some of the tasks a leadership team must take up if a school is to succeed.

Fourth, videotapes or video clips are needed of (a) teachers using best practices, and (b) teachers engaged in productive study groups. Teachers need to see and learn from other teachers who are succeeding.

Fifth, the long-term nature of a reform effort needs to be stressed up front because school staff or district staff may get impatient or discouraged with slow growth. To maintain momentum, leaders need to share evidence of progress, both in students' reading scores and in teachers' instructional practices. Finally, teachers need to celebrate these successes on their sustained journey to school wide reading improvement, especially in the heart of the reading process, reading comprehension instruction, and assessment.

REFERENCES

Bergman, J. L. (1992). SAIL—A way to success and independence for low-achieving readers. *The Reading Teacher, 45,* 598–602.

Blachowicz, C., & Ogle, D. (2001). *Reading comprehension: Strategies for independent learning.*

Brown, R., Pressley, M., Van Meter, P., & Schuder, T. (1996). A quasi-experimental validation of transactional strategies instruction with low-achieving second grade readers. *Journal of Educational Psychology, 88,* 18–37.

Fullan, M. (1999). *Change forces: The sequel.* Philadelphia: Falmer.

Fullan, M. (2002). Educational reform as continuous improvement. In W. D. Hawley & D. L. Rollie (Eds.), *The keys to effective schools: Educational reform as continuous improvement.* Thousand Oaks, CA: Corwin.

Hawley, W. D. (Ed.). (2002). *The keys to effective schools: Educational reform as continuous improvement.* Thousand Oaks, CA: Corwin.

Knapp, M. S. (2002). *Teaching for meaning in high-poverty classrooms.* New York: Teachers College Press.

Lieberman, A., & Miller, L. (2002). Transforming professional development: Understanding and organizing learning communities. In W. D. Hawley (Ed.), *The keys to effective schools: Educational reform as continuous improvement* (pp. 74–85). Thousand Oaks, CA: Corwin.

National Reading Panel. (2000). Report of the National Reading Panel. Washington, DC: National Institute for Child Health and Human Development.

Newmann, F. M. (2002). Achieving high-level outcomes for all students: The meaning of staff-shared understanding and commitment. In W. D. Hawley (Ed.), *The keys to effective schools: Educational reform as continuous improvement* (pp. 28–42). Thousand Oaks, CA: Corwin.

Pressley, M. (2002). *Effective beginning reading instruction: The rest of the story from research.* Washington, DC: National Education Association.

Pressley, M. (2002). *Reading instruction that works: The case for balanced teaching* (2nd ed.). New York: Guilford.

Pressley, M., Wharton-McDonald, R., Allington, R., Block, C. C., Morrow, L., Tracey, D., et al. (2001). A study of effective first-grade literacy instruction. *Scientific Studies of Reading, 5*, 35–58.

Raudenbush, S. W., Bryk, A. S., & Congdon, R. (2000). *HLM: Hierarchical Linear and Nonlinear Modeling* (Version 5 [computer software]). Chicago: Scientific Software International.

Snow, C., Burns, S., & Griffin, P. (Eds.). (1998). *Preventing reading difficulties in young children*. Washington, DC: National Academy Press.

Taylor, B. M. (2002). *Characteristics of teachers who are effective in teaching all children to read*. Washington, DC: National Education Association.

Taylor, B. M., Pearson, P. D., Clark, K., & Walpole, S. (2000). Effective schools and accomplished teachers: Lessons about primary grade reading instruction in low-income schools. *Elementary School Journal, 101*(3), 121–166.

Taylor, B. M., Pearson, P. D., Peterson, D. S., & Rodriguez, M. C. (in press). The CIERA School Change Framework: An Evidence-Based Approach to Professional Development and School Reading Improvement. *Reading Research Quarterly*.

Taylor, B. M., Pearson, P. D., Peterson, D. S., & Rodriguez, M. C. (2003). Reading growth in high-poverty classrooms: The influence of teacher practices that encourage cognitive engagement in literacy learning. *Elementary School Journal, 104*, 3–28.

Taylor, B. M., Peterson, D. S., Pearson, P. D., & Rodriguez, M. C. (2002). Looking inside classrooms: Reflecting on the "how" as well as the "what" in effective reading instruction. *Reading Teacher, 56*, 270–279.

Taylor, B. M., Pressley, M., & Pearson, P. D. (2002). *Research-supported characteristics of teachers and schools that promote reading achievement*. Washington, DC: National Education Association.

Valli, L., & Hawley, W. D. (2002). Designing and implementing school-based professional development. In W. D. Hawley (Ed.), *The keys to effective schools: Educational reform as continuous improvement* (pp. 86–96). Thousand Oaks, CA: Corwin.

11

Attending to the Nature of Subject Matter in Text Comprehension Assessments[1]

Annemarie Sullivan Palincsar
Shirley J. Magnusson
Ellen Pesko
Maria Hamlin
University of Michigan

In this chapter, we report on exploratory research investigating elementary students' comprehension of text in a domain-specific manner, using a specially designed text. In addition, the assessment context was designed with an eye to reducing the limitations that students with impoverished content-specific prior knowledge may have in building adequate mental representations of the text. Prior to describing this research, we present an argument for the significance of this type of inquiry.

Reading research has provided firm evidence of the important role that prior knowledge plays in comprehension, whether viewed from schema theory (Anderson & Pearson, 1984; Rumelhart, 1981) or from a construction-integration model of reading (Kintsch, 1988). One thorny issue for test developers is the design of comprehension assessments that are not simply measures of prior knowledge. Allington, Chodos, Domaracki, and Truex (1977), for example, determined that students accurately answered 23% to 31% of the comprehen-

[1]This research was supported under the Educational Research and Development Centers Program, PR/Award Number R305R70004, as administered by the former office of Educational Research and Improvement, U.S. Department of Education. It was also supported by the U.S. National Science Foundation.

sion questions included in four commonly used diagnostic reading measures without reading the passages.

Test developers have sought ways to attempt to account for the role that prior knowledge plays in measures of reading comprehension. For example, the designers of the Michigan Educational Assessment Program included multiple-choice questions designed to assess students' prior knowledge before administering the passage comprehension items. Comprehension scores were then calculated factoring in the knowledge children brought to the text.

Another approach to addressing this challenge has been the general practice of designing assessments that measure students' ability to understand texts about a range of different topics. For example, in his analysis of popular reading tests that are used in developmental placement decisions, Behrman (2000) listed the following among the topics featured in one level of the test: spiders, air pollution, moral justice, adolescence, and business ethics. However, research suggests that the practice of using content-general reading assessments is problematic, for a number of reasons.

First, there is only a modest case for the criterion-related validity of content-general tests.[2] For example, Byrnes (1995), in a review of 33 studies (reported between 1988–1994), reported that in 83% of the studies in which the role of general and domain-specific skills was examined, domain-specific skills were far more important than general abilities in predicting performance. These findings held up whether the dependent measures involved fast responding, strategies, or metacognition.

Content-general reading tests fail to recognize the significant and dynamic relation between comprehension and prior knowledge (Pearson & Hamm, this volume; Valencia & Pearson, 1987). Furthermore, comprehension is not a unitary ability but rather represents a set of content-based abilities that reflect unique domain knowledge and related strategies (Alexander & Kulikowich, 1994; Langer, 1994). The case for domain-specific comprehension assessments is perhaps even more compelling when applied to the assessment of comprehension of science texts, which are replete with features that demand different forms of text processing (Dee-Lucas & Larkin, 1988). For example, typical science text imposes linguistic demands, mathematical demands, and graphic demands on the reader, with the significance of the demand determined by the degree of integration of these features.

There are two related arguments for this exploratory research, one of which is that, as a field, we have a relatively good theoretical understanding of the structure and content of narrative text; however, there are no comparably

---

[2]It should be noted that this type of research has been conducted exclusively with adult populations.

well-developed theories of the representation of exposition, although it is recognized that exposition is not nearly as homogenous in structure as narrative (Lorch & van den Broek, 1997).

Finally, most comprehension research has examined how readers construct horizontal connections between concepts or events and has not focused on the construction of vertical relations (e.g., relating subordinate ideas to superordinate ideas, interpreting sequences of statements in support of a generalization). In conclusion, there is a significant role for research on reading comprehension that seeks to inform our understanding of assessments that take into account the role of prior knowledge, as well as domain-specific demands and text features. In the next section, we describe the text and activity we designed with these issues in mind.

DESIGNING TEXTS AND CONTEXTS TO ASSESS COMPREHENSION IN DOMAIN-SPECIFIC WAYS

The Text

The text was informed by the design of texts that we have used in earlier research (Magnusson & Palincsar, 2004; Palincsar & Magnusson, 2001). It was a two-page excerpt from the notebook of a fictitious scientist. The text begins with the scientist (Lesley) identifying a real-world phenomenon that puzzled her. Specifically, Lesley was biking with two friends when one friend challenged them to a race. Each friend predicts that, due to his or her physical characteristics (vis-à-vis weight and ability to pedal hard or fast) he or she will win the race. In this way, the problem situation sets the stage for the exploration of the two variables that affect motion: mass (weight) and force (pedaling effort). To Lesley's surprise they all tie, and she decides to investigate this problem, beginning her investigation by modeling the situation. She thinks aloud about what the model must include to be analogous with the biking situation; she poses the research question (i.e., "How does the amount of force on a bike affect its speed?") to her research group, and presents her investigative setup in a labeled figure. She proceeds to make a prediction (i.e., "with more force, the cart will go faster"), and she presents data she collected in a table (times to hundredths of seconds) for several trials (depending on the variability of her data) at five amounts of different force. She then argues that the data support her prediction (i.e., "additional force increased the motion of the cart"). She decides to average those data for the purpose of helping others see the pattern that she sees in the data, commenting that the pattern in the data is interesting because "the times do not decrease by the same amount."

There are specific features of this text that are noteworthy given the purpose of our inquiry. First, in addition to the linguistic elements, it contains graphic representations (figures, tables) and mathematical information; features that are characteristic of scientific text. Contrary to some naturally occurring science text (Dee-Lucas & Larkin, 1988), these features are well integrated, easing some of the burden on the reader. Second, the content features scientific reasoning (e.g., the use of modeling, the process of recording observations and drawing on those observations as evidence to support or refute particular hypotheses). This is a noteworthy characteristic for at least two reasons; first, because it speaks to one of the goals of science instruction, which is that students learn not only the canonical knowledge of science (i.e., scientific conceptions), but that they also learn how that knowledge is generated and verified. The experimental text is possibly one way in which this type of knowledge can be communicated to learners. The design is also interesting because it is conceivable that it provides a way of supporting children's interpretation of the text; that is, Lesley is engaged in her own "extended think-aloud" as she sets about designing an investigation, conducting and analyzing her investigation, and generating knowledge claims from the investigation. Having access to Lesley's thinking may support students as they construct their own mental representation of the text.

The Context

There are at least three common procedures often used to identify children's sense-making with these texts: "think-aloud," retelling, or question answering. We initially piloted the use of think-aloud, but determined that the vagueness of the students' think-alouds left us with many more questions than they addressed. We then designed an interview protocol that combined retelling with question asking; that is, with virtually each of eight segments into which the text was divided, the child was first asked to respond to a general prompt such as, "What does Lesley write about in this section of her notebook?" or, "What do we learn in this next section of her notebook?" However, we supplemented the retelling prompt with specific questions. As Goldman, Varma, Sharp, and Cognition and Technology Group at Vanderbilt (1999) have documented, question answering allows children to reveal more of what they understand than does retelling; in part because of the linguistic production demands associated with retelling. Hence, following the general retelling prompt, the interview proceeded with more specific questions that addressed particular issues and opportunities within the text. Furthermore, if the student included inaccurate information in responding to a question, the interviewer was prompted to assist the student to get back "on course" so that the interview was as productive as possible; for example, interviewers were urged to support the student by referring the child directly back to information in the notebook text.

The participants were 24 fourth-grade students from four schools that principally serve students from low socioeconomic status families and are racially diverse. Twelve of the participants were girls. Teachers were asked to nominate "typically achieving readers" for whom the decoding of the text would not be particularly challenging. The vast majority of the participants chose to read the text aloud, providing confirmatory evidence that they were not challenged by the decoding demands of the text. To our knowledge, none of the children had studied motion (the topic of the assessment text) during the academic year in which this research took place.

The interview took place in a space outside of the classroom and was captured via the use of an audiotape recorder. The interviewer began the assessment by introducing herself [3] and then asking the student to complete a brief (four-item) assessment that was used to assess the children's prior knowledge of concepts that were central to the notebook text excerpt. For example, in the case of motion, the four items assessed the student's understanding of relations between time-speed, force-speed, speed-mass, and speed-mass-force. The interviewer then introduced the task to the student:

We have designed a new kind of text that we call a scientist's notebook text. The scientist is named Lesley Park and she writes in this notebook to share her thinking as she conducts investigations to answer questions about the world around us. We need your help to learn what children think about as they read this notebook text. I will ask you to read the notebook text, one section at a time. At the end of each section, I will ask you several questions. You are welcome to look back at the notebook text as often as you would like, if it would be helpful to you.

The children were offered the choice to read each segment of the text to themselves or aloud. Questions were asked following the reading of each segment of the text. Each interview ranged from 30 to 45 minutes, depending on the amount of prompting required and the rate at which the child decoded the text. Following the interview, children were invited to share any additional thoughts they had or any questions they were left with following the reading of the text.

[3]The authors gratefully acknowledge research assistant Jane Cutter, who joined Maria Hamlin and Ellen Pesko in the conduct of the interviews reported in this chapter.

Rating the Students' Prior Knowledge

The prior knowledge measures were multiple choice and were coded for accuracy. One item (time-speed), was worth a single point, two items were worth 2 points (force-speed, speed-mass), and one item (speed-mass-force relations) was worth 3 points, reflecting the variable demands of the four items. Children who earned 2 points or less were designated as having "low prior knowledge." Children who earned 4 points were designated as having "low-medium prior knowledge." Children who earned 5 points were designated as having "medium to high prior knowledge," and children earning 8 points were designated as having "high prior knowledge." The outcomes of the prior knowledge measure are presented in Table 11.1.

Scoring the Interviews

Each interview was transcribed by a professional transcribing service. We lost data for a total of five students due to recording problems ($n = 3$), or because of the poor quality of the interview ($n = 2$).

We conducted two forms of coding with these data. The first focused on generating a set of claims regarding what the transcripts revealed about the students' ability to make sense of the graphic, mathematical, and syntactic issues present in the text. In this analysis, we examined the following: (a) interpretation of a figure illustrating the setup for Lesley's investigation, (b) interpretation of data tables, and (c) indications that the students were engaged in scientific reasoning with the text (e.g., able to identify why times might vary in trials, able to identify when differences in times are significant, able to relate the type of data collected to the instrumentation). The second analysis, which is the one reported in this chapter, was conducted for the purpose of determining how the child's mental representation of the text developed over the course of reading each segment. To support this analysis, we first

TABLE 11.1
Results of Prior Knowledge Measure

Level of Prior Knowledge	Number of Students
Low	2
Low-medium	5
Medium-high	9
High	3

identified the opportunities the text afforded in each segment (see Table 11.2). In addition, we identified whether the information necessary to respond accurately to the question was explicitly identified in the text, or required the child to engage in inferencing. A possible total of 8 points was associated with explicit questions and a total of 9 points was associated with inferential questions. We then scored each child's transcript, blind relative to the results of the prior knowledge assessment, in relation to the opportunities. Partial points were possible for several of the items.

An overall picture of the findings, reported for the four prior knowledge groups in terms of the explicit and inferential items, is presented in Fig. 11.1. Recall that there were 8 points possible on the explicit items and 9 points possible on the inferential items. The average score for the explicit items was 5.9 (with the scores ranging from 3 to 8) and the average score for the inferential items was 4.4 (with a range from 0 to 9). Although five students attained higher scores on the inferential than the explicit questions, typically, the students achieved higher scores on the explicit items.

We discuss the findings according to specific questions we asked of these data. Given the limited numbers of students (particularly within each of the four categories), we are reporting these data in descriptive rather than inferen-

TABLE 11.2
Opportunities and Points-Types Possible Across the Text

Segment	Opportunity	Points-Type
1	**Context setting**: Lesley and her two friends all think they will win the race because of their different characteristics, which vary in terms of mass and force.	2-explicit
	Problem definition: How did the three bikers reach the park at the same time?	1-inference
2	**Modeling**: General definition.	1-inference
	Identifies question guiding investigation.	1-explicit
3	**Identifies** each of the **analogues** in the problem.	2-explicit
	Holding the phenomenon in mind, **evaluates** the model.	2-inference
	Holding the phenomenon in mind, **predicts** how the investigation will be conducted.	2-inference
4	**Predicts** findings.	1-explicit
	Draws a **relation** between Lesley's reasoning and the biking phenomenon.	2-inference
5	Draws a **conclusion** from data: the greater the force, the faster the cart.	1-explicit
6	**Represents data for clarity**.	1-explicit
7	**Identifies pattern** in the data.	1-inference

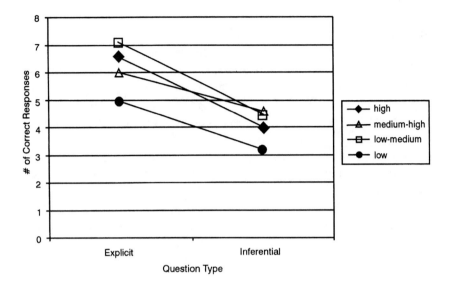

FIG. 11.1. Performance on text interview.

tial terms. For each question, we use excerpts from the transcripts to investigate the findings from the scored data. Table 11.3 provides an advance organizer, identifying the range of factors we found useful to characterizing the performance of the students participating in this study.

Prior to reporting findings for specific questions, we summarize—as a point of comparison—the protocol for one student, JH (a male student with medium-high prior knowledge), who earned the highest number of points on the interview. Following his reading of the biking phenomenon, JH completely and accurately described the context adding that "everybody had like different qualities to win." Drawing on his everyday rather than a scientific notion of modeling, JH associated modeling with making miniature versions of something. When asked about the figure Lesley uses to represent her model, JH did a complete accounting of the model, identifying each feature of the physical model and what each represented in the biking problem. Furthermore, he critiqued the representation, noting that the heavier person would need to be three blocks, Lesley would be two blocks, and Felicia would be one block. When responding to that portion of the text in which Lesley offers her prediction, JH commented, "she explained it (the model) to us and told us what she thought before she did the model." He correctly identified her prediction and indicated why he agreed with her thinking. When examining the data table, he accurately labeled each part of the table

TABLE 11.3

Factors Useful to Characterizing Students' Performance Interpreting Experimental Text

Extent to Which Students Engaged in the Following:
- Consistent and flexible use of prior knowledge
- Effective reasoning from the text in the absence of prior knowledge
- Metacognitive awareness and strategic activity
- Accommodating to lexical demands
- Meeting working memory demands
- Vertical integration across the text
- Productive use of text features (e.g., diagram, data table, graph)

and noted when there was not the full complement of trials. Prior to reading Lesley's conclusion, JH identified the pattern that the time with the fewest washers was the slowest and the time with the most washers was the fastest. When he went on to read Lesley's conclusion, he commented that her conclusion is "just like I said." His response to the averaging question was vague ("we did a mean, median, and average or something a long time ago, but I forgot how to do it"), but in responding to the prompt about the pattern in the data, JH calculated the differences in increments for several of the trials to illustrate Lesley's point.

TO WHAT EXTENT DOES PRIOR KNOWLEDGE PREDICT STUDENTS' PERFORMANCE ON THE TEXT INTERVIEW?

In a typical reading comprehension assessment, one would expect that there would be a positive relation between the content-specific prior knowledge measure and performance responding to the interview questions, across both the explicit and inferential items, but perhaps especially on the inferential items, with which students are asked to reason beyond the information that is presented in the text, an activity that would be enabled through the use of one's prior knowledge (Bransford & Johnson, 1972; Dooling & Lachman, 1971).

Clearly there are limitations to drawing conclusions about students' prior knowledge from a brief four-item assessment (although the assessment was designed to sample the central concepts addressed in the notebook excerpt). Nevertheless, it is interesting to note that performance among the high, medium-high, and medium-low students on both the explicit and inferential questions is not easily predicted by students' prior knowledge. To explore this finding, we draw on excerpts from the interviews with select children. The most instructive cases are those in which prior knowledge is the least predictive for the case of both high and low prior knowledge children.

Examining the Cases of High Prior-Knowledge Children

There were only three children (all boys) who responded accurately to all of the prior knowledge measures (SD, LD, and MS). Although SD was successful with all of the prior knowledge items, he was inconsistent in bringing this prior knowledge to bear in interpreting the text. To elaborate, although SD had an accurate understanding of the force-mass-motion relation, he identified the question that Lesley is investigating as the following: "how things with mass in different weights and different lengths effect um, how they move and how fast they move." This is in contrast to the question Lesley has written, which is, "How does the amount of force on a bike affect its speed?" On the other hand, he was one of very few students who drew a complete relation between the way in which Lesley is modeling the problem and the phenomenon itself; in response to the question probing the relation between the model and the actual bike race, SD commented, "Cause there's force like how strong your ... or big your legs are ... how fast they can peddle. And there's mass like how much they weigh." Furthermore, he was troubled that Lesley has not included the study of mass in her notebook. In reference to whether there is more in her notebook, SD asked the following: "Does it tell you about force and mass?"

I: Yeah ... she does go on to investigate mass.

SD: 'Cause that's what I was thinking ... just, I think mass would make some difference.

In fact, SD is a case where it is essential to look at his processing of the text over time (a matter we consider later). For the first half of the interview, his responses were fairly sketchy and superficial; by the second half, when he was asked whether he agreed with Lesley's conclusions from her investigation, he was troubled that she has not considered all of the important variables in the biking phenomenon. The following exchange occurred at the conclusion of the interview, when SD was invited to share any questions he had following his reading of the notebook text:

SD: What about mass?

I.:   So, you're curious to know about mass and how mass
        [SD: because] would affect that?

SD: Because it seems kind of unfinished.

I: Unfinished?

SD: Without the mass part.

LB, another student who accurately responded to each of the prior knowledge questions, earned the maximum number of points possible on the explicit
items, but was more challenged by the inferential items. For example, as LB
studied the table in which Lesley presents the time data by trials for each of five
amounts of force, he was asked the following: "Why didn't Lesley complete a
fourth trial when she was investigating two and three washers?" LB responded
as follows: "I don't know what she means by trial ... if I knew what she meant by
trial, I could probably figure it out." As an additional illustration, although LB's
retelling of the context was complete and accurate, capturing the role that the
bikers' physical characteristics could have played in the outcome of the race, he
had considerable difficulty bringing his understanding of the phenomenon, as
well as his understanding about mass-force-motion relations to his sense-making of the text, when assessed through the inferential items. For example, despite his facility responding to the interview items that assessed his ability to use
the information explicitly provided in the text about how Lesley is conducting
the investigation and what conclusions she drew from her investigation regarding the relation between force and speed, when he finished the notebook text
he was asked the following: "So why do you think they (the cyclists) did get
there at the same time? LB failed to draw on either his prior knowledge or the information in the text and said the following: "I think their weight weren't much
different, because if you're skinny you can go fast, if you're muscular you can go
fast, and if you're just in between those you can go fast. So I think that's why."

MS, the third student to respond accurately to all of the prior knowledge
measures, was similarly challenged by the inferential items. Although the prior
knowledge measure indicated that he was aware that differences in mass are related to differences in motion, when he was asked to comment on why Lesley
was surprised about the outcome of the race, given the differences in her
friends, MS commented as follows: "It doesn't really matter if you're heavier,
like ... it doesn't really matter what you are as long as you can like sort of ride a
bike. They're like equal in skill in riding a bike and so, it doesn't really matter if
they're heavier or anything."

MS's description of the model was very sparse; although each part of the
model is carefully labeled, he noted only that there is a cart and a string to pull

it. He did not comment on the ways in which the model represents the phenomenon, and he did not identify how (with the weight of the washers on the pulley) the cart will move. Furthermore, although he completely and accurately identified the types of information in the table, when asked, "What do we learn about motion from this table?" he responded, "I don't know. Well, I guess you learn (long pause). I don't know. It takes different times depending on ... I don't know."

These examples are significant because they point out ways in which this assessment is tapping more than students' prior knowledge. The text and context provide evidence relative to students' ability and inclination to flexibly use not only their prior knowledge, but also the information provided in the text, to support comprehension. This dynamic interaction between existing knowledge structures that have been acquired through prior experiences, and available information from on-going experiences (such as the reading of new text), figures prominently in a number of models of text comprehension. Anderson (1984) referred to this interaction as *instantiation*; whereas Kintsch and his colleagues (Mannes & Kintsch, 1987; van Dijk & Kintsch, 1983) referred to it as a *situation* model of comprehension. Ausubel (1963) described this process as *ideational scaffolding*. The text and task employed in this research provide a glimpse of high prior knowledge readers failing to successfully negotiate the interface between prior knowledge and novel information.

Examining the Cases of Low Prior Knowledge Children

There were two children who answered only the most basic question about time-speed relation on the prior knowledge measure, KC and KS (girls). KC is particularly interesting because she scored above the mean on the explicit items of the interview. The transcript reveals that KC gave a complete retelling of the bike race context, including the reason why Lesley was surprised that the bikers had finished the race at the same time. When KC commented on Lesley's decision to model the bike problem, she included the observation that Lesley is "trying to find something that will be a bike, represent a bike, represent the different weights of the three of them." Despite her limited prior knowledge, KC is productively engaged in interpreting the text; in fact, in contrast to KC, we saw few instances of children spontaneously including in their retellings of this segment of the text, reference to changing the weight, or reference to the phenomenon. There were two factors that appeared to interfere with KC's sense-making. One was that she did not recognize that mass and weight are interchangeable in this context; although she had spontaneously identified the importance of being able to change the weight in the initial description of how this problem should be modeled, when she encountered Lesley's description of how she will model the problem, she did not make this same connection:

> I: When you think of the bicycles, who might have more mass? Do you remember in the beginning? [No response] Do you think one of them had more mass?
>
> KC: No.
>
> I: You think the mass was about the same?
>
> KC: Yah.

More problematic, however, is the observation that, midway through the text, KC began to think about other variables that would affect the motion of a bike; furthermore, she switched from a horizontal plane context to an inclined plane context (traveling down a hill):

> KC: Like some people like to be careful and have their hands on the break a lot. So that kind of slows them down. And some people like their hand just like on the handlebars. And if they have to stop they quickly move their hands onto the breaks. Or if … they just pedal backwards if they don't have hand breaks.
>
> I: So how does her prediction [that with more force, the cart will go faster] compare to her understanding of the bike race?
>
> KC: I don't know.
>
> I: Think about … she's predicting that … her prediction is that with more force the cart will go faster. So, how does … does that seem like the bike race?
>
> KC: Yah, kind of because the different people weigh different things and the different weight might help. And another prediction would be like … something that goes with this would be that if one person was pushing forward on their bike a lot then that would make them go down the hill faster … it's kind of like you're bringing your weight back. But if you're like this …. Forward on the bike, then it makes you …

KC's responses provide insight into why the criterion-related validity of reading measures may be problematic in predicting performance within a domain. In this case, KC's speculations about other variables and contexts interfere with her sense-making of this particular text; on the other hand, in the context of inquiry experiences in science, her thinking about other factors that might influence the motion of a bike, such as how the rider sits on the bike (changing the aerodynamics), and the geography of the physical context (rolling down a hill vs. pedaling on a flat surface), could be very productive in advancing inquiry on the topic of motion.

In contrast to KC, KS, the second low prior knowledge student, was one of the four lowest performing children in the interview context; furthermore, she had a markedly different profile from KC. Her retelling of the context was incomplete, making no reference to the physical characteristics of the riders, nor to the surprise ending. She was challenged using the information in the text to support her understanding; for example, although Lesley comments that she will "add mass ... in different amounts to represent our different weights," KS asks what is mass. Reading the statement, "My race with Germane and Felicia made it seem that differences in force and mass do not affect motion, but maybe the relationship is just complex," KS inaccurately paraphrased the text to say, "The mass doesn't have anything to do with the motion." There was also a disparity between some of her declarative statements about the information in the text and the application of this information to the problem at hand in the text. For example, when asked to evaluate Lesley's prediction that "with more force the cart will go faster," KS commented as follows: "... they might have had the same speed of going and like ... since they start off together they will ... um, as they start pedaling they might be pedaling at the same time and you could get there at the same time."

Perhaps in part because her understanding of the context and the relevant conceptual issues appears to be quite fragile, KS was most significantly challenged when she came to the data table, although interpreting her sense-making of the table is confounded by the difficulties she experienced identifying the information in the table. For example, she needed significant support to identify the parts of the table, impeding her ability to draw conclusions from the table.

We conclude this discussion with the presentation of one additional child who scored in the low-medium range on the prior knowledge measure. BW (girl) is a particularly interesting child because, although she has only low-medium prior knowledge, she is quite actively engaged in sense-making with the text. Her interview provides evidence of the ways in which this assessment context can reveal the strategic nature of (some) children's sense-making activity as they interact with text. After a complete and accurate retelling of the biking context, when she read that Lesley has decided to model the situation—but before reading how she will model the situation—BW conjectured that Lesley should get a "toy car that has wheels and add a ball or pencil and put it on top" so that she can "figure out what mass can do to things that move." When she encountered Lesley's figure depicting how she will model the phenomenon, she expressed concern that the washer may not be enough to make the cart move. She expressed this insight at the same time that she disclosed, "really, I don't even know what a washer is. I know what a clothes washer is, but I don't know if they're talking about that kind of washer." BW initially thought that the three blocks on the cart in the figure stood for three people; however, she revised her thinking in a manner that made the text consistent with the phenomenon when she noted, "I made a mistake. So, what I mean to say is that, I think she's trying to see how fast the bike can move with one person on it. I think the three blocks are representing the bigger person, to see how fast it'll move." BW not only spontaneously identified Lesley's prediction about the relation between force and speed, but she also went on to explain that this prediction made sense to her: "... Like if you put more force on a bike, or more force on roller blades, or more force on a scooter, or a skateboard, the more force you have, the faster it'll go."

BW's interview is particularly interesting at the point that she was interpreting the data table. Her initial comment about the time data was that the differences in the times are "really not all that different." BW spent approximately 15 min reading through and discussing the data table. What became clear, with the assistance of the clarifying questions asked by the interviewer, was that she was having difficulty reading times to the hundredths of a second and determining whether the times were greater or lesser. However, she was extremely persistent, and when she read Lesley's conclusion that her (Lesley's) prediction was correct, she returned to the data table, conceding that the "the force increases the motion of the cart, it makes it kinda go a little bit faster ... not all the way faster, but a little bit." This comment led to another round of exchanges about how to evaluate the differences across the trials in terms of the numbers of seconds each trial took. This exchange culminated in BW's statement: "Oh! You just brought something to my head ..." She then proceeded to reread each of the lines of data for every trial run for each of the five amounts of force, concluding: "So, I do agree with her conclusion. I just noticed that. So I do agree with her conclusion."

The differences in the performances of KC, KS, and BW, as well as the differences among the high prior knowledge students, point to ways in which this assessment context is providing information about individual differences among students relative to constructing coherent and sensible meaning from text through their interactions with surface level features of the text, with visuals, and with the content of the text. In addition, we see interesting variations in ways in which students are integrating visuals with text, as well as integrating information across the text.

What is the evidence that, in this context, children use—or fail to use—the support provided in the text to construct accurate mental representations of the text and how does this activity provide instructionally useful comprehension assessment information?

We mentioned, in the cases described earlier, that SD was an example of a student who achieved greater clarity over the course of responding to the text. There were several children for whom this was the case, with the most striking example being BR (boy, low-medium prior knowledge). Although BR described the bike context completely and accurately, he did little else that was productive with the first half of the text. In fact, he made several erroneous statements about Lesley's thinking (for example, suggesting that Lesley thinks that force and mass do not affect motion). When BR encountered Lesley's data table, we see a clear difference in his response to the text; he fluently labeled and interpreted the information in the table. When asked "from this table, what can we learn about Lesley's investigation?" BR responded as follows: "The more mass—I mean force—does actually affect the speed." When asked how it affects the speed, BR added, "Well, it says that it um [looking at the data in the table] five washers it says 31 hundredths of a second, but it says one washer, 65 hundredths of a second so it does actually go faster ... [I- "which?"] with five washers." From this point on, BR began to look like a much more competent reader and thinker. For example, he was critical of Lesley for drawing conclusions about the bike race from the situation she had modeled, noting the following: "They [the bikers] actually control the motion." We don't have sufficient information to understand this shift in BR's sense-making with the text; it may be that the inclusion of the data table, laying out the trials with various amounts of force, concretized the problem in a way that the text by itself had not. Although the mathematical demands associated with making sense of the data table appeared to impair some students' performance, for BR, the linguistic demands of the first half of the text may have been more challenging. Given the frequency with which numerical information is used in science (particularly in the study of the physical sciences), this form of mixed genre text may provide a more accurate picture of the skills that children like BR bring to the comprehension of science text.

We now turn the discussion to several students who were particularly challenged in constructing accurate mental representations of the text for the purpose of exploring what this context can reveal about students' comprehension challenges. Because we do not have a sufficiently large enough sample to identify patterns in students' profiles, we use the sample we have to generate hypotheses about the challenges students experienced. The case of MW (girl, medium-high prior knowledge) is particularly instructive. MW proceeded smoothly through the initial part of the interview; she understood the context and accurately described how Lesley would model the problem (she even criticized the investigative setup for its failure to take into account the differences in the weights of the bikers). She then came to a point in reading the text where she decided that this was a problem of mass and gravity.[4] MW resituated the problem on an inclined (rather than horizontal) plane, and proceeded down a path that was replete with the naïve conceptions that people hold about the speed of objects of different masses down inclined planes (Driver & Erickson, 1983). The case of MW is revealing in several respects: she is a classic example of a reader overrelying on top-down processing of the text and in so doing, her monitoring (metacognitive activity) becomes focused on finding evidence to support the schema she has imposed on the text, rather than focused on the internal consistency of the text itself.

We conclude with a presentation of the data for two students who experienced significant difficulty with this assessment, focusing on what their interviews revealed about their respective approaches to text. DP (boy, medium-high prior knowledge) was challenged from the beginning of the text. Although he accurately read the text aloud, in his retelling of the first segment, there were but two bikers racing; when he was referred back to the text, he identified Jermaine and Felicia, but did not appear to realize that, because this was written in the first person by Lesley (who refers to herself as "I"), there was a third person involved in the race. When asked what Lesley wrote about in the second segment, he asked if he could reread the text and extracted a sentence—although not the main idea—for his retelling. He identified the question Lesley was investigating as the following: "How they both got down to the finish line at the same time" and had to be redirected to the text for the question, "How does the amount of force on a bike affect its speed?" His response to what Lesley meant when she said she would "model the situation" was that "she'll probably like, go over and ask questions." This pattern continued for the remainder of the interview, eventuating in DP commenting toward the end of the interview, "I wish I was smart." Although one would be hesitant to draw conclusions about DP's reading from this one interview, there are a number of hypotheses that one could explore. DP's lexical knowledge might be suspect. The words *model, trial, washers,* and *conclude* were all unfamiliar to him and he was not strategically using context to support his understanding of those words. Although he had a fair degree of prior knowledge specific to motion, he seemed

---

[4]The switch appears to have been triggered by a discussion of Lesley's observation that the greater the force, the faster the speed. MW interjected that she thinks weight has "something to do with it … because if you're heavier and you're going downhill the more heavier you are, the more you push out. If you're lighter, you're more likely to go slower or something."

reluctant to use that prior knowledge, especially in drawing inferences from the text. Finally, the data table in Lesley's notebook placed considerable demand on children's working memory; if they were unfamiliar with data tables—as seemed the case for DR—they were confronted with the tasks of both identifying the information in the data table and interpreting that information for the purpose of generating or evaluating claim statements.

RJ, another boy with medium-high prior knowledge, presents a different profile that is especially interesting when thinking about the design of comprehension assessments that reflect domain-specificity. We argued that, to be maximally useful, comprehension assessments should measure not only students' conceptual understanding, but also their syntactic knowledge; their understanding of how knowledge claims are generated and tested within the disciplines. RJ presented the profile of a child who seemed especially challenged with those aspects of the text that call for the deployment of syntactic knowledge. For example, he didn't think it was a good idea for Lesley to model the bike race, proposing instead that "she should just race again to see if it will happen again." As another example, although other students made certain appropriate assumptions regarding the investigation Lesley is conducting (for example, that Lesley is using the same cart for each trial), RH thought the carts might be different, which made his interpretation of the data table regarding changes in motion as a function of changes in force difficult for him to interpret: Issues that need not have been problematic interfered with his sense-making of the text. At the end of the interview, when RH was asked about Lesley's conclusion regarding the role of force in motion, RH, drawing on a textbook definition of force, made the following general statement: "Force makes a difference because if we didn't have force … like force is pushing or pulling so if we didn't have that then nothing could move." His statement is not an adequate match with the data and claims that Lesley presents in her notebook.

DISCUSSION

The purpose of this research was to investigate what children's interactions with a text would reveal about their comprehension activity when both the text and context in which their comprehension was assessed were designed to reflect the epistemological dimensions of the physical sciences. In our discussion, we consider our findings in terms of the following: the text itself, the nature of the context, and possibilities for future research.

Scientific texts are not, of course, monolithic. Goldman and Bisanz (2002) have presented a functional analysis of six genres of science text, each of which serves a different societal role from raising awareness to advancing knowledge. The text that we designed was a hybrid of exposition, narration, description, and argumentation. In addition, the text contained features that are frequently present in science text, including diagrams and tables. The intraindividual, as well as interindividual, variations in students' activity relative to these different genres and features suggest that this text provided a useful stimulus for assessing comprehension. Although some students' prior knowledge and experience was quickly evoked by Lesley's first-person account of the bike race, other students took a more active stance when presented with the investigative setup or when asked to evaluate Lesley's argument. Although some students relied heavily on the linguistic information in the text, other students appeared to be more supported by the data table and, in fact, reconstructed their understanding of the linguistic information, following their interpretation of the data table.

The interview context, which blended retelling with question-answering, was productive to the extent that it revealed how children's mental representations of the text were unfolding across each segment of the text. The questions were designed to be consistent with engaging the students in "reasoning along" with Lesley; for example, the students were asked to predict Lesley's activity, to draw conclusions from her data, and to critique her thinking. In this fashion, the reading task was situated as one of constructing and revising coherent and sensible meaning. This context was particularly sensitive to revealing the metacognitive profiles of students. Although some students (e.g., MW), demonstrating "schema blindness" (Spiro & Myers, 1984), tenaciously imposed their preconceived ideas on the text and continued to rely on these ideas—even in the face of contradictory evidence—other students monitored for consistency between their representation and information encountered in the text and made adjustments in the course of reading.

Within the limits of this investigation (e.g., the small sample size and the brief assessment of prior knowledge), there are, nevertheless, some findings we think are especially provocative. Although the text and context were sensitive to prior knowledge (i.e., the low-knowledge children were the poorest performing on the interview), it is not the case that prior knowledge was predictive of performance for children who brought even a modicum of prior knowledge to this task; recall that the students with low-medium prior knowledge earned more points on the explicit items than any other prior knowledge group and earned as many points on the inferential items as did the medium-high prior knowledge students. Thus, the context provided the opportunity to study whether and how children made flexible use of the information provided in the text to support their comprehension. Furthermore, as one would expect, the task was sensitive to children's capacity to respond to explicit versus inferential questions. Although a handful of children did better on the inferential items, the majority performed better on the explicit items.

Beyond providing a glimpse of the role that prior knowledge played in children's sense-making with the experimental text, it was possible to generate a number of other hypotheses regarding the reading comprehension skills of children in this context. For example, there were interesting interindividual differences in the lexical and semantic processing of the text; for some children (e.g., DP, KC), the terminology in the text impeded their progress, whereas others (e.g., BW) compensated for their unfamiliarity with the terminology by constructing meaning from larger chunks of text. Given our goal of identifying issues that are germane to conducting comprehension assessments that are domain-sensitive, we think the cases of KC and RJ are particularly instructive. Recall that KC's performance on the interview was not particularly strong; nevertheless, her capacity and inclination to go beyond the text in considering other variables relevant to the study of motion would portend well for her performance in an inquiry-based science class. In contrast, RJ's apparent lack of experience engaging in scientific inquiry disadvantaged him in this context. Finally, we could hypothesize about the role that working memory demands posed by the features particular to this text played in children's comprehension activity. Children who immediately apprehended the biking phenomenon and drew relations between the model and its analogues at a phenomenological level were clearly advantaged in following Lesley's argument when she engaged in her investigation. Furthermore, children who were familiar with the activity of deriving information from tables were advantaged in interpreting and applying that information to the problem at hand. Finally, we thought that there were interesting differences in the ways in which children made vertical versus horizontal inferences across the text; with some students (e.g., BW) actively integrating and revising their representations of the text (working vertically, as well as horizontally), whereas others (e.g., RH) appeared to focus principally on horizontal processing of the text.

We can also consider the implications of this research for the design of text comprehension assessments that reflect domain-specific text and text use. To design domain-specific comprehension assessments, one needs to consider the features, structure, and purposes of text use particular to domains. For example, we argued that the inclusion of multiple features, such as prose, tables, and illustrations, was important to the design of this experimental assessment because these are features commonly found in science text; hence, children's sense-making with these features, and ability to coordinate the information contained in these various features, is likely to be predictive of their learning with science text (both trade books and basals). Turning to the structure of the text, the content of this experimental text was presented in terms of a scientific argument. This structure presented readers with a richer context for interpreting the text than, for example, the presentation of facts (i.e., statements or formulae about the relations between force and motion); within this structure, a broader range of comprehension questions could be asked, some of which were focused on students' ability to both identify and evaluate the scientific reasoning in which Lesley was engaged. To adopt this principle of text construction, developers would need to consider the ways in which various domains conduct and report their scholarship; for example, a domain-specific comprehension task in history might engage students in interpreting and evaluating alternative narratives.

There are several directions future research might take. The hypotheses we generated earlier regarding what this assessment context revealed about the comprehension profiles of our participants could be explored by designing instruction informed by these hypotheses and examining students' responses to the instruction. Recalling that the students who participated in this study were identified by their teachers as "typically achieving" readers, it would be useful to conduct this inquiry with a broader range of readers. It is conceivable that readers must have a certain threshold of comprehension skill before we are able to learn anything particularly useful from this form of assessment.[5] Additionally, given the questions we raised at the beginning of the chapter related to the criterion-related validity of domain-general reading tests, it would be useful to compare students' performance in the experimental context with their performance on a traditional measure of comprehension. In addition, it would, of course, be worthwhile to examine the predictive validity of the experimental task vis-à-vis performance in an inquiry-based instructional context. Among the issues to be examined relative to predictive validity is the role that the specific topic plays in the assessment, as well as whether there are certain dimensions of the experimental task that are more predictive of students' engagement in scientific reasoning across topics.

REFERENCES

Alexander, P. A., & Kulikowich, J. M. (1994). Learning from physics text: A synthesis of recent research. *Journal of Research in Science Teaching, 31,* 895–911.

Allington, R. L., Chodos, L., Domaracki, J., & Truex, S. (1977). Passage dependency: Four diagnostic oral reading tests. *Reading Teacher, 30*(4), 369–375.

Anderson, R. C. (1984). Some reflections on the acquisition of knowledge. *Educational Researcher, 13*(9), 5–10.

Anderson, R. C., & Pearson, P. D. (1984). A schema theoretic view of basic processes in reading comprehension. In P. D. Pearson (Ed.), *Handbook of reading research* (Vol. 1, pp. 255–292). New York: Academic.

Ausubel, D. (1963). *The psychology of meaningful verbal learning: An introduction to school learning.* New York: Grune & Stratton.

Behrman, E. H. (2000). Developmental placement decisions: Content-specific reading assessment. *Journal of Developmental Education, 23,* 12–16.

---

[5]Indeed, there were several students for whom we did not share transcript data because their comprehension was so poor, it was difficult to discern where the breakdown was occurring.

Bransford, J., & Johnson, M. K. (1972). Contextual prerequisites for understanding: Some investigations of comprehension and recall. *Journal of Verbal Learning and Verbal Behavior, 11*, 717–726.

Byrnes, J. P. (1995). Domain specificity and the logic of using general ability as an independent variable or covariate. *Merrill-Palmer Quarterly, 41*, 1–24.

Dee-Lucas, D., & Larkin, J. (1988). Attentional strategies for studying scientific text. *Memory and Cognition, 16*, 469–479.

Dooling, D. J., & Lachman, R. (1971). Effects of comprehension on retention of prose. *Journal of Experimental Psychology, 88*, 216–222.

Driver, R., & Erickson, G. (1983). Theories-in-action: Some theoretical and empirical issues in the study of students' conceptual frameworks in science. *Studies in Science Education, 10*, 37–60.

Goldman, S. R., & Bisanz, G. (2002). Toward a functional analysis of scientific genres. In J. Otero, J. A. Léon, & A. C. Graesser (Eds.), *The psychology of science text comprehension* (pp. 19–50). Mahwah, NJ: Lawrence Erlbaum Associates.

Goldman, S., Varma, K. O., Sharp, D., & the Cognition and Technology Group at Vanderbilt. (1999). Children's understanding of complex stories: Issues of representation and assessment. In S. G. Goldman, A. C. Grasser, & P. van den Broek (Eds.), *Narrative comprehension, causality, and coherence* (pp. 135–160). Mahwah, NJ: Lawrence Erlbaum Associates.

Kintsch, W. (1988). The role of knowledge in discourse comprehension: A construction-integration model. *Psychological Review, 95*, 163–182.

Lorch, R. F., & van den Broek, P. (1997). Understanding reading comprehension: Current and future contributions of cognitive science. *Contemporary Educational Psychology, 22*, 213–246.

Magnusson, S. J., & Palincsar, A. S. (2004). Learning from text designed to model scientific thinking in inquiry-based instruction. In E. W. Saul (Ed.), *Crossing borders in literacy and science education* (pp. 316–339). Newark, DE: International Reading Association.

Mannes, S. M., & Kintsch, W. (1987). Knowledge organization and text organization. *Cognition and Instruction, 4*, 91–115.

Palincsar, A. S., & Magnusson, S. J. (2001). The interplay of first-hand and text-based investigations to model and support the development of scientific knowledge and reasoning. In S. Carver & D. Klahr (Eds.), *Cognition and instruction: Twenty five years of progress* (pp. 151–194). Mahwah, NJ: Lawrence Erlbaum Associates

Rumelhart, D. (1981). Schemata: The building blocks of learning. In J. T. Guthrie (Ed.), *Comprehension and teaching: Research reviews* (pp. 3–26). Newark, DE: International Reading Association.

Spiro, R. J., & Myers, A. (1984). Individual differences and underlying cognitive processes in reading. In P. D. Pearson (Ed.), *Handbook of research in reading* (pp. 245–278). New York: Longman.

Valencia, S., & Pearson, P. D. (1987). Reading assessment: Time for a change. *Reading Teacher, 40*(4), 726–732.

van Dijk, T. A., & Kintsch, W. (1983). *Strategies of discourse comprehension.* New York: Academic.

12

Issues of Validity and Reliability in Early Reading Assessments

Robert D. Carpenter
Eastern Michigan University

Scott G. Paris
University of Michigan

Reading assessments in Grades kindergarten through third (K–3) have become more numerous and important in the past 10 years because research has shown that early diagnosis and remediation of reading difficulties can improve reading achievement (Snow, Burns, & Griffin, 1998). The Report of the National Reading Panel (NRP; 2000) identified five essential skills to assess and teach in primary grades: the alphabetic principle, phonemic awareness, oral reading fluency, vocabulary, and comprehension. The same five skills were endorsed in the "Reading First" part of the No Child Left Behind Act of 2001 (2001) Federal legislation as fundamental in K–3 education. Assessment of these essential skills can inform teachers and parents about children's strengths and weaknesses and thus provide diagnostic information for appropriate instruction. This is a formative use of assessment data. The same five skills can also be assessed to provide summative evidence of individual progress over time and comparative information about relative achievements of groups of students. New K–3 reading assessments often have both purposes, especially because accountability is a cornerstone of the No Child Left Behind Act of 2001 (2001) legislation.

One consequence of the renewed emphases on scientific evidence about early reading achievement is that some states have developed batteries for assessing literacy skills in students in K–3. The assessments are designed to be used in classrooms by teachers yet yield summative assessment data. For example, Virginia created an assessment called the Phonological Awareness Literacy Screening (PALS), Texas designed the Texas Primary Reading Inventory (TPRI), Illinois created the Illinois Snapshots of Early Literacy (ISEL), and Michigan developed the Michigan Literacy Progress Profile (MLPP). These batteries include multiple assessments of the five essential skills emphasized by the NRP (2000), along with additional skills and knowledge. These state-wide assessments share many similarities such as one-on-one assessment, teachers' control and administration of the assessments, repeated testing in primary grades, and immediate usefulness of the assessment information.

The MLPP was designed to serve both formative and summative purposes for multiple stakeholders, and it includes a battery of tasks that are similar to the PALS, TPRI, and ISEL. It can serve as a representative case study of other early reading assessments regarding issues of reliability and validity. The MLPP was created and revised between 1997 and 2002 by the Early Literacy Committee, a group of many teachers, supervisors, and reading experts throughout the state, who reported to the Michigan Department of Education. The MLPP was incorporated into professional development throughout the state to enhance teaching effectiveness and children's early literacy skills. To date, more than 20,000 Michigan teachers have participated in workshops about the MLPP and implications for both classroom assessment and instruction. However, there were no initial validation studies of the MLPP because of the continuous revisions of the MLPP tasks, procedures, and scoring. We were part of a team of researchers at the University of Michigan and Michigan State University who conducted research to test the reliability and validity of the MLPP during its development. This chapter reports evidence on some of the assessment tasks in the MLPP battery that remained unchanged for several years and that reflect the five essential skills identified by the NRP (2000). We discuss the data briefly and then examine some thorny issues about reliability and validity of early reading assessments, with a special emphasis on issues regarding assessment of comprehension.

MEASUREMENT ISSUES

The NRP report (2000) and the subsequent No Child Left Behind Act (2001) legislation place important emphasis on using reliable and valid assessments to document student learning. However, there may be different perceptions of what is meant by reliability and validity for policymakers. For example, Cronbach (1988) identified five different perspectives on validity, the functional, the political, the operational, the economic, and the explanatory, each valuing different aspects of what is considered validity. He compared the research perspective to the policy perspective and stated that the "scientific argument and political argument are different in degree rather than kind, the scientific having a longer time horizon, more homogeneous participants, and more formal reasoning" (pp. 6–7). These differences may lead to different criteria for establishing reliability and validity. For example, the list of Reading First approved assessments is dominated with standardized and publisher-produced tests, with very few state-generated or formative assessments included. The result is a highly constrained notion of reliability and validity that values assessments with strong psychometric properties over authenticity. This approach may work for discrete assessments (e.g., letter identification), but the constraint becomes more restrictive for complex cognitive processes like reading comprehension and the result is a narrowing of the types of assessments that may meet the psychometric criteria of validity.

Measuring reliability and validity has a long history in educational assessment and the procedures have been debated for many years. Traditional assessments are usually validated empirically by using correlational analyses to measure test–retest reliability and the components of criterion validity including concurrent and predictive validity. Most "standardized" assessments are considered valid measures because items are selected to maximize reliability and criterion validity. Group data are analyzed to ensure that subscales are similar but not identical, that questions differentiate students in the population, and that the scores approximate a normal distribution. Psychometricians, policymakers, and administrators usually describe these tests as "good, fair, unbiased, or objective" summative assessments of student ability. Validity is evaluated according to characteristics of the data because the psychometric criteria were used to select the items. More recent views of consequential validity and generalizability expand the traditional views of validity.

In contrast, formative assessments are developed with greater emphases on construct validity and diagnostic usefulness. Unlike summative assessments that are typically administered once or twice each year, formative assessments are given regularly by teachers to guide instructional decisions for individual students. However, formative assessments are considered by some educators to be "subjective or biased" (Madaus, 1994) with "questionable reliability" (Shavelson, Baxter, & Gao, 1993) because they do not have the levels of reliability and validity found on high-stakes standardized tests. Thus, research on the reliability and validity of state-designed early reading assessments is situated precariously between the purposes and criteria of formative and summative assessments. In trying to meet both goals, the tests run the risk of being criticized for doing neither as well as tests that serve only one purpose. However, if an assessment battery could be both formative and summative, it would benefit educators and students. We address four main questions in this examination of the MLPP. First, how reliable are MLPP assessments when administered by different individuals? Second, do scores on MLPP assessments correlate well with similar individually administered early reading assessments? Third, how do scores on MLPP assessments correlate with standardized reading assessments at the same time? Fourth, how well do MLPP assessments predict standardized reading test scores given 1 to 3 years later?

Measuring Reliability

The importance of reliability is to ensure consistent scores across settings, examiners, and administration conditions, the assumption being that a more consistent assessment is a more accurate estimate of ability. Reliability is usually measured with four techniques: (a) test–retest reliability, (b) equivalent form reliability, (c) internal consistency, and (d) interrater reliability. In this study, we measured test–retest reliability by administering the same task to children within a small window of time (2–6 weeks). This method is typically used when only a single form of a test is available or if a researcher is interested in measuring the influence of the test administrator on scores. The assumption behind test–retest reliability is that the skill being measured is stable. If the skill changes over time and is consistent across all individuals (e.g., all children score 5 points higher when they take a test the second time) then "carryover" (e.g., practice effects) can occur which would increase the reliability coefficient (Kaplan & Saccuzzo, 2001). However, if the change over time varies across individuals or if maturation differentially affects scores, then the reliability will be reduced. Often some individuals will recall more information from a test than others or be exposed to a learning situation that is beneficial to the outcome being measured (Aiken, 1997). The strength of test–retest reliability is that the same items and forms are used and the measure of reliability is one of individual consistency rather than item consistency. The weakness is the possibility of carryover effects influencing the results by overestimating or underestimating the reliability coefficient.

Measuring Validity

The validity of an instrument determines whether the assessment is measuring the construct of interest, in the intended manner, and without unintended consequences. Recently the notion of validity has undergone significant revision, with researchers adding the interpretation of results and the consequences of testing as important components of validity (Linn, 1998a, 1998b; Messick, 1995, 2000; Moss 1992, 1998). The shift of validity away from characteristics of the assessment to the impact on test-takers and the validity of inferences is the most notable shift in thinking since the original *Standard for Educational and Psychological Tests and Manuals* (American Psychological Association, 1966, referred to as the *Standards*) was published (Linn, 1993).

Traditionally, validity has been conceptualized in three parts: content, criterion, and construct validity (Messick, 1993). Content validity refers to the coverage of the knowledge domain in an assessment and is typically measured by using parallel forms, by examining errors, and by analyzing content relevance. Criterion validity can be evaluated by comparing test scores to an established criterion measure collected at approximately the same time (concurrent validity) or compared to a criterion that was assessed after the initial testing (predictive validity). Construct validity examines whether an assessment measures an unobservable mental process by using multiple methods of professional judgment, internal consistency, and convergent and discriminant evidence of correspondence with other assessments. These three notions of validity are still prevalent and popular in the literature.

However, researchers have debated the traditional components of validity, questioning their relation to each other and evaluating whether additional factors should be considered. For example, it was only a few years after Cronbach and Meehl introduced the term *construct validity* in the *Standards* in 1954 and in their follow-up article (Cronbach & Meehl, 1955) that Loevinger (1957) questioned whether construct validity was the same as the more accepted views of validity. She argued that content and criterion validity were actually subcomponents of construct validity. Almost 20 years later, Messick (1975) reiterated Loevinger's perspective when he wrote that, "all measurement should be construct referenced" (p. 957).

A second shift in the components of validity occurred in the 1970s as Cronbach and others began reconceptualizing validity as the quality of inferences that could be made rather than whether a test and its items were "valid." Cronbach (1971) is largely credited with this shift as he explained the following: "One validates, not a test, but an interpretation of data arising from a specified procedure" (p. 447). The shift occurred as other aspects of testing, such as consequences, were beginning to be considered as part of validity. Messick (1975) argued that validity should include some evidence of the consequences of the assessment before one could evaluate whether an assessment was valid. However, it was not until the 1980s that the field began to regard validity as a quality of the inferences that could be made rather than solely as a test characteristic.

The 1985 version of the *Standards* makes this shift clear in the explanation of validity, "Validity is the most important consideration in test evaluation. The concept refers to the appropriateness, meaningfulness, and usefulness of the specific inferences made from test scores ..." (American Education Research Association, American Psychological Association, & National Council on Measurement in Education, 1985, p. 9). However, the *Standards* still relied on content, criterion, and construct validity to evaluate whether inferences were valid based on the evidence provided. To establish whether the MLPP is valid, we chose to first determine whether the measure met traditional criteria for validity including content, criterion, and construct validity. Follow-up studies are being conducted to evaluate the validity of the inferences that can be made using the MLLP.

EMPIRICAL STUDIES OF THE MLPP

Participants and Procedures

We selected several different samples of children attending Michigan school districts with very different demographic profiles. The schools were selected because of their representative communities and because the teachers were already implementing the MLPP in their classrooms. The schools served urban, suburban, and rural communities and the total sample was representative of Michigan students. More than 1,000 students participated in the studies over a period of 4 years, and there were approximately equal numbers of boys and girls, approximately equal numbers of students at Grades kindergarten, 1, 2, and 3, and approximately 60% were White, 20% were African American, and the remaining students included Hispanic, Asian American, and multiracial children. Data were collected by a group of graduate and undergraduate research assistants who were trained to administer the assessments to individual children.

Measures

The MLPP includes six enabling tasks and five milestone behavior assessments that measure four of the five essential skills identified by the NRP report (2000). The enabling tasks include letter-sound identification, phonological awareness, concepts of print, hearing-recording sounds, known words, and sight word-decodable word lists. These tasks are considered enabling because the skills enable students to perform well on the reading and writing milestone assessments. They are necessary precursors and foundational skills for reading development, and they reflect two of the five essential skills: the alphabetic principle and phonological awareness. All six enabling tasks were assessed in our research. The MLPP milestone assessments include oral language, writing, oral reading fluency, comprehension, and attitudes and self-perceptions. We assessed the reliability and validity only for the MLPP milestone tasks of oral reading fluency and comprehension because they were two of the five essential skills and because the tasks did not undergo revisions like the other milestone tasks.

The MLPP allows teachers to use a variety of informal reading inventories (IRIs) to provide measures of oral reading accuracy, rate, fluency, and comprehension. The IRIs used by participating schools were the Qualitative Reading Inventory–II (QRI; Leslie & Caldwell, 1995), the Basic Reading Inventory (BRI; Johns, 1997), and the Developmental Reading Assessment (DRA; Beaver, 1997). The QRI and BRI are similar because both contain word lists ranging from preprimer through 12th grade and both include narrative and expository passages ranging from preprimer through the eighth grade. Unlike the QRI, most BRI passages include the same number of words (100) and the same number of questions to assess comprehension (10). The DRA employs little books that range from kindergarten to fifth-grade levels, but the version we used did not include comprehension questions for quantitative analyses. All assessments were individually administered according to the manuals.

Children's oral reading accuracy and fluency were obtained by scoring miscue analyses from tape-recorded sessions as children read leveled passages. Accuracy was measured as the percentage of words read correctly. More fluent readers would be expected to read text with few miscues, few meaning-changing miscues, and with high rates of self-corrected miscues. Prosody, another feature of fluency, was rated as a child read a passage using a 4-point rubric (1 = *all word-by-word reading*, 2 = *mostly word-by-word reading*, 3 = *mixed word-by-word reading and phrased reading*, and 4 = *fluent, phrased reading*). Retelling was measured after the completion of the passage and scored as the percentage of propositions recalled and the number of key ideas recalled. Comprehension was assessed using questions from each manual and the scores were converted to percentages to allow comparison across passages. All children read multiple passages to determine their instructional levels of reading, so the data are reported for both the lowest and highest level passages separately. The lowest level passages were generally read with 95% to 100% oral reading accuracy, and the highest level passages were read with 90% to 95% accuracy. The method allows an assessment of various reading skills (e.g., fluency and comprehension) on texts that are read easily and texts that are more challenging, yet both are within the range of the child's abilities to decode most of the words.

One advantage of using IRIs to assess comprehension is that children's understanding is evaluated with minimal confounds due to decoding differences. The typical procedure for administering IRIs (also used by teachers and researchers in this research) is to identify and assign passages in which children read at least 90% of the words accurately. Thus, children may read different levels of text, but their comprehension is assessed on texts that they can at least decode most of the words. This is in sharp contrast to procedures in standardized tests where children at a given grade level all read the identical texts. Those children who cannot decode easily may display poor comprehension because they cannot read enough words in the passage to make sense of it. This confound in the assessment of comprehension is most severe for beginning readers who are likely to have the greatest variability in decoding proficiency, so it is a serious issue for all early reading assessments. The MLPP was designed to assess children's comprehension skills on passages that they could read independently, so it is predicated on procedures similar to IRIs. The liability of overestimating a child's comprehension skills on an easy passage that could be decoded successfully was considered less important than the problem of underestimating a child's comprehension skills on passages that were too difficult to read many of the words.

However, the use of different leveled passages in IRIs confounds comparisons of performance across passages and time (Paris, 2002). We used two procedures to solve this problem. Both methods created unidimensional scales to compare results across passage levels to evaluate oral reading accuracy, percent propositions recalled, and questions correct both within and between subjects and repeated administrations. In the first method, the data for each dependent variable were rescaled using difficulty values derived from the Degrees of Reading Power (DRP) analyses of each QRI passage. The DRP difficulty was calculated based on the words in the text, sentence length, and syntactic complexity. The DRP values for each passage range from a low of 30 for the preprimer passage to a high of 65 for the junior high passage. We created scaled scores for each dependent variable by multiplying percentages correct by the passage's DRP value. For example, the scaled scores for comprehension were computed according to the following equation: (percentage correct ÷ 100 + 1) × DRP difficulty = Comprehension DRP scaled score. If children answered four of eight questions correctly on the most difficult passage, their scores would be 97.5 ((.50 + 1) × 65)), and if they answered four out of eight on the easiest passage, their score would be 45 ((.50 + 1) × 30)). The constant of 1 was used to avoid zero scores for children who did not answer any comprehension questions correctly. This procedure resulted in scores that ranged from 30 to 130.

The BRI data were scaled using a second method to allow comparisons across passages and levels, but instead of using DRP units, we used Item Response Theory (IRT) and Rasch modeling techniques. IRT procedures are used in most large-scale standardized tests, but when the same passages are given to all students at a given grade, the resulting IRT scores confound decoding and comprehension abilities. IRT scores may provide better measures of comprehension with leveled passages and may be a more accurate way to scale data from IRIs. Individual estimates of students' ability are generated based on data collected on each passage by calculating item difficulty as generated by children's performance rather than a text readability formula like the DRP. However, using IRT to scale the data requires data on every item, and those were unavailable in the data collected using the QRI and DRA.

Concurrent validity of the MLPP was tested using the Texas Primary Reading Inventory (TPRI) and the Gates–MacGinitie Reading Test (GMRT). The TPRI was selected because it is very similar to the MLPP in terms of grade level, types of assessment tasks, and individual administration. We administered the TPRI to a subsample of children who were tested by teachers and researchers. Participants were randomly selected with approximately equal numbers in each grade from kindergarten through second grade (K–2). (The TPRI is designed for K–2 students only so no Grade 3 students participated in the TPRI validity study.) The TPRI was administered in the same 2- to 4-week window after initial teacher administration of the MLPP. The GMRT was selected because it is an established standardized assessment frequently used with young children with documented psychometric properties. The GMRT is a group-administered assessment with format and procedures that are similar to other standardized assessments, such as the Iowa Test of Basic Skills (ITBS) and the Michigan Educational Assessment Program (MEAP) that are used to gauge educational quality across the state.

Predictive validity of the of the MLPP was evaluated using data collected with two group-administered standardized assessments. The first assessment, the GMRT, was also used to study concurrent validity. It provides standardized scaled scores for vocabulary and comprehension beyond first grade. The second assessment was the MEAP test. Fourth-grade reading data were used in our analyses. The MEAP test is part of the group-administered state assessment in Michigan designed to measure the State Board of Education's recommended curriculum. The reading test consists of two reading passages, one narrative or story selection and one informational selection. A set of comprehension questions follows each passage. Scores are reported individually for each passage selection. Scaled scores for both story and information texts were used to test the predictive validity of the MLPP.

SUMMARY OF THE FINDINGS

The MLPP appears to have sufficient content validity, measuring four of the five essential skills. The alphabetic principle is measured by the tasks that require children to identify lower case and upper case letters and to match letters and their corresponding sounds. Phonemic awareness is measured by the rhyming (using both supply and choice tasks), blending (including both onset and rime), and phonemic segmentation tasks. The MLPP measures oral reading fluency through the number of miscues, types of miscues, reading rate (words correct per minute), and prosody (utilizing a 4-point scale). Reading comprehension is measured by retelling and comprehension questions. The MLPP has no vocabulary measure.

Overall, the test–retest reliability of the MLPP appears strong, as shown in Tables 12.1 and 12.2. The reliabilities were stronger for discrete tasks, such as letter identification and sight word identification, than oral reading tasks. The MLPP enabling tasks were very reliable, with overall high correlations for letter identification ($r = .96$, $p < .001$), phonemic awareness ($r = .93$, $p < .001$), hearing and recording sounds ($r = .93$, $p < .001$), and letter sound identification ($r = .86$,

TABLE 12.1
Test-Retest Correlations for the Michigan Literacy Progress Profile Enabling Skills

	Overall	Kindergarten	First Grade
Concepts of print	.56	.54	.43
	$p < .001$	$p < .001$	$p = .024$
	($n = 75$)	($n = 47$)	($n = 28$)
Letter identification	.96	.95	.35
	$p < .001$	$p < .001$	$p = .071$
	($n = 75$)	($n = 47$)	($n = 28$)
Letter sound identification	.86	.78	.66
	$p < .001$	$p < .001$	$p < .001$
	($n = 61$)	($n = 33$)	($n = 28$)
Phonemic awareness	.93		.93
	$p < .001$		$p < .001$
	($n = 44$)		($n = 44$)
Hearing and recording sounds	.93		.93
	$p < .001$		$p < .001$
	($n = 21$)		($n = 21$)
Known words	.73		.73
	$p < .001$		$p < .001$
	($n = 22$)		($n = 22$)

TABLE 12.2
Test-Retest Correlations for the Michigan Literacy Progress Profile Oral Reading and Milestone Assessments

	Overall	First Grade	Second Grade	Third Grade
Sight word identification-lowest	.67 $p < .001$ ($n = 81$)	.94 $p = .001$ ($n = 8$)	.51 $p = .001$ ($n = 38$)	.76 $p < .001$ ($n = 35$)
Sight word identification-highest	.74 $p < .001$ ($n = 101$)	.78 $p = .001$ ($n = 20$)	.53 $p = .001$ ($n = 43$)	.84 $p < .001$ ($n = 38$)
Oral reading rate-lowest	.87 $p < .001$ ($n = 50$)		.95 $p < .001$ ($n = 26$)	.57 $p < .01$ ($n = 24$)
Oral reading rate-highest	.77 $p < .001$ ($n = 50$)		.81 $p < .001$ ($n = 26$)	.62 $p = .001$ ($n = 24$)
Oral reading accuracy-lowest	.36 $p < .05$ ($n = 50$)		.34 $p = .09$ ($n = 26$)	.40 $p = .05$ ($n = 24$)
Oral reading accuracy-highest	.53 $p < .001$ ($n = 105$)	.40 $p = .06$ ($n = 23$)	.50 $p < .001$ ($n = 46$)	.80 $p < .001$ ($n = 36$)
Oral Reading retelling-lowest	.53 $p < .001$ ($n = 50$)		.51 $p < .01$ ($n = 26$)	.56 $p < .01$ ($n = 24$)
Oral reading retelling-highest	.53 $p < .001$ ($n = 50$)		.68 $p < .001$ ($n = 26$)	.39 $p = .06$ ($n = 24$)
Oral reading comprehension-lowest	.73 $p < .001$ ($n = 50$)		.77 $p < .001$ ($n = 26$)	.68 $p < .001$ ($n = 24$)
Oral reading comprehension-highest	.35 $p < .05$ ($n = 49$)		.36 $p = .08$ ($n = 26$)	.30 $p = .17$ ($n = 23$)

$p < .001$). More complex tasks, such as the known words activity, also demonstrated strong correlations between initial and follow-up administration ($r = .73$, $p < .001$). The reliability coefficient for the concepts of print task was lower than the other MLPP tasks ($r = .54$, $p < .001$), but still significant.

The test–retest reliabilities for the oral reading measures on the MLPP were also strong. The highest reliabilities were found on sight word identification ($r = .71$, p $< .001$) and oral reading rate as measured by words correct per minute ($r = .82$, p $< .001$). The test–retest reliability for oral retelling was significant but moderate for both the lowest and highest passages that children read ($r = .53$, p $< .001$). Oral reading accuracy and comprehension also demonstrated significant test–retest correlations for both the lowest and the highest passages. However, the reliability was stronger for accuracy on the highest passage and stronger for comprehension on the lowest passage, perhaps because of increased variances at those levels. Scaling the sight words and oral reading measures by DRP units resulted in very high reliabilities for all measures. Some measures, such as oral reading accuracy and word recognition, may have high reliabilities because they measure automatic word decoding that may be more stable across testing than comprehension and memory for passages that may improve with a second reading. Such carryover or learning effects are expected in retesting children's reading of identical passages so the appropriate target level of reliability is debatable at least and may be set lower than for enabling tasks.

Two features of analyzing reliability emerged that have implications for early reading assessments. First, correlations calculated within grades were generally lower than correlations calculated across grades. The multigrade analysis provided a broader range of scores and more cases. Second, correlations fluctuated by grade level due to grade level differences in learning. For example, Table 12.1 shows a correlation of $r = .35$ for letter identification at first grade but a correlation of $r = .95$ at kindergarten. This is a surprising but provocative finding. We think it is due to the ceiling-level performance of first graders on letter identification coupled with the fact that Pearson correlations do not consider tied scores and are therefore influenced by a few cases (usually outliers) when most scores are tied. In general, high correlations are observed for the reliability of enabling tasks only when floor and ceiling effects are avoided.

Concurrent validity of the MLPP tasks was established in comparisons with the TPRI and the GMRT. All MLPP enabling tasks were significantly correlated with scores on the TPRI (see Table 12.3). Correlations with the GMRT were moderate to strong for most tasks, but the small sample size for some analyses reduced the power and significance of the correlations. The MLPP letter identification task demonstrated the strongest concurrent validity with both the TPRI ($r = .92$, p $< .001$) and the GMRT ($r = .82$, p $< .01$). Letter sound identification on the MLPP was also significantly related to the TPRI ($r = .54$, p $< .01$) and the GMRT ($r = .55$, p $= .05$). The total score for phonemic awareness was significantly related to total phonemic awareness on the TPRI ($r = .77$, p $< .001$) but not with the phonemic awareness subtest on the prereading level of the GMRT. The concepts of print task in the MLPP was moderately, but not

TABLE 12.3

Concurrent Validity of the Michigan Literacy Progress Profile Enabling Tasks and the Texas Primary Reading Inventory (TPRI) and Gates-MacGinitie Reading Test (GMRT)

	Overall	TPRI Kindergarten	First Grade	GMRT Total Correct
Concepts of print				.45 $p = .12$ $(n = 13)$
Letter identification	.92 $p < .001$ $(n = 31)$	.92 $p < .001$ $(n = 31)$		.82 $p < .01$ $(n = 13)$
Letter sound identification	.54 $p < .01$ $(n = 29)$	.54 $p < .01$ $(n = 29)$		.55 $p = .05$ $(n = 13)$
Phonemic awareness	.77 $p < .001$ $(n = 60)$	.55 $p < .001$ $(n = 39)$	.44 $p = .06$ $(n = 19)$	.19 $p = .53$ $(n = 13)$

significantly, correlated with the literacy concepts section of the GMRT. Concepts of print was not assessed on the TPRI.

The MLPP oral reading assessments were also related significantly to both the TPRI and the GMRT (see Table 12.4). The concurrent validity correlations were strongest for the scaled sight word task with both the TPRI ($r = .79$, $p < .001$) and the GMRT ($r = .91$, $p < .001$). Reading rate and oral reading accuracy on the MLPP were only compared to the TPRI. Both correlations were significant with stronger correlations on reading rate ($r = .86, p < .001$) than oral reading accuracy ($r = .55, p < .01$). The percentage of propositions recalled on the MLPP was also significantly related to GMRT comprehension ($r = .70, p < .001$). Propositions were not compared to the TPRI because it does not include a retelling component. Comprehension questions answered correctly were significantly correlated with the GMRT ($r = .80, p < .001$) but were not significantly related to the TPRI ($r = .39, p = .06$). The lower correlation with the TPRI is probably due to ceiling effects because 85% of children answered four or more of the five TPRI questions correctly on their grade-level TPRI passages.

The concurrent validity analysis revealed features very similar to those found in the reliability analysis. Concurrent correlations were stronger for

TABLE 12.4

Correlations Between Michigan Literacy Progress Profile (MLPP) Oral Reading and the Texas Primary Reading Inventory (TPRI) and Gates-MacGinitie Reading Test (GMRT)

MLPP Measure	TPRI	GMRT
Sight word identification	.79 $p < .001$ ($n = 26$)	.91 $p < .001$ ($n = 35$)
Reading rate	.86 $p < .001$ ($n = 24$)	
Propositions recalled		.70 $p < .001$ (n = 52)
Oral reading accuracy	.55 $p < .01$ ($n = 24$)	
Oral reading comprehension	.39 $p = .06$ ($n = 24$)	.80 $p < .001$ ($n = 52$)

multi-age samples than single grade samples. Restricted ranges, due to floor and ceiling effects on the MLPP or the TPRI, strongly influenced the significance of the correlations. For example, the correlation between comprehension questions on the MLPP and the TPRI were low for each grade, but most children were at ceiling on the TPRI, with over 85% correctly answering four or five out of five comprehension questions. Distributions in both the measure under review and the external criterion used to establish validity can strongly influence the results of the analysis. In addition, discrete tasks, such as letter identification, demonstrated stronger concurrent validity than more complex tasks. It is important to look beyond the initial response that this must indicate that the enabling tasks are more valid than the measures of complex tasks such as comprehension because there is more task variability on items measuring more complex cognitive processes. For example, letter identification is measured using the same 26 letters on all assessments. Variability is only introduced by the procedures (e.g., identifying all or a subset of the letters). In contrast, comprehension is measured using different passages that vary in decoding difficulty, length, and topic, with a different number and type of question asked on each assessment. The variability in the task introduces many sources of variation into the correlation and reduces the strength of association. Perhaps assessments of more complex cognitive tasks should be examined using a different standard of validity than more discrete tasks.

The predictive validity of the MLPP was moderate to strong with an overall correlation of $r = .45$ across all tasks and all longitudinal analyses in different samples. The data revealed significant correlations for 74.1% of all analyses. Correlations declined across time with a higher overall correlation for the 6-month prediction ($r = .64$) than the 1- ($r = .46$), 2- ($r = .38$), or 3- ($r = .33$) year analyses. The decline was evident for both enabling skills and oral reading data predicting the GMRT or the MEAP. The MLPP was a stronger predictor of scores on the GMRT ($r = .50$) than performance on the MEAP ($r = .35$). The finding is likely due to the use of the GMRT for shorter-term predictions.

The predictive correlations for MLPP tasks and the GMRT are shown in Table 12.5. They are consistently significant and strong for the oral reading measures. Predictive correlations were more similar across sections of the MLPP for predicting GMRT scores (oral reading $r = .45$ and enabling $r = .43$) than the MEAP (oral reading $r = .36$ and enabling $r = .23$). One contributing factor to the lower predictive power for the enabling tasks with the MEAP could be the 3 years between initial assessment and MEAP testing. Another factor could be the greater similarity between MLPP tasks and GMRT tasks than between MLPP and MEAP tasks. The differences are partly due to the developmental appropriateness of MLPP for children in Grades K–2 whereas the MEAP reading tasks are appropriate for older children who can read independently. The GMRT is designed to be appropriate for both beginning and proficient readers, with the lower level tests orally administered to prereaders or beginning readers.

A longitudinal sample of children who attended summer school throughout Michigan was included to test the predictive validity of the oral reading assessments using IRT-scaled data instead of DRP-scaled data. These children received the BRI and item-level information was coded so that IRT scales could be calculated for each dependent variable. The MLPP tasks analyzed in this section were scaled sight word list, oral reading accuracy, propositions recalled, and comprehension. The correlations with MEAP scores are shown in Table 12.6. It should be noted that different samples of children were used for each analysis because data were only collected at two time points. As a result, the 1-year predictive analysis utilized the third-grade summer school data whereas the 2- (i.e., second grade) and 3- (i.e., first grade) year predictions were calculated with younger children. The sight word vocabulary scores significantly predicted MEAP story and information scores 1 ($r = .21, p < .05$), 2 ($r = .43, p < .001$) and 3 years ($r = .41, p < .001$) after initial assessment. MLPP accuracy scaled

TABLE 12.5

Predictive Validity of the Michigan Literacy Progress Profile (MLPP) Tasks With Gates-MacGinitie Reading Test (GMRT) Scores

MLPP Task	MLPP Sample		District C Sample		
	6-Month Prediction	1-Year Prediction	1-Year Prediction	2-Year Prediction	3-Year Prediction
Concepts of print	.43 $p < .001$	.34 $p < .01$	.15 $p = .45$	.41 $p < .05$	.51 $p < .01$
Letter identification	.46 $p < .001$	.40 $p < .01$			
Letter sound identification	.73 $p < .001$	.68 $p < .001$			
Total phonemic awareness	.60 $p < .001$	.64 $p < .001$	.01 $p = .96$	.41 $p < .05$	.32 $p = .06$
Hearing and recording sounds	.68 $p < .001$	.73 $p < .001$	.42 $p < .05$	.27 $p = .14$	.35 $p < .05$
Sight word list scaled	.89 $p < .001$	.84 $p < .001$	.60 $p < .001$	.57 $p < .001$	.68 $p < .001$
Accuracy lowest passage scaled-Degrees of Reading Power (DRP)	.67 $p < .001$	.74 $p < .001$	.50 $p < .05$	.57 $p < .001$	.58 $p < .01$
Accuracy highest passage scaled-DRP	.66 $p < .001$	.74 $p < .001$	.72 $p < .001$	.58 $p < .001$	.59 $p < .01$
Propositions recalled lowest passage scaled-DRP	.63 $p < .001$	.57 $p < .001$	.10 $p = .69$	.33 $p < .01$	.35 $p = .11$
Propositions recalled highest passage scaled-DRP	.67 $p < .001$	.65 $p < .001$	.41 $p < .001$	.22 $p = .06$	.24 $p = .28$
Comprehension lowest passage scaled-DRP	.56 $p < .01$	.53 $p < .001$	.05 $p = .86$	.48 $p < .001$	.22 $p = .33$
Comprehension highest passage scaled-DRP	.61 $p < .001$	.68 $p < .001$	.60 $p < .001$	.33 $p < .01$	.12 $p = .58$

Note. The MLPP sample included rural and urban schools. District C was a suburban district.

TABLE 12.6

**Predicting Michigan Educational Assessment Program
(MEAP) Scores With Item Response Theory Scaled Scores
on the Basic Reading Inventory (BRI)**

BRI Task	1 Year	2 Year	3 Year
Sight word list scaled			
MEAP story	.21	.43	.41
	$p < .05$	$p < .001$	$p < .001$
	$(n = 129)$	$(n = 181)$	$(n = 121)$
MEAP information	.27	.44	.39
	$p < .01$	$p < .001$	$p < .001$
	$(n = 129)$	$(n = 181)$	$(n = 121)$
Oral reading accuracy			
MEAP story	.13	.08	.30
	$p = .15$	$p = .29$	$p = .001$
	$(n = 128)$	$(n = 181)$	$(n = 119)$
MEAP information	.17	.17	.20
	$p = .05$	$p < .05$	$p < .05$
	$(n = 128)$	$(n = 181)$	$(n = 119)$
Propositions recalled			
MEAP story	.26	.05	.02
	$p < .01$	$p = .53$	$p = .81$
	$(n = 127)$	$(n = 176)$	$(n = 114)$
MEAP information	.24	.04	−.09
	$p < .01$	$p = .57$	$p = .36$
	$(n = 127)$	$(n = 176)$	$(n = 114)$
Comprehension			
MEAP story	.37	.14	.21
	$p < .001$	$p = .07$	$p < .05$
	$(n = 129)$	$(n = 180)$	$(n = 119)$
MEAP information	.34	.11	.15
	$p < .001$	$p = .13$	$p = .12$
	$(n = 129)$	$(n = 180)$	$(n = 119)$

using IRT significantly predicted scores on the MEAP information passage across all time points (1 year $r = .17, p < .05$; 2 year $r = .17, p < .05$; and 3 year $r = .20, p < .05$), but only predicted MEAP story scores 3 years after initial assessment ($r = .30, p = .001$). The IRT scaled propositions recalled only predicted scores one year after original testing ($r = .20, p < .05$). Oral reading comprehension significantly predicted scores on the MEAP story passage 1 year ($r = .37, p < .001$) and 3 years ($r = .21, p < .05$) after initial assessment. Comprehension also predicted scores on the MEAP information passage 1 year later ($r = .34, p < .001$).

Sight word identification was scaled for comparisons by giving children full credit (20 points) for each word list that was below the highest word list attempted. The average word list score was higher for children in the 1-year predictive sample ($M = 110.9$) than the 2-year ($M = 82.0$) or 3-year ($M = 58.9$) predictive samples. The decline was expected because the age of the children declined with each sample, as third-grade data were used for the 1-year prediction, second-grade data for the 2-year prediction, and first-grade data for the 3-year prediction. The MLPP sight word list was a significant predictor of both the MEAP story passage and information passage scores 1, 2, and 3 years after initial assessment. The predictions of scores on the MEAP story section were low, but significant for 1-year ($r = .21, p < .05$) and stronger for 2- ($r = .43$, $p < .001$) and 3-year analyses ($r = .41, p < .001$). The correlational pattern between the MLPP sight word list and the MEAP information section was similar, with lower significant correlations for the 1-year prediction ($r = .27, p < .01$) and stronger correlations for the 2- ($r = .44, p < .001$) and 3-year ($r = .39$, $p < .001$) samples.

ISSUES IN EVALUATING THE RELIABILITY AND VALIDITY OF EARLY READING ASSESSMENTS

The exploration of the reliability and validity of the MLPP raises important issues that should be considered when establishing the validity and reliability of early reading assessments. How these issues are resolved will influence the validation process and ultimately the types of assessments used with young readers. The following five issues were discovered in this research and should be considered when determining the reliability and validity of early reading assessments.

Issue 1—Discrete Skills Can Be Measured More Easily and Consistently Than Complex Reading Skills, and This Can Make Reliability Higher for Simple Tasks

The complexity and difficulty of items vary across different skills assessments and influence reliability and validity correlations between assessments. Some reading tasks, such as letter identification and concepts of print, contain a discrete set of items that can be assessed as either known or unknown. Discrete skills are measured more consistently across administration because knowledge of the correct answer is highly specific and independent of other information. Answers will be consistent across closely timed administration if no instruction or assistance is given to learn the particular piece of information (e.g., the letter "B"). The result is strong test–retest correlations and a reliable task.

More complex cognitive skills, such as comprehension, will vary more across administrations because they require multiple complex processes. To comprehend a passage, one needs to be able to decode words, relate the words to prior knowledge, and to generate situation and text models with explicit and implicit meaning. Prior experience, whether in general or with a specific text, is an important part of understanding a passage. Repeated exposure to the same information or text will influence a reader's level of understanding by easing the burden of decoding and by providing information about the content of the text from earlier readings. The effects of repeated reading will vary by individuals because some will recognize more words automatically or remember more information than their peers. These individual differences produce a wide range of changes in comprehension among children from initial to subsequent testing that leads to lower reliabilities of complex reading skills.

To illustrate the point for reliability calculations, consider the patterns of means on the letter identification task and passage comprehension. Average scores on letter identification changed little from initial assessment ($M = 50.3$) to retest ($M = 49.4$). The total number of letters children knew at each testing was consistent across administration and resulted in strong reliability correlations ($r = .96, p < .001$). In contrast, the means for percentage of comprehension questions correct on the highest MLPP passage varied from teacher ($M = 50.6$) to researcher ($M = 65.9$) administration. The increase was over half a standard deviation. The increase suggests that children learned text information from the initial assessment and the result was greater comprehension on the second reading. However, the growth was not consistent across children and resulted in lower test–retest reliability for comprehension. It is the combination of task complexity and difficulty of the material that may contribute to differential learning from first to second testing, leading to lower reliability coefficients for comprehension compared to discrete skill assessments.

Issue 2—Some Reading Skills Develop Rapidly in K–2 So Floor and Ceiling Effects May Be Evident at Some Grades, and the Skewed Distributions Can Attenuate Correlations

Traditional approaches to validity and reliability assume normally distributed data and linear growth of skills. However, some enabling skills such as letter identification and concepts of print may approach asymptote by Grade 2. In fact, many enabling skills may exhibit nonlinear growth in K–3 and the skewed distributions can affect the reliability and validity correlations. The distributions of data for the MLPP enabling tasks varied widely across tasks and ages. For example, there was very strong test–retest reliability for the letter identification task with kindergarten children ($r = .95$, $p < .001$) and a low, nonsignificant reliability coefficient for first-grade children ($r = .35$, $p = .07$). The data show high means for both groups (kindergarten, $M = 48.2$ out of 54, and first grade, $M = 53.7$), but a very low standard deviation for first-grade children ($SD = 0.8$) when compared to their kindergarten schoolmates ($SD = 8.7$). This indicates a highly skewed distribution for first-grade children with all children correctly identifying 52 or more out of the 54 letters. Preschool children know few letters and by the end of first grade they know most or all of the letters. The reliability of the measure is only strong when the scores exhibit a large range and variance with a more normal distribution, typically before the end of first grade.

Another example of skewed distributions is evident with the concurrent validity between MLPP blending and the TPRI blending tasks. Kindergarten children were given the task at the beginning of the school year and expectedly scored at the bottom of the distribution, with 87.5% scoring a zero on the MLPP, resulting in a mean of 0.5 out of 8 ($SD = 1.4$). In contrast, first-grade children were assessed on the same task at the end of their second year in school and were at ceiling on both the MLPP ($M = 7.5$, $sd = .08$) and the TPRI ($M = 4.8$ out of 5, $SD = 0.4$). The resulting concurrent validity correlation was significant for kindergarten children ($r = .50$, $p < .05$) but not for first graders ($r = .36$, $p = .06$). The rapid development of knowledge on blending phonemes from the beginning of kindergarten to the end of first grade influenced the distribution of scores. Thus, the degree of skill mastery when children are assessed is an important factor that influences the reliability and validity of early reading assessments (Paris, in press).

Issue 3—Scaling Procedures Are Required to Analyze Reading Scores Derived From Leveled Texts

The issue of scaling is most evident when comparing scores on reading across the MLPP, TPRI, and the GMRT. The MLPP includes raw data that can be converted to percentages or scaled using DRP units. The TPRI also includes raw data that can be converted into percentages, but the number of comprehension questions is limited to five questions and no DRP units were available for TPRI passages. The result was low concurrent validity between the MLPP and TPRI because children answered most or all of the TPRI questions correctly. The MLPP, with its graded word lists and passages, required some type of scaling to compare the results to the standardized scaled scores of the GMRT. Using DRP units to create a unidimensional scale was one method to account for text difficulty among the MLPP passages. The result was strong concurrent validity between the MLPP and the GMRT. If raw percentages were used for the MLPP, then the dimension of passage level difficulty would not have been considered. In this case, the concurrent validity would have been less meaningful because children who answered 85% of the questions on a first-grade passage would be considered as proficient as children who answered 85% of comprehension questions on a fifth-grade passage. Using DRP scaling procedures helped to disentangle the differences in passage difficulty from differences in individual performance (Paris, 2002).

We discovered that the DRP scaling procedure produced stronger correlations among tasks across grade levels because variance by grade is inherent in the scale. Greater variability among the scores between grades inflates the strength of the relations between two correlated tasks. Thus, Table 12.5 shows higher predictive correlations for DRP-scaled scores than was evident with IRT scaling procedures. Table 12.6 shows lower, but still significant, predictive correlations using IRT scores derived from the BRI. We think the IRT procedure is better than the DRP scaling procedure because it is based on estimates of individual ability and item difficulty rather than readability scores. IRT also allows separate IRT scales for any dependent variable, so it is more precise.

Issue 4—Children Vary in the Cognitive Resources and Automatic Skills They Utilize When Reading a Passage So Developmental Proficiency May Affect Some Tasks More Than Others

Children's cognitive capacity may influence the reliability of assessments of complex activities such as comprehending more than discrete skills such as letter identification. Task difficulty also influences the impact of cognitive resources on reliability and validity. The prior example of reading comprehension is an important illustration of the impact of cognitive attention on evaluations of reliability. The test–retest reliability for the lowest MLPP passage ($r = .73, p < .001$) was stronger than the reliability for the highest passage ($r = .35, p < .05$). The average percentage of questions answered correctly did not differ greatly on the lowest passage (from $M = 72.6$ to $M = 72.1$), but differed by almost two thirds of a standard deviation on the highest passage (from $M = 50.6$ to $M = 65.9$). It may be that the higher-level passages required more cognitive attention to decoding during the first reading and less on subsequent readings, freeing cognitive resources for comprehending the text. In addition, the more difficult passages provided more room for growth because scores were not constrained by ceiling effects. Maybe the second reading helped some children improve their understanding of the passage. The differences in the amount of improvement may vary by individual cognitive characteristics such as attention and memory.

Issue 5—Differences in Assessment Content and Procedures Can Influence Reliability and Validity Correlations

Differences in procedures occurred across task administration and examiner. For example, both the MLPP and TPRI use children's performance on the word lists to determine the appropriate passage to use with a particular child. However, the MLPP includes nine word lists ranging from a preprimer to junior high level with 20 words per list (a total of 180 words), and the TPRI includes a single list of 20 words of varying difficulty. The MLPP passage administered to an individual child may range from beginning reading (preprimer) to advanced reading (junior high) based on his or her word list score, whereas the TPRI passages are constrained to three slightly below, at, or slightly above, grade level. The result is that children on the MLPP were reading passages at an instructional level and many of the children read TPRI passages at an independent level as demonstrated by high levels of accuracy (95.6%) and comprehension (85%). The high number of children who answered all questions correctly on the most difficult passage (54.2%) indicates that many of these children were at ceiling on the TPRI task. The result was a highly skewed distribution and lower concurrent correlations between the MLPP and the TPRI. The GMRT included multiple passages that increased in difficulty to determine a child's reading score. The result was a wider range of scores that more closely corresponded with DRP-scaled performance on the MLPP.

The context of the testing situation may also contribute to differences in reliability and validity of an assessment. For example, children read MLPP passages at a much faster rate, but with many more miscues, the second time they read with researchers than they did with classroom teachers. Accuracy in School A declined almost two thirds of a standard deviation on the highest passage (from 97.1% to 95.1%), yet comprehension scores improved over half a standard deviation for these same children (from 50.6% to 65.9%). It may be that children attended less to the pronunciation of the words when reading for a stranger, thereby freeing more attention to comprehend the passage. Children's perceptions of the testing situation, their familiarity with the examiner, and their motivation, may all influence test–retest reliability data. The differences in context are difficult to ascertain from this study because teachers always administered the tasks before researchers.

IMPLICATIONS FOR ASSESSMENTS
OF K–3 COMPREHENSION

Assessing enabling skills is relatively straightforward with young children because the same skills and knowledge can be assessed repeatedly until mastery is achieved. That applies to letter identification, phonics, the alphabetic principle, concepts of print, and most aspects of phonemic awareness. Perhaps that is why these skills are the predominant measures in K–3 reading assessments. Comprehension is different; it continues to develop into adulthood and it depends greatly on the specific texts and questions used in the assessment, because difficulty and familiarity can vary widely. Comprehension poses additional problems that are unresolved. For example, are assessments of listening or viewing comprehension appropriate for children who cannot decode many words? How similar are they to the cognitive processes involved in reading comprehension? Does reading comprehension always depend on decoding proficiency or can it be assessed independently? How many passages can young children read before fatigue becomes a factor? Do the types of questions asked influence the comprehension assessment? Is retelling a comprehension assessment? These questions become more troublesome for beginning readers who are learning to decode words at the same time they are learning how to comprehend what they read, hear, and view.

Traditional comprehension tests for older children skirt these questions. Traditional standardized tests present children at the same grade with the same variety of passages and ask the same questions of everyone. Often, students read many brief passages that are fragmented bits of information about a variety of topics. The tests are usually administered in groups and students usually respond to multiple-choice questions by filling in bubbles on answer sheets. Children in Grades 1 to 3 often have difficulty with group-administered tests because they may lose their place on the answer sheets, may be confused by the multiple-choice options, may not know how to spell the answer they want to supply, may try to complete the test quickly, or may become anxious about their performance. Despite the standardized procedures, uniform content, and quantitative data available from group-administered reading tests, teachers and parents need to be sensitive to the problems that may weaken the validity of the test scores.

The MLPP allows teachers to use various IRIs, both the content and procedures, to gather information about children's comprehension with methods more appropriate for K–3 students. The assessments are administered individually, multiple passages or little books are used, and the texts are "genuine" in the sense of being familiar and similar to usual classroom reading materials. Furthermore, the passages vary for children depending on their relative decoding abilities. This is a fundamental and crucial assumption about assessing comprehension in beginning readers. The MLPP confirms the IRI procedures that attenuate the influences of decoding differences by assigning leveled texts to children according to their decoding abilities. Although this levels the field for decoding proficiency, it complicates the interpretation of comprehension results. Despite a long history of use, IRIs never confronted the problem of comparing performance over passages and time in quantitative ways. There has been no satisfactory answer provided to the following question: "How can 80% comprehension of easy text at Time 1 be compared to 50% comprehension of more difficult text at Time 2?" In our research, we created two procedures for scaling data: one by the DRP formula for text difficulty and one based on empirical estimates of item difficulty and personal ability (i.e., a two-factor Rasch model). The IRT procedures that we used to scale the item difficulty as well as the proficiency level of the test taker appear to be useful.

Our research also revealed that test–retest reliability of comprehension should be expected to be lower than skills that do not change with one additional exposure to the stimuli. Reading a passage twice can change the rate, accuracy, prosody, and comprehension markedly for some children so reliability may be lower. Likewise, concurrent and predictive validity will be influenced by the similarity of test items and formats. Genre and prior knowledge are additional variables that may influence comprehension assessments, and they need to be studied more.

The difficulty of assessing comprehension among beginning readers may be why so few states have designed early comprehension assessments. PALS does not include a comprehension component. ISEL has only two questions. TPRI has five questions for each of nine passages. All of these batteries devalue comprehension in assessment and instruction by failing to include rich and diverse measures of children's understanding of text. The MLPP is the only state-designed test that makes comprehension a priority in K–3 assessment and provides teachers with sophisticated tools to assess how children construct meaning from texts. More work is clearly needed to create additional assessments that go beyond commercial IRIs and assess the rich variety of comprehension skills and strategies that teachers present to students in their classrooms.

CONCLUSIONS

Our research on the MLPP has shown that the battery of tasks has reasonable test–retest reliability and strong evidence of concurrent and predictive validity.

These are the traditional measures of reliability and validity and the MLPP meets these criteria for the enabling tasks and oral reading measures that we examined. Because these reading tasks are closely aligned with four of the five essential skills (vocabulary was not included originally in the MLPP) in the No Child Left Behind Act of 2001 (2001) legislation, the MLPP appears to be a qualified assessment for use in K–3 classrooms for both formative and summative purposes. Teachers in Michigan have become knowledgeable about the MLPP, and more importantly, about the essential skills in early reading development so that they can instruct them better. Early reading assessment in Michigan is coupled with professional development and that link is essential for instruction to improve.

It is important to look beyond correlations when examining issues of reliability and validity of early reading measurements. Low reliability may result from a highly skewed distribution rather than a poor assessment. In addition, reliabilities for more discrete tasks could be stronger simply because of the discrete skills being assessed rather than the method of measurement. As reading tasks become more complex and assessments focus on comprehension rather than enabling skills, greater variability among children is expected, greater learning from repeated testing occurs, and estimates of reliability and validity may decrease in power. At the same time, construct validity, developmental appropriateness of assessments, and the consequences of assessment, become more important. Thus, traditional notions of psychometric reliability and validity are only rudimentary criteria to evaluate the usefulness of early reading assessments. The hard work lies ahead as researchers try to create better assessments of early reading development at the same time they create better ways to evaluate validity and reliability of assessments for young children.

REFERENCES

Aiken, L. R. (1997). *Psychological testing and assessment* (9th ed.). Needham Heights, MA: Allyn & Bacon.
American Educational Research Association, American Psychological Association, & National Council on Measurement in Education. (1985). *Standards for educational and psychological testing* (Rev. ed.). Washington, DC: American Educational Research Association.
American Psychological Association. (1966). *Standards for educational and psychological tests and manuals*. Washington, DC: American Psychological Association.
Beaver, J. (1997). *Developmental reading assessment*. Glenview, IL: Celebration Press.
Cronbach, L. J. (1971). Test validation. In R. L. Thorndike (Ed.), *Educational measurement* (2nd ed., pp. 443–507). Washington, DC: American Council on Education.
Cronbach, L. J. (1988). Five perspectives on the validity argument. In H. Wainer & H. I. Braun (Eds.), *Test validity* (pp. 3–18). Hillsdale, NJ: Lawrence Erlbaum Associates.

Cronbach, L. J., & Meehl, P. E. (1955). Construct validity in psychological tests. *Psychological Bulletin, 52,* 281–302.

Johns, J. L. (1997). *Basic reading inventory* (7th ed.). Dubuque, IA: Kendall/Hunt.

Kaplan, R. M., & Saccuzzo, D. P. (2001). *Psychological testing: Principles, applications, and issues* (5th ed.). Belmont, CA: Wadsworth.

Leslie, L., & Caldwell, J. (1995). *Qualitative reading inventory–2.* New York: Addison Wesley Longman, Inc.

Linn, R. L. (1993). Current perspectives and future directions. In R. L. Linn (Ed.), *Educational measurement* (3rd ed., pp. 1–10). Phoenix, AZ: Oryx Press.

Linn, R. L. (1998a). Partitioning responsibility for the evaluation of the consequences of assessment programs. *Educational Measurement: Issues and Practice, 17*(2), 28–30.

Linn, R. L. (1998b). Validating inferences from National Assessment of Educational Progress achievement-level reporting. *Applied Measurement in Education, 11,* 23–47.

Loevinger, J. (1957). Objective tests as instruments of psychological theory. *Psychological Reports, 3,* 955–966.

Madaus, G. F. (1994). A technological and historical consideration of equity issues associated with proposals to change the nation's testing policy. *Harvard Educational Review, 64,* 76–91.

Messick, S. (1975). The standard problem: Meaning and values in measurement and evaluation. *American Psychologist, 30,* 955–966.

Messick, S. (1993). Validity. In R. L. Linn (Ed.), *Educational measurement* (3rd ed., pp. 13–103). Phoenix, AZ: Oryx Press.

Messick, S. (1995). Validity of psychological assessment: Validation of inferences from persons' responses and performances as scientific inquiry into score meaning. *American Psychologist, 50,* 741–749.

Messick, S. (2000). Consequences of test interpretation and use: The fusion of validity and values in psychological assessment. In R. D. Goffin (Ed.), *Problems and solutions in human assessment: Honoring Douglas N. Jackson at seventy* (pp. 3–20). Norwell, MA: Kluwer Academic.

Moss, P. A. (1992). Shifting conceptions of validity in educational measurement: Implications for performance assessment. *Review of Educational Research, 62,* 229–258.

Moss, P. A. (1998). The role of consequences in validity theory. *Educational Measurement: Issues and Practice, 17*(2), 6–12.

National Reading Panel. (2000). *Teaching children to read: An evidence-based assessment of the scientific research literature on reading and its implications for reading instruction.* Washington, DC: National Institute on Child and Human Development.

No Child Left Behind Act of 2001, Pub. L. No. 107–110, paragraph 115, Stat. 1425. (2001).

Paris, S. G. (2002). Measuring children's reading development using leveled texts. *Reading Teacher, 56*(2), 168–170.

Paris, S. G. (in press). Re-interpreting the development of reading skills. *Reading Research Quarterly.*

Shavelson, R. J., Baxter, G. P., & Gao, X. (1993). Sampling variability of performance assessments: Performance assessment [Special issue]. *Journal of Educational Measurement, 30*(3).

Snow, C. E., Burns, M. S., & Griffin, P. (1998). *Preventing reading difficulties in young children.* Washington, DC: National Academy Press.

13

Commentary on Three Important Directions in Comprehension Assessment Research

Michael Pressley
Katherine R. Hilden
Michigan State University

The three chapters we read for this volume provided enormous food for thought about comprehension, its development through instruction, and its assessment, as well as teaching and assessment of reading more generally. We also found the chapters inspiring of good questions, which we emphasize in this commentary. These three authoring teams offered admirably scholarly position papers, ones that characterize well the cutting edge of thinking about literacy. This is real ongoing science, rather than science as being redefined in documents such as the National Reading Panel (2000) report, which is merely a selective history and interpretation of past scientific work. These authors are doing what characterizes good science—carefully researching problems that have not been well studied as the start of a journey to a brighter future for literacy instruction in American schools. We offer here some suggestions to these journeyers, hoping we can make their trip more interesting for them and significant for future generations of American students.

CARPENTER AND PARIS

As residents of Michigan, we feel better about the state's standardized Michigan Literacy Progress Profile assessment (the MLPP is given to students in kindergarten through second grade) after reading Carpenter and Paris's (this volume)

305

intelligent analysis of its reliability and validity. We are certain that most readers of the chapter noticed that this analysis was anything but straightforward, anything but formulaic. At every turn, the authors had to consider many factors that could impact their conclusions. We are particularly impressed by their sensitivity to the distortions that floor and ceiling effects can cause with respect to assessment of reliability, and thus, validation of assessments. The hope in constructing a test of phonemic awareness or beginning word recognition is that students will eventually hit the ceiling. When that happens, it is virtually certain that reliability will be low because of a scaling artifact: That is, when there is zero variability (which is the case when everyone attains a perfect score or everyone gets a zero), reliability is necessarily low. Although it might seem such a simple point, this is a simple point that many attempting to validate tests often ignore. There needs to be painstaking attention to the distributional characteristics of an assessment's data if a competent psychometric evaluation is to be conducted. All too often, we know that the test data get thrown into a computer and the correlations come out, accepted at face value. If the correlation is near zero, it must mean the test is unreliable. Not necessarily; it may be that none of the children can do any of the items on the test or all of the children can do all of the items.

As we reflect on Carpenter and Paris's (this volume) work, we also reflect on the fact that there are new tests of reading popping up everywhere. The pressures to test flowing out of the No Child Left Behind legislation (107th Congress, 2002) are causing many states to develop assessments. Unfortunately, we doubt whether the country has the manpower to do the type of careful work that Carpenter and Paris have reported in this volume. We fear that many of these assessments are being developed and then implemented that are far from completely evaluated. In fact, that was true of the MLPP, for this analysis from Carpenter and Paris comes only after the test has been operational in Michigan for a few years.

Consider an extreme case of dissemination of a measure in the absence of extensive validation. The Dynamic Indicators of Basic Early Literacy Skills (i.e., DIBELS; Good & Kaminski, 2002) is a set of early reading measures tapping the development of fluency. Although the University of Oregon group that developed DIBELS has generated a great deal of reliability data, there is very limited validation data, limited to predictive validity (i.e., performance on the DIBELS predicts performance on other reading tests, although the correlations are often statistically significant but modest; see their Web site: http://dibels.uoregon.edu). Yes, the performance of DIBELS increases when students experience a curriculum aimed at increasing word level fluency compared to when they experience curricula that are not so focused (e.g., Kamps et al., 2003). There is also some evidence that DIBELS correlates concurrently with other standardized measures of reading as well as teachers' ratings of reading achievement (Elliott, Lee, & Tollefson, 2001). Yet, according to the DIBELS Web site, this assessment system will be used this year in over 4,000 American schools to assess more than 850,000 children. Because this volume addresses comprehension assessment, we point out that DIBELS now includes an Oral Reading Fluency and Retell Fluency scale for third graders that the authors advertised as providing comprehension data. We cannot find any validation of the DIBELS with respect to comprehension in the literature. That the test requires 1 min of oral reading aloud followed by simple recall of the words read (yes, the number of words recalled is the comprehension measure) raises substantial doubts about whether this evaluation could possibly be tapping comprehension validly. Yet, it is out there being administered to children across the land as part of making decisions about whether they need additional comprehension instruction.

We do not think that measures should be used to make decisions about instruction in general or about specific children before the measures are well understood and evaluated. We also think that to understand such measures well will require the type of reflective and intelligent psychometric work carried out by Carpenter and Paris (this volume) and by other sophisticated and thorough scientists. Unfortunately, this is unlikely to be the norm given the fiscal and temporal resources as well as the specialized expertise that such work demands. Thus, we think that a metamessage of Carpenter and Paris's chapter is that it is unwise to continue down the assessment path on which the nation is currently following. It makes no sense to proliferate beginning reading tests. Rather, we think that it makes sense to make high investment in a few assessments, with this the only hope of getting assessments that are valid. This includes studying the assessments' consequential validity. It is imperative that assessments inform practitioner and policymaker decisions in ways that it was designed to inform. It is time to demand that children only be assessed with measures that are well understood.

One other point made very well by Carpenter and Paris (this volume) is that comprehension is much more difficult to assess than lower-order reading skills, from letter and sound skills to word recognition and vocabulary. Between their discussion of this problem and the many challenges of assessing comprehension presented in other chapters of this volume, we suspect that readers are persuaded of this point. Although educators should never rely on single assessments for any decision making, this point is especially important to emphasize when highly reliable assessments cannot be obtained for a construct, such as comprehension. In general, such a situation calls for aggregation across assessments, with the reliability of such an aggregation always greater than the reliability of any of the individual indicators (see Rushton, Brainerd, & Pressley, 1983). In addition, because comprehension is multifaceted, it is hard to imagine single measures that would capture well its many qualities. That is, valid assessment of comprehension requires multiple measures of comprehension. In short, with respect to comprehension, what is going to be needed are batteries that measure comprehension in various ways (i.e., with different types of texts read, different types of test items, different directions at the time of reading, etc.). That comprehension is only likely to be measured satisfactorily with extensive batteries provides additional motivation for narrowing the field of tests.

The idea of a few (or even one) national test batteries testing reading comprehension deserves consideration for another reason. Carpenter and Paris (this volume) should convince readers that developing excellent reading assessments is costly. That said, we feel the country should expend the costs to do comprehension assessment well. Nonetheless, the educational resources of the country are very scarce relative to the demands on them. That requires that there be intelligent economies in the system. One such intelligent economy is to invest heavily in the development of a few excellent tests, ones that are well understood through careful, thoughtful, scientific evaluation. Those who receive this charge, and we think this charge is coming because the country is currently being overwhelmed by assessment requirements as well as criticisms of state-developed assessments, should fold Carpenter and Paris into the conversation from the start. They have as good a vision about how to do such work as we have encountered.

TAYLOR AND PEARSON

The fundamental question that Taylor and Pearson (this volume) address is whether teachers can benefit from school reform efforts geared toward improving their reading instruction, and thereby their students' reading achievement? Do the teachers benefit from professional development in a workshop style? Also, what role do assessments and best practices in reading instruction play in this professional development? Because we know that very little comprehension instruction is occurring in the elementary grades, inquiry about professional development geared toward increasing comprehension instruction should become a paramount target of reading researchers.

The tentative conclusions offered by Taylor and Pearson (this volume) are that change requires considerable effort. There were lots of weekly and monthly meetings for the teachers who were trying to change. And, when all was said and done, Taylor and Pearson found no quick fix or magic bullet. When Pam El-Dinary and Pressley studied teachers in Montgomery County who were trying to become comprehension strategies teachers, they found that only the minority succeeded (Pressley & El-Dinary, 1997). Alysia Roehrig (2003), who has worked with us to develop interventions to teach primary teachers to be more like the most effective primary teachers (see Pressley, Allington, Wharton-McDonald, Block, & Morrow, 2001), has documented that year-long, intensive mentoring works well for a third of the teachers, produces some change for another third of the teachers, and has little to no impact on the remaining third of the teachers. Was it coincidence that nothing happened in a third of the schools that Taylor and Pearson studied? This said, their discussion of school-level factors relating to success of professional development was interesting and deserves further consideration. Best practices typically improved in the highest reform schools and did not improve in the lower performing schools. Taylor and Pearson listed many characteristics of high reform schools such as dedicated principals and school leaders, teacher buy-in, and dedication to long-term goals. For schools to join the CIERA School Change Project, 75% of teachers had to agree to participate, so wiliness to participate may be a necessary but not sufficient condition for successful reform in a school.

Recently in Colorado, Pressley sat with state officials who thought about what kind of assessments could be administered that would be most helpful to teachers in figuring out which reading skills to target with instruction. He would have liked to have known more from Taylor and Pearson (this volume) about how assessments informed the teachers they studied as they experienced the professional development described in the chapter in this volume. Based on what is detailed in the chapter, excellent comprehension assessment seemed to inform teachers about how to adjust, inform, and reform their practice. The teachers found most helpful their own observations and informal assessments. Not surprising to us, the teachers did not find the tests by the building or district to be useful, and Taylor and Pearson did not present any evidence that those tests were helpful to teachers. This, of course, begs the following question: How useful do teachers find the state and nationally mandated standardized tests? In the 10 years of research in our group on exceptional and not so exceptional elementary literacy teachers (for a review, see Pressley et al., 2003b), we have not observed one instance where a classroom teacher used standardized test data to make instructional decisions about a student. There needs to be serious inquiry about how teachers do and could use tests as part of deciding whether the expanding national investment in testing should continue.

Taylor and Pearson (this volume) called for more video clips of best practices. It is a call we are hearing often. That said, the most effective teachers rarely teach skills in any way that is easy to frame with a camera. Rather, the best teachers do more scaffolding than whole group teaching, more opportunistic teaching than the scope-and-sequence instruction that is easy to capture with the camera lens. As Roehrig (2003) has been working with teachers, she has been videotaping excellent teachers as they teach and reflecting with novice teachers about large segments of teaching that are filled with effective practices. Somehow we think this shows best practices at their best better than isolated video clips. Still, we are having a hard time conceiving how to scale up what Roehrig is doing. Video clips of best practices may be a start. In any case, we are certain that it makes sense to study the impact of images of excellent teaching on teachers. For instance, how much can teachers learn from video clips? What goes on when they experience video clips? And how can such clips be formatted so they are most effective?

We close by noting that as much as we admire the work of Taylor and Pearson (this volume), those who know the work of our group know that we favor longer-term observations than did the CIERA investigators. Our experience has been that the rich case studies developed by our group have done much good in informing the educator community about what effective instruction is really like (see Pressley et al., 2001). Although description is valued lowly in this post-National Reading Panel era, where experimentation and hypothetical-deductive testing is receiving ringing endorsement, we wish we could read more in-depth cases about the professional development documented in this chapter. Science that informs and transforms the education of teachers is going to be concrete, in the form of images, or at least imaginable from verbal descriptions.

PALINCSAR, MAGNUSSON, PESKO, AND HAMLIN

Palinscar, Magnusson, Pesko, and Hamlin (this volume) conducted an exploratory study to investigate students' comprehension activity while reading a domain-specific text that was designed to reflect the characteristics (both in content and process) of the physical sciences. They collected data from 24 typically achieving fourth-grade readers who could decode the texts. Perhaps the study's greatest contribution lies in the individual profiles of comprehension difficulties experienced by readers. For instance, some readers lacked sufficient prior knowledge, whereas others did not activate prior knowledge to make inferences. In contrast, other readers overrelied on what they knew about the topic before encountering the text.

Also, Palinscar and her colleagues captured individual differences in knowledge that seemed to affect working memory demands. For example, those students who proved unfamiliar with data tables had difficulty simultaneously identifying information in the tables and interpreting it. Also, students differed in their metacognitive awareness and cognitive processes that can be affected by monitoring. Thus, some readers adjusted their text representations based on new information they encountered whereas others did not. In short, this research group confirmed that reading comprehension is complex in nature and is influenced by text (domain-specific science text), activity (retelling and answering questions), and reader factors (e.g., prior knowledge; RAND Reading Study Group, 2002).

Given the researchers' goal of studying how domain-specific prior knowledge impacts students' reading comprehension, it was disappointing that prior knowledge did not prove more predictive of students' comprehension performance in this study. One possibility is that the four-question prior knowledge assessment was simply too brief, after all, consisting of only four questions. One of the challenges associated with studying the impact that prior knowledge has on reading comprehension is the way that prior knowledge is assessed. The hypotheses about prior knowledge advanced by this group deserve additional study.

It makes great sense to figure out the processes that students employ to understand science texts. Palincsar et al. (this volume) chose to assess processing with retellings and question-asking. We worry that this approach may have prompted students to process the text differently than they would have on their own. As one of their students commented, "Oh, you just brought something to my head" (p. 271). Thus, it seems that this assessment gauges what students are capable of with guidance instead of what they normally do while reading. In future work, we'd recommend tapping processing by cuing as little as possible, perhaps reflecting additionally on how children might be led to produce verbal protocols of their reading processes as they read, with at least a few examples in the literature that children can so report (Brown, Pressley, Van Meter, & Schuder, 1996; McGuire & Yewchuk, 1996; Meyers, Lytle, Palladino, Devenpeck, & Green, 1990).

CONCLUSION

Each of these chapters reported extremely innovative work, the kind of work that only comes from individual scientists (or a few scientists working together), reflecting hard on the state of understanding about instruction and achievement at present and how knowledge about literacy instruction might be advanced intelligently. Excellent science begins as bits and pieces of advance that requires consumers to sift through it and find inspiration, rather than certain conclusions. Certain conclusions about the problems explored by Carpenter and Paris (this volume), Taylor and Pearson (this volume), and Palincsar et al. (this volume) are years away. That said, there was plenty in these chapters to provide practitioners and policymakers incentive to consider doing business differently in the near future. It is a mistake to think that science should not impact schools and the institution of education until dozens of studies on a problem have been completed by a variety of research groups, a position advanced by the National Reading Panel (2000).

A possible, and we think important, next step for these researchers would be to study the consequential validity of their assessments. Messick (1988) defined consequential validity as the impact or consequences an assessment has for its stakeholders. Carpenter and Paris (this volume) investigated the validity and reliability of one such high-stakes test, the MLPP. Paris (2000) believed that high-stakes tests have many negative, often unnoticed consequences attached to them, including promotion of low-level thinking, misdirection of student motivation, disadvantaging minority and poor students, and negatively impacting the instructional focus in the classroom toward the coverage of the tests. Although these assessments were designed to inform teachers, parents, and administrators about how students are learning, the tests are also often used in unintended ways, for example, to judge school and teacher quality and determine grade retention. Further research, including on the MLPP, should continue to examine the effects of the unintended consequences of high-stakes tests and how to best reduce such consequences.

Taylor and Pearson's chapter (this volume) motivated us to think about how we assess teachers' reading comprehension instruction. Certainly, as teachers provide students feedback as they use comprehension strategies to actively construct meaning when reading, it makes good sense to provide teachers feedback about their instruction when they are involved in professional development. With regard to consequential validity, further research should examine what teachers do with this feedback, specifically how it affects their instruction.

We ask Palinscar et al. (this volume) how their assessments would impact teachers' reading comprehension instruction. We can easily envision good comprehension instructors pulling out students with similar comprehension difficulties in small group lessons where they could tailor their instruction to a specific deficit. An assessment such as the one studied by Palincsar and her colleagues has the potential to impact intelligently elementary teachers' reading comprehension instruction of domain-specific texts.

A final point that we make is that we are disappointed that none of the contributors to the conference considered very seriously the possibility of verbal protocol analyses as part of comprehension assessment. Verbal protocol analyses seem well suited to providing a window into how readers construct meaning from a text. Typically, when conducting verbal protocols, participants verbally report what they are thinking or feeling as they read a text. Verbal protocol analyses then capture the processes the readers use to make sense of texts before, during, and after reading. Much of what we know about reading comprehension processes has resulted from previous verbal protocols provided by adult readers (Pressley & Afflerbach, 1995). For example, Wyatt, Pressley, El-Dinary, and Stein (1993) examined how 15 professional-level social scientists comprehend journal articles in their areas of study. The result was a very complete catalog about what social scientists can do when they read articles that matter to them professionally.

Since the appearance of the Pressley and Afflerbach (1995) summary of the verbal protocols literature, we have been involved in many conversations about how verbal protocols might be used to assess comprehension. To date, however, we know of no serious attempts to transform this research tool, one that has been in use for about a century (Duncker, 1926; James, 1890) and one that has proven useful in dozens of research studies, into an assessment that can be used by reading clinicians and educators. Perhaps this is because many researchers believe that developing readers are unable to provide useful verbal protocols. Verbalizing thoughts while reading might overwhelm children's cognitive resources, and therefore, this methodology would not provide an accurate portrayal of children's reading comprehension. Also, younger readers may not provide accurate think-alouds because they may not have sufficient metacognitive awareness of what they are thinking while reading.

However, occasionally, researchers have collected verbal protocols from elementary students (Brown, Pressley, Van Meter, & Schuder, 1996; McGuire & Yewchuk, 1996; Meyers et al., 1990). Thus, Brown et al. (1996) compared the verbal protocols of second graders who had experienced traditional reading instruction to a form of comprehension strategies instruction for reading. They triangulated the verbal protocol analysis with analysis of retellings and standardized assessments. The verbal protocol data not only converged with other measures that the comprehension instruction improved reading comprehension over more traditional instruction, it also helped answer the more important question of why.

Therefore, at least initial support exists for pursuing verbal protocol analyses as an assessment tool for reading comprehension. As we encourage additional research and development on the assessment directions in the chapters we reviewed, we also encourage research and development of verbal protocol analyses. A major finding of Pressley and Afflerbach (1995) is that whenever researchers have looked for relations between reported comprehension processing and actual comprehension, they have found them (Pressley & Afflerbach, 1995, pp. 105–107). There is plenty of reason to believe that think-alouds during reading can be valid indicators of skilled and not-so-skilled reading.

REFERENCES

Brown, R., Pressley, M., Van Meter, P., & Schuder, T. (1996). A quasi-experimental validation of transactional strategies instruction with low-achieving second grade readers. *Journal of Educational Psychology, 88*, 18–37.

Duncker, K. A. (1926). A qualitative (experimental and theoretical) study of productive thinking (solving of comprehensible problems). *Pedagogical Seminary, 33*, 642–708.

Elliott, J., Lee, S. W., & Tollefson, N. (2001). A reliability and validity study of the Dynamic Indicators of Basic Early Literacy Skills–Modified. *School Psychology Review, 30*, 33–49.

Good, R. H., & Kaminski, R. A. (Eds.). (2002). *Dynamic indicators of basic early literacy skills* (6th ed.). Eugene, OR: Institute for the Development of Educational Achievement. Retrieved Feb. 1, 2004, from http://dibels.uoregon.edu

James, W. (1890). *The principles of psychology*. New York Holt.

Kamps, D. M., Wills, H. P., Greenwood, C. R., Thorne, S., Lazo, J. F., & Crocket, J. L., et al. (2003). Curriculum influences on growth in early reading fluency for students with academic and behavioral risks: A descriptive study. *Journal of Emotional and Behavioral Disorders, 11*, 211–224.

McGuire, K. L., & Yewchuk, C. R. (1996). Use of metacognitve reading strategies by gifted learning disabled students: An exploratory study. *Journal of the Education of the Gifted, 19*, 293–314.

Messick, S. (1988). The once and future issues of validity: Assessing the meaning and consequences of measurement. In H. Wainer & H. I. Braun (Eds.), *Test validity* (pp. 33–45). Hillsdale, NJ: Lawrence Erlbaum Associates.

Meyers, J., Lytle, S., Palladino, D., Devenpeck, G., & Green, M. (1990). Think-aloud protocol analysis: An investigation of reading comprehension strategies in fourth- and fifth-grade students. *Journal of Psychoeducational Assessment, 8*, 112–127.

National Reading Panel. (2000). *Teaching children to read: An evidence-based assessment of the scientific research literature on reading and its implications for reading instruction: Reports of the subgroups*. Washington, DC: National Institute of Child Health and Development.

107th Congress. (2002). *The no child left behind act of 2002*. Washington, DC: United States Congress.

Paris, S. (2000). Trojan horse in the school yard: The hidden threats in high-stakes testing. *Issues in Education, 6*, 1–16.

Pressley, M., & Afflerbach, P. (1995). *Verbal protocols of reading: The nature of constructively responsive reading*. Hillsdale, NJ: Lawrence Erlbaum Associates.

Pressley, M., Allington, R., Wharter-McDonald, R., Block, C. C., & Morrow, L. M. (2001). *Learning to read: Lessons from exemplary first grades*. New York: Guilford.

Pressley, M., & El-Dinary, P. B. (1997). What we know about translating comprehension strategies instruction research into practice. *Journal of Learning Disabilities, 30*, 486–488.

RAND Reading Study Group. (2002). *Reading for understanding: Toward an R & D program in reading comprehension*. Santa Monica, CA: Author.

Roehrig, A. D. (2003). *The effects of mentoring on beginning teacher effectiveness and student outcomes*. Unpublished doctoral dissertation, University of Notre Dame, Notre Dame, IN.

Rushton, J. P., Brainerd, C. J., & Pressley, M. (1983). Behavioral development and construct validity: The principle of aggregation. *Psychological Bulletin, 94*, 18–38.

Wyatt, D., Pressley, M., El-Dinary, P. B., & Stein, S. (1993). Comprehension strategies, worth and credibility monitoring, and evaluations: Cold and hot cognition when experts read professional articles that are important to them. *Learning and Individual Differences, 5*, 49–72.

Part IV

Large-Scale Assessments of Reading Comprehension

14

Assessment of Young Children as They Learn to Read and Write

Terry Salinger
American Institutes for Research

Early childhood educators and researchers have historically distrusted standardized measures of young children's learning (National Association for the Education of Young Children [NAEYC], 1988), and current legislation mandating new waves of testing has focused renewed attention on assessment practices. To contextualize the discussion of current practice and current concerns, this chapter begins by briefly reviewing the history of early literacy assessment and discussing the enduring issues surrounding assessment practices. Issues have largely centered on the appropriateness of the assessment practices and of the instruments used, the nature of information that is collected and the uses to which it is put, and impact of assessment practices on instruction for young children.

Testing of young learners was relatively uncommon before 1965. The practice has increased constantly since then, largely motivated by political agendas and needs. The influx of federal and state money to schools, the requirement for accountability measures, the necessity of measuring attainment of academic standards, the alarms raised by the 1983 publication of A *Nation at Risk* (National Commission on Excellence in Education, 1983), and the need to measure students' "readiness" to see if they have met the National Educational Goals Panel's goal of "all children ready for school" by age 5—these have all motivated the rise in testing. In 1988, NAEYC catalogued the uses of tests: for entry into and exit from kindergarten, for placement, and for early tracking.

As testing increased, early childhood educators and researchers began to voice their distrust and often-vehement disapproval for testing (NAEYC, 1988; Shepard, 1991, 1994, 1997, 2000). Lorrie Shepard was an early and vocal opponent of inappropriate use of tests with young learners. Her publications in both the measurement literature and the more popular educational outlets like *The Kappan* have been wide ranging—in some, cautions against the misuse of screening tests, and in others, suggestions for the role of "dynamic" assessments in creating a learning culture within classrooms. Constance Kamii, in her 1990 book for NAEYC, *Achievement Testing in the Early Grades: The Games Grown-ups Play*, contended that the rush to test is motivated by the "vote-getting game," the "looking good game," the "keep-my-job game," and the "buck-passing game." In this still-relevant volume, Vito Perrone (1990) suggested that "[u]sed as they are in many settings for major educational decisions, the various tests clearly limit the educational possibilities of children" (p. 3).

In 1998, perhaps recognizing that the testing movement was getting out of hand, the National Educational Goals Panel (NEGP, 1998) proposed sensible purposes for assessment of children in their early years of development. Acknowledging that states and local agencies need to gather information for monitoring young children's living and social conditions, the report stressed that the use of standardized tests should be restricted because "[b]fore age 8, standardized achievement measures are not sufficiently accurate to be used for high-stakes decisions about individual children and schools. Therefore, high-stakes assessments intended for accountability purposes should be delayed until the *end of third grade (or preferably fourth grade)*" (NEGP, 1998, p. 21, emphasis added).

STANDARDIZING THE ASSESSMENT
OF YOUNG LEARNERS

Cautionary words not withstanding, use of standardized testing in the early grades has been common, and the recent "No Child Left Behind" (NCLB) legislation includes provisions that will instantiate testing firmly in kindergarten to Grade 3 classrooms across the country. Many states use the most common commercial standardized tests, which provide national norms for comparative purposes but do not necessarily measure all components of state academic standards. Other states chose to develop their own tests to ensure alignment to their state academic standards or have contracted with testing companies to "customize" norm-referenced products. Customized tests serve the accountability machinery better than off-the-shelf tests (Linn & Hambleton, 1991). Testing companies can document their tests' alignment with local and state

standards so that commercial, off-the-shelf, standardized tests can be featured
as integral parts of state or local reform efforts. Additionally, many testing companies can, for a fee, provide criterion-referenced interpretations of test results,
specialized reports for parents, highly individualized score reports, and instructional material to help teachers "understand" how their curricular approach is
reflected in a test given nationwide (Farr, 1992).

Testing companies have also added new item types and "authentic" texts to
their products. For example, children as early as Grade 1 may now encounter
both multiple-choice and constructed-response questions about the "passages"
they read on standardized tests. Even when these "passages" are drawn from
"authentic" sources or written by children's authors, the context in which children read, think, and write is still that of a standardized test, with all that signi-
fies. The bubbles they fill in may be larger than those on tests for older children,
but the context is still the same.

WHY TESTING CAN BE INAPPROPRIATE

The current imperative to test young learners presents many problems, above
and beyond an aversion to this kind of testing. The first is the appropriateness of
the tests themselves. Many variables can influence how a child performs on a
test, including the health or mental state of a child on testing day, her or his level
of distractibility or inability to sit still, the child's familiarity with testing routines, or even the teacher's demonstrated attitudes toward the test. The children's book, *Testing Miss Malarkey* (Finchler, 2000), is not a complete
exaggeration in its depiction of a school community's preparation for standardized tests. The gym teacher teaches stress-reducing yoga, parents give pop quiz-
zes on bedtime reading, and the cafeteria serves "brain food" such as fish.

Another set of variables might be thought of as mechanical. Young learners
can easily make mistakes by accidentally marking the wrong box on the test
sheet, overlooking a question, or missing a word while reading a text. Such "errors" mask a child's real knowledge and understandings on the particular testing day and hence may underestimate what the child knows and can do.
Perrone (1990) reminded us that even something as seemingly innocuous as
breaking one's pencil midtest can cause a child to lose focus on the test he or she
is taking.

The singularity of the testing event is also problematic. Standardized tests
are efficient—given on one or two days and then sent away to be scored. But
learning to read and write is hardly efficient for most children. The data these
tests yield are limited, frozen in time, and reflective of students' performance,
well-being, and mood at the moment of testing. As children learn, they progress

along a developmental trajectory that includes both acquisition of knowledge about literacy and also numerous skills and strategies. The most valuable information is where children are on that trajectory and how they are orchestrating what they are learning. Thus, the information reported by a standardized test may also be seriously flawed simply because it is old. Results may not be reported to parents or teachers until months after the test administration, and children may have progressed far beyond the formal picture presented of their achievement. Even for accountability purposes, data that are flawed for individual students skew the representation of group status.

Similarly, the very sense of reading achievement as the accumulation of discrete skills is problematic, although the current parlance of five essential components of reading merges discussion of instructional foci with the messy cognitive activities involved in learning to read. Test results reported as subscores for discrete skills or clusters of skills are quantitative and defy the notion of a developmental trajectory. They tell what students have or have not mastered at a given point and perpetuate a deficit model by emphasizing areas in which students need "to improve." It is true that commercial test reports are often in the form of a "profile" of student strengths and weaknesses, but even when presented as a compensatory model ("children are good in this, less good in this ..."), deficits will undoubtedly draw more attention than strengths. If Stanovich's (1984) finding that it is impossible to find single elements or subsets of elements that are the cause of children's potential reading difficulties is to be trusted, the deficit model makes even less sense.

The impact of tests on classroom practice can be immense. Horror stories are common about teachers being encouraged to "teach to the tests" used to evaluate their students, especially if the tests are "aligned" to local standards (Hoffman, Roser, & Worthy, 1998; Paris, 2000). This practice, whether effected by using test-prep material or practice items, or by drilling on specific behaviors or facts, results in unequal and uncontrolled variability in instructional practice prior to testing and in actual test administrations. Teaching to the test can alter the meaning of test scores, in that comparisons across students, schools, districts, and other focal units are skewed by the unequal opportunities some students received. Haladyna (Haladyna, Nolen, & Haas, 1991; also Mehrens & Kaminski, 1989) referred to this as "test score pollution."

At another level, test preparation practice can reduce the conceptualization of literacy to the constructs assessed on the test, effectively defining and narrowing the instructional program students experience. Thus, children in low-performing schools may receive a diet of skill-and-drill activities that limits their view of the value of reading and writing and may curtail the momentum of students who can progress normally. Likewise, students in high-performing schools who genuinely need a more prescriptive instructional program may be overlooked because it is the "above average" students who set the pace (National Research Council, 1998).

The final, ironic problem is that customization of testing programs for state-level assessment, especially as part of a reform effort, has been shown to be less effective than anticipated. Large-scale assessment programs in North Carolina, Kentucky, and Arizona, which included literacy measures, were expected to motivate change in curriculum and instruction. Studies of these efforts have suggested that the tests did not provide teachers with enough guidance to bring about change, and, in Arizona especially, not enough professional development was provided to increase teachers' capacity to teach to meet curricular mandates (Valencia & Wixson, 1999).

It is logical to ask why use of standardized tests is so pervasive. Answers are simple to generate and discussed throughout this book. Paper-and-pencil tests are efficient and relatively economical, even with constructed-response items. They provide normative data to facilitate comparisons of local students to students nationwide, although such data report nothing about instructional programs or the context of students' lives. Standardized tests also come with a tacit "guarantee" that they have been developed according to rigorous professional standards (AERA, APA, & NCME, 1999), so their reports can be "trusted" to be valid and reliable measures of the constructs being measured. This "guarantee" has considerable power over many end users of the test development process. Shepard (2000) has reported on a collaborative study with teachers to develop alternate assessments for teacher administration; she found that the teachers even considered classroom-based assessment as "an official event, separate from instruction" (p. 5).

CLASSROOM-BASED ASSESSMENTS AND MULTIPLE FORMS OF EVIDENCE

Responding to their concerns about standardized tests, teachers, administrators, and researchers have sought to formalize and legitimize classroom-based assessment procedures such as those Shepard (Shepard et al., 1996) sought to develop. This is especially true at the lower grade levels, where instruction is apt to include considerable direct teacher–student interaction. Because the information they yield about students' learning is gathered in different learning contexts, at different points in time, and with differing levels of independence versus scaffolding, such assessments are often thought of as an antidote to the one-time-only measurement of standardized tests. Information gathered through classroom-based measures can have immediate utility for teachers and more meaning for parents than standardized tests scores. Classroom-based assessment can serve numerous purposes, from informing instruction to gathering data for classroom, school, and district accountability needs. The term "multiple forms of evidence" is often used to describe the accumulated data about students.

There are several different forms of classroom-based assessments that seek to collect, evaluate, and report multiple forms of evidence about student learning. In some cases, groups of early childhood teachers and administrators have responded to their distrust for other forms of assessments or to the demand for accountability by developing early literacy assessments that embody their theoretical perspectives about emergent literacy instruction and their conviction that teachers are the best evaluators of children's academic growth. In other situations, classroom-based programs have been purchased for use in early childhood classes. These range from systems like *Work Sampling, The Primary Language Record* and *Fox in a Box*, to more recent assessments like the *Texas Primary Reading Inventory*, the DIBELS (or Dynamic Indicators of Basic Early Literacy Skills) or the PALS or Phonological Awareness Literacy Screening. Both locally-developed and commercial classroom-based tests are discussed next.

LOCALLY DEVELOPED ASSESSMENTS

Locally developed classroom-based literacy assessment systems have many common characteristics. The work of Clay (1985), Holdaway (1979), Sulzby (1991; Teale & Sulzby, 1986), and others, has informed the development of many such systems. Tasks include curriculum-embedded or on-demand activities and often mimic situations similar to their everyday classroom routines. Thus, running records (Clay, 1985), story retellings (Morrow, 1988), invented spelling tests, tasks like "Concepts of Print" (Clay, 1985), and analysis of collections of student writing, are common. Anecdotal records, vocabulary or sight-word lists, self-assessments (McKenna & Kear, 1999), motivation inventories (Gambrell, Palmer, Codling, & Mazzoni, 1999), and other tasks or inventories (Parker et. al., 1999), round out the collection of evidence. In most systems, data are collected throughout the year for teachers to document and chart the range of skills and strategies students are acquiring.

Approaches to classroom-based assessment fall into two distinct categories. In the first category, the assessment system consists of distinct tasks that are administered either at scheduled times throughout the year or at times specified within the scope and sequence of the instructional program. Teachers administer and score tasks and use data to monitor student progress; results can immediately influence instruction. Individual tasks have integrity within an underlying theoretical perspective, but they exist as stand-alone data collection instruments. Scores they yield do not necessarily contribute to a profile of growth in multiple aspects of literary learning.

In the second model, tasks are administered throughout the year to document progress along a theoretically-grounded developmental trajectory. Work is kept in a folder of some sort, is shared at parent conferences, and usually travels as a whole or in summary with children from grade to grade to provide "receiving" teachers with concrete examples of students' progress during the previous year. Thus, there are multiple forms of evidence of student work, collected at multiple points in time and in multiple learning contexts. Often data from the individual tasks contribute to placement on a developmental continuum that describes how students orchestrate knowledge, skills, and abilities at different points in literacy learning.

Assessment systems in Bellevue, WA (Valencia & Place, 1994), Cambridge, MA, New York (New York State Department of Education, 1999), and Michigan (Michigan Department of Education, 1998), all exemplify portfolio approaches to early literacy portfolios. The South Brunswick, NJ, school district was among the first to create and validate a developmental continuum aligned to the data collection in its early literacy portfolio (Salinger & Chittenden, 1994). Its evolution through seven consecutive drafts paralleled teachers' increasing understanding of sound early literacy instruction and of the ways in which students demonstrate learning development was motivated by an innovative local administrator and guided by a team of researchers from Educational Testing Service. The assessment system developed for the School District of Philadelphia represented another example of such a system (Chester, Maraschiello, & Salinger, 2000). Again, local teachers were intimately involved in the development of the system under the guidance of researchers from the American Institutes for Research. The literacy assessment was paralleled by a classroom-based early mathematics assessment aligned to the district's kindergarten to Grade 3 mathematics standards. Table 14.1 shows the components of the system as it was originally planned.[1]

---

[1]Development of the Philadelphia Kindergarten to Grade 3 Assessment system began during a time of intense school reform in the district. The innovative superintendent David Hornbeck envisioned a district offering its teachers vast amounts of professional development and parents tremendous opportunities for involvement in the schools. Development of the assessment was to be informed by the existing Balance Literacy Framework and was guided by researchers from the American Institutes for Research. Changes were made throughout the developmental period because of demands from the test development committee and the assessment requirements of Title I and of the Reading Excellence Act program. Best practice in assessment development did not always win out over the demands of local educators determined to maintain a reading program built firmly on the use of the many series of "trade" books that are readily available. The need to assess students according to the core dimensions of the Reading Excellence Act necessitated a move to more subskills assessment than local educators originally wanted. Ultimately, the system was dismantled as the district responded to state take-over and the assignment of approximately one-third of the schools to control by the Edison Corporation, a for-profit company that had bid for governance of the district.

TABLE 14.1

Original Plan for the Philadelphia Kindergarten to Grade 3 Literacy Assessment

Activity	Literacy Aspects Assessed/ Observed	Mode of Administration	Overlap with Other Assessments / Comments
Assessment of prerequisite skills			
Concepts of print	Familiarity with book handling skills; purposes for reading; vocabulary of instruction	Individual	The prerequisite skills tasks were used to assess entry skills in kindergarten or when students transferred into class midyear; results were not used to place children on the developmental continuum.
			The tasks formalized the observations teachers made of students as they got to know them.
Alphabet knowledge survey	Letter recognition	Individual	
Rhyme awareness activity	Phonemic awareness	Small group	
Assessment of foundational skills			
Monster spelling test	Phonemic awareness/letter-sound correspondence	Group	Spelling observed in the context of writing activities
Sight word activity	Orchestration of prerequisite skills; ability to read familiar words; decoding	Individual	Writing activities; oral reading

Comprehension tasks

Story retelling	Listening comprehension; familiarity with story structure; ability to recall, select, organize, summarize information	Individual	Oral language Reading comprehension Difficulty with the oral retelling could indicate that students were not familiar with story structure and needed more opportunities to listen to and discuss what they heard.
Running record	Reading rate and fluency; pacing in oral reading; accuracy of decoding strategies; comprehension as indicated by orchestration of text and answers to questions	Individual	
Running record	Reading rate and fluency; pacing in oral reading; accuracy of decoding strategies; comprehension as indicated by orchestration of text and answers to questions	Individual	Story retelling reading comprehension
Reading comprehension	Comprehension ability to orchestrate emergent and developing reading skills	Individual	Story retelling and writing
On-demand tasks	Reading comprehension; problem solving; research and organization skills; writing	Individual scores; could be group tasks	Reading comprehension; writing; these were designed to augment the individual tasks in both the literacy and mathematics assessments

(continued)

TABLE 14.1 (continued)

Activity	Literacy Aspects Assessed/Observed	Mode of Administration	Overlap with Other Assessments/Comments
Writing Assessment			
Writing assessments	Orchestration of prerequisite skills; familiarity with story structure and conventions of writing; syntax; vocabulary	Individual	Measures of reading, spelling reflected in writing
Surveys			
Oral language survey	Facility with oral language in multiple settings	Checklist format	Teachers were trained to listen to students and observe them as they interacted orally with peers
Literacy survey	Students' out-of-school experiences	Individually-administered by teacher or student completed	Modeled after an interest inventory; this gave teachers insight into students' literacy experiences and knowledge about reading and writing

The development of local assessments reflects the work of dedicated teachers and represents invaluable opportunities for professional development. From a measurement perspective, however, there is little research about the validity and reliability of classroom-based assessments. The local nature and relative newness of some of the assessment systems may well explain this lack of data. Validity and reliability considerations are discussed later, but it is worth noting at this point that many local assessment systems will not pass muster for use within federally-funded programs such as "Reading First." Although well-conceived and theoretically-grounded, states and districts cannot demonstrate that assessments meet the rigorous psychometric requirements imposed by Federal legislation. The South Brunswick early literacy portfolio is one example of a local assessment for which validity data were collected (Bridgeman, Chittenden, & Cline, 1995; Chittenden & Spicer, 1993), but the validation studies were conducted as part of a research agenda funded in part by Educational Testing Service. Validity studies planned for the Philadelphia Kindergarten to Grade 3 literacy system fell victim to budget cuts as the district underwent state take-over.

COMMERCIALLY DEVELOPED ASSESSMENT SYSTEMS

There is an increasing supply of commercially developed packages for classroom-based assessment. Systems like "Work Sampling," "Fox in a Box," the "Texas Primary Reading Inventory," and the "PALS" are available commercially. Others, like the DIBELS, can be downloaded from a Web site. Systems such as these have the advantage of considerable conceptual and psychometric power behind them. Data are available to support scores derived from the assessments; users can more or less trust that the tests have been field-tested and possess some degree of construct validity.

Technical reports do exist for instruments such as these. They most often reveal careful attention to psychometric details but can also show subtle problems with the assessments. Hintze, Ryan, and Stoner (n.d.) conducted a study of the concurrent validity and diagnostic accuracy of the DIBELS by using a validated, commercial test of phonological processing. Their results were most interesting vis-à-vis diagnostic accuracy. They found that the DIBELS recommended cut scores were so sensitive that "use of these cut-scores led to a very high percentage of true positives; however, this came at the expense of an exceeding number of false-positives" (Hintze et al., n.d., p. 16). Although it is desirable that a test can identify those students who truly need intervention early in their reading careers, schools need to be cautious when using tests that overidentify potentially struggling readers. This is another form of "test pollution," one that can certainly direct the instructional program (for individuals and for classes as a whole) in very prescribed directions.

Impressive technical reports are also available for the Texas Primary Reading Inventory or TPRI (Center for Academic and Reading Skills & Texas Institute for Measurement, Evaluation, and Statistics, n.d.; Foorman, et al., n.d.). The TPRI spans all the essential components of reading and does not give comprehension short shrift. In discussing false positives, the report of the 1998 edition of the assessment raises important points about all classroom-based systems:

> Even when various phonological awareness and related skills are assessed at the end of kindergarten or beginning of first grade, the link with the development of actual reading skills is not simple. A variety of indirect factors may impinge on the assessment of reading precursor skills that might also produce both false positive and false negative errors. For example, a child may do well on phonological aware-ness measures because of intense training or extensive literacy experiences, but still struggle with the development of word recognition skills because the training did not include a print component. Similarly, false positive errors may reflect the assessment of children from communities where many families have limited re-sources and are from diverse cultural and linguistic backgrounds with less expo-sure to English literacy-related activities. (Hintze, Ryan, & Stoner, n.d., p. 12)

Existence of careful studies to back up commercial or quasi-commercial tests is reassuring, but that does not make them necessarily better than locally-developed versions of the same sort of instrument. As with any assessment, it is essential to look carefully at the purpose for which assessments have been developed and to determine if their use is congruent with their purpose. Put another way, for an assessment to be useful, it must assess the constructs of in-terest in their entirety. For example, the TPRI is intended to be comprehen-sive, whereas many other readily-available assessments are not. The DIBELS and the PALS do not contain comprehension assessments; they have been de-signed for screening of specific components of beginning reading. They don't claim to do anything else, although the developers of the DIBELS attest to the predictive validity of their instruments. Scores on DIBELS subtests are sup-posed pinpoint exact areas of instruction that students need if they are to ad-vance toward reading competency by Grade 3. However, the distinct areas assessed by the DIBELS constitute only part of the entire constellation of learning that students must encounter if they are to become readers, and over-dependence on DIBELS results to shape instruction can seriously limit stu-dents' literacy experiences. Although they may learn to decode flawlessly, students may not gain experience actually using reading to learn or to achieve enjoyment.

ISSUES FOR LOCALLY DEVELOPED
OR COMMERCIAL ASSESSMENTS

Classroom-based assessments, either locally developed or commercial, posed numerous challenges. These include their technical characteristics, especially validity, scoring procedures and reliability, the burden placed on teachers and students, and the need for intense and ongoing professional development.

TECHNICAL CONSIDERATIONS

Validity and reliability are technical properties that must be considered as any assessment system or standardized test is evaluated. Standardized tests are often touted for their strong psychometric properties, their validity and reliability in measuring learning or other constructs. The classical definitions of validity and reliability apply when considering classroom-based assessments, but the ways in which they play out is often less rigorous than in traditional test development. Administration procedures, scoring, and score interpretation cannot be as highly standardized as in a testing program in which tests arrive, shrink-wrapped, and accompanied by scripted administration protocols and directions for returning booklets to a scoring center.

The validity of any assessment must be considered from various perspectives. Construct validity is the first important perspective, and the determination of construct validity at the beginning of an assessment project is essential. Test developers—groups of educators or professional test makers—must determine how the constructs to be measured are defined and how achievement on the assessments will be construed. This preliminary step to determine and clarify constructs is essential for numerous reasons. At the most practical level, it can provide extraordinary professional development. As they identify the constructs to be measured, teachers express in concrete terms the benchmarks of early literacy growth and negotiate their views with other professionals to reach consensus on what it means to move along a continuum toward literacy. Often, as in South Brunswick, a developmental continuum or scale is developed to express stages of growth, and this expression itself can go through numerous drafts before it is used as part of an assessment system.

Achieving face validity is also important. When teachers say that they don't like a standardized test because it doesn't test what they teach, they are saying that they disagree with the constructs on which the test is built; the test lacks face validity. Assessment systems that reflect routine classroom practice have inherent face validity because the distinction between instruction and assessment is blurred. But face validity is weak if it means the same trivial instruction is assessed repeatedly in the classroom. Burden, as discussed later, can also decimate face validity.

The extent to which classroom-based assessments can predict students' performance in subsequent years is perhaps their most important characteristics. Although it is perhaps excessive to imbue classroom assessments with formal predictive validity, they should provide information about how well students are progressing toward measurable goals, such as proficiency on an externally-developed and professionally-scored standards-based test. Teachers, administrators, and parents need to have confidence that the measurements taken as part of a classroom assessment are adequate to discriminate those students who are progressing well and those who need extra instruction, some intervention, or even additional, finer-grained testing to forestall later failure. Administrators in Philadelphia replaced their demand for predictive validity from the kindergarten through third grade (K–3) system with the statement that there should be "no surprises" when students took the high-stakes Grade 4 standardized tests. What they meant was that the kindergarten to Grade 3 assessments had to be rigorous enough that they could identify students whose progress toward a predetermined proficiency score at Grade 4 was in doubt and diagnostic enough that teachers could identify weaknesses and intervene early.

To be effective, scores derived from assessments must capture the full range of performance students might demonstrate in a given year, with relatively little floor or ceiling effect. Inflated scores—the ceiling effect—may mean that teachers do not understand the appropriate expectations to place upon students if students are to achieve beyond the early childhood grades or have not fully conceptualized the component skills that cumulatively result in solid comprehension. Scores that are deflated because students cannot make sense out of supposedly authentic tasks represent equally flawed measurement. Data gathered in these ways do not provide adequate information about how students are progressing toward an external, often high-stakes accountability benchmark.

The Philadelphia K–3 assessment can provide an example of how well-intentioned local test development can jeopardize the psychometric rigor of an assessment system (Chester, Maraschiello, & Salinger, 2000). Books from common series of trade books were to be set aside for the reading comprehension tests that were part of the system at all grade levels (see Table 14.1). Teachers on the test development committee held fast to Fountas and Pinnell's (1999) version of readability and, against the recommendations of the researchers advising them on assessment development, seemed to select the easiest books at each level for inclusion on the list of "benchmark" books. In this case, "easy" spanned both linguistic and content characteristics, resulting in a selection of books that offered so few linguistic and semantic challenges that the assessment provided little evidence of how students were actually orchestrating their learning. Children could answer the questions posed, but the validity of the measurement itself was doubtful for the simple reason that the books were too easy. Assessment results offered the false reassurance that students were making adequate progress toward a Grade 4 test that contributed to promotion decisions. The grade four SAT–9 scores verified the developers' predictions that students weren't in fact reading well, and an individually-administered alternative reading test, the "Grade 4 Second Chance Tests" (Baldi, Skidmore, & Ritter, 1999), confirmed the prediction. There had, in fact, been surprises, as teachers' grading systems were found to be faulty by both a commercial standardized test and by the locally-developed but psychometrically sound alternative test.

Finally, the consequential validity of any assessment must be considered. This term refers to the effects that a test or assessment system has on the system into which it is introduced. Ideally, the effect should be positive. Classroom-based assessments yield huge quantities of rich, descriptive data. Learning to quantify data reliably is one aspect of implementing the system, but it does not speak to consequential validity. Teachers must grow and change in their ability to make sense of what they see and to act on the information they gather. Only deeply-instantiated change will attest to consequential validity, and evidence of this level of change may not be readily apparent until long after a system is put in place. Interim evidence of change as teachers and students learn to live with the system reinforces its importance. Yet, as is discussed later, even small levels of change will not be sustained without ongoing, intense, professional development.

The consequences of classroom-based assessments may, of course, not be positive. Overemphasis on the content of the subtests within the general scheme of early literacy assessment—such as the phonemic awareness or phonics subtests of an instrument like the DIBELS—can reify test content as curriculum and propel tests to greater prominence than their developers would claim. The weakness inherent here is that the assessments have the potential to focus teachers' and administrators' attention too narrowly and away from students' actual orchestration of skills as can be demonstrated by fluent oral reading and comprehension. "Attention" in this context can mean instructional time, but it can also mean self-congratulatory overconfidence that kids are in fact making great progress toward reading independence, just as the use of relatively easy books skewed the results of the Philadelphia comprehension measures. The TPRI technical report acknowledges this potential testing misuse. Developers and marketers of screening tests would, of course, never advocate that fluent reading of extended prose and comprehension be relegated to later grades, but the danger inherent in their narrow focus remains.

SCORING AND ASSESSMENT RELIABILITY

It is most often teachers who assign the scores to assessment tasks they administer or to pieces of evidence collected into a portfolio. In South Brunswick, Philadelphia, New York State, and other locales, teachers analyze student evidence
to determine placement on a developmental continuum or set of scales. In the
best of situations, accuracy of this assignment accrues from teachers' understanding of the constructs of the assessment, the nuanced levels of the developmental continuum, and the multiple ways students can actually demonstrate
achievement. In other assessments, teachers score individual tasks, record results in what one hopes is a user-friendly data capture sheet, and probably sum
the scores to get a sense of how students are doing overall. Some locales are ex-
perimenting with hand-held data capture devices to lessen teacher burden—
and to ensure that teachers won't make errors in calculating total scores.

It is reasonable to ask about the accuracy of teacher-derived scores and
about the reliability of these tests. When assessments serve a classroom-level
purpose, teachers will undoubtedly use contextual knowledge to supplement
what student evidence says about performance. Teachers want their students to
do well, for the sake of their students and for their own sake as well. However,
when assessments serve an external purpose as well, scores or placement on a
continuum must be reliable and objective. Here, reliability means that someone
familiar with the constructs of the assessment but unfamiliar with individual
children will be able to interpret student evidence in the same way as the
classroom teacher.

If there is to be any chance for objective, accurate scoring of student tasks
and subsequently meaningful aggregation of data, scoring guides must be detailed, objective, comprehensive, and still easy to follow. Additionally, teachers
should receive adequate training on scoring procedures and score interpretation, but procedures for scoring may seem very abstract when presented as part
of more general procedural training as a new assessment system is introduced. It
is primarily within the act of scoring—applying specified criteria to assign ratings to many examples of student work—that teachers learn how scoring differs
from routine, more contextualized grading practices.

To reinforce the need for precise and objective scoring, many assessment
systems use trained, external scorers who do not know the children to sec-
ond-score the collected work of a sample of students. Second scoring produces measures of interrater reliability, that is, checks on how accurately
classroom teachers have scored their own students' collected work so that
teacher judgments can be "recalibrated" as needed. High levels of interrated
reliability have been reported in South Brunswick (Bridgeman, Chittenden,

& Cline, 1995) and in New York State (Falk, Ort, & Moirs, 1999). The process of second scoring student work provides excellent opportunities for professional development in that participants in these exercises must closely examine and internalize not just scoring rubrics but also the standards that the rubrics represent. Researchers studying the New York State Early Literacy Profile (Falk et al., 1999) used teacher surveys to determine the value of the assessment system. They found that

> by asking teachers to look at evidence of student learning (as it is manifested in student work) in relation to standards (as described in the Profile scales), teachers perceive themselves to have increased their knowledge of individual students, to have become better informed about the capacities of their students in relation to literacy progress, and to have received guidance about what they need to do next to support the forward development of their students. (Falk et al., 1999, pp. 40–41)

BURDEN *Summarice #17*

Burden on teachers and students can be as great a problem with commercially-available tests as with locally-developed ones. Classroom-based assessment tasks are similar to but must be more refined than routine classroom activities. Significant amounts of evidence must be collected to support students' scores, evidence from tasks that are not so trivial as to be inconsequential, or so ambitious as to disrupt classroom life. They must be administered at numerous times during the year in systematic, standard ways, and they must produce credible, unambiguous evidence. That's a tall order, one that takes time to accomplish. Educators, parents, and unions complain about the ways in which standardized tests rob students of teaching time, but classroom-based assessments can do the same thing, especially if the assessment requires teachers to administer tasks individually. No one will dispute the value of one-on-one interaction with students over some aspect of literacy learning, but this time can be costly. Some of the time spent administering assessment tasks may be "quality" time, some will be time spent handling logistics, and some will be time spent disciplining the rest of the class. Johnston (1987) wrote that "simple classroom management skills are part of evaluation expertise. Without a well managed classroom in which children have learned to work independently, a teacher cannot step back from instruction and watch the class as a whole, or work uninterrupted with particular individuals" (p. 745).

Burden imposed on teachers can weaken the face validity of even the most popular classroom-based assessment. Burden can take two forms: first, the actual time and energy spent assessing individual students, and second, the time needed to analyze and report student data. Most teachers already engage in some form of assessment practice, which they judiciously base on their needs and their knowledge of their students. They conduct frequent, relatively informal checks on students' understanding, often noting what they observe in writing but perhaps more frequently translating their observations into immediate, precise, instructional change. Conducting a miscues analysis is a good example of another, more structured informal assessment: data collection is somewhat more formalized, and actual primary data are collected for comparison to previously-collected data. These assessment practices do not necessarily impose a burden on teachers because they are so well-integrated into classroom practice.

Another level of assessment—sometimes termed *finding out*—involves both assessing all students in routine, standardized ways and also abstracting information from administration of assessments such as running records or invented spelling tests (Chittenden, 1991; Engel, 1990). This level of assessments yields individual and group data that can be quantified for use both inside and outside the classroom. It has been argued (Engel, 1990) that the process of quantifying data is less meaningful to teachers than collecting information in more informal ways. Teachers may balk at collecting data systematically about all students and not become vested in analyzing student work thoroughly enough to aggregate data in the systematic way needed for external purposes such as accountability. If teachers do not understand the process for extracting data from analysis of student work or if time pressures push them to do so in a haphazard way, the reliability of their scoring will be suspect. At the classroom level, teachers' faulty scoring can be compensated for by their attention to other details of instruction. It is, however, this "finding out" data that needs to be reported to higher levels, and if it is inadequate, an accountability system dependent on classroom-based information may falter.

What's the answer to the burden issue? Obviously, it's less testing. But there are other possible ways to address this issue. Many classroom-based systems lack decision or branching rules to tell teachers-as-test-administrators when to stop administration of tasks that are too difficult, where to enter into a body of testing materials based on performance in previous test administrations, and directions in which to branch if students seem to be doing marvelously well on particular sections of a test. Adaptive testing is efficient because the reliability per unit of testing time tends to be greater with such a test. Adaptive testing can also minimize the floor and ceiling effects, a definite problem when tests or components of a larger test battery are designated as appropriate for a particular grade level or period during a school year (say, middle of kindergarten). Testing children at what seems to be their zone of proximal development makes sense both for screening and diagnosis.[2]

TRAINING AND PROFESSIONAL DEVELOPMENT FOR CLASSROOM-BASED ASSESSMENT SYSTEMS

Implementation of a classroom-based assessment system can be successful only if accompanied by rigorous training at the outset and comprehensive, ongoing professional development. The hard work of those individuals who developed the conceptual framework of the assessment must be transmitted in understandable ways to the teachers who will implement the system in their classrooms. Teachers must become knowledgeable about and take ownership of the constructs being assessed, master the instructional practices inherent in these constructs, and also learn the procedures for administering and scoring classroom-based tasks. Teachers have to become data-gatherers in a way that may be new to them because they are being asked to interpret students' responses to relatively standardized tasks and make inferences from what they see and hear. The validity of their inferences will rest not on their enthusiasm for the assessment system (although that is valuable) but on their understanding of the way the system reflects emergent literacy principles. Interpretations that are imprecise, superficial, or faulty about one assessment task may be ameliorated by accuracy on other tasks, but too much dependence on a compensatory scoring system will weaken the validity of the system as a whole. Teachers must learn to push themselves beyond their usual intuitive interpretation of what they observe, and they must be supported both intellectually and professionally as they learn to do this. This is a huge burden for teachers and districts

Professional development efforts must continue after initial implementation of a classroom-based assessment system because such systems are neither self-evident nor self-sustaining. Ongoing efforts can help teachers refine their procedural understanding of the system and concomitantly hone their skills as interpreters of student literacy behavior. These efforts are essential because the presence of a classroom-based assessment system alone will not be enough to sustain instructional change and improvement. For example, in one extensive study, researchers (Shepard et al., 1996) found that introducing a performance-based assessment system revealed that although teachers knew about the curricular frameworks to which the assessments were aligned, instruction

---

[2]It is interesting to note that the battery of tests for the Early Childhood Longitudinal Study is adaptive. All children receive a "routing" test that determines which tasks within a large pool of tasks will be administered to them.

was not congruent with the frameworks. Thus, professional development efforts designed to introduce the new assessments had to be refocused toward instructional change. The researchers concluded that long-term professional development was needed to support both instruction and assessment innovation. Teachers in South Brunswick, NJ, cited the need for ongoing professional development and focused efforts for new teachers as missing elements in the implementation over time of the Early Literacy Portfolio (Salinger & Chittenden, 1994).

Classroom-based assessment has the potential to enhance teachers' skills and impact on student learning; these changes were discussed earlier as consequential validity. However, change can be superficial unless the infrastructure is created to give teachers time and support to learn not only how to administer the assessment system skillfully but also how to mine its results to the fullest. Research on school reform attests to the need for such support, and only with focused, ongoing support can classroom-based assessment of literacy fulfill its role as the agent for reform that both enhances teaching and learning and replaces more traditional measures of literacy growth.

CURRENT FEDERAL LEGISLATION AND ITS INFLUENCE ON EARLY LITERACY ASSESSMENT

Until recently, the main questions seemed to be why and when to assess young learners. The passage of NCLB legislation has broadened the questions. Two key features of NCLB are particularly relevant to this discussion. First, "Reading First," the ambitious intervention program for kindergarten to Grade 3 students, mandates specific kinds of data collection and a three-tiered assessment routine. Second, NCLB mandates testing of all students in reading and mathematics in Grades 3 to 8.

The ideal that NCLB represents includes initial screening, diagnostic assessment and intervention, and thorough progress monitoring for children in kindergarten to Grade 3. This assessment triad should equate to the following sequence: (a) quick, initial screening of all students; (b) more intense diagnostics tests for students whose screening tests indicated need; and (c) intervention and ongoing assessment. These steps are in preparation for the eventual achievement test to be given in Grade 3. In the ideal, the emphasis here should be on intervention and eventual. Within such a plan, children have ample opportunities to show what they know and can do and to demonstrate those areas where they need some level of intervention—before being confronted with a high-stakes test at Grade 3. The plan, in and of itself, is a strong one, at least so long as what is being advocated makes sense conceptually and practically and will not result in unintended negative consequences.

Consequences are important here, both positive and negative. From a positive perspective, real attention is being paid to the reality that many children reach upper elementary grades unable to read successfully enough to progress academically. NCLB tries to address this problem and propose some solutions. Second, there is recognition that too many children have been relegated to special education as a way to get them out of mainstream education and mainstream testing. In theory, this isn't going to happen anymore because children will be screened, diagnosed, and given intervention early and systematically. Third, the "Reading First" statute and guidance place a strong emphasis on professional development, family literacy, teacher training, and libraries. These emphases suggest that the program is envisioned as comprehensive and reaching out into the communities that can and should support children's literacy growth.

Negative consequences are possible, too. Three forms of assessment are to be used in "Reading First" classrooms, and assessment and intervention are supposed to take place throughout the year. In theory, this makes excellent sense and bodes well for real change. Venezky and Winfield (1979) found that consistent use of data on student performance is a hallmark of effective schools as they investigated high-poverty schools that demonstrated strong achievement. More recently, the CIERA Beat the Odds study (Taylor, Pearson, Clark, & Walpole, 2000) affirmed the same thing.

However, who is going to be doing this monitoring and will they know how to administer the assessments, score them if needed, interpret results accurately, and then follow up as appropriate to tailor instruction or provide intervention? The answer is that teachers are supposed to do all this. Experienced teachers will be able to accomplish these tasks successfully, especially if administration, scoring, and interpretation directions are clear and thoughtful, if they have good classroom management skills or maybe small classes or an aide, and if they see the value of what they are doing and of the instruments they are using to assess their students. This is a monumental order, and with all due respect to teachers, many will not be able to accomplish these feats.

Reasons for possible teacher failure range along a continuum that spans their own inexperience to the vicissitudes of students' attendance. Additionally, teachers may simply not see the value in what they are being asked to do; here "value" and "face validity" are inextricably linked. The reality is that teachers in elementary grades seem neither to be interested in nor knowledgeable about assessment. Block, Oakar, and Hunt (2002) compared the aspects of literacy instruction, kindergarten to Grade 5, which were most valued by classroom teachers and by researchers. Their report showed no indication that the respondents placed any importance on knowledge of assessment procedures or use of data to inform instruction.

Block et al.'s (2000) findings are hardly reassuring as one contemplates the assessment responsibilities that teachers currently face, unless, of course, the assessments are so standardized, so routinized, so prescriptive, that they cannot capture the nuances of learning. The nuances of learning are demonstrated by patterns of behaviors that students show in repeated interactions with text. We can question the extent to which teachers using a prescribed screening and diagnostic test will be able to detect and act on the pattern in students' reading behaviors if they have to spend countless minutes per year assessing students within the structure of a three-part system. Recognizing, understanding, and taking action on patterns of behavior and productive and counterproductive strategies constitute true diagnostic teaching. An externally-imposed system of assessments (whether locally-developed or commercial) must include extensive training and very detailed scoring guides and rubrics if teachers are to learn how to handle the logistics of the system and make sense out of the data they are gathering, but such materials and training can never capture the entire range of idiosyncratic ways in which students tackle the tough work of learning to be literate.

A key criticism of standardized tests is the extent to which they can narrow the curriculum and negatively shape instruction. There are several indicators of potential curricular narrowing within the Reading First guidance and within the larger NCLB statute. For example, the emphasis on phonemic awareness and other basic skill elements of reading may overshadow the implied "balance" of instructional emphases in the five components of reading, especially for students who continue to struggle even when given a heavy diet of phonemic awareness and phonics. It is also worth noting what is omitted from the five basic components: motivation to read is absent from the list.

The need for districts that receive Reading First funding to demonstrate improvement within 3 years to maintain funding will establish a teach-to-the-test mentality that can be as severe as that imposed by external, norm- or criterion-referenced measures. Just as classes take on different "personalities" with each successive group of students, individual school results can be volatile from year to year; 3 years seems hardly enough time to evaluate programmatic success. The comprehensiveness of the measures required for Reading First equates to costs for states and districts that aren't already using a three-tiered assessment system in kindergarten to Grade 3; state departments of education may well institute the same testing system state wide so that there is uniformity across Reading First and non-Reading First classrooms, thus quite literally, letting Reading First define the curriculum nationwide.

The Grade 3 reading achievement test that is required by NCLB will further dictate instructional and curricular decisions. The specificity of content standards for K–3 reading and writing has varied widely across the country, with some states delineating precise benchmarks for early grades and others providing less guidance or prescription. Lack of specificity is true for upper grade standards in some states as well. The requirement for Grade 3 to 8 achievement testing in reading and math forces states to develop or test clearly-articulated specifications and to conduct standard setting exercises that create clear targets for student attainment.

State and local educational administrators, state school boards, and parents are going to want guarantees that students are progressing through the early grades right on track for passing scores at Grade 3. One, perhaps sanguine, view of this situation is that the kindergarten through Grade 2 assessments should "predict" performance at Grade 3, but this view is shortsighted both conceptually and instructionally. It is not just Donald Graves who is saying that testing is not teaching. Bob Linn (Linn, Baker, & Betebenner, 2002) recently questioned whether gains on a state test generalize to other measures of achievement, such as the National Assessment of Educational Progress. The question stems from "concerns that the narrow focus on teaching to a state test may produce inflated gains in scores and because the fundamental concern is with improved achievement, not just higher test scores" (Linn et al., 2002, p. 6). The seemingly positive triad of assessment approaches advocated by Reading First has as great a potential to narrow curriculum as would the imposition of standardized, paper-and-pencil tests on our very youngest learners.

CONCLUSIONS

Finally, it can be good to take a step back and look at the national landscape. The legitimization of classroom-based assessments for young learners and the acceptance of the validity and utility of teacher-collected data represented important steps forward for both assessment and early childhood education. The repeated arguments throughout the last decade from researchers like Lorrie Shepard, Constance Kamii, Ted Chittenden, Brenda Engel, and others were heard and acted on in positive ways. A new model—multiple forms of evidence—was introduced into the lexicon of teachers, administrators, parents, and researchers. Having participated in the development of the South Brunswick early literacy portfolio and having led the development of the Philadelphia K–3 Assessment (which has been replaced by the DIBELS district wide), I can assure my readers that these were exciting times.

Reading First and provisions for the early grades in NCLB seem at first to affirm positive directions in assessment for young learners. But if, as we are being told, few states will be able to measure their schools successfully against the rubric put forth by NCLB and the need for "adequate yearly progress," states will deliberately or inadvertently begin to play some of the games Constance Kamii (1990) elucidated. Standards set for Grade 3 will drive instruction and assessment at the lower grades, resulting in classroom-based assessments that are selected and used primarily to predict scores on this benchmark test. Standards for proficiency on this important test may well be selected, as were books for the Philadelphia assessment, to maximize scores, rather than to reflect students' more rigorous comprehension needs in later grades. Essentially, standards will be lowered and easier tests will be created or adopted, and educators and policymakers will hope that somehow the National Assessment of Educational Progress at Grade 4 will not reveal what has happened.

Ultimately, if young students' understandings about literacy happen to coalesce into a battery of skills and strategies that can be used for real learning, rather than just test taking, that will be fortunate. But young learners have a way of foiling the games that adults play, sometimes by motivating their own learning in positive directions (see Chittenden & Salinger, 2001), but more often by closing themselves off from instruction that does not engage them. We may be producing a generation of students for whom we can check off mastery of certain basic componential skills but who cannot go on to become real readers, real users of literacy in all subjects and in life. If somehow this bleak picture does not materialize and students overcome the regime of classroom-based testing that seems to be imminent, it will because of teachers who skillfully eke out time for careful instruction, rather than because the current legislative mandates have been appropriately interpreted.

REFERENCES

American Educational Research Association (AERA), American Psychological Association (APA), & National Council on Measurement in Education (NCME). (1999). *Standards for educational and psychological testing.* Washington, DC: Author.
Baldi, S., Skidmore, D., & Ritter, S. (1999). *Developing alternatives to traditional standardized assessments: The Philadelphia "Second-Chance" assessments.* Washington, DC: American Institutes for Research.
Block, C. C., Oakar, M., & Hunt, N. (2002). The expertise of literacy teachers: A continuum from preschool to grade 5. *Reading Research Quarterly, 37,* 178–207.
Bridgeman, B., Chittenden, E., & Cline, F. (1995). *Characteristics of a portfolio scale for rating early literacy.* Princeton, NJ: Educational Testing Service.
Center for Academic and Reading Skills & Texas Institute for Measurement, Evaluation, and Statistics. (n.d.). *Technical report: Texas Primary Reading Inventory (1998–1999 edition).* Houston: University of Texas–Houston Health Science Center & University of Houston.
Chester, M., Maraschiello, R., & Salinger, T. (2000, April). *Kindergarten to grade 3 assessments in Philadelphia: Development of an innovative system.* Paper presented at the American Educational Research Association annual meeting, New Orleans, LA.

Chittenden, E. (1991). Authentic assessment, evaluation, and documentation of student performance. In V. Perrone (Ed.), *Expanding student assessment* (pp. 22–32). Alexandria, VA: Association for Supervision and Curriculum Development.

Chittenden, E., & Salinger, T. (2001). *Inquiry into meaning: An investigation of learning to read.* New York: Teachers College Press.

Chittenden, E., & Spicer, W. (1993, September). *The South Brunswick literacy portfolio project.* Paper presented at the New Standards Project: English Language Arts Portfolio Meeting, Minneapolis, MN.

Clay, M. M. (1985). *The early detection of reading difficulties* (3rd ed.). Auckland, NZ: Heinemann.

Engel, B. (1990). An approach to assessment in early literacy. In C. Kamii (Ed.), *Achievement testing in the early grades: The games adults play* (pp. 119–134). Washington, DC: National Association for the Education of Young Children.

Falk, B., Ort, S. W., & Moirs, K. (1999). *Using classroom-based assessment on a large scale: Support and reporting on student learning with the Early Literacy Profile.* Paper presented at the annual meeting of the American Educational Research Association, Montreal, Quebec, Canada.

Farr, R. (1992). Putting it all together: Solving the reading assessment puzzle. *The Reading Teacher, 46,* 26–37.

Finchler, J. (2000). *Testing Miss Malarkey.* Markham, Ontario: Fitzhenry & Whiteside.

Foorman, B. R., Fletcher, J. M., Francis, D. J., Carlson, C. D., Chen, D, & Mouziaki, A., et al. (n.d.). *Technical report: Texas Primary Reading Inventory* (1998 ed.). Austin: Texas Education Agency.

Fountas, I. C., & Pinnell, G. S. (1999). *Matching books to readers: Using leveled books in guided reading, K–3.* Portsmouth, NH: Heinemann.

Gambrell, L., Palmer, B. M., Codling, R., & Mazzoni, S. A. (1999). Assessing motivation to read. In S. J. Barrentine (Ed.), *Reading assessment: Principles and practices for elementary teachers* (pp. 215–232). Newark, DE: International Reading Association.

Haladyna, T., Nolen, S. B., & Haas, N. S. (1991). Raising standardized achievement test scores and the origins of test score pollution. *Educational Researcher, 20*(5), 2–7.

Hintze, J. M., Ryan, A. L., & Stoner, G. (n.d.). *Concurrent validity and diagnostic accuracy of the dynamic indicators of basic early literacy skills and the comprehensive test of phonological processing.* Amherst, MA. Author.

Hoffman, J., Roser, N., & Worthy, J. (1998). Challenging the assessment contest for literacy instruction in first grade: A collaborative study. In C. Harrison & T. Salinger (Eds.), *International perspectives on reading assessment: Theory and practice* (pp. 166–181). London: Routledge.

Holdaway, D. (1979). *The foundations of literacy.* Sydney, Australia: Ashton Scholastic.

Johnston, P. (1987). Teachers as evaluation experts. *The Reading Teacher, 40,* 744–748.

Kamii, C. (Ed.). (1990). *Achievement testing in the early grades: The games grown-ups play.* Washington, DC: National Association for the Education of Young Children.

Linn, R. L., Baker, E. L., & Betebenner, D. W. (2002). Accountability systems: Implications of the requirements of the "No Child Left Behind Act of 2001." *Educational Researcher, 31*(6), 3–26.

Linn, R. L., & Hambleton, R. K. (1991). Customized tests and customized norms. *Applied Measurement in Education, 4,* 185–207.

McKenna, M. C., & Kear, D. J. (1999). Measuring attitude toward reading: A new tool for teachers. In S. J. Barrentine (Ed.), *Reading assessment: Principles and practices for elementary teachers* (pp. 199–214). Newark, DE: International Reading Association.

Mehrens, W. A., & Kaminski, J. (1989). Methods for improving standardized test scores: Fruitful, fruitless, or fraudulent? *Educational Measurement: Issues and Practice, 8*(1), 14–22.

Michigan Department of Education. (1998). *Michigan in literacy progress portfolio.* East Lansing, MI.

Morrow, L. M. (1988). Retelling stories as a diagnostic tool. In S. M. Glazer, L. W. Searfoss, & L. M. Gentile (Eds), *Reexamining reading diagnosis: New trends and procedures* (pp. 128–149). Newark, DE: International Reading Association.

National Association for the Education of Young Children. (1988). NAEYC position statement on standardized testing of young children 3–8 years of age. *Young Children, 43*(3), 42–47.

National Commission on Excellence in Education. (1983). *A nation at risk: The imperative for educational reform.* Washington, DC: Author.

National Educational Goals Panel. (1989). *Principles and recommendations for early childhood assessment.* Washington, DC: Author.

National Research Council. (1998). *Preventing reading difficulties in young children.* Washington, DC: National Academy Press.

New York State Department of Education. (1999). *Early literacy profile.* Albany, NY: Author.

Parker, E. L., Armengol, R., Brooke, L. B., Carper, K. R., Cronin, S. M., & Denman, A. C., et al. (1999). Teachers' choices in classroom assessment. In S. J. Barrentine (Ed.), *Reading assessment: Principles and practices for elementary teachers* (pp. 68–72). Newark, DE: International Reading Association.

Paris, S. (2000). Trojan horse in the schoolyard: The hidden threats in high-stakes testing. *Issues in Education, 6,* 1–16.

Perrone, V. (1990). How did we get here? In C. Kamii (Ed.), *Achievement testing in the early grades: The games grown-ups play* (pp. 1–14). Washington, DC: National Association for the Education of Young Children.

Salinger, T., & Chittenden, E. (1994). Analysis of an early literacy portfolio: Consequence for instruction. *Language Arts, 71,* 446–452.

Shepard, L. A. (1991). The influence of standardized tests on early childhood curriculum, teachers, and children. In B. Spodek & O. N. Saracho (Eds.), *Yearbook in early childhood education* (Vol. 2, pp. 295–305). New York: Teachers College Press.

Shepard, L. A. (1994). The challenges of assessing young children appropriately. *Phi Delta Kappan, 76,* 206–213.

Shepard, L. A. (1997). Children not ready to learn? The invalidity of school readiness testing. *Psychology in the Schools, 34,* 85–97.

Shepard, L. A. (2000). The role of assessment in a learning culture. *Educational Researcher, 29*(7), 1–14.

Shepard, L. A., Flexer, R. J., Hiebert, E. H., Marion, S. F., Mayfield, V., & Weston, J. T. (1996). Effects of introducing classroom performance assessments on student learning. *Educational Measurement: Issues and Practice, 15*(3), 7–18.

Stanovich, K. E. (1984). The interactive-compensatory model of reading: A confluence of developmental, experimental, and educational psychology. *Remedial and Special Education, 5*(1), 11–19.

Sulzby, E. (1991). Assessment of emergent literacy: Storybook reading. *The Reading Teacher, 44,* 498–500.

Taylor, B. M., Pearson, P. D., Clark, K., & Walpole, S. (2000). Effective schools and accomplished teachers: Lessons about primary grade reading instruction in low income schools. *Elementary School Journal, 101,* 121–166.

Teale, W. H., & Sulzby, E. (Eds.). (1986). *Emergent literacy: Writing and reading.* Norwood, NJ: Ablex.

Valencia, S. W., & Place, N. A. (1994). Literacy portfolios for teaching, learning, and accountability: The Bellevue Literacy Assessment Project. In S. W. Valencia, E. H. Hiebert, & P. P. Afflerbach (Eds.), *Authentic reading assessment: Practices and possibilities* (pp. 134–156). Newark, DE: International Reading Association

Valencia, S. W., & Wixson, K. K. (1999). *Policy-oriented research on literacy standards and assessments* (CIERA Report No. 3–004). Ann Arbor: University of Michigan Center for the Improvement of Early Reading Achievement.

Venezky, R. L., & Winfield, L. (1979). *Schools that succeed beyond expectations in teaching reading* (Technical Report No. 1). Newark, DE: Department of Educational Studies, University of Delaware.

15

Single Instrument, Multiple Measures: Considering the Use of Multiple Item Formats to Assess Reading Comprehension

Jay R. Campbell
Educational Testing Service

As with any endeavor in the area of educational measurement, assessing reading comprehension with a single test necessarily poses some limitations. Among the threats to reliability and validity in the use of a single instrument is the possibility that the content of the test does not fully represent the construct, and that the test taker is in some way disadvantaged due to the range of content that may be represented. The goal of the test developer is always to maximize the representativeness of the content sampled for the test, making it possible to generalize results to the content domain.

Of course, the task would be easier if the test developer could utilize unlimited testing time, materials, and procedures to ensure the broadest possible domain coverage. The reality, however, is that tests must be developed that represent a balance between breadth and depth of domain coverage with the practical considerations of testing time and test-taker burden. In the current educational reform and testing policy environment, this is increasingly a real concern. More and more, single instruments are being used to track student progress, monitor effectiveness of reading programs, and hold educators accountable for learning outcomes.

How then can we measure reading comprehension with single instruments that maximize the interpretive value of test results? Moreover, given that available testing time and resources are not unlimited, what are the construct-relevant features that should be accounted for in a measure of reading comprehension? Two features are most apparent—the types of comprehension processes expected to be demonstrated by test takers, and the types of reading passages or texts that test takers are expected to be able to read and comprehend. In a blueprint for test development, these two features are typically accounted for in a process-by-content matrix that details the proportion of testing time to be devoted to each.

There is little debate that a range of comprehension processes and text types should be represented on a single instrument measuring reading comprehension. Although they vary from instrument to instrument, the process components of most test blueprints typically account for such cognitive processes as recall, inference, interpretation, and evaluation. Few educators would be willing to place much interpretative value on test results based on an instrument that did not include some range, if not hierarchy, of reading processes in the comprehension questions posed to test takers. Similarly, most educators undoubtedly expect that a valid assessment of reading comprehension will include a range of text types (e.g., literary, expository, informative) to ensure complete domain coverage. Ensuring the representation of comprehension processes and text types on an assessment is very much about ensuring the generalizability of test results to the domain of reading comprehension.

One feature of testing that is not always accounted for to the same degree in reading comprehension test blueprints is the mode of response that test takers will use to demonstrate their comprehension abilities. Indeed, the response mode most typically utilized on standardized tests of any subject area is one that requires test takers to answer a question by selecting from a list of optional responses—the multiple-choice item format. The usefulness of this rather economical and reliable item format for assessing most educational constructs is widely accepted. Despite ongoing criticisms from some educators, it remains the mainstay of standardized testing—and with good reason. Numerous validity studies over decades have continued to demonstrate the validity and usefulness of this response mode—not to mention the clear advantage in terms of reliability and efficiency in scoring.

The question posed by this chapter and the focus of the research highlighted is whether relying solely on a multiple-choice item format to assess reading comprehension poses any threat to the validity of assessment. More specifically, is the coverage of the domain (i.e., reading comprehension) at all threatened by the use of a single mode of response? Is anything gained by using multiple modes of response on a single test of reading comprehension? Are test takers advantaged or disadvantaged in any way by reliance on a single mode of response? These questions become more compelling as test developers and test users feel pressured by high-stakes accountability testing to ensure the most objective instrument possible. In such an environment, it would be fair to ask if using a less objective (more open-ended) response mode is really necessary to ensure the validity of test-score interpretations.

ADVANTAGES AND CRITICISMS OF MULTIPLE-CHOICE ITEM FORMAT

There are solid psychometric, economic, and fairness rationales for the ubiquitous use of the multiple-choice format for assessing educational constructs. First, the reliability of scoring procedures may be viewed as a major advantage over subjective and impressionistic methods for rating test-taker performance. It may be assumed that a response format in which predetermined correct answers are identified, and in which test takers are given a standard set of options from which to choose the correct answer, should minimize the disadvantages inherent in procedures that require subjective, human rating. Consequently, the multiple-choice format may be viewed as potentially more fair to individual test takers. Second, because multiple-choice questions can typically be answered quickly, more questions can be included in a single test, increasing the potential for maximizing coverage of the domain being assessed. Third, rather sophisticated statistical analyses procedures (e.g., Item Response Theory or IRT) may extend the potential interpretations that can be made from scores on tests using multiple-choice questions. Finally, the ease and cost-efficiency of scoring multiple-choice questions clearly offers faster and cheaper score reporting (Bennett & Ward, 1993, p. ix).

Nevertheless, restriction of response has been a concern voiced by some critics as long as there has been multiple-choice testing. These concerns may have reached a crescendo in the early 1990s, when the enterprise of educational testing was very much influenced by calls for more authentic, real-world, performance-based methods. For example, Resnick and Resnick (1992) argued strongly that multiple-choice testing is a remnant of outdated views of thinking and learning processes. They described the assumptions underlying this item format as being responsible for causing a "decomposability" and "decontextualization" of the curriculum in which cognitive abilities were being taught and assessed as collections of isolated skills independent of contexts in which they might be applied. In contrast, they argued that the higher-order thinking skills, which should be the goal of instruction, are more than simply a sum of skills and are highly contextualized.

In their use as a tool for measuring reading comprehension, multiple-choice questions received additional and more specific criticism. Some critics suggested that the ability to select the correct answer from a list of options may have little to do with students' reading comprehension abilities. In fact, some studies have produced results indicating that test takers perform equally well on reading comprehension multiple-choice questions without actually reading the passages associated with them, or that multiple-choice item difficulty has less to do with the reading passage and more do to with nonpassage factors (Katz & Lautenschlager, 2001; Katz, Lautenschlager, Blackburn, & Harris, 1990). Moreover, some researchers and educators were concerned about the implications for reading instruction, suggesting that repeated exposure to these types of tests could lead students to develop artificial reading strategies that are counterproductive in actual reading experiences (Winograd, Paris, & Bridge, 1991).

The most often cited criticism of multiple-choice testing in reading assessment has been that a single, correct answer to a comprehension question must be identified. Clearly, many theories of reading would seem to contradict this notion. For example, prior knowledge may be viewed as a critical part of the reader's interpretations of a text. But, as Valencia and Pearson (1987) pointed out, "The diversity in prior knowledge across individuals as well as the varied causal relations in human experiences invite many possible inferences to fit a test or question" (p. 731). Consequently, forcing test takers to select a predetermined correct answer, even when at least some of the "incorrect" options may be plausible from divergent perspectives, could be viewed as resulting in test scores that do not accurately reflect the extent to which test takers may be able to construct meaning from text.

In one review of several large-scale standardized tests of reading comprehension, Murphy (1998) concluded that most suffered from serious flaws related to quality of texts, items, and the interaction of text and items. She categorized the items in six different standardized tests in terms of their textual focus, and determined that 22% to 53% of the items required no focus on continuous discourse. The majority of items focused only on meaning that resided at a sentence, phrasal, or word level. She concluded that "the standardized tests of the early 1990s appear to be operating with a very restricted definition of reading …" (p. 55).

ITEM FORMAT VALIDITY STUDIES

As described earlier, there are many sound reasons why the multiple-choice item format became so widespread in standardized educational testing. Perhaps because of its ubiquitous use, the multiple-choice item format has been the focus of extensive validity research. For many researchers, questions about the usefulness of this format for assessing higher-order, critical thinking skills was a driving force behind their studies. A recurring question has been whether multiple-choice questions impose undesirable measurement constraints that are not present when test questions are formatted to allow a free or open-ended response from the test taker. And more generally, are the two item formats equivalent in terms of their measurement value and the underlying construct being assessed by either?

The summary of results from studies examining the comparability of multiple-choice and constructed-response item formats, or the validity of either type, may be viewed as somewhat inconclusive. Are the two item formats comparable in assessing educational constructs? During the last four decades, some researchers found few or no differences in how the two item formats functioned (Bracht & Hopkins, 1970; Choppin & Purves, 1969; van den Bergh, 1990; Weiss & Jackson, 1983). Other researchers, however, did uncover differences in the amount or type of information about test takers' abilities revealed through the different item formats (Birenbaum & Tatsuoka, 1987; Heim & Watts, 1967; Manhart, 1996; Ward, Frederiksen, & Carlson, 1980).

Many of the studies conducted to examine the usefulness or comparability of multiple-choice and constructed-response item formats have relied primarily on statistical methods. For example, Bridgeman and Rock (1993) used factor analyses of test scores on the Graduate Record Examination (GRE) General Test to determine that open-ended and multiple-choice versions of the same analytical test items were measuring essentially the same construct. Similarly, Lukhele, Thissen, and Wainer (1994) concluded, using IRT methods, that "there is no evidence to indicate that these two kinds of questions are measuring fundamentally different things, at least for domains such as those represented by AP chemistry or U.S. history" (p. 245). A factor-analytic approach used by Manhart (1996), however, did uncover a significant distinction between the two item formats.

Other studies conducted specifically in the context of assessing reading have failed to produce a definitive answer to the item-format comparability issue. For example, Ward, Dupree, and Carlson (1987) administered equivalent sets of multiple-choice and constructed-response reading comprehension questions to college students. Their exploratory factor analysis revealed only a weak effect, suggesting that there were minimal differences in the constructs being assessed by the two types of items. van den Bergh (1990) investigated the possibility that different intellectual abilities were involved in answering multiple-choice and constructed-response reading questions. He examined the relation between third-graders' scores on equivalent multiple-choice and constructed-response reading questions, and their scores on a series of tests of semantic abilities based on Guildford's structure of the intellect (SI) model. Because none of the SI abilities were differentially related to item type, van den Bergh concluded that "students seem to construct their answers to multiple-choice items to the same degree as when they answer open-ended reading comprehension items" (p. 10). Relying on sophisticated IRT scaling procedures to examine the dimensions of reading comprehension measured by multiple-choice and constructed-response item types on the 1992 National Assessment of Educational Progress (NAEP), Mazzeo, Yamamoto, and Kulick (1993) did conclude, however, that "... the inclusion of the extended constructed-response items probably provide a broader definition of the achievement construct implicitly defined by the item pool" (p. 23).

PROCESS VALIDITY AND ITEM FORMAT

The issue of how well the construct is represented by the content of a test is central to test validity. Construct representation may be studied through a variety of methods—from simple correlations between scores on equivalent tests to more sophistical modeling and scaling procedures. Reading comprehension may be viewed as a unique construct among the many that are typically assessed with educational tests. It is, perhaps, a construct that has more to do with process than the accumulation of a knowledge base. As such, questions about the construct representation of reading assessment instruments (including the usefulness of different item formats) must always include some focus on the cognitive processes underlying test-taker performance.

Lindquist (1951) pointed to the importance of this type of validity investigation when he stated that "the most important consideration is that the test questions require the examinee to do the same things, however complex, that he is required to do in the criterion situations" (p. 154). Similarly, Embretson (1983) proposed that considerations of content representativeness in judging validity must include examinations of process representation. That is, validity studies should determine the degree to which processes elicited by assessment tasks adequately represent the range and depth of processes associated with the construct being measured. Messick (1989) also emphasized the analyses of processes underlying item or task performance in his seminal discussion of validity in educational measurement.

It would seem then, with regard to item format, one aspect of construct representation to be considered is whether the use of a single item format restricts the demonstration of reading processes on a measure of reading comprehension. Furthermore, if the use of a single item format restricts the range of processes engaged by test takers, does that restriction truly result in construct underrepresentation? How can we answer this question? It would certainly take more than one study, and more than one method. Many of the studies cited earlier may be viewed as addressing this issue, at least in part, through statistical procedures (e.g., factor analyses, regression models, scaling procedures). These represent important methods of inquiry that provide many of the pieces to the assessment puzzle. Yet another route to investigating issues of process validity involves a more direct, albeit less quantitative, approach—that would be asking test takers to reveal the thinking processes they are engaging while answering reading comprehension test questions.

The use of protocol analysis or "think-alouds" has been used extensively to investigate the cognitive processes associated with a variety of activities, from creative productions to problem-solving tasks. As a tool for reading researchers, think-aloud procedures have proven to be invaluable for exploring and describing the processes of reading (Afflerbach & Johnston, 1984; Kucan & Beck, 1997; Pritchard, 1990). Pressley and Afflerbach (1995) compiled an extensive inventory of reading processes that have been revealed through think-aloud procedures. Researchers who use this methodology are often guided by the suggestions made by Ericsson and Simon (1984/1993) in designing their protocols. Ericsson and Simon argued that, with appropriate controls, asking the participant to tell what he or she is thinking as he or she completes a particular task can reveal important thinking processes underlying task completion without seriously altering those processes.

Several studies have been conducted using this methodology to investigate processes and strategies associated with reading tests. A few that have focused on the issue of item format are worth noting. Each examined the issue in slightly different ways and with different research questions. But, together they begin to build a knowledge base of the effects of item format on construct representation—in particular, process validity—in assessing reading comprehension.

Langer (1987) administered one portion of a standardized reading comprehension test to 26 third graders. As students read the assessment passage, they were periodically asked to describe what they were thinking about the text—their evolving "envisionment" of the text. Subsequently, the multiple-choice comprehension questions were presented without the response options, and participants were asked to provide an answer. Participants were then shown the response options and asked to explain why they preferred one of the options over the others.

The students in this study often selected incorrect options based on what the researcher considered to be plausible interpretations of the text. Langer (1987) observed that some students appeared to be disadvantaged by the multiple-choice questions, in that they were unable to demonstrate their under-standing of the text through the selection of the supplied options. Based on how students discussed the passage as they were reading and their subsequent selec-tion of multiple-choice response options, Langer concluded that "standardized tests do not measure the processes involved in the construction of meaning from a text nor do they evaluate an individual's ability to manage those processes" (p. 243).

Farr, Pritchard, and Smitten (1990) used retrospective and introspective think-alouds to examine the thought processes of 26 college seniors in reading a passage and answering multiple-choice questions on a test of reading compre-hension. Few differences were observed between passage reading or question answering in the strategies used by the participants. Generally, the strategies ap-peared to be driven by the test questions. That is, participants tended to rely on the questions to direct their searching or skimming of the passages to locate an-swers to the multiple-choice questions. Little attention seemed to be given to overall understanding of the passage.

The researchers suggested that the reading strategies observed may have lit-tle resemblance to what readers typically do during nontest situations. They emphasized, however, that searching text for specific information is a common strategy used in reading expository or informative texts—the type of reading that characterizes most school reading experiences. Thus, they concluded that "the study supports the construct validity of multiple-choice reading compre-hension tests for one general kind of reading task, but that the relation of such tests to other particular reading tasks is left unanswered" (Farr et al., p. 224).

Cordón and Day (1996) examined the differences in reading strategies used by high school sophomores and juniors who anticipated answering multiple-choice questions after reading a passage and those who simply were asked to read the passage for overall meaning (a more naturalistic reading situation). To examine these differences, they administered a reading test to 128 participants in two con-ditions: (a) reading passage with multiple-choice questions, presented as a typical standardized reading test, and (b) reading passage with multiple-choice questions replaced by a single question about the passage's main idea.

The results of their think-aloud procedure indicated that these subjects used significantly more strategies in the typical standardized test condition than when being asked simply to read for overall meaning. Participants in the stan-dardized test condition were more likely to reread, paraphrase text, and draw on prior knowledge to understand the text than participants in the overall mean-ing condition. It was interesting to note, however, that although the amount of strategy use differed between the two conditions, the actual pattern of strategy use was similar. The researchers concluded that, "perhaps the standardized reading test is not as artificial a task as some of its detractors would suggest" (Cordón and Day, 1996, p. 292).

Yet another study conducted by the author utilized stem-equivalent multiple-choice and constructed-response questions to examine the influence of item format on cognitive processes engaged by eighth graders on an assessment of reading comprehension (Campbell, 1999). The use of stem-equivalent items allowed for a study of item format effects while controlling for content. This may be an important variable in making comparisons between item format, because test developers who use both format types tend to rely on one or the other for particular skills. Without controlling for content, the results of any comparative study may have as much to do with differences in content as with differences in response format.

For the purpose of this investigation, 74 eighth graders from a large, urban school district were asked to "think aloud" as they answered a combination of both item types. Twelve pairs of stem-equivalent items, six pairs accompanying a literary text and six pairs accompanying an informative text, comprised the instrument used in this study. The stem-equivalent items and their accompanying texts were randomly assigned across participants to ensure that individual participants were not answering the same question twice in different formats. Each participant took both a set of literary and a set of informative questions—counterbalanced across participants to control for order and placement effects. Participants were asked to think aloud after they had read the passage and began answering the set of comprehension questions following the passage.

Across the entire set of items in this study, the constructed-response version of comprehension questions was more likely, on average, to elicit a higher-level process of constructive thinking about the text. That is, slightly more than half of the think-aloud protocols associated with items formatted as constructed-response questions demonstrated an attempt to connect ideas across the text to make an interpretation, to infer meaning, to evaluate information, or to generalize across specific ideas. For the multiple-choice versions of these same questions, such processes were observed less than one third of the time. It should be pointed out that not all the questions required such a high-level of thinking process, and some could be answered with simple recall. This is an important attribute of reading questions that must be considered in such comparability studies.

Examining the individual pairs of stem-equivalent items more closely, however, revealed that the apparent advantage of a constructed-response format on average did not hold true for certain types of questions. Moreover, there appeared to be some item-format-by-text interaction, wherein the item-format effect seemed more apparent among the informative text comprehension questions, and much less so among the literary text comprehension questions. It may be that the issue of process validity and item format is quite complex—one that involves considerations of text type, item-text interactions, and of course, individual test-taker differences.

At this point in the discussion, however, it would be more interesting perhaps to see exactly what it was that students said they were thinking about as they answered the multiple-choice and constructed-response questions in this study.

Profiles of Two Eighth Graders' Thinking Processes in Answering Multiple-Choice and Constructed-Response Reading Comprehension Test Questions

This qualitative analysis of two eighth graders' thinking processes reveals the potential for individual test taker differences in the item format effects described earlier. The first participant profiled is an African American male eighth grader who performed quite well on the set of questions he answered, receiving full credit for each of his responses. The second participant profiled is an African American female eighth grader who was only able to answer half of the questions correctly.

Profile of High-Performing Test Taker. For this participant, returning to the stimulus passage was a common strategy during his initial consideration of each question. Regardless of the item format, he almost always indicated that he was looking back through the text immediately after reading the question. His use of textual support, however, varied somewhat depending on the format of the item. With several of the constructed-response questions, he returned to the text, sometimes a second time, to confirm his answer or to search for additional support to use in his written answer. He did not rely on the text for confirmation after deciding on an answer to the multiple-choice questions. Instead, identifying one of the options that came close to his preconceived answer appeared to be sufficient confirmation.

As an example of these subtle differences, two excerpts from his verbal reports based on the literary passage questions are presented. The first shows this participant's thinking about a multiple-choice question. The second shows his thinking about a constructed-response question. The complete questions are presented, followed by the transcript of his verbal reports.

Multiple-Choice Question:
What does the phrase "brandishing a pistol" mean in the story?
  A. Cleaning its barrel
  B. Carefully aiming it at a moving target

C. Holding it in a threatening manner [correct option]

D. Loading ammunition into it

Transcript of Verbal Report:

Student: *First I'm thinking about brandishing a pistol—what does it mean—I know it has something to do with holding it—swinging it or something.*

Researcher: [What's going through your head?]

Student: *Brandishing—I think cleaning—it has something to do with cleaning—I'm going back to see if I can find it in the story.*

Researcher: [What's going through your head as you're doing that?]

Student: *I remember a part where it says a soldier walks up to her, points a gun at her—I went back—thinking—holding it in a threatening manner.*

Researcher: [What thoughts did you have?]

Student: *Cause I was thinking—cleaning a barrel—but they didn't do that awhile ago back in the old days—I guess he says—brandishing a pistol and looking at her cruelly, so I guess he was holding it in a threatening manner.*

Constructed-Response Question:

For Anne Frank, what was "the something I can do"?

Transcript of Verbal Report:

Student: *It says for Anne Frank, what was the something that I can do.*

Researcher: [What's going through your head right now?]

Student: *I'm going back to read the story, cause I don't remember it.*

Researcher: [What are you thinking?]

Student: *What that has to do with the story—the something that I can do—I guess the something that she can do is write a diary and hope that someone will find it if she ever got caught and know it was wrong to hate the Jews.*

Researcher: [Other thoughts with number 2?]

Student: *Yea, I was thinking, maybe she wrote the diary, hoping maybe—I just thought she wrote the diary just in case something happened to her—someone would find it, try to stop what was going on—now, I'm going back to read it to see if there are any mistakes, see if there's anything more I want to put down.*

Differences between the two item formats in this student's thinking processes were not overwhelming for the entire set of questions he answered. With each of the questions he answered about the literary text, there was some evidence of interpretation or inferencing in answering both the multiple-choice and the constructed-response questions. However, the manner in which these constructive thinking processes unfolded differed slightly. With the multiple-choice questions, he seemed to be "filtering" his thinking about the text through the options. That is, he used the language of the options to reconstruct his own thinking about the text. In the multiple-choice example shown earlier, the participant indicates he had the response option in mind when he returned to that part of the text ("I went back—thinking—holding it in a threatening manner"). Here, he would seem to be using the portion of the text in which the phrase "brandishing a pistol" appears to evaluate the option he has tentatively selected as his answer. It did not appear that he simply recognized the correct answer; rather, he used at least two of the options provided to reconstruct his thinking about the text.

The level of engagement this participant demonstrated with the literary passage questions was not nearly as apparent in his thinking about the informative passage questions. The following two excerpts from this participant's think-aloud reports based on the informative passage questions illustrate this difference in text engagement.

Constructed-Response Question:
What was one of the most important legacies that Dorothea Dix left to us?

Transcript of Verbal Report:
Researcher: [What are you thinking with number 1?]
Student: *About what this lady did—what did she achieve.*
Researcher: [What's going through your head?]
Student: *I'm trying to remember the story—go back to the story—the main idea—I'm going back to the story.*
Researcher: [What's going through your head as you're doing that?]
Student: *I'm trying to see if I can come up with any more to support my answer.*
Researcher: [Any more thoughts?]
Student: *No, not really.*

Multiple-Choice Question:
What was one of Dorothea Dix's goals that was mentioned in the passage?

A. Establishing a trust fund for teachers of people with mental illness
B. Finding a cure for mental illness
C. Establishing asylums in Russia and Turkey
D. Getting national laws enacted to improve living conditions in asylums [correct option]

Transcript of Verbal Report:

Researcher: [What's going through your head now?]

Student: *Just reading the question—now, I'm going back to find something in the story.*

Researcher: [What's going through your head as you're doing that?]

Student: *Skimming the paragraphs—trying to find—trying to find important things she did.*

Researcher: [What thoughts did you have?]

Student: *Well, I found something important—I looked for the main idea—I guess that's what it was asking for—I found a couple things—then I found one that was important—tried to connect it to one of the answers.*

Possible reasons for the difference in engagement between the literary and informative sets of comprehension questions may include genre or text effects. That is, the participant may simply not have been as deeply engaged or interested in the informative text as he was with the literary text. There may also have been a fatigue factor involved because his informative questions came during the last half of his testing session. It may also be possible that the set of questions associated with the informative text, regardless of format, were simply not written in a manner that elicited from him the constructive thinking processes that were evidenced in his thinking about the literary passage questions. Whatever the reason, this high-performing participant's verbal reports on the literary passage questions showed only subtle format effects, whereas his verbal reports on the informative passage questions showed little or no such effects.

Profile of Average-Performing Test Taker. This average-performing participant responded to the same set of comprehension questions as the previously profiled participant. Her verbal reports also reveal some item format effects, but clearly different from those observed with the high-performing participant.

In response to the literary passage questions, this average-performing participant demonstrated little or no focus on the text in her thinking about the comprehension questions. Only minimal references to the text were observed. For the most part, she attempted to answer the questions without thinking about or returning to the passage. Furthermore, the format of the individual item did not seem to influence her engagement with the text. The following two excerpts from her verbal reports on the literary passage questions demonstrate this.

Multiple-Choice Question:

What does the phrase "brandishing a pistol" mean in the story?
   A. Cleaning its barrel
   B. Carefully aiming it at a moving target
   C. Holding it in a threatening manner [correct option]
   D. Loading ammunition into it

Transcript of Verbal Report:

Researcher: [What are you thinking about with question number 1?]

Student: *Carefully aiming it at a moving target—Holding it in a threatening manner.*

Researcher: [Can you tell me what you were thinking?]

Student: *Well, basically—when they say brandishing a pistol—means probably pointing it at her face—probably pointing at something they don't got no business pointing at.*

Constructed-Response Question:

For Anne Frank, what was "the something I can do"?

Transcript of Verbal Report:

Student: *Something she can do means—she probably can do a lot—Well, maybe she didn't think she could do.*

Researcher: [Can you tell me what you were thinking?]

Student: *I was thinking about the something that I can do—in the poem it said something that I can do—you can do it, do it—so that means whatever she could do, she probably had did it.*

Only minimal engagement with the passage content is seen in these two excerpts from her thinking about the literary passage questions. As shown in the following excerpts from her verbal reports based on the informative passage questions, however, the degree of her focus on the text increased.

Constructed-Response Question:

What was one of the most important legacies that Dorothea Dix left to us?

Transcript of Verbal Report:

Student: *She left them to think that mentally ill was not a crime—they took the people who were sick and they built a lot of mentally ill hospitals, all because she had died—they thought of her and they—when they build the hospitals—she left them a lot—she left them that mentally ill was not bad—and after she died—they built the mentally ill hospitals.*

Researcher: [Any other thoughts with question number 1?]

Student: *No.*

Multiple-Choice Question:

What was one of Dorothea Dix's goals that was mentioned in the passage?
  A. Establishing a trust fund for teachers of people with mental illness
  B. Finding a cure for mental illness
  C. Establishing asylums in Russia and Turkey
  D. Getting national laws enacted to improve living conditions in asylums [correct option]

Transcript of Verbal Report:

Student: *One of her goals was to keep the mentally ill—not to think of them bad—and she was teaching people with mentally ill—that was her goal. I think it's number A, establishing a trust fund for teachers with mentally ill—no, finding a cure for mentally illness—that's what I think number 2 is.*

Researcher: [Can you tell me what you were thinking?]

Student: *Because she did a lot for the mentally ill people and if you could find a cure for that, then wouldn't be mental illness.*

On the set of comprehension questions associated with the informative passage, this participant's focus on text increased. As shown earlier, her thinking about the first informative question moved easily from a focus on local text meaning to a causal inference about text ideas. Having constructed some interpretive understanding with the first question, she relied on this interpretation to begin thinking about the next question. The understanding she had developed with the first question, however, did not fit well with the second question. As a consequence, she selected an incorrect answer without thoughtful consideration of all the options, or further consideration of the text.

The following two items that this participant answered (excerpts from verbal reports not shown) revealed a similar pattern. The next question after the multiple-choice question shown earlier required a constructed response. It had a totally different content focus, and the participant returned to the text to construct a new understanding. Her thinking on this question moved from a focus on global text meaning to an appropriate connective interpretation of local text meaning. This resulted in her being able to provide an appropriate written response. However, the next question, formatted as a multiple-choice item, was about a part of the text that she did not recall or understand. Consequently, she selected an incorrect option based on a key term she recognized from the passage.

For this average-performing test taker, there appeared to have been some format effects in the thinking processes elicited by the informative passage questions. She displayed more text focus and more constructive thinking on the constructed-response questions than she did on the multiple-choice questions. It may also be of note that she was more successful with the constructed-response questions—receiving full credit to all of her responses to the constructed-response items, and providing an incorrect answer to each of the multiple-choice questions. With the informative passage questions, this participant tended to select a multiple-choice option as her answer without careful consideration of the text. In contrast, the lack of options from which to choose on the constructed-response questions appeared to force her to consider the text and to engage in deeper thinking about text ideas to construct an answer.

Summary of Test Taker Profiles.   The thinking processes engaged by these two profiled test takers were quite different. Moreover, the item format effects observed were different for each participant. For the high-performing participant, the format effect seemed to be one of seeking textual support to confirm his answer. With the constructed-response questions, he typically returned to the text a second time to look for additional support to verify his answer. With the multiple-choice questions, he appeared to rely on the options for confirmation—in some sense, the options helped to scaffold and direct his thinking about the text. Conversely, the average-performing participant featured in the second profile appeared to have been disadvantaged at times by the multiple-choice questions. At least with the informative passage questions, she was more likely to think about the text or return to the text when answering constructed-response questions. This forced interaction with text would seem to have contributed to her greater success with the constructed-response questions.

Item Format As a Construct Representation Issue

Many of the studies cited earlier that explored item format effects framed the issue as one of comparability. Conclusions from these studies included statements like the following:

- There is no evidence to indicate that these two kinds of questions are measuring fundamentally different things.
- The two item formats appear to be equivalent or nearly so.
- The multiple-choice and constructed-response items appear to assess the same characteristics.

The point to be made here is that comparability of item formats should not be viewed as the only issue. In fact, to ensure an acceptable degree of homogeneity on a test of reading comprehension, different item formats should not be assessing completely different constructs. If one item format is assessing a different construct from the other, then perhaps one should be excluded. Ideally, a single test of reading comprehension is composed of items that all measure the same construct (i.e., reading comprehension). The argument could be made that it is not a question of whether the item formats are equivalent or that they measure different constructs, but rather does the use of a single item format narrow the definition of the construct undesirably—and conversely, does the use of more than one item format broaden the definition of the construct being measured to a desirable degree?

If we rely on studies that demonstrate the equivalence of multiple-choice and constructed-response item formats in assessing reading comprehension to argue against the use of the more expensive and time-consuming constructed-response formats, it could be that we have missed an important point. Reading comprehension is not a neat and easily defined construct. This may be one reason why there have always been so many conflicting theories on the nature and development of reading comprehension. The process of gaining meaning from text and demonstrating that understanding is very much influenced by individual factors. Cognitive style, prior knowledge, personal interest, and level of engagement are among the many individual characteristics that can influence the way someone approaches a reading situation—and thus, can influence the way reading comprehension performance is demonstrated on a measurement instrument.

This is clearly why most test developers would never rely on a single passage to measure someone's ability to comprehend text. The need to present a variety of texts in terms of topic, genre, difficulty, language use, or structure, on a single reading assessment instrument, is well understood and accepted. If reading ability was measured with the use of only one passage, we understand well why it could not be a valid measurement for all test takers. The nature of any one text could present disadvantages to certain test takers due to issues like level of interest or variance in related prior knowledge. Could we not view the issue of item format similarly?

The studies cited earlier that relied on protocol analysis (think-aloud) methods help to make this point. None of them seemed to suggest that the multiple-choice format was completely devoid of any measurement value for assessing reading comprehension. For example, Farr, Pritchard, and Smitten (1990) made it clear that they felt the processes test takers used to answer the multiple-choice questions were a good representation of one type of reading situation—but, they went on to make the point that it is questionable whether these processes can be generalized further to other reading situations. Here, the possibility of construct underrepresentation seems clear. Even Langer (1987), whose conclusions seemed most negative with regard to the multiple-choice format, seemed to concede that not all children were disadvantaged by this format type.

The excerpts of two students' verbal reports and the profiling of their cognitive processes from the Campbell (1999) study would seem to make this point in a very concrete, albeit more anecdotal, manner. Of particular note in this qualitative analysis of the cognitive processes elicited by two eighth graders on an assessment of reading comprehension was the fact that the lower performing student, in fact, appeared to gain some advantage from having to provide a written response. She was encouraged to think about the text and attempt to understand it to provide a response to the constructed-response items. With the multiple-choice items, she seemed comfortable to use a less mentally strenuous approach. For this test taker, a single test composed of only multiple-choice questions may not have provided enough incentive for her to truly demonstrate the full range of her comprehension abilities.

Beyond the possible advantages and disadvantages of item format for individual test takers, it should also be considered that focusing on the issue of comparability between item formats narrows our view of the construct from the start. If we are only concerned that they are comparable in their measurement value, we may be ignoring the common sense notion that there simply are facets of comprehension that cannot be assessed with multiple-choice questions. In defining the construct of reading comprehension, do we want to include the ability to find textual support of an interpretation or evaluation? Do we value the ability to connect text information to information beyond the text? Can more than one interpretation be acceptable and supported by the same text? Is it desirable that readers be able to paraphrase, evaluate arguments, compare and contrast information, or critique the quality of a text in their own words? If the answer is affirmative to any of these questions, how then can we ignore the possibility that relying solely on multiple-choice questions to assess reading comprehension may result in an underrepresentation of the construct?

IMPLICATIONS OF MULTIPLE ITEM FORMATS IN ASSESSING READING COMPREHENSION

The main argument put forth here is that the question of item format should not be an either–or proposition. It would seem that the lack of conclusiveness in findings regarding the comparability of multiple-choice and constructed-response item formats, or their respective advantages, in assessing reading comprehension, suggests that the study of item format effects should be moved beyond whether one or the other needs to be excluded. There may be strong economic and efficiency reasons for wanting to rely solely on multiple-choice questions. There may be strong reasons related to instructional consequences for wanting to rely solely on constructed-response questions. Perhaps it is time, however, to recognize the advantages and disadvantages of both item formats— and begin to focus on how each can be better used to maximize the construct representation of reading assessment and to maximize the opportunities for individual test takers to demonstrate their reading abilities.

A combination of carefully crafted multiple-choice and constructed-response questions may be the most valid approach to assessing reading comprehension. The problem is that item format decisions are not always grounded in a solid research-based understanding of which format is most appropriate for particular skills or abilities. When distributions of item format are specified in a test blueprint, it is often simply a statement of the overall percentage of items that should be formatted in a particular manner. It typically does not go on to provide the test developer with information about how item format decisions should be made or how the range of skills and abilities should be distributed across item format types.

We may already have some information (based in part on common sense) about what types of comprehension skills are best assessed by either format. But this knowledge has not been formalized in any way. If we knew, for example, that comprehension questions intended to assess global understanding were more likely to elicit the desired cognitive process when formatted as a constructed-response item, or that vocabulary knowledge was best assessed through multiple-choice questions, this could be an important guiding principle for test developers—and thus, should be accounted for in the test specifications. Until we have such a solid research base, it may be useful for test developers to incorporate investigations of process validity into their test development procedures. For example, the administration of pilot test items in one-on-one think-aloud sessions to determine how students are likely to answer the question could be just as important as having yet another test developer or committee of experts review the item for content validity.

As further research is conducted in this area, several unanswered questions stand out. First, we know that reading test items cannot be evaluated independent from the passage; their effectiveness and validity are very much dependent on their relation to the text. Future studies of item format effects should include a broad range of stimulus materials to control for possible text effects and item-text interactions. Second, it is very likely that developmental differences influence the effect of item format. Studies should be conducted on more than one age group or grade level to examine this issue. Relatedly, it would be important to investigate format effects in relation to test-taker proficiency. As demonstrated in the profiling of test-taker thinking presented earlier in this chapter, the effect of item format on test takers of differing abilities may not be as expected. Some have argued that requiring students to provide a written response may disadvantage lower performing students who would find the combination of reading and writing a detriment to their being able to demonstrate their reading abilities. As shown in that one example, however, the lower performing student in fact had greater success with the constructed-response questions than with the multiple-choice questions. But, clearly, this issue needs further research and investigation.

In conclusion, let us remind ourselves that the enterprise of educational measurement should have as its goal more than just the assigning of a numeric value to a person or a group of people. Most of us recognize that we are called on as researchers, educators, and test developers to support the educational achievement of all students. Assessment is fundamental to education in that it guides policy decisions, holds education systems and educators accountable, assists teachers in making instructional decisions, and provides feedback to students and parents. With so much depending on the assessment instruments we develop and use, it is imperative that we remain relentless in our pursuit of the most useful, valid, and fair methods for measuring educational constructs. Although we must always balance the pragmatic constraints of testing time and resources with the ability to maximize the interpretative value of our testing instruments, we must be sure that the procedures we use are informed fully by research, theory, and concern for the impact on individuals.

REFERENCES

Afflerbach, P., & Johnston, P. (1984). Research methodology: On the use of verbal reports in reading research. *Journal of Reading Behavior, 16,* 307–322.

Bennett, R. E., & Ward, C. W. (Eds.). (1993). *Construction versus choice in cognitive measurement: Issues in constructed response, performance testing, and portfolio assessment.* Hillsdale, NJ: Lawrence Erlbaum Associates.

Birenbaum, M., & Tatsuoka, K. K. (1987). Open-ended versus multiple-choice response formats: It does make a difference for diagnostic purposes. *Applied Psychological Measurement, 11,* 385–395.

Bracht, G. H., & Hopkins, K. D. (1970). The communality of essay and objective tests of academic achievement. *Educational and Psychological Measurement, 30,* 359–364.

Bridgeman, B., & Rock, D. A. (1993). Relationships among multiple-choice and open-ended analytical questions. *Journal of Educational Measurement, 30,* 313–329.

Campbell, J. R. (1999). *Cognitive processes elicited by multiple-choice and constructed-response questions on an assessment of reading comprehension.* Unpublished doctoral dissertation, Temple University, Philadelphia, PA.

Choppin, B. H., & Purves, A. C. (1969). A comparison of open-ended and multiple-choice items dealing with literary understanding. *Research in the Teaching of English 3,* 15–24.

Cordón, L. A., & Day, J. D. (1996). Strategy use on standardized reading comprehension tests. *Journal of Educational Psychology, 88,* 288–295.

Embretson, W. S. (1983). Construct validity: Construct representation versus nomothetic span. *Psychological Bulletin, 93,* 179–197.

Ericsson, K. A., & Simon, H. A. (1993). *Protocol analysis: Verbal reports as data.* Cambridge, MA: MIT Press. (Original work published 1984)

Farr, R., Pritchard, R., & Smitten, B. (1990). A description of what happens when an examinee takes a multiple-choice reading comprehension test. *Journal of Educational Measurement, 27,* 209–226.

Heim, A. W., & Watts, R. B. (1967). An experiment on multiple-choice versus open-ended answering in a vocabulary test. *British Journal of Educational Psychology, 37,* 339–346.

Katz, S., & Lautenschlager, G. J. (2001). The contribution of passage and no-passage factor to item performance on the SAT reading task. *Educational Assessment, 7,* 165–176.

Katz, S., Lautenschlager, G. J., Blackburn, A. B., & Harris, F. H. (1990). Answering reading comprehension items without passages on the SAT. *Psychological Science, 1,* 122–127.

Kucan, L., & Beck, I. L. (1997). Thinking aloud and reading comprehension research: Inquiry, instruction, and social interaction. *Review of Educational Research, 67,* 271–299.

Langer, J. A. (1987). The construction of meaning and the assessment of comprehension: An analysis of reader performance on standardized test items. In R. O. Freedle & R. P. Duran (Eds.), *Cognitive and linguistic analyses of text performance* (pp. 225–244). Norwood, NJ: Ablex.

Lindquist, E. F. (1951). Preliminary considerations in objective test construction. In E. F. Lindquist (Ed.), *Educational measurement* (pp. 119–184). Washington, DC: American Council on Education.

Lukhele, R., Thissen, D., & Wainer, H. (1994). On the relative value of multiple-choice, constructed-response, and examinee-selected items on two achievement tests. *Journal of Educational Measurement, 31,* 234–250.

Manhart, J. J. (1996, April). *Factor analytic method for determining whether multiple-choice and constructed-response tests measure the same construct.* Paper presented at the annual meeting of the National Council on Measurement in Education, New York.

Mazzeo, J., Yamamoto, K., & Kulick, E. (1993, April). *Extended constructed-response items in the 1992 NAEP: Psychometrically speaking, were they worth the price?* Paper presented at the annual meeting of the National Council on Measurement in Education, Atlanta, GA.

Messick, S. (1989). Validity. In R. Linn (Ed.), *Educational measurement* (3rd ed., pp. 13–103). New York: Macmillan Publishers.

Murphy, S. (1998). *Fragile evidence: A critique of reading assessment.* Mahwah, NJ: Lawrence Erlbaum Associates.

Pressley, M., & Afflerbach, P. (1995). *Verbal protocols of reading: The nature of constructively responsive reading.* Hillsdale, NJ: Lawrence Erlbaum Associates.

Pritchard, R. (1990). The evolution of introspective methodology and its implications for studying the reading process. *Reading Psychology: An International Quarterly, 11,* 1–13.

Resnick, L. B., & Resnick, D. P. (1992). Assessing the thinking curriculum: New tools for educational reform. In B. R. Gifford & M. C. O'Connor (Eds.), *Changing assessment: Alternative views of aptitude, achievement, and instruction.* Boston: Kluwer Academic.

Valencia, S., & Pearson, P. D. (1987). Reading assessment: Time for a change. *Reading Teacher, 40*(7), 726–732.

van den Bergh, H. (1990). On the construct validity of multiple-choice items for reading comprehension. *Applied Psychological Measurement 14,* 1–12.

Ward, W. C., Dupree, D., & Carlson, S. B. (1987). *A comparison of free-response and multiple-choice questions in the assessment of reading comprehension* (Research Report No. 87–20). Princeton, NJ: Educational Testing Service.

Ward, W. C., Frederiksen, N., & Carlson, S. B. (1980). Construct validity of free-response and machine-scorable forms of a test. *Journal of Educational Measurement, 17,* 11–29.

Weiss, D., & Jackson, R. (1983). *The validity of descriptive tests of language skills: Relationship to direct measure of writing skill ability and grades in introductory college English courses* (Report LB-83-4; ETS-RR-83-27). New York: College Entrance Examination Board.

Winograd, P., Paris, S., & Bridge, C. (1991). Improving the assessment of literacy. *Reading Teacher, 45*(2), 108–116.

16

Dimensions Affecting the Assessment of Reading Comprehension

David J. Francis
University of Houston

Jack M. Fletcher
University of Texas Health Science Center—Houston

Hugh W. Catts
University of Kansas

J. Bruce Tomblin
University of Iowa

The assessment of reading comprehension has a long and storied history in educational research (Pearson, 1998). There are multiple approaches to the assessment of reading comprehension, reflecting the evolution of theory and pedagogical shifts in reading education and assessment. The recent report of the Rand Reading Study Group (2002) identified three broad categories that represented the outcomes of reading comprehension. The outcomes were as follows: (a) knowledge, which involves successful comprehension of the content, integration of new content with previously stored information, and critical evaluation of the information; (b) application, which represents the utility of content when it is applied to practical problems and tasks; and (c) engagement, which reflects involvement with the ideas, experience, and style of the text. It is clear that the assessment of reading comprehension is multidimensional. Yet many contemporary assessments of reading comprehension involve only the assessment of content knowledge. Comprehension of print that addresses the integration and evaluation of the information is infrequently assessed. Even rarer are assessments that address application or engagement.

Even when assessing content knowledge, many instruments employ a unitary form of assessment, such as the sole use of short passages and multiple-choice answer formats. These presentation and response formats are usually reliable and allow for valid inferences about readers' understanding of text, but they also have limitations. Moreover, there is often little variation in the type of material that must be comprehended. It is especially apparent on high-stakes assessments that both the type of material that must be comprehended and the response formats are often restricted. As comprehension assessment often influences instruction, particularly because of high-stakes testing, it is important to broaden the assessment of reading comprehension and to develop methods that incorporate multiple outcomes, multiple presentation formats, and multiple response formats. Otherwise, the understanding of how well a person comprehends what is read will depend on how comprehension is assessed, with little generalization beyond the method itself. Obviously, what aspects of reading comprehension are assessed depend on the purposes for which the assessment is undertaken, and this will influence how the instruments are constructed. However, any instrument should permit assessments that are not method dependent.

PURPOSES OF THIS CHAPTER

In the remainder of this chapter, issues involved in moving beyond the method dependence that characterizes many current approaches to the assessment of reading comprehension is discussed. First, we attempt to make the case that basic research in the measurement of reading comprehension needs to be supported by the profession and by funding agencies, and generally is not except in the service of developing a specific instrument, usually for commercial purposes. To do such research, it is important to anchor the research in psychometric theory and method, particularly those components that address construct validity and scaling, and to integrate psychometric theory with multiple theories that guide the process of reading acquisition, including theories of reading development, instruction, and comprehension.

For the purposes of this chapter, demonstration of reliability is assumed for any assessment and is not addressed, except to mention here that developers must consider the variety of sources of error variability in readers' performance in assessing test reliability. For example, if an assessment of comprehension relies on expert judgment of reader responses, such as in scoring story retells or open-ended responses, it is imperative that the scoring process be evaluated for reliability, in addition to examining more standard elements of score consistency, such as consistency in student responses across repeat assessments, or consistency in response across different questions for the same text. Nothing in the foregoing should be construed to imply that all aspects of reliability are equally important in all contexts, or even that reliability in general maintains the same importance in all contexts. Certainly, although not inconsequential, unreliability of teacher judgments of student performance on low-stakes classroom assessments is of lesser concern than reliability of expert judges on a high-stakes end-of-year assessment. In a sense, errors in the teacher's judgments may lead to less effective instruction for the student over time, whereas errors in the judges' ratings on end-of-year exams could lead to the promotion of students not prepared to handle work at the next grade level, or to retention of students who are prepared. Surely, the greater consequential validity of the end-of-year exams carries with it an increased burden for high reliability and for a more thorough assessment of test reliability. Whereas test developers vary considerably in their thoroughness with respect to evaluating the psychometric properties of assessments, especially those used for low-stakes decisions, this chapter presumes that assessments are reliable. Thus, we are able to focus more fully on the issue of validity of inferences based on test scores and on the dimensions affecting the assessment of reading comprehension beyond notions of error in the sense of inconsistency.

After making the case for basic research on the assessment of comprehension, issues involved in methods of assessment, especially presentation and response formats, are discussed. The essential point is that variations in presentation and response formats influence what we know about a person's reading comprehension. To better understand comprehension and its assessment, we begin with the premise that there is no single best way to assess reading comprehension, but rather that there are dimensions of both stimulus (i.e., text) selection, stimulus presentation (e.g., layout and use of visual aids, hypertext, etc.), and response format (e.g., fixed choice, open response, etc.) that affect student performance on comprehension assessments. At the same time, we maintain the working notion that reading comprehension is best understood as a latent construct, that is, as an unobserved ability whose presence is inferred on the basis of patterns of observable test performance. That is to say, that reading comprehension is latent in the observed test performance, not latent in the individual. Consequently, multimethod approaches to assessment are critical, along with research addressing the dimensionality of different assessments, and relations among variations in methods. Again, a key factor is to approach the study of these issues from a measurement perspective, for it is only through adoption of such a perspective that research can determine if a dimension represents (a) a fundamental aspect of comprehension (i.e., that it is inextricable from comprehension); (b) a dimension of assessment that affects comprehension, but is not itself considered a fundamental aspect of comprehension; or (c) a characteristic of the tester that affects performance on comprehension assessments, but is itself distinguishable from comprehension.

The role of theory and the purposes of assessing reading comprehension are also discussed. Methods of assessment will vary depending on the theory of comprehension, just as the classification of dimensions as belonging to (a) or to (c), discussed earlier, will be heavily influenced by theory. For example, motivation might clearly seem to belong to (c), a characteristic of the individual that affects performance on an assessment, but is itself distinguishable from comprehension. For example, motivation can be manipulated independently of the assessment (e.g., by providing incentives for performance or effort). However, at the same time, motivation can also be directly affected by the assessment, such as when students are tested using materials that they find intrinsically interesting, or motivating to read. Because the interest one feel's in reading a given piece of text is likely to be quite person-specific, even in the presence of strong external motivation to read, eliminating or controlling motivation as a source of variability in a single test score may be difficult, if not impossible. Thus, precisely how motivation enters into the assessment of comprehension will depend in part on one's theory of comprehension and the methods employed in its assessment. If the argument over (a) and (c) seems strained with respect to motivation, substitute decoding ability for motivation in the foregoing example. Is decoding ability a dimension of comprehension, or a separate ability that can be measured independently, but which impacts comprehension, or is decodability simply a feature of the text which interacts with other text properties and reader characteristics to impact comprehension? We conclude this section by presenting data from several studies that examined the relations among decoding and reading comprehension using samples of different ages and ethnic composition, and some popular approaches to the assessment of reading comprehension. This section provides concrete examples of how latent variable structural equation models can be used as representations of measurement theory to test explicit hypotheses about the structure of reading comprehension assessments and their links to component processes of reading. In the final section of the chapter, we conclude by outlining some potential research questions. We do not pretend to propose an exhaustive list of questions. Rather, we suggest a set of questions that seem to us to command the immediate attention of reading researchers.

The sequence of these three sections varies from how they are usually presented, in which theory leads to method and both are subjected to some type of analysis. This reversal is deliberate and is intended to highlight the importance of beginning the research with an explicit attempt to incorporate measurement theory into the research. Reading comprehension research must begin with recognition of the role of measurement theory as it pervades even the most subtle decisions about assessment and measurement, including the decisions of those who reject the idea that reading comprehension can and should be measured. Approaching the assessment of comprehension from a measurement theory point of view confers the advantage of making explicit the distinctions among (a), (b), and (c), as well as the relations and possible interactions among them as reflected both in the underlying theory of comprehension and in its assessment. Both method and theory are influenced by goals and purposes more than is commonly acknowledged, and thus, we must consider the context in which comprehension assessment is to take place throughout this chapter. Although we do not make explicit reference to context and how context might alter postulated or demonstrated relations, the reader is reminded that forever lurking in the background are the potentially significant effects of context on the assessment of student performance as well as on the relations among important dimensions of reading. Unfortunately, a thorough discussion of context and its potential effects on comprehension assessment would necessitate a chapter in its own right.

MEASUREMENT THEORY
AND READING COMPREHENSION

The differences in what is understood about a person's reading comprehension from different assessment purposes and formats is an empirical question that can be approached from the perspective of measurement theory. These theories and the attendant methods are well developed, but infrequently used to their full potential. Their application as part of an aggressive approach to the development of enhanced procedures for the assessment of reading comprehension would help address and potentially resolve some of the conflicts that have emerged over what constitutes proficient comprehension and how to assess it.

Modern measurement theory has evolved from classical test theory, in which notions about individuals' test performance emanate from weak true-score theory. In this framework, observed performance is comprised of two independent components, an underlying true-score component and error (Nunnally & Bernstein, 1994). However, in this framework, the true-score component for an individual is defined simply in terms of the expected value of an individual's scores on the assessment, giving rise to notions of repeated assessment on the same instrument under identical conditions, or repeated assessment on parallel or *tau-equivalent* (i.e., true-score equivalent) instruments. In the classical test-theory frame of reference, true scores are inextricably linked to the specific assessment. There is no necessary implication that this score reflects some underlying latent ability. Although such a possibility is not ruled out, neither is it required.

Disaffection with weak true-score theory and its untestable assumptions about the nature of true scores led psychometricians to develop a more compelling theory of modern psychological measurement (Lord & Novick, 1968). At the heart of this modern theory of psychological measurement lies the notion of strong true scores, or abilities, whose values at any given moment in time for a particular individual are potentially knowable, albeit indirectly through the responses of individuals to items on tests. In this theory of measurement, the ability is unchanged by changing the items on the test, provided that the new items measure the same underlying dimension as the original items, albeit with potentially different difficulties and validities. If one simply knows the relation between the items and the latent abilities (i.e., the difficulties and validities), then it would be possible to consistently estimate the abilities of individuals despite changes in the test items. Fundamental to this modern theory of measurement are two interrelated and testable assumptions. The first states that abilities are invariant across changes in the items, whereas the second states that the properties of items are invariant across people. Both assumptions, it turns out, are actually properties of tests and abilities that follow directly from an assumption of unidimensionality. Although a complete discussion of measurement theories in general, and item response theory, in particular, is beyond the scope of this chapter, suffice it to say that theories differ in their assumptions about the statistical properties of test scores. In general, the stronger assumptions of item response theory imply that the item parameters and test scores will possess certain properties. If the item parameters and test scores do not possess these properties, then we can reject the model implied by the theory as a reasonable model for the test.

The factor analytic model can similarly be employed to examine the structure of tests even when those tests are conceptualized under classical test theory. However, the linear factor analytic model has some limitations for dealing with item level data that are scored in binary (i.e., correct–incorrect) or ordered categorical (i.e., 0, 1, 2, 3) formats because the assumption of linear regression of item responses on the factor will not hold. The linear factor analytic model provides a better characterization of inter-test relations, and can be effectively employed to study the dimensionality of test batteries. With modern approaches to estimating linear factor analysis models, models of intertest relations can be formulated and explicitly tested, thus allowing researchers to take a hypothesis testing approach to examining test dimensionality, or intertest relations.

The history of reading comprehension assessment reflects considerable disagreement about its underlying dimensions. Early attempts to measure and evaluate the components of reading comprehension rarely suggested that reading comprehension was a uni-dimensional concept. Rather, the discussion was about the number of components necessary to support an adequate assessment of reading comprehension. Indeed, early assessments of reading comprehension reflected attempts to incorporate multiple presentation and response formats in an attempt to assess these different components. For example, some of the dimensions of reading comprehension appeared to include oral vocabulary, prior knowledge, and the ability to infer beyond the content. Whether assessments that attempted to measure these three components were adequate, as well as how well a particular assessment device measured these components, are questions that could have been addressed through research. Part of the problem at the time was that statistical methods were not widely available to address these types of questions in an explicit way.

Today, methods for constructing and assessing the properties of a measurement device are widely available and easily accessed in many computer packages. Latent variable methods, such as confirmatory factor analysis, help specify the latent variables assessed by a measurement device and have the additional advantage of potential restraint by the theory guiding the construction of the instrument (Francis, Fletcher, & Rourke, 1988). Item response models (Baker, 1992; Hambleton & Swaminathan, 1985) help assess not only the difficulty level of a specific item, but also permit interval scaling for the assessment of change, assessment of the dimensionality of a set of items, and specification of the range of items (in terms of "ability scores") that characterize a particular measurement device. The floor and ceiling of the device and its capacity for assessing specific latent variables at different levels of ability or points in development can be evaluated. Such evaluations can be revealing not only about the tool itself, but may also contribute to substantive issues on how these capabilities develop and relate to other capabilities.

To illustrate, Schatschneider, Francis, Foorman, Fletcher, and Mehta (1999) applied item response theory to a seven-subtest battery of phonological awareness tests widely employed in research and recently released through a publisher (Wagner et al., 1999). They found that phonological awareness was essentially a unitary construct that varied on a continuum of complexity. The simplest assessments involved initial sound comparison and rhyming, whereas the most complex assessments involved elision of medial phonemes. Hence, how well phonological awareness skills are related to reading outcomes may involve how and when such skills are assessed. These data were used in the development of the Texas Primary Reading Inventory (Foorman, Fletcher, & Francis, 2004), a teacher administered inventory of early reading skills designed to help plan instruction. The results of Schatschneider et al. (1999) helped the authors select items at different grade levels and to order them according to level of difficulty. This resulted in a shorter instrument, saving teachers valuable time. Item response theory was also used to order a set of words according to difficulty level so that children could read a list of words and the teacher could then pick a comprehension story with words that were at the child's level of decoding ability. This approach permitted an assessment of reading comprehension that was not dependent on word recognition ability and which minimized the number of stories a child would have to read to assess this domain.

As in the early days of research on the assessment of reading comprehension, assessment of the dimensionality within and across reading comprehension tasks is of critical importance. Given the multiple methods characteristic of reading comprehension assessment, there may well be fewer dimensions than is commonly hypothesized and stronger relations across different methods than is believed. There is a strong tendency to argue polemically over method when systematic measurement research would help specify the imperfections inherent in any singular approach to assessment, or perhaps more importantly, the commonalities across the hypothetically different dimensions assessed. The assessment of reading comprehension is inherently difficult as it is not a process that can be directly observed (Pearson & Hamm, this volume). In other words, unlike oral reading, comprehension is not a directly observable phenomenon. Rather, we observe the products of reading comprehension. Thus, any attempt to assess reading comprehension is inherently imperfect.

This imperfection is not unique to the assessment of reading comprehension, but one can argue reasonably, as do Pearson and Hamm (this volume), that the assessment of reading comprehension is perhaps more indirect than is the assessment of other reading processes, such as decoding ability, fluency, and vocabulary. Comprehension must be inferred on the basis of individuals' responses to questions aimed at eliciting the level of the readers' understanding of the material which has been read. This indirectness in the assessment of comprehension increases the variability in comprehension scores which is attributable to aspects of the assessment, such as response format, text selection, text difficulty, background knowledge, and so forth. In a sense, the comprehension score will generalize less well to other assessments of comprehension than we might expect for a score reflecting a student's ability to decode. From a measurement perspective, the differences across various methods for assessing reading comprehension reflect degrees of imperfection in how well a particular indicator measures the underlying latent variable (Nunnally & Bernstein, 1994) because our measures are rarely pure and never completely reliable. Approaches to measurement need to incorporate multiple indicators to enhance the precision with which the underlying latent variables are measured. Relying on a single approach to assessment of a complex latent construct, such as reading comprehension, leads to "mono-operation bias" (Cook & Campbell, 1979). Unfortunately, little research exploring the dimensionality or generalizability of comprehension assessments exists in contemporary reading research. In fact, the most recent edition of the *Handbook of Reading Research* (Kamil, Mosenthal, Pearson, & Barr, 2000) had no chapter on assessment or measurement. Themes involving assessment and measurement were common, but often simply expressed negative feelings about standardized or high-stakes testing. It is critical to revitalize this area of research and enhance its acceptability to the reading community.

Variations in Methods

The view of reading comprehension assessment expressed earlier reflects a decidedly trait-oriented measurement perspective. However, it is not necessary to adopt a trait oriented measurement perspective to adopt a "measurement" oriented perspective. Our adoption of this particular perspective is not intended to minimize or diminish the importance of other perspectives, but rather reflects our orientation to the challenge of assessing reading comprehension. Every perspective on measurement carries with it certain assumptions that ground the method in practice, only some of which can be challenged empirically. Although there are some who feel that the measurement issues in comprehension are so difficult and complex that no psychometric approach would ever be adequate, we would argue that because of its complexity, many measurement perspectives can and should be brought to bear on the study of reading comprehension and that these different perspectives can, and should, be contrasted to one another where possible, such as when perspectives make different predictions about the same phenomenon. Too often, perspectives are rejected on the grounds that their assumptions are untenable without consideration for the perspectives' ability to predict and explain phenomena of interest.

Regardless of the measurement perspective one adopts, there is little disagreement regarding the complexity of reading comprehension, the importance of measuring it well, nor the many factors affecting it, and consequently, its measurement. One such factor is the method of soliciting information back from the reader to gauge the reader's comprehension. It may be desirable, for example, to interview the comprehender or to engage groups of comprehenders in activities that will make the processes of comprehension more visible (e.g., "think-alouds"). Such an interactive approach to response solicitation will result in richer and more complex depictions of comprehension than constructed-response, or closed-format methods of response, such as multiple choice. At the same time, the latter approaches may lend themselves more readily to efficiently and reliably ranking individual readers on the extent of their understanding of the text, or judging their level of understanding against some proficiency criterion, but may fail to capture more nuanced understanding or misunderstanding on the part of the reader.

There is no question but that the *processes* underlying reading comprehension are not visible on a paper-and-pencil task. This includes strategies, interactions, and related factors. However, even if one chooses to focus on assessment of the comprehension process, as opposed to comprehension itself, a measurement perspective can be applied. For example, some of the process or interactive approaches involve different forms of discourse analysis where the comprehenders' oral or written responses are transcribed and coded according to some type of rubric. The discourse analysis and rubric itself are grist for the psychometrician's mill as measurement is involved. Rubrics can be complicated, such as those involved with discourse analysis, or relatively simple, such as the use of multiple choice or cloze. The specific approach to assessment is not what is important. Rather, what is important is to recognize that the approach taken to comprehension assessment, both in terms of what the person is asked to read and how he or she is asked to demonstrate his or her understanding, influences what we understand about the reader's level of comprehension. To understand the role that these factors play on the reader's comprehension, these dimensions of the assessment can be manipulated, and estimates derived which apply across a range of texts and response formats. Alternatively, one could focus more explicitly on measuring (i.e., quantifying or describing qualitatively) the influence that text features and response format exert on each particular readers' comprehension.

Presentation Formats.   In terms of presentation formats, that is, what the person is asked to read, distinguishing between constructed and authentic tasks barely scratches the surface in terms of the complex issues that affect the choice of materials on which to assess reading comprehension. The difficulty of the passage, which can be measured along many dimensions, including surface features of the text (e.g., decodability, sentence length), vocabulary demand, propositional complexity, and intersentential complexity, will influence its usefulness for measuring reading comprehension at different points in development, that is, at different levels of reading proficiency. For a passage to be useful in assessing reading comprehension, it must be matched in difficulty to the abilities of the reader. Yet the assessment of passage difficulty is not straightforward as suggested by the variety of dimensions along which complexity can be measured. Commonly applied readability formulae will give different indications of difficulty level depending on how they weight vocabulary, syntax, and other features of the text. Few readability formulae take into account propositional complexity or intersentential complexity. In addition to the difficulty level of the text as assessed independently, text structure can interact with readers' prior knowledge and ability to make text more or less difficult to understand (Calisir & Gurel, 2003).

There are numerous structural features of texts that may influence comprehension and proficient comprehenders learn to use their knowledge of text structure to facilitate comprehension. Goldman and Rakestraw (2000) summarized this research, showing that readers use knowledge of structure to process text, that knowledge of text structure develops with time and exposure to different genres, and that helping teachers become aware of text structure leads to enhanced student learning. Finally, genre (e.g., expository vs. narrative texts) has long been argued to be important (Graesser, Golding, & Long, 1996; Weaver & Kintsch, 1996). Some large-scale assessments (e.g., NAEP) commonly mix formats and include passages that vary in structural features and genre. However, NAEP is often seen as weak in the specification of difficulty level and the need for a better floor to the assessment, reflecting issues with the assessment of difficulty level (Pearson & Hamm, 2001).

Response Formats. Comprehension assessments also vary in response formats. Multiple-choice and cloze formats are common in commercially available devices and often reflect the lower expense of developing and processing these types of formats. These methods are often criticized, as the provision of a correct response does not appear to necessarily require that the person read the text. Other approaches that are also potentially economical have been developed to address this problem (see Pearson & Hamm, this volume), such as interview techniques and alternative multiple-choice formats. Alternative response formats often involve recording oral or written responses to stories. Such methods are more difficult to score and require more effort to establish reliability. They may confound reading comprehension with the person's capacity for producing narrative or written discourse. However, any assessment of reading comprehension measures more than one latent variable, so this issue can be addressed. More recently, sentence verification techniques have emerged and also show strong overlap with other response formats (Carlisle, 1989; Royer, Hastings, & Hook, 1979). Campbell (this volume) provided an extended discussion of research on the effects of item-response format on the assessment of comprehension.

Pearson and Hamm (this volume) also discussed classroom-based observational methods (e.g., think-alouds) and approaches to performance assessment that attempted to take into account the social component of reading comprehension. They noted that, although promising, these forms of assessment struggle with issues of reliability, validity, and generalizability, and they noted the importance of repeated assessment over many such tasks to establish confidence in one's estimates of students' abilities. Although these latter approaches are different from the sorts of assessments that typically characterize commercially available instruments, they can be incorporated into an assessment framework, integrated with more directly quantitative approaches and examined for reliability and validity. Such observational approaches can be reliable and do demonstrate validity, but their reliance on flexible selection of stimulus materials and on observational methods for obtaining, coding, and scoring student responses requires that one document evidence of reliability and validity whenever such methods are employed because these properties are less transportable than those of standardized stimulus and response procedures. The few studies that relate traditional assessments of reading comprehension with more authentic, discourse-based assessments show surprisingly high correlations across assessment methods (Fuchs, Fuchs, & Maxwell, 1988; Hannon & Daneman, 2001). However, research of this sort is sorely needed, as those studies that have been done to date tend to be limited by small and restricted samples and relatively narrow age ranges.

In an effort to make this process more explicit, in the next section we turn to several examples involving data from several longitudinal studies with which we have been involved. Each of these studies was concerned, at least in part, with the relation between decoding skill and comprehension. Thus, we use data from these studies to explicitly examine the relation between decoding and comprehension, and in so doing, ask whether comprehension measures function as a single factor.

Data-Based Examples

The foregoing sections make clear that reading is multidimensional in its presentation to the reader, in what is expected of the reader, in the contexts in which reading occurs, and in the purposes which reading serves. For assessment of reading comprehension to be successful, we must be clear of its purposes and mindful of its consequences. The data for the examples are taken from several studies funded by NICHD, all of which looked at early reading skill. Given the focus on early reading skill, each of the studies examined word reading, phonological awareness, vocabulary and verbal ability, and word reading efficiency or fluency, as important skills in determining reading comprehension. These studies were first and foremost research investigations of student skills and abilities and their interrelations. Although in some cases, the focus was on specific groups of children, such as children with Specific Language Impairment (SLI) or children at risk for reading problems, the overriding purposes of each study necessitated that large numbers of elementary school children were participating. As a consequence, the studies were limited in the early phases to individualized assessment of reading related skills and reading comprehension, and because of the number of children involved and the research emphasis of the particular studies, it was necessary to use assessments that were easily and readily scored using objective criteria. These forces place constraints on the class of assessment materials that could be used. In particular, it was not possible in any of these studies to use open ended questioning or retelling as the primary response format as such procedures would have been prohibitively time consuming given the large numbers of students participating in the studies, and the funds available to complete all facets of the research projects.

For some purposes, the choice of assessment may have minimal impact on the decisions that we reach. For example, in evaluating students, the choice of which assessment to use appears to have only minimal bearing on final decisions about the relative positions of students (Campbell, this volume). However, that is not to say that the choice of assessment is inconsequential. Certainly, when assessment is used to determine the effects of instruction, the goals of instruction should be explicitly linked to assessment. Given that different response types tend to engage different thought processes (Campbell, this volume), reliance on a single response format in state assessments may adversely narrow instruction. The same could be said for limiting assessment to a single genre of text, or overly restricting factors affecting text difficulty, and vocabulary demand. Thus, it is important in any assessment decision to keep in mind the purpose of assessment and to realize that different purposes of assessment (e.g., ranking students on ability, evaluating the effectiveness of classroom instruction) often necessitate different decisions regarding the specific assessment, or approach to assessment, to use. Insofar as it is arguably impossible for any single assessment to serve all purposes equally well, focusing assessment decisions first and foremost on the purpose of assessment increases the likelihood of sound assessment decisions.

Although it's clear that limiting response type is undesirable in the context of state-wide assessments to gauge the effects of classroom instruction, this link between response type and cognitive processes may also bear on research findings on reading comprehension. If an assessment engages certain cognitive processes based on the types of text involved or the response formats employed, then research findings may be biased in favor of factors related to those processes. For example, if the assessment fails to engage students in evaluation and integration of information, then research will find negligible effects for the higher order linguistic and cognitive abilities that subserve these processes in comprehension, or the instructional practices that develop those abilities and processes. Psychometrically motivated research can help to shed light on the extent to which such factors may be operating in the research literature. To see how psychometrically motivated research might work in this way, we consider, in the context of our examples, the role of decoding in comprehension by drawing on the results of several different studies with samples from different populations.

Table 16.1 shows correlations over time between the Woodcock Reading Mastery Test Passage Comprehension scores (WRMT; Woodcock & Johnson, 1977), and WRMT Decoding composite scores (Letter Word and Word At-

TABLE 16.1

**Correlation Between Decoding and Comprehension
on the Woodcock-Reading Mastery Test (WRMT)
From Grades 1 to 9 (N = 395)**

WRMT Decoding	WRMT Comprehension								
				Grade					
Grade	1	2	3	4	5	6	7	8	9
1	.89	.79	.73	.69	.64	.66	.66	.61	.65
2	.75	.83	.78	.74	.70	.70	.71	.68	.69
3	.70	.74	.77	.74	.71	.75	.72	.72	.71
4	.64	.71	.74	.73	.70	.74	.72	.68	.70
5	.58	.63	.68	.67	.70	.69	.67	.66	.66
6	.59	.65	.67	.68	.67	.69	.67	.66	.66
7	.53	.61	.65	.65	.68	.69	.69	.66	.68
8	.49	.58	.62	.62	.64	.65	.65	.63	.63
9	.52	.58	.60	.62	.60	.63	.63	.61	.63

Note. The elements in the table are correlations (rounded to two decimals) between decoding and comprehension measured on the WRMT at Grades 1 through 9. The row index gives the grade of assessment for decoding and the column index gives the grade of assessment for comprehension. All scores are taken from the WRMT and are scaled scores.

tack). The WRMT measure of Passage Comprehension is a cloze-based procedure, whereas the Decoding composite is based on reading of words in isolation. The Letter Word subtest uses real words whereas the Word Attack subtest measures phonological decoding skills through the reading of pseudowords. The data in Table 16.1 are derived from the Connecticut Longitudinal Study (CLS; Shaywitz, Shaywitz, Fletcher, & Escobar, 1990). The CLS sample is an epidemiologic sample from Connecticut, largely White, middle to upper income children with very low attrition (over 90% retention through Grade 9; see Shaywitz et al., 1990, for a more detailed description of the sample, and Francis, Shaywitz, Stuebing, Shaywitz, & Fletcher, 1996, for a description of individual student growth over time in these skills from this sample). Focusing here explicitly on the correlation between decoding and comprehension, we see that the correlations are uniformly high, but clearly are substantially higher in the early grades than in the later grades. Specifically, the correlation of decoding measured in Grade 1 with comprehension ranges from 0.89 when comprehension is also measured in Grade 1 and gradually declines to 0.65 when comprehension is measured in Grade 9. At the same time, tracing the diagonal of the table highlights the within-grade correlation between the two abilities. Here again, we see that the correlation is highest in Grade 1 and gradually declines over time to 0.83 in Grade 2, to 0.77 in Grade 3, and so on, until reaching a low of 0.63 in Grade 9. This pattern of correlations is indicative of the increasing complexity of reading comprehension suggesting that reading comprehension is less heavily determined by decoding skill in later grades. However, this same pattern of declining correlations could also signal reduced variability in either decoding skill or reading comprehension in later grades as measured on the WRMT.

Table 16.2 expands on the data in Table 16.1 by including a second measure of reading comprehension, the Formal Reading Inventory: Silent Reading (FRI) score (Wiederholt, 1986), along with the Woodcock–Johnson–Revised (Woodcock & Johnson, 1989) measure of reading comprehension (WJPC). The Woodcock–Johnson–Revised measure of reading comprehension is similar in format to the measure from the WRMT used in the CLS, whereas the Formal Reading Inventory measures silent reading comprehension through the reading of graded passages and answering of questions. In addition, Table 16.2 includes a measure of reading vocabulary from the Woodcock–Johnson–Revised (WJ vocabulary) as well as a measure of vocabulary taken from the Wechsler Intelligence Scale for Children–Revised (WISC) (Wechsler, 1974). In this case, the data were collected over a more narrow time frame, namely Grades 1 and 2, but the sample is more economically and racially diverse. The data were collected as part of a large normative sample ($N = 945$) from three

TABLE 16.2

Correlations Among Woodcock-Johnson-Revised (WJR) Passage Comprehension and Formal Reading Inventory (FRI) Silent Reading with WJR Decoding Subtests and Vocabulary

	Grade 1		Grade 2	
Predictor	WJRPC	FRI	WJRPC	FRI
WJR: Letter–Word (22)	0.84	0.44	0.81	0.45
Standard Score	< .0001	< .0001	< .0001	< .0001
	613	578	545	541
WJR: Word Attack (31)	0.75	0.42	0.70	0.40
Standard Score	< .0001	< .0001	< .0001	< .0001
	615	580	546	542
WJR Reading Vocabulary (32)	0.79	0.48	0.83	0.49
Standard Score	< .0001	< .0001	< .0001	< .0001
	614	580	545	541
WISC–R: Vocabulary	0.33	0.21	0.41	0.27
Scale Score	< .0001	< .0001	< .0001	< .0001
	613	581	546	542

Note. All correlations are rounded to two decimals. FRI = Formal Reading Inventory Silent Reading Comprehension scaled score; WISC–R = Wechsler Intelligence Scale for Children–Revised; WJR = Woodcock–Johnson–Revised scaled score. Sample size and *p-value* given below correlation.

schools in Houston, Texas, and is roughly balanced for gender and was mixed with respect to racial composition: White (54%), African American (18%), Hispanic (15%), Asian (12%). See Schatschneider et al. (1999) for a detailed description of the sample.

The relations in Table 16.2 show a marked similarity to those of Table 16.1 insofar as correlations between the WJPC and measures of decoding are high in Grade 1 (0.84 and 0.75) and are only slightly lower (0.81 and 0.70, respectively) in Grade 2. In contrast, the correlations with the FRI are similar in Grades 1 and 2 and substantially lower than for WJPC. In addition, a somewhat different pattern is observed for correlations involving reading vocabulary. In this case, correlations are somewhat higher for Grade 2 WJPC than for Grade 1 (0.83 vs. 0.79 with WJ Reading Vocabulary and 0.41 vs. 0.33 for WISC Vocabulary), which is similar to the pattern seen for FRI (0.49 vs. 0.48

for Grade 1 vs. Grade 2 with WJ Reading Vocabulary, and 0.27 vs. 0.21 for Grade 1 vs. Grade 2 with WISC Vocabulary, respectively). Although the grade differences in correlations are small for both decoding and for vocabulary, they are of opposite direction, and the decoding correlations show the same pattern as in Table 16.1, whereas the vocabulary correlations show the pattern expected by theory, which says that reading comprehension becomes more complex with age as the linguistic demands of text increase. Although this caveat is typically preserved for later grades (typically Grade 4 and beyond), the pattern seen here is consistent with that expectation. Nevertheless, we neither confirm, nor can we rule out, on the basis of these observed patterns, the possibility that the two comprehension measures serve as distinct measures of a common underlying construct known as reading comprehension. To address this question more explicitly requires a more advanced data analytic plan, specifically latent variable structural equation modeling (Bollen, 1989; Francis, 1988; Francis, Fletcher, & Rourke, 1988).

The final sample comes from a longitudinal study of oral and written language development being conducted by Bruce Tomblin at the University of Iowa's Child Language Research Center (CLRC), Hugh Catts at the University of Kansas, and their colleagues. Children in this study were recruited in kindergarten and followed longitudinally in Grades 2, 4, and 8. Grade 10 assessments were in progress at the time of this writing, The sample was a subsample of children participating in a longitudinal study of language impairments in children. In Grades 2 and 4, data were available on 570 children in one of four groups: Typically developing controls ($n = 268$), children with specific language impairments (SLI; $n = 117$), children with nonspecific language impairments (NLI; $n = 91$), and children with low nonverbal cognitive abilities ($n = 94$). For detailed information on the sample and the criteria for the four subgroups, see Tomblin and Zhang (1999) and Rice, Tomblin, Hoffman, Richman, and Marquis (in press).

Table 16.3 provides correlations for the CLRC sample between three measures of reading comprehension (WRMT Passage Comprehension, WRM–PC; Gray Oral Reading Comprehension score, GORT; and the Diagnostic Assessment Battery, DAB–2) and composite measures of decoding skill (combination of WRMT Letter Word Identification and Word Attack), receptive language, and a measure of fluency at Grades 2 and 4. Table 16.3 again shows patterns of correlations similar to those seen in Tables 16.1 and 16.2 with larger correlations between decoding and comprehension as measured by the WRMT Passage Comprehension, and declining correlations between decoding and comprehension over time, here from Grade 2 to Grade 4. Within grade correlations between decoding and comprehension in Grade 2 are 0.89, 0.67, and 0.61,

TABLE 16.3

Correlations for Three Comprehension Measures With Language, Decoding, and Fluency at Grades 2 and 4 for Child Language Research Center Sample (N = 570)

	Grade 2			Grade 4		
	WRMTPC	*DABS*	*GORT C*	*WRMTPC*	*DABS*	*GORT C*
Language	0.60	0.64	0.61	0.63	0.62	0.62
Grade 2	< .0001	< .0001	< .0001	< .0001	< .0001	< .0001
Decoding	0.89	0.67	0.61	0.79	0.53	0.46
Grade 2	<.0001	< .0001	< .0001	< .0001	< .0001	< .0001
Language	0.59	0.62	0.59	0.65	0.64	0.63
Grade 4	<.0001	< .0001	< .0001	< .0001	< .0001	< .0001
Decoding	0.85	0.64	0.57	0.84	0.55	0.49
Grade 4	<.0001	< .0001	< .0001	< .0001	< .0001	< .0001
Fluency	0.77	0.62	0.57	0.72	0.50	0.42
Grade 4	<.0001	< .0001	< .0001	< .0001	< .0001	< .0001

Note. All correlations are rounded to two decimals. DABS = Diagnostic Assessment Battery Comprehension Score; GORT = Gray Oral Reading Test Comprehension Score; WRMTPC = Woodcock Reading Mastery Test Passage Comprehension scaled score. Decoding = composite of Word Attack and Letter Word from the Woodcock Reading Mastery Test; Language = composite of standardized receptive language measures including listening comprehension and receptive vocabulary; Fluency = Test of Word Reading Efficiency (Torgesen, Wagner, & Rashotte, 1999).

respectively, for the three comprehension measures in comparison with correlations between decoding and comprehension within Grade 4 which equal 0.84, 0.55, and 0.49. In contrast, correlations with receptive language appear to be stable or slightly increasing.

Although the consistency of the pattern across the three tables is interesting, the presence of multiple measures of comprehension across multiple time points in the CLRC sample allows examination of more precisely formulated hypotheses about the relations among the measures. The WRMT–PC, DAB–2, and GORT are all purported to measure reading comprehension, albeit in significantly different ways, for example WRMT–PC is a cloze-based reading test whereas GORT requires children to read short passages that are graded in difficulty and then answer multiple-choice questions over each passage. The questions call for a variety of factual and inference-based responses. The student continues reading more difficult passages until a ceiling is reached. The DAB–2 requires silent reading of passages followed by answering of open-ended questions. Each of the measures correlates reasonably high with the other comprehension measures and with factors known to be associated with reading comprehension, such as receptive language, decoding skill, and fluency. Do these three measures reflect a latent ability in the factor analytic sense, that is, an underlying ability which no one test measures perfectly, but which all measures reflect somewhat imperfectly?

A strong version of this idea would say that the three tests share one thing in common, and it is this commonality which reflects the underlying process of reading comprehension. In general, reading comprehension theorists reject the notion that reading comprehension is unidimensional. However, given a dataset with multiple comprehension measures, such as the CLRC dataset, it becomes possible to empirically evaluate this hypothesis in specific contexts. Precisely because such psychometric hypotheses carry with them very specific assertions about the relations among the observed variables, these hypotheses are testable. In particular, the notion of one or more latent dimensions to the comprehension measures carries with it specific assertions about (a) relations among the comprehension measures themselves, (b) relations of each of the comprehension measures to other variables that are related to the proposed comprehension construct, as well as (c) relations to variables not related to the proposed construct. These assertions are falsifiable in a given dataset, which allows one to explicitly test the dimensionality hypothesis and to determine the extent to which the model provides a reasonable approximation to the data. It is this process of model fitting and testing, and the analysis of model misfit, which makes psychometric models useful for studying the properties of tests in general, as well as for studying how these properties change or remain invariant across specific contexts of interest.

In what follows, we present a pair of models for the measures of Table 16.3 in an effort to determine the structure of these comprehension measures, but more importantly to demonstrate the utility of latent variable modeling for addressing questions about reading comprehension assessments. To begin, we specify a model of reading comprehension at Grades 2 and 4 where comprehension at each grade is measured by the three measures collected at a specific time point. However, the model further allows that measures have sources of systematic variance outside of the comprehension construct which account for test-specific correlation over time, but do not account for intertest correlations within-time, or overtime for different tests. That is, the DAB–2 contains specific sources of variability unrelated to the reading comprehension construct that cause the DAB–2 to correlate from Grade 2 to Grade 4 in a manner not predicted by the DAB–2's relation to the comprehension constructs at

Grades 2 and 4 and the relation between the two comprehension constructs. Similar relations are posed for the WRMT–PC and the GORT. Model 1 is analogous to the model shown in Fig. 16.1, but with the measures of language and decoding omitted, and in their place we simply estimate the correlation between the two reading factors. Also, because the design of the study involves four groups, Model 1 was actually fit constraining the pattern and value of the factor loadings, and the interfactor correlations to be equivalent across all four groups. This model of unidimensionality within grade with test specific relations over time and factor loadings and factor correlations constrained equal across the four groups of students fits the data quite well ($\chi^2_{(32)}$ = 28.62, p = .6357, RMSEA = 0.00). In Model 1, the 15 covariances among the six variables in each of the four groups (60 covariances in all) are being explained by the six factor loadings, the three intrameasure cross-time relations (i.e., test specific variation over time), and the correlation between factors. The correlation between comprehension factors, which is estimated at 0.85, indicates a high degree of stability in comprehension as measured by these assessments from Grade 2 to Grade 4.

The model of Fig. 16.1 introduces language and decoding constructs at Grade 2 as predictors to Model 1. The model stipulates that the factors exert the same influence on comprehension for the four groups, although the effects are allowed to differ at Grades 2 and 4. This model is consistent with the notion that reading becomes more complex at later ages, but is still determined by decoding and language skill, albeit in comparable ways for the four groups of participants. One other critically important aspect of the model in Fig. 16.1 is the allowance that not all of the variability among the two reading comprehension factors is required to be explained by their mutual relations to the language and decoding factors. Rather, the model allows for nonzero residual correlation between the two comprehension factors. The parameter estimates of the model in Fig. 16.1 corroborate expectations with respect to the relations between the two comprehension factors and the two predictors. In particular, the effects of the language factor are stronger at Grade 4 (γ = 0.35 in Grade 4 as compared to γ = 0.22 in Grade 2), whereas the effects of the decoding factor are stronger at Grade 2 (γ = 0.84 in Grade 2 as compared to γ = 0.64 in Grade 4). However, it is important to keep in mind that, despite this opposite shift in the magnitude of the regression coefficients, the decoding factor exerts a stronger influence on comprehension at both grades than does the language factor.

Perhaps more importantly, the outstanding fit of Model 1 is lost by the introduction of these two predictor factors ($\chi^2_{(112)}$ = 327.16, p < .001, RMSEA = 0.12) and the need to place constraints on the error variance

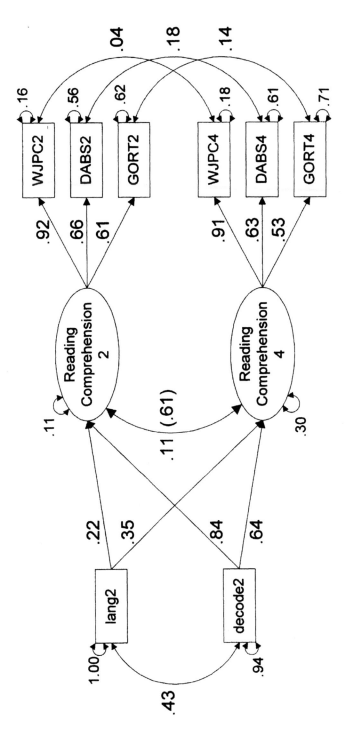

FIG. 16.1. Multigroup unidimensional model for reading comprehension within Grades 2 and 4 with language and decoding at Grade 2 as predictors (CLRC Sample). *Note:* Standardized covariance (correlation) is shown in parentheses; Chi-square = 327.16, d.f. = 112, $p < .001$, RMSEA = 0.12.

across groups to get the models to estimate. Possibly with larger samples in the disability groups, this constraint would not be required, but it was impossible to obtain parameter estimates without the constraint once the predictors were introduced into the model. It is tempting to argue that the loss of fit is due to the rather rigorous constraints across groups on the relation between the predictors and the comprehension factors. Unfortunately, relaxing these constraints and fitting the model in such a way that allows these parameters to vary across groups does not result in a well fitting model ($\chi^2_{(91)} = 277.07$, $p < .001$, RMSEA $= 0.12$), and again, the constraint on error variances is necessary to get the model to estimate, although this constraint was not necessary prior to the introduction of the predictors.

Overall, the model fit is not particularly strong, especially in light of the strong support for the model without predictors. Introducing the predictors into the model increases our power for discriminating among the different measures of comprehension, and falsifying the unidimensionality hypothesis. Lack of fit in the model tends to come from the somewhat stronger relation between decoding and WJPC than the other two measures, and their somewhat greater relation with language. It should be noted that the model allows for test specific relations over time for each of the three comprehension measures. The model also allows that not all of the correlation between the two comprehension factors over time (which is substantial, viz. .88) is due to their respective relations with decoding and language. Thus, the model fully accounts for correlation between the two comprehension factors and among pairs of measures from the same assessment over time. These potential sources of misfit have been eliminated in the model. Thus, lack of fit in the model must be attributable to other aspects of the model, including the constraint on error variance across groups, but also the constraint that all comprehension measures at a given time point have a common relation with decoding and language, such that the only source of difference between comprehension measures in these relations stems from differential validities and thus affects all relations in comparable ways.

This finding raises the possibility that overreliance on a single measure of comprehension in the research literature, in this case the WJPC, could have the effect of diminishing the importance of language skills over time in favor of decoding skills because of the generally stronger relation between WJPC and decoding than the other two measures. Inclusion of multiple measures mitigates this potential for methodological bias somewhat, but the comprehension measures in this study do not function as a single factor in a reflex indicator model (i.e., in the typical factor analytic sense). By formulating and testing an explicit measurement model for the set of observed relations among measures, we have obtained considerably more information about how the tests actually function than by simply examining the matrices of correlations.

FUTURE DIRECTIONS

The foregoing discussion suggests many possible directions for future research that would follow from a commitment to research on the measurement and assessment of reading comprehension that takes advantage of the advances in psychometric theory and advances in reading theory over the past two decades. One important set of research questions simply takes existing frameworks for assessment and does comparative studies of the item properties, dimensionality, and generalizability of the existing devices on well-specified samples that receive common subsets of these devices. Another set of questions focuses on components of different frameworks that lack adequate development and attempts to develop assessments of those components (e.g., application and engagement). Across both approaches, some common questions could be addressed, including the following: (a) What are the important components of reading comprehension? (b) Does reading comprehension exist on a single, inseparable dimension? If not, what are the different dimensions, components, and outcomes that must be assessed? (c) What are the most productive approaches to the assessment of reading comprehension? How do we incorporate and evaluate the various presentation and response formats that lead to differences in assessment results? Do these differences have implications for instruction? (d) How well does a particular assessment device assess individual differences, variation attributable to sociocultural factors, and performance at different levels of proficiency? Finally, another set of research questions involves attempts to extend research beyond assessment of knowledge into application and engagement as discussed in the Rand report (2002) as the three outcomes of reading comprehension. Procedures for assessing these alternative outcomes of reading comprehension are in a rudimentary state of development.

There has been decidedly little work that has examined reading comprehension assessment from the position of measurement theory. Most such research has focused on single assessments in efforts to build individual assessments or to study factors affecting a particular assessment, or the features of specific approaches to assessment. For example, Greene (2001) has shown that appropriately designed cloze tests can be used to measure readers' comprehension of macropropositions in text, but require that items target connective propositions explicitly. That is, typical cloze procedures that automatically eliminate every n^{th} word will not routinely achieve this purpose. In contrast, studies are rare that examine the performance of a large sample of students of various ages, abilities, and backgrounds on a variety of common reading comprehension assessments to examine the dimensionality of those assessments and whether the factors affecting different assessments exert similar influence on different assessments, a proposition which underlies the notion of unidimensionality. If different comprehension assessments tap a single common dimension, then correlations of different comprehension measures with factors that affect reading comprehension will differ only as a function of the validities of the different comprehension assessments. Test specific relations with other factors, or relations that do not follow the pattern predicated by the unidimensionality hypothesis, will lead to rejection of the unidimensionality hypothesis, which leads to advances in our theoretical understanding of reading comprehension, its assessment, and the factors affecting it. We have attempted to show in the preceding examples how such models can be fit. These models can also be easily extended to examine how particular assessment properties might vary across groups of readers (e.g., Pomplun & Omar, 2001), or through explicit manipulation of the context under which comprehension has been assessed, such as through manipulation of students' motivation to perform on the assessment.

Although some studies examining the properties of reading comprehension assessments across groups of students have been reported, more such work is needed involving broader age samples and wider arrays of assessments. The foregoing is intended only to convey to the reader the many advantages afforded to the study of reading comprehension through the fitting and testing of explicit models for the measurement properties and cognitive determinants of reading comprehension assessments. As advances in statistical theory continue to occur at a rapid pace and convergence across models and software breaks down barriers that prevent access to these models, substantive researchers' ability to test their explicit theories about reading comprehension and its assessment will continue to improve. As our tests of hypotheses become more comprehensive and more closely matched to the explicit theories from which they derive, our theories of comprehension and our strategies for its assessment will continue to improve and be better understood.

ACKNOWLEDGMENTS

This research was supported in part by grants HD 28172, PO1 HD31952, HD 30995, P01HD 21888, and P01 HD39521 from the National Institute of Child Health and Human Development, and grant P50 DC 002746 from the National Institute of Deafness and Communication Disorders. The opinions expressed in this publication are those of the authors and do not necessarily reflect the opinions or official positions of the funding agencies.

REFERENCES

Baker, F. B. (1992). *Item response theory: Parameter estimation techniques*. New York: Marcel Dekker.

Bollen, K. A. (1989). *Structural equation modeling with latent variables*. New York: Wiley.

Calisir, F., & Gurel, Z. (2003). Influence of text structure and prior knowledge of the learner on reading comprehension, browsing and perceived control. *Computers in Human Behavior, 92,* 135–145.

Carlisle, J. F. (1989). The use of the sentence verification technique in diagnostic assessment of listening and reading comprehension. *Learning Disabilities Research, 5,* 33–44.

Cook, T. D., & Campbell, D. T. (1979). *Quasi-experimentation: Design and analysis issues for field settings*. Chicago: Rand McNally.

Foorman, B. F., Fletcher, J. M., & Francis, D. J. (2004). Early reading assessment. In W. Evers & H. Walberg (Eds.), *Testing student learning, evaluating teaching effectiveness* (pp. 81–126). Stanford, CA: Hoover Institution Press.

Francis, D. J. (1988). An introduction to structural equation models. *Journal of Clinical and Experimental Neuropsychology, 10,* 623–639.

Francis, D. J., Fletcher, J. M., & Rourke, B. P. (1988). Discriminant validity of lateral sensorimotor tests in children. *Journal of Clinical and Experimental Neuropsychology, 10,* 779–799.

Francis, D. J., Shaywitz, S. E., Stuebing, K. K., Shaywitz, B. A., & Fletcher, J. M. (1996). Developmental lag versus deficit models of reading disability: A longitudinal individual growth curves analysis. *Journal of Educational Psychology, 1,* 3–17.

Fuchs, L. S., Fuchs, D., & Maxwell, L. (1988). The validity of informal reading comprehension measures. *Remedial and Special Education, 9,* 20–28.

Goldman, S. R., & Rakestraw, J. A. (2000). Structural aspects of constructing meaning from text. In M. L. Kamil, P. B. Mosenthal, P. D. Pearson, & R. Barr (Eds.), *Handbook of reading research* (Vol. III, pp. 311–335). Mahwah, NJ: Lawrence Erlbaum Associates.

Graesser, A., Golding, J. M., & Long, D. L. (1996). Narrative representation and comprehension. In R. Barr, M. Kamil, P. Mosenthal, & P. D. Pearson (Eds.), *Handbook of reading research* (Vol. II, pp. 171–205). Mahwah, NJ: Lawrence Erlbaum Associates.

Greene, B. B. (2001). Testing reading comprehension of theoretical discourse with cloze. *Journal of Research in Reading, 24,* 82–98.

Hambleton, R., & Swaminathan, H. (1985). *Item response theory: Principles & applications*. Boston: Kluwer Publishing.

Hannon, B., & Daneman, M. (2001). A new tool for understanding individual differences in the component processes of reading comprehension. *Journal of Educational Psychology, 93,* 103–128.

Kamil, M. L., Mosenthal, P. B., Pearson, P. D., & Barr, R. (Eds.). (2000). *Handbook of reading research* (Vol. III). Mahwah, NJ: Lawrence Erlbaum Associates.

Lord, F., & Novick, M. R. (1968). *Statistical theories of mental test scores*. Reading, MA: Addison-Wesley.

Nunnally, J. C., & Bernstein, J. (1994). *Psychometric theory* (3rd ed.). New York: McGraw Hill.

Pearson, P. D. (1998). Standards and assessment: Tools for crafting effective instruction? In F. Lehr & J. Osborn (Eds.), *Literacy for all: Issues in teaching and learning* (pp. 264–288). New York: Guilford.

Pomplun, M., & Omar, M. H. (2001). The factorial invariance of a test of reading comprehension across groups of limited English proficient students. *Applied Measurement in Education, 14,* 261–283

Rand Reading Study Group. (2002). *Reading for Understanding.* Santa Monica, CA: RAND Corporation.

Rice, M. L., Tomblin, J. B., Hoffman, L., Richman, W. A., & Marquis, J. (in press). Grammatical tense deficits in children with SLI and nonspecific language impairment: Relationships with nonverbal IQ over time. *Journal of Speech, Language, and Hearing Research.*

Royer, J. M., Hastings, C. N., & Hook, C. (1979). A sentence verification technique for measuring reading comprehension. *Journal of Reading Behavior, 11,* 355–363.

Schatschneider, C., Francis, D. J., Foorman, B. R., Fletcher, J. M., & Mehta, P. (1999). The dimensionality of phonological awareness: An application of item response theory. *Journal of Educational Psychology, 91,* 439–449.

Shaywitz, S. E., Shaywitz, B. A., Fletcher, J. M., & Escobar, M. D. (1990). Prevalence of reading disability in boys and girls: Results of the Connecticut Longitudinal Study. *Journal of the American Medical Association, 264,* 998–1002.

Tomblin, J. B., & Zhang, X. (1999). Are children with SLI a unique group of language learners? In H. Tager-Flusberg (Ed.), *Neurodevelopmental disorders: Contributions to a new framework from the cognitive neurosciences* (pp. 361–382). Cambridge, MA: MIT Press.

Torgesen, J. K., Wagner, R., & Rashotte, C. (1999). *Test of word reading efficiency.* Austin, TX: PRO-ED.

Wagner, R., Torgesen, J., & Rashotte, C. (1999). *Comprehensive test of phonological processes (CTOPP).* Austin, TX: PRO-ED.

Weaver, C. A., & Kintsch, W. (1996). Expository text. In R. Barr, M. Kamil, P. Mosenthal, & P. D. Pearson (Eds.), *Handbook of reading research* (Vol. II, pp. 171–205). Mahwah, NJ: Lawrence Erlbaum Associates.

Wechsler, D. (1974). *Manual for the Wechsler Intelligence Scale for Children–Revised.* San Antonio, TX: Psychological Corporation.

Wiederholt, J. L. (1986). *Formal reading inventory.* Austin, TX: PRO-ED.

Woodcock, R. W., & Johnson, M. B. (1977). *Woodcock–Johnson Psychoeducational Test Battery.* Boston: Teaching Resources.

Woodcock, R. W., & Johnson, M. B. (1989). *Woodcock–Johnson Psycho-Educational Battery–Revised.* Allen, TX: DLM.

17

The Influence of Large-Scale Assessment of Reading Comprehension on Classroom Practice: A Commentary

Karen K. Wixson
Joanne F. Carlisle
University of Michigan

Large-scale assessments have traditionally been used for purposes external to the classroom such as monitoring of educational programs or large numbers of students. In contrast, other types of assessment have typically been used to address purposes internal to the classroom, such as instructional decision making for individual students. However, as the stakes associated with large-scale instruments have increased, their influence on educational practice at all levels has increased as well. The differences between assessments traditionally used for internal and external purposes create a set of tensions that need to be explored when considering the influence of large-scale assessments on educational practice in the classroom—where it really matters (Wixson, Valencia, & Lipson, 1994). This means attending to the nature of these assessments as well as the purposes for which they are used.

CONCERNS ABOUT MEASURES USED FOR INTERNAL AND EXTERNAL PURPOSES

Many thoughtful critics have voiced concerns about the validity of the large-scale assessments used for external purposes, whereas others are equally concerned about the reliability of the assessments used for internal purposes (cf. Linn, Baker, & Dunbar, 1991). Large-scale assessments of reading comprehension are generally criticized as being atheoretical, lacking a basis in current theories or the processes by which students understand written texts (Francis, Fletcher, Catts, & Tomblin, this volume; Snow, 2003). The recent RAND Reading Study Group placed the need to improve assessment of reading comprehension on center stage (RAND Reading Study Group, 2002). They specified the importance of building a stronger connection to theories of reading comprehension and making use of theories of measurement of reading, and they called for an infusion of research to devise better methods of assessing reading comprehension

The differences between the large-scale assessments and assessments used for purposes internal to the classroom make clear issues that need to be addressed in considering how large-scale assessments can or should influence classroom practice. For example, because the emphasis in large-scale assessments used for external purposes is so often on evaluating reading programs, all that is required are fairly global scores. The specific items on these tests are not generally of importance to consumers, so they are often comprised of items that are a "proxy" for the actual knowledge or performance of interest. In contrast, reading assessments designed for internal purposes are used to make more immediate and specific instructional decisions and therefore are likely to be more closely related to curricular content and instructional strategies. Often they are direct measures of what students have learned over a limited period of time or with respect to specific outcomes (Linn et al., 1991). The emphasis is on process, effort, and individual growth. Most importantly, the results are intended to be directly applicable to teachers and students.

There are also concerns about the effects of the norming process on large-scale assessments, even when efforts have been made to address higher-level outcomes and more authentic assessment formats. When tests are normed, validity and performance criteria are often considered secondary to the need for a normal distribution of students' scores that is relatively stable over time. Items that do not discriminate among students (i.e., those that are generally too difficult or too easy) are often discarded regardless of their curricular importance or value. This results in tests that are not as consistent with the curricular outcomes or frameworks from which they were derived as was intended. In contrast, internal assessments are designed to promote the attainment of instruction goals (Cole, 1988). Teachers certainly do not expect a normal distribution after instruction. Instead, they would be inclined to set performance criteria for students, teach to those criteria, and then expect a change in performance after instruction and practice.

Differences in the frequency of administration, time, cost efficiency, and format of assessments used for external and internal purposes are also of concern. The large-scale assessments used for external purposes are used with such large numbers of students that efficiency and economy are valued highly. This has led to heavy reliance on group, paper-and-pencil, and short-answer tests that compare individual and group performance to the performance of a normative sample or to some external set of criteria or standards. Even when tests use more authentic assessments, the scoring and results are generally done at some distance from the classroom. However, the scores reported from large-scale assessments are more easily reported to policymakers and the public at large than those from assessment used for internal purposes.

Tensions between assessments used for internal and external purposes are further heightened when one type of assessment is privileged over another as a source of information in high stakes situations. High stakes assessment involves serious decisions and consequences to either individuals (e.g., high school graduation) or groups (e.g., sanctions or public display of results). High stakes incline teachers to teach to the content reflected in reports related to these assessments, which can result in a narrowing of the curriculum (cf. Airasian & Madaus, 1983; Shepard, 1989). The stakes associated with results of large-scale assessments can overwhelm other aspects of the internal–external relations. Political uses and public reporting that do not match the intent or capture the complexity can undermine even the best assessments of reading comprehension.

CURRENT EFFORTS TO IMPROVE ASSESSMENTS OF READING COMPREHENSION

Given this context, we looked to the authors of the three chapters in this section of this volume for their views on the role of large-scale comprehension assessment in educational practice. How are the tensions between assessments used for internal and external purposes best resolved? Have changes in the design of large-scale reading comprehension measures better aligned them with theories of reading comprehension? What are the current issues and research efforts that stand to advance our knowledge of effective comprehension assessment? What progress (if any) has been or is being made to improve large-scale reading comprehension assessment, especially given that the influence of these assessments may be greater because of their links to state and federal policies (Valencia & Wixson, 2000)? In response to these questions, we found three themes that cut across the chapters: (a) an increased emphasis on theories of reading and of measurement in designing reading comprehension assessments; (b) a reiteration of the importance of having coherent systems of assessments, including closer alignment of the design of assessments used for external and internal purposes; and (c) an increased emphasis on the need to improve consumer's knowledge of the nature and purposes of different forms and uses of comprehension assessments.

EMPHASIS ON THEORIES OF READING AND MEASUREMENT

The validity of reading comprehension assessments is central to both educators and psychometricians. A test is worthless unless it assesses the content and processes that it purports to assess. This is a formidable problem for the assessment of reading comprehension because, as Francis et al. (this volume) reminded us, comprehension processes are not observable. They do not lend themselves to direct observation or measurement. Francis et al. also pointed out that educators and researchers do not agree on the processes involved in constructing meaning. Agreement on the construct of reading comprehension has turned out to be an elusive goal. In fact, Campbell (this volume) suggested that this goal may be impossible to achieve:

> Reading comprehension is not a neat and easily defined construct.... The process of gaining meaning from text and demonstrating that understanding is very much influenced by individual factors. Cognitive style, prior knowledge, personal interest, and level of engagement are among the many individual characteristics that can influence the way someone approaches a reading situation—and thus, can influence the way reading comprehension performance is demonstrated on a measurement instrument. (p. 363)

Similar comments are made by Salinger (2001; this volume) and Francis (Francis et al., this volume), both of whom reminded us that reading has numerous purposes and that reading may involve different processes, depending on the outcome task, the nature of the text, and so on. With the acknowledgment that reading comprehension cannot be reduced to a "neat" construct comes the realization that comprehension assessments may need to sample a variety of reading behaviors by using different types of passages and different response formats or by gathering multiple sources of evidence, as is pointed out in all three chapters.

Campbell (this volume) argued that because practical realities (e.g., time, test-taking burdens) force us to rely on a single measure to assess reading comprehension, these single measures need to tap different reading processes and purposes to represent the construct of reading comprehension. With this in mind, he and others have carried out studies of response formats. The particular focus has been on constructed responses and the ways that these might either be more informative than multiple-choice responses or else useful in conjunction with this more traditional format. The outcome of the studies he discussed indicates that constructed responses will not alone address the shortcomings of large-scale reading comprehension tests, but will align the tests more with current views of comprehension. They provide a sample of students' thinking about texts and offset the common criticism that multiple-choice responses contribute to the illusion that there is "one right answer." Most theorists believe that each reader constructs meaning from text by linking what is previously known with what is "new" in the passage—a view of comprehension that is not compatible with "one right answer."

Francis and colleagues (this volume) agreed that assessment of reading comprehension must be multidimensional. However, they believed that effective assessment cannot be accomplished by use of a single measure:

> As comprehension assessment often influences instruction, particularly because of high stakes testing, it may be important to broaden the assessment of reading comprehension and to develop methods that incorporate multiple outcomes, multiple presentation formats, and multiple response formats. Otherwise, the understanding of how well a person comprehends what they read will depend on how comprehension is assessed, with little generalization beyond the method itself. (p. 370)

Similarly, Salinger (this volume) argued that multiple forms of evidence are needed to gather information about students' reading for different purposes (e.g., educational, policymaking; see also Salinger, 2001).

In addition to the importance placed on construct validity, Salinger (this volume) presented consequential validity as a major concern. The idea is that assessment measures ought to be evaluated with regard to the uses to which the information from the test is put. What are the consequences of administering and reporting a particular test? The concern for the consequences of testing reflects the tensions created by "accountability" issues, as described by Wixson, Valencia, and Lipson (1994). At about the same time, Wiggins (1993) called for a redefinition of accountability, asking the following: "To whom are schools truly accountable—in the sense of morally responsible?" He went on to say that

if the answer was "the school's clients (not oversight agencies), then standardized testing has little to do with accountability, since the client's satisfaction or
dissatisfaction will be due more to routine and direct indicators" (Wiggins,
1993, pp. 256–257). In Wiggins's view, the place to effect change was at the
level of the local school or classroom; the locus of control also ought to be at the
local level: "We will never understand or achieve accountability until we see
that tests per se do not provide it, but mechanisms that increase responsiveness
to clients do" (p. 263).

As a group, the three authors have not focused attention on the major issue
of consequential validity as it arises from the current uses of large-scale assessments for evaluating the status and well-being of schools under the No Child
Left Behind Act of 2001. In this respect, the chapters are not giving voice to
concerns of a large number of researchers and scholars (e.g., Linn, Baker, &
Betebenner, 2002). In her discussion of consequential validity, Salinger (this
volume) concentrated on the growing emphasis on classroom-based measures
to monitor progress of the students and evaluate the instructional materials and
methods. With regard to classroom-based measures, used for evaluation at the
local level, she pointed out that simply using a measure for progress monitoring
does not assure us that concerns for either construct or consequential validity
will be addressed. If the assessments are narrowly focused (i.e., not representative of reading skills for that age or grade level) or if the measures themselves are
not trustworthy (i.e., lacking reliability or validity), all is for naught. Further, re-
placing the assessments used for external purposes with those used for internal
purposes does not necessarily solve the problems of validity (construct and consequential). A measure that constitutes an internal assessment of reading
comprehension might or might not be a useful and valid means for monitoring
of educational progress.

COHERENCE OF SYSTEMS FOR ASSESSING
READING COMPREHENSION

Wixson et al. (1994) identified various ways that external and internal assessment systems could become more aligned, two of which seem particularly relevant today. One way is by having external assessments take on more of the
characteristics of internal assessments, thus offering the possibility that they
might serve the purposes of both types of assessment (e.g., assessing knowledge in
the domain of reading of large groups, and also providing information about students' comprehension and their response to instructional materials and methods). The other is by having stakeholders (e.g., school administrators, teachers)
work together to assure understanding and coordination of interpretations of the

results of information garnered from large-scale assessments and classroom assessments. In our reading of the three chapters, we found some evidence for both of these trends, but perhaps only because we looked hard to find it.

The first of these possibilities (that external assessment might come to be more like internal assessment) has clearly become an active area of research. For example, the research Campbell (this volume) reported in his chapter has yielded results that suggest the effectiveness of constructed-response formats as an alternative to multiple-choice items. Constructed responses (e.g., oral or written explanations of the students' thinking) are increasingly incorporated into state reading assessments, as well assessments in other content areas (e.g., science). In Michigan, not only are there constructed-response items on recent revisions of the Michigan Educational Assessment Program, but there are also Web-based activities and guidelines for students and others who want to learn how to respond to such items. It is in the area of response formats that external assessments are coming closer to resembling classroom-based assessments of comprehension. In addition, Francis and his colleagues, (this volume, citing the results of a study by McEnery, 1999) suggested that it may not be important that the texts in tests do not look like real books. In short, in studying the design and use of different response formats, large-scale assessments are attempting to address the criticism that they lack construct validity. We see the recognition that assessments need to sample the types of mental processes that readers use as a sign of progress in the world of reading comprehension assessment.

Campbell (this volume) noted that although at present, a combination of multiple-choice and constructed-response questions may be the most valid approach to assessing comprehension, numerous questions still need to be answered. Some concern item format decisions that test-makers must make— decisions that go beyond simple percentages of each type of item that make up a specific test. He pointed out that items cannot be evaluated independent of the passage, and that not all types of questions lend themselves to one type of response. He also indicated that developmental differences may affect the usefulness of different item formats. As Francis et al. (this volume) pointed out, considerable work remains if we are to understand the impact of variations in response formats on assessment of comprehension.

If standardized, large-scale assessments are becoming more like internal assessment measures, is it also true that stakeholders are increasingly working to develop coordinated and coherent testing systems within their schools and districts? We found little evidence in the discussion of the three authors of this possible means of resolving the tension between external and internal assessment. Salinger (this volume) came the closest to suggesting that there is a movement toward more coordinated systems of assessment in reading, and this is evident from her discussion of the requirements of assessment in the Reading First initiative (Part B of No Child Left Behind or NCLB). As she pointed out, NCLB requires that districts with Reading First funding need to include methods for initial screening, diagnostic assessments, progress monitoring, and year-end standardized testing in reading. At least in the conception of this system, there is the implication that information from each type of reading assessment plays a role in determining appropriate reading instruction for students and making sure that such instruction is effective in addressing the students' needs during the year, not just at the end of the year. Still, coherence in a deeper sense depends on the buy-in of the educators working with the system. The responsibilities for gathering and interpreting the data from these different types of reading assessments is not a trivial problem, as Salinger recognized. Thus, overall, we are hearing little from the three authors that suggests a movement in this important direction.

We also note that states are attempting to link their reading assessments more closely to the state standards for reading and language arts, and in so do-ing, are moving to create external assessments that may serve "internal" func-tions. The crucial connection, however, is that the stakeholders within districts and schools must learn how to interpret and work with the results of such tests if they are in fact going to have an impact on educational practices in the class-room. We read with interest Salinger's (this volume) description of a study car-ried out in New York in which teachers were learning to evaluate test results. The researchers were studying the New York State Early Literacy Profile, using teacher surveys to determine the value of the assessment system. They found that when teachers had to look for evidence of student learning in relation to standards, they felt that they acquired a better understanding of their students' progress in literacy. These teachers apparently felt that the process provided them with the guidance they needed to learn how test results could be used to support their students' learning. Salinger seemed to be suggesting that without such guidance for teachers, the design of this state test and its link to state stan-dards were not enough to make the results useful for educational purposes. Thus, it is not enough to focus on the content and item types of reading compre-hension assessments if the goal is to make it likely that test results are used to improve reading instruction in the classroom.

EDUCATORS' KNOWLEDGE OF THE NATURE AND PURPOSES OF COMPREHENSION ASSESSMENTS

As Salinger and Campbell (this volume) pointed out, a major problem with all assessments of reading comprehension, external or internal, commercial or lo-cally developed, is that of extracting useful and appropriate information from results. Francis et al. (this volume) added that a specific device may not be well suited for its state purpose, such as the attempt to use a norm-referenced test for accountability of instructional planning. Further, the purpose for which a test was devised may not be the same as the uses to which test information is put. Issues concerning test administration, too, arise as we consider the knowledge and experience of teachers. It seems likely that in the world of reading assessments, there is a general belief that classroom-based assessments are readily interpreted and the information can be incorporated into the evaluation and planning of instruction. However, as Salinger indicated, test interpretation of classroom measures, whether commercially developed or locally developed, can be as problematic as interpretation and appropriate use of information from large-scale assessments.

We agree wholeheartedly with Salinger (this volume) that teachers have to become data gatherers, but need to do so in a knowledgeable way. It is becoming clear that teachers need a more complete understanding of technical characteristics of tests (e.g., reliability). They need a better understanding of testing practices (including test design and administration) to avoid pitfalls that will lessen the value of the results. The problem of improving teachers' knowledge of assessment practices and their ability to interpret test results is what Salinger called a "huge burden." Nonetheless, it is a necessary direction in which we need to move.

Salinger (this volume) reminded us that large-scale assessments are thought of as robbing teachers and students of valuable time for classroom instruction and learning. However, inappropriately selected or designed classroom-based measures have the same effect. We might all agree that classroom-based assessments have the potential to enhance teachers' skills and thus students' learning. However, this potential won't be realized unless significant changes take place in the preparation and professional development offered to teachers.

WHERE ARE WE HEADED?

Our reading of the three chapters has shown some convergence on issues that still need to be addressed. Among the high-priority items are the following:

1. To reflect authentic reading comprehension processes and activities, there is a need for multidimensional assessments. Salinger (this volume) and Francis et al. (this volume) saw the need for multiple forms of evidence, whereas Campbell (this volume) discussed the "practical realities" which may force us to rely on a single assessment tool.
2. Comprehension assessments need to be developmentally sensitive. They need to link the notion of "component skills" to the construct of read-

ing. Without this link, an emphasis on subskills may result in students not adequately engaged in real literacy for real purposes.

3. There is a continuing need to resolve tensions between "measurement theory" and "reading theory" as they relate to assessment of reading comprehension. Currently, popular standardized reading tests have the advantage of meeting basic criteria for reliability and concurrent or predictive validity; they are less successful at meeting acceptable criteria for construct (and consequential) validity.

4. Progress in the study of response and presentation formats is heartening but needs to be extended to cover various contexts of reading. Here, too, tests used for "external" purposes need to be more aligned to views of reading comprehension. Studies of classroom-based measures are needed to provide assurance that they have good technical characteristics.

We also see that there are areas in which relatively little progress has been made. These include (a) the development of coherent, integrated systems of reading comprehension assessment; and (b) the improvement of teachers' knowledge of assessment principles and practices. At a broader level, we suggest that a major indication of progress would involve consumers' taking responsibility for evaluating the assessment measures they are using and for contributing to efforts to balance the influence of assessments used for external and internal purposes. A partnership between researchers and educators would be a starting point.

In the absence of a system to hold schools and teachers accountable locally, that is accountable to students, parents, and community members, it is likely that large-scale assessments will be increasingly influential on classroom practice. The process of devising coordinated assessment systems is not the responsibility of researchers alone but rather depends on the joint efforts of researchers and educators at the school and district levels. Finally, wise use of information from reading assessments, whether for external or internal purposes, depends on teachers and school administrators who have sufficient knowledge and experience to understand the power of aligning assessment and instruction.

REFERENCES

Airasian, P., & Madaus, G. (1983). Linking testing and instruction: Policy issues. *Journal of Educational Measurement, 20*, 103–118.

Cole, N. (1988). A realist's appraisal of the prospects for unifying instruction and assessment. In C. V. Bunderson (Ed.), *Assessment in the service of learning* (pp. 103–117). Princeton, NJ: Educational Testing Service.

Linn, R. L., Baker, E. L., & Dunbar, S. B. (1991). Complex, performance based assessment: Expectations and validation criteria. *Educational Leadership, 20*(7), 15–23.

Linn, R. L., Baker, E. L., & Betebenner, D. W. (2002). Accountability systems: Implications of requirements of the No Child Left Behind Act of 2001. *Educational Researcher, 31*(6), 3–16.

McEnery, P. (1999). *The role of context in comprehension of narrative text in first graders.* Unpublisherd doctoral dissertaion, University of Houston.

No Child Left Behind Act of 2001, Public Law No. 107–110, 115 Stat. 1425 (2002).

RAND Reading Study Group. (2002). *Reading for understanding: Toward an R and D program in reading comprehension.* Santa Monica, CA: RAND Publication.

Salinger, T. (2001). Assessing the literacy of young children: The case for multiple forms of evidence. In S. B. Neuman & D. K. Dickinson (Eds.), *Handbook of early literacy research* (pp. 390–404). New York: Guilford.

Shepard, L. A. (1989). Why we need better assessment. *Educational Leadership, 46*(7), 4–9.

Snow, C. E. (2003). Assessment of reading comprehension. In A. P. Sweet & C. E. Snow (Eds.), *Rethinking reading comprehension* (pp. 192–206). New York: Guilford.

Valencia, S., & Wixson, K. K. (2000). Policy-oriented research on literacy standards and assessment. In M. Kamil, P. B. Mosenthal, P. D. Pearson, & R. Barr (Eds.), *Handbook of reading research* (Vol. III, pp. 909–935). Mahwah, NJ: Lawrence Erlbaum Associates.

Wiggins, G. P. (1993). *Assessing student performance.* San Francisco: Jossey-Bass.

Wixson, K. K., Valencia, S. W., & Lipson, M. Y. (1994). Issues in literacy assessment: Facing the realities of internal and external assessment. *Journal of Reading Behavior, 26*(2), 315–337.

Author Index

Subject Index

A

Ability, 53
Accountability issues, 399–400
Assessment dimensions, 371–373, 375
Assessment of reading comprehension system, 6–9, 100–102, *see also* Comprehension assessment
issues, 9–11
Assessment practices, 13–14
past anomalies and omens, 17–19

B

Basic Reading Inventory (BRI), 133, 135, 179–180, 285, 293, 295, 299
Book reading levels, 50–52
lexile scaling techniques, 51

C

California Learning Assessment System (CLAS), 41–42, 225–230
California Achievement Test (CAT), 177
model, 226
Center for Improvement of Early Reading Achievement (CIERA), xi, xii, 237–239, 250, 252–254, 309–310, 339

Howard elementary school, 243–253
Changing demographic patterns, 16
Classroom-based assessment, 39–40, 323–341
burden, 335–337
Cloze procedure, 23–24, 378–379, 391
Cognitive psychology, 29
and assessment, 30–33
Illinois pilot of 1986, 34–36
Commercially-developed assessment, 329–337
Comprehension
and decoding, 72, 382, 384, 386
and oral reading, 132–141, 167, 172–174
and print knowledge, 142–147
in young children, 108–109, 114–119, 320–342
K–3, 279–303
miscues, 167–169, 170–172
preschool comprehension, 119–125
study groups, 237–243
word factors, 161–162
Comprehension as nonunitary construct, 93, 96–100, 169
subskills, 96–97
Comprehension assessment, 4–5, 86–91, 179–181
accountability, 399–400
domain-specific, 259–265, 277